THE STRUGGLE FOR CANADIAN SPORT

Canadian sports were turned on their head between the world wars. Swamped by the rise of consumer culture and severely weakened by the Depression, the middle-class amateur men's organizations steadily lost their dominance. In *The Struggle for Canadian Sport* Bruce Kidd illuminates the complex and fractious process that produced the familiar contours of Canadian sport today – the hegemony of continental cartels such as the NHL, the enormous ideological power of the media, the overshadowed participation of women in sports, and the strong nationalism of the amateur Olympic sports bodies.

Kidd focuses on four major organizations of the period: the Amateur Athletic Union, the Women's Amateur Athletic Federation, the Workers' Sport Association, and the National Hockey League. Each became a focal point of debate and political activity, and they often struggled with each other. Each had different goals: The AAU sought 'the making of men' and the strengthening of English-Canadian nationalism; the WAAF promoted the health and well-being of sportswomen; the WSA was a vehicle for socialism; and the NHL was concerned with lucrative spectacles.

These national organizations stimulated and steered many of the resources available for sport and helped expand opportunities. They enjoyed far more power than other cultural organizations of the period, and they attempted to manipulate both the direction and the philosophy of Canadian athletics. Through control of the rules and prestigious events and their countless interventions in the mass media, they shaped the practices and coined the language Canadians used to discuss sports. The successes of each group, as well as the groups' confrontations with one another, were crucial in shaping modern Canadian sport.

The Struggle for Canadian Sport adds to our understanding of the material and social conditions under which people created and elaborated sports and the contested ideological terrain on which sports were played and interpreted.

BRUCE KIDD, a former world-class distance runner, is director of the School of Physical and Health Education, University of Toronto. He is the author of several books on Canadian sports, including *Tom Longboat* and, with John Macfarlane, *The Death of Hockey*.

BRUCE KIDD

The Struggle for Canadian Sport

UNIVERSITY OF TORONTO PRESS
Toronto Buffalo London

© University of Toronto Press Incorporated 1996
Toronto Buffalo London
Printed in Canada

Reprinted 1997, 1999, 2002

ISBN 0-8020-0717-1 (cloth)
ISBN 0-8020-7664-5 (paper)

Printed on acid-free paper

Canadian Cataloguing in Publication Data

Kidd, Bruce, 1943–
    The struggle for Canadian sport

    Includes bibliographical references and index.
    ISBN 0-8020-0717-1 (bound) ISBN 0-8020-7664-5 (pbk.)

    1. Sports – Canada – Societies, etc. – History – 20th
    century.   2. Sports – Canada – History – 20th century.
    I. Title.

    GV585.K53 1996   796'.0971   C95-933273-1

The excerpt from Michael Ondaatje's *In the Skin of a Lion* (Toronto: McClel-
land and Stewart, 1987) on pages 159–60 is reproduced with the permission
of the author. Some of the material in chapter 4 appeared as ' "We Must
Maintain a Balance between Propaganda and Serious Athletics": The
Workers' Sports Movement in Canada, 1924–36,' in Morris Mott, ed., *Sports
in Canada: Historical Readings* (Toronto: Copp Clark Pitman, 1989), 247–64;
and 'Radical Immigrants and the Workers' Sports Federation of Canada,' in
George Eisen and David Wiggins, eds., *Ethnicity and Sport in North American
History and Culture* (Westport, Conn.: Greenwood, 1994), 201–20.

This book has been published with the help of a grant from the Humanities
and Social Sciences Federation of Canada, using funds provided by the
Social Sciences and Humanities Research Council of Canada.

University of Toronto Press acknowledges the financial assistance to its
publishing program of the Canada Council and the Ontario Arts Council.

FOR PHYLLIS

Contents

Acknowledgments

This long, oft-interrupted enterprise might never have been completed were it not for the encouragement and support of many people. Chris Armstrong, who supervised it when it was a doctoral thesis, Rob Beamish, Steve Hardy, and Ester Reiter sustained my resolve when other projects and proscrastination took over my life, and they were extremely helpful throughout. Harold Averill of the University of Toronto Archives, Sylvia Doucette and Pierre Labelle of the Canadian Olympic Association Archives, David Fraser and John Smart of the National Archives of Canada, Gretchen Ghent of the University of Calgary Library, Michael Moir of the Toronto Harbour Commission Archives, Cheryl Rielly of Canada's Sports Hall of Fame, and the staff of the Archives of Ontario were invaluable in locating useful collections. I am also grateful to the men and women of the Hockey Hall of Fame and from provincial and local archives and sports museums who responded to my queries. Tom Babits, Tim Hutton, and Nancy Moran provided research assistance. Anne Clark Ayres, Mabel Beech, Kay Conacher Findlay, Harvey Haid, Walter Kaczor, Fred Kazor, Helen Lenskyj, Margaret Lord, Irene McInnis, Dorothy Medhurst, Emmanuel Orlick, and Gladys Gigg Ross lent me scrapbooks, documents, and personal correspondence and helped me locate other athletes and officials of the interwar period. Helen Gurney, Sydney Halter, David Kashtan, and Jim Worrall responded to draft chapters about the organizations in which they were involved. Irving Abella, Norman Baker, Craig Heron, Varpu Lindström, Brian Pronger, Michael D. Smith, Paul Thompson, and University of Toronto Press editors Rob Ferguson, Gerald Hallowell, and John Parry made useful suggestions along the way.

I must also acknowledge my debt to the countless men and women who have played, schemed, argued, and rejoiced with me during a lifetime's involvement in sports, and my relationship to that experience. No investigator can expect to be completely independent of her or his data, but I stand closer to my subject than many. My parents, Margaret Easto Kidd and Roby Kidd, introduced me to the pleasures and politics of sports at an early age. I have enjoyed personal relationships with many of my informants for many years, particularly Fred Foot, Helen Gurney, Margaret Lord, Bob Osborne, and Jim Worrall, through collaborations, controversies, and changes, and at one time or another interacted with others in this history, such as the late Conn Smythe. If I am kinder to amateurism than most people are, it may be because I am proud to have been an amateur myself once upon a time and have ever since been immersed in the structures and battles that amateurism initiated. I bring to this story the experiences and blind spots of someone 'on the inside.'

A number of friends and colleagues have helped me make sense of sports. Varda Burstyn and Heather Jon Maroney struggled for many years to help me see and confront the patriarchal ideologies of sports. Stephen Clarkson, Peter Fitting, David Kidd, Paul Thompson, and Mel Watkins helped me place the analysis within the broader struggles for Canadian culture and provided much-appreciated emotional support. My greatest intellectual debt is to the small but flourishing network of sports scholars. Rob Beamish, Peter Donnelly, Rick Gruneau, Ann Hall, Steve Hardy, Jean Harvey, John Hoberman, Carl James, Charles Korr, Helen Lenskyj, John MacAloon, Don Macintosh, Margaret MacNeill, Alan Metcalfe, Morris Mott, Brian Pronger, Geneviève Rail, Jim Riordan, Don Sabo, Barbara Schrodt, Patricia Vertinsky, David Whitson, Brenda Zeman, and many others will see their influence in the pages that follow. I hope that they will regard this book as a small contribution to the ongoing 'interrogation' of sports in Canadian society.

My partner, Phyllis Berck, who has lived with this project much longer than she ever bargained for, has made innumerable helpful suggestions along the way. Moreover, she keeps me sane by reminding me that the joys of physical activity are best experienced with lactic acid in the out-of-doors and organizes the adventures to make that possible. Her steady support and her zest for life are warmly sustaining.

The book is dedicated to her.

Percy Williams won the 100-yard dash at the first British Empire Games in Hamilton in 1930 with his famous finishing leap.

Canadian team travelling to London for the 1934 British Empire Games and the Women's World Games. Train and boat travel to European competitions often took its toll in lost fitness.

The Toronto Granites (in white), who easily won the 1924 Olympic hockey tournament in Chamonix, France, were considered one of the best teams of the interwar period.

Sprinters Josie Dyment and Myrtle Cook. Cook, a world-record holder and member of the gold medal 4 x 100 metre Olympic relay team in Amsterdam in 1928, became a sportswriter for the *Montreal Star*.

Throughout the interwar period, Canadian amateurs sought the patronage of powerful corporations and the state. From left, E.W. Beatty, president of the Canadian Pacific Railway; Governor General Viscount Willingdon; Prime Minister R.B. Bennett; and Ontario premier Howard Ferguson review the opening ceremonies of the British Empire Games in Hamilton, 1930.

Dorothy Walton, world singles
badminton champion.

The Edmonton Grads, the winningest team in Canadian sports history.

Female athletes were rarely allowed to forget that they had ventured onto male terrain.

The Women's Amateur Athletic Federation, annual meeting, 26 November 1927. In the back row are Alexandra Gibb (second from left) and Mabel Ray (fourth from left).

For years, the best seat in the house at baseball games at Sunnyside Park in Toronto was a park bench. By 1930, however, after years of steady attendance, fans could finally watch from the comfort of permanent bleachers.

Canada's first women's Olympic team leaves Toronto's Union Station for the 1928 Amsterdam games. From left: Myrtle Cook, Jean Thompson (hidden from view), Ethel Smith, Ginger Catherwood (who accompanied sister Ethel), Florence Bell, Ethel Catherwood, Bobbie Rosenfeld, Marie Parkes, and Dorothy Prior.

Communist leader Tim Buck is carried by members of the Workers' Sports
Association into a rally at Maple Leaf Gardens, Toronto, 1934.

Women's gymnastics team from the Jewish Workers' Sports Association of Toronto, 1927.

Yritys women's gymnastics group, Camp Tarmola, Toronto, 1935.

Whether indoors or out, gymnastic pyramids were a favourite form of training and performance for Finnish-Canadian clubs.

Finnish-Canadian ski race in South Porcupine, 1943.

After the 1924–5 regular season, the first-place Hamilton Tigers went on strike in an effort to be paid for the play-offs. The NHL refused to negotiate, and the team was sold to a New York group to become the Americans.

Lester Patrick tried to develop
'syndicate hockey,' an entire league
controlled by a single corporation,
with the Pacific Coast League prior to
the First World War.

Frank Calder, a Montreal sportswriter,
became the NHL's first president. He
deserves much of the credit for
turning an often uncooperative
coalition of owners into an efficient
cartel.

Walter Knox, renowned multi-event track-and-field champion and coach of the 1912 and 1920 Canadian Olympic teams. During the 1920s, the Ontario Athletic Commission sent him around the province to instruct boys in schools and clubs.

Hugh Plaxton, star of Canada's gold-medal hockey team in 1928, was unsuccessful in his 1937 bid to have Parliament create a national ministry of sport.

Conn Smythe turned the failing
Toronto franchise into the NHL's
flagship team.

Foster Hewitt, publicity director of
Maple Leaf Gardens, the charismatic
voice of 'Hockey Night in Canada.'

British Columbia's Pro-Rec Mass Display, Vancouver Forum, 1939.

THE STRUGGLE FOR CANADIAN SPORT

Introduction

Once the preserve of upper-class British males, sports are now played and watched at some point by virtually everyone. They have become by far the most popular of the many forms of physical culture practised in Western societies. Ambitious parents teach them to their children before they can walk. In 1992, a national study found that 9.6 million Canadians over the age of 15 had competed in sports during the previous 12 months.[1] Most participants derive great pleasure from their efforts. In the east end of Toronto, where I grew up, the adults relished playing as much as their kids. 'You win a few and lose a few,' one friend's mother, whose fastball team we followed at Coxwell Stadium, told us after every game, 'but the ones that hurt the most are the ones rained out.'

The numbers participating are even greater for spectatorship. Thousands of Canadians attend prestigious events such as the Stanley and Grey cups, and millions follow the World Series, the World Cup of soccer, and the Olympic, Commonwealth, and Pan-American Games on radio and television. Households, schools, and public and private enterprises organize their schedules around them. In the increasingly atomized post-modern world, these events provide rare moments of collective experience and the affirmation of membership in a 'community.' When Team Canada takes on the rest of the world in ice hockey, or a Canadian 'franchise' plays in the World Series, most of the country shuts down to watch.

We should not, however, exaggerate the extent to which such events collapse social barriers. In stadiums such as Toronto's SkyDome, the cost of tickets and the seating arrangements, which prominently elevate two tiers of private boxholders and give 'club' seatholders privileged access to restaurants, sustain and extend social hierarchy. Most people watch television sports in their own homes and their own neighbourhoods. But sports do create broad communities of language and cultural experience.

The great popularity of sports and athletes has encouraged a mushrooming commerce. Participants buy and rent specialized equipment and clothing and organize their holidays around sports events and adventures; public and private institutions build facilities and provide instructional services; and fans purchase admission tickets, radios, TVs and VCRs, souvenir sweatshirts, trading cards, specialty magazines, and videos to follow and identify with their favourites. The interest in sports has served as a tremendous stimulus to the transportation and communications industries, and these in turn have furthered the popularity of sports. In the nineteenth century, the railway companies added to their passenger traffic and encouraged intercity competition by offering reduced fares to players and spectators and by publicizing results over their telegraph lines. In the twentieth century, the automobile and airlines industries have grown in step with sports in much the same way. Today, production and distribution of sporting commodities and services are inextricably integrated with the mass media as well, in what scholars call 'the sports-media complex.' Newspapers devote entire sections to sports. In 1993, the public and private networks in Canada telecast a total of 2,800 hours of sports; the cable channels – The Sports Network (TSN) and Reseau des Sports – provide sports programming around the clock. Other enterprises also contribute to the production of sports spectacles and the images and narratives that emanate from them. Cities and urban tourism are designed around sports stadiums. Theologian Michael Novak calls those structures 'the cathedrals of the modern world.'[2]

Sports have long attracted the attention of the Canadian state. In the nineteenth century, governors general patronized and legislators regulated them, even prohibiting activities such as prizefighting.[3] Today, governments invest in them. The federal government, through the Fitness and Amateur Sport Act of 1961, directs, finances, and controls Canadian preparation and participation in international competition, largely in the interests of reinforcing and publicizing Canadian identity and 'the ideology of excellence.' The provinces do the same in vying for national honours, while municipalities build facilities for citizens' recreation and professional sports.[4] The efforts of politicians to exploit sports' popularity and of political commentators to draw on sports' imagery have a similar history. In 1924, the Liberal party advertised 'a good program of sports' at the 'grand demonstration' in honour of William Lyon Mackenzie King, probably Canada's least athletic prime minister.[5] Editorial cartoonists drew King and his principal opponent, Conservative leader Arthur Meighen, as boxers in the ring. After Quebec's 1994 provincial election, the Parti Québécois introduced its successful candidates with a fanfare of the familiar hockey refrain, 'He shoots, he scores!'

It is impossible to describe modern life accurately without some account of sports. Though often trivialized as 'just entertainment' or the 'playpen of society,' these activities have considerable social impact. They provide many of us with significant formative experiences. To race or shoot a puck is not only to exercise a skill, but to embody, express, and elaborate a complex code about self and culture – in short, to acquire an identity. Barry Nye, former president of the Commonwealth Games Association of Canada, says that one can tell a person's personality from the sport he or she plays. The identities encouraged by sports are usually multifaceted. During the pleasure/pain of exertion, the shouts and surprises of competition, and the often-unhurried camaraderie with teammates, the sporting quest tutors competitors in the expectations and boundaries of self-display and interpersonal relations and the geography, history, and hierarchies of their lives. Sports teach us above all about the gendering of bodies, social opportunity, and performance, especially the requirements and rewards of 'masculinities.'[6] This is not to romanticize the pedagogy of sports. Increasingly, as Canadians learned from the Dubin Inquiry (1988–90), some athletes at the highest levels of competition learn how to cheat and to risk their health, as well as how to win.[7] Those excluded from sports often feel bitterness and marginalization. The women who grew up in the celebrated hockey towns of western Canada enjoyed few of the sorts of affirming experiences the men so fondly remember.[8] But in each of these cases, sports played a vital role in people's lives.

For the spectator, too, the cultural influence of sports is deeply felt. Sports stir the passions and excite the imagination, often in unforgettable ways. The artistry of a brilliant play and the adrenalin generated by a close contest speed up the heart and lift us out of ourselves in a visceral identification that can seem like transcendence. It is not only the most famous, nationally affirming accomplishments, such as Paul Henderson's last-minute goal against the Soviet team in the 1972 hockey series, or Angela Chalmers's stirring finishes in the Commonwealth Games of 1990 and 1994, that produce such exhilaration. I have felt the same in a high-school gym. Sports animate a rich, dense tapestry of mythological and symbolic narratives. Some of them are deeply encoded. Roland Barthes once suggested that with hockey 'man has taken the elements of immobile winter / the frozen land, and suspended life / and fashioned them into a rapid, vigorous sport.' The spirit of 'sacrifice' so frequently attributed to Olympic athletes draws on centuries-old vocabularies of military and religious victimization. Advertisers inscribe the athlete with images of the closely knit production unit or the finely tuned machine.[9]

Other metaphors and identities, such as trials and triumphs of individuals and teams, are more readily understood and expressed. In the late 1900s, the marathon duels between Toronto-based Onondaga runner Tom Longboat and British sensation Alf Shrubb widely evoked Aesop's fable of the tortoise and the hare. The hundreds of southern Ontario fans who travelled to watch, and the thousands more who followed the races by newspaper wire, always feared that the Old Country speedster would someday outlast their adopted favourite, the slower but relentlessly confident 'Canadian.' The 'Battles of Alberta' between Calgary and Edmonton teams evoke similar rivalries of place and political tradition. In fact, sports provide a ready source of associations to the groups and regions whose allegiances they bear. Cheering for a team for the first time is often as significant as first communion or crossing a frontier. Sam Hoffman, the father of runner Abby Hoffman, once told me that he first knew he had won acceptance as a Jewish immigrant in the small Ontario town of Omemee when several new acquaintances asked him to accompany them to a game the local hockey team was playing against neighbouring Peterborough.

Athletes from subordinate and disadvantaged groups, such as Jackie Robinson, Marilyn Bell, Rick Hansen, and Alwyn Morris, dramatize the aspirations of their communities for democratic rights and a fairer share of social resources. These relationships have not always been appreciated. In 1881, after Toronto City Council honoured Ned Hanlan for winning the world's rowing championship, Goldwin Smith complained that 'no part of the affair is more offensive than the suggestion that Canada is indebted to a professional oarsman for redemption from obscurity and contempt.'[10] Occasionally, athletes protest that they are not 'role models.' But they are powerless to turn off the popular identification. In 1955, hundreds of hockey fans rioted in the Montreal Forum and then rampaged through the downtown, smashing windows and stealing goods, to protest National Hockey League president Clarence Campbell's decision to suspend the Canadiens' Maurice 'Rocket' Richard for the rest of the season. Many French-speaking Québécois regarded the suspension of the charismatic Richard as symbolic of the harsh discrimination they were receiving at the hands of the English-speaking minority during the corrupt Duplessis era. Commentators suggest that the defiant 'hockey riots' presaged Quebec's 'quiet revolution.'[11]

Today, those in power seek to mobilize popular identification with athletes for commercial and political ends. Corporations pay millions to have stars such as Silken Laumann and Joe Carter endorse their products, community standing, and ideology. Pierre Trudeau consciously encouraged development of Teams Canada to personify his vision of pan-Canadian unity and shore up the legitimacy of the federal state, at a time of intensifying Quebec nationalist and western regional challenges. Joe Clark sought to use sports to promote Canada's image abroad, Brian Mulroney to boost his ambition to link Canada more closely with the United States. In 1988, within minutes of Ben Johnson's bedevilled victory at the Olympic Games in Seoul – the apparent triumph of a poor immigrant of colour, assisted by a public program, in the most contested of global competitions – the deputy minister of fitness and amateur sport gleefully told me that 'now the prime minister can call the (free trade) election!'

Not surprisingly, such important sites of socialization and symbolization have become terrains of endless intervention, negotiation, and contestation, as individuals and groups seek to influence and control the values and practices that sports privilege and the rewards and status they confer. These efforts take many forms, from the shouts and deeds of athletes, parents, and coaches, to the rulings of referees and governing officials, the moralizing of sportswriters, the investments of governments and corporations, and the demands of sponsors. They shape not only the nature, extent, and meanings of opportunities but the identities and social commentary that sports provide.

The perennial Canadian war of words about fighting in hockey, for example, is a debate at once about sports, gender, and social policy. At its most immediate, it affects decisions about who is encouraged to play and how such experience is provided and understood – no small matter in a country where some 1.4 million children and adults regularly play the game. But while the actual discussion may never stray from the language of rules, interpretation, and enforcement, the subtexts reveal competing codes of masculinity and approaches to violence. The celebrated Wayne Gretzky is loved by some and hated by others for his refusal to join in the prohibited but widely encouraged practice of fighting and thereby to declare himself in favour of a version of masculinity that prefers intelligence and skill to brute strength and intimidation and opposed to the view that every frustration justifies physical retaliation. These allegiances can complicate other loyalties. I grew up with male Torontonians who cheered for the Montreal Canadiens because they resented the conservative defensive play and pugnacious 'beat-em-in-the-alley' tactics of Toronto Maple Leaf president Conn Smythe. Even those who have no interest in sports wonder about the relationship between the mass media's often-uncritical depiction of fighting in hockey and the plague of male violence against women and children. Thousands intervene in these struggles about identity, discourse, and practice, but some have significantly more power to affect the outcome than others. As several decades of scholarship and public inquiries have argued, the National Hockey League, along with its media partners, continues to tolerate, if not legitimate, hockey thuggery, despite the best efforts of governments, educators, and such players as Gretzky to abolish it.[12]

Such struggles influence and are influenced by the society in which they take place. They are also structured by the outcomes of such efforts in earlier generations. This book presents an analysis of the major contending interests in Canadian sports during the years between the first and second world wars. Participants and spectators may have played and watched games primarily for pleasure, but the organizers had additional motives. The four major groups whose ambitions are followed in this study – the 'nation-builders' of the Amateur Athletic Union (AAU), the feminists of the Women's Amateur Athletic Federation (WAAF), the revolutionaries of the Workers' Sports Association (WSA), and the capitalists of the National Hockey League (NHL) – sought to shape the way people defined themselves and to enhance social, economic, and ideological goals. They insisted on fierce loyalty, usually punishing those who broke ranks. One of them – the NHL – was successful beyond its wildest dreams, while the others encountered a bewildering mix of achievement and failure. The study attempts to show why the NHL triumphed and the consequences for Canadian sports as a whole. I argue that the particular transformations of this period have shaped the structure of Canadian sport as much as anything before or since.

Despite the cultural, economic, and political importance of sports, Canadian historians have generally neglected them. Perhaps they have been discouraged by advisers and colleagues who 'reproved [them] for wasting time indulging [their] interest in sports,' as Syd Wise was by Arthur Lower.[13] Or perhaps they have been too caught up as fans to take a critical stance. Though there has been during the last two decades a rapid growth of historical writing about American, Australian, and British sports, exploration of the Canadian experience lags behind. At the time of writing, there is barely a handful of published, full-length scholarly historical treatments.[14]

Much of what we do know has been produced by such journalists as W.A. Hewitt, Henry Roxborough, Scott Young, Eric Whitehead, Brian McFarlane, William Houston, and Alison Griffiths and David Cruise, or such gifted amateurs as Charles Coleman, whose three-volume, self-published history of the Stanley Cup is still an essential reference.[15] But relying on these works can be problematic. Few of them have references, making it extremely difficult to verify statements of fact, particularly for the early years, for which few records remain. The prolific Roxborough is particularly frustrating in this respect. What's more, most journalistic histories deal solely with the winners of the quest for sporting dominance, such as the established commercial leagues. They implicitly tend to use 'modernization' frameworks, which treat what has been achieved as desirable and inevitable, while glossing over the doubts and alternatives that even those who succeeded often held or considered and ignoring the clubs, sports, and regions that do not conform to the pattern. For example, it is frequently asserted that immediately following the First World War lacrosse 'failed' as a sport because the men who controlled it did not turn it into a successful commercial spectacle in the manner of NHL hockey.[16] Yet lacrosse has hardly disappeared. It is still played and watched enthusiastically in several parts of Canada. From his experience as a professional player, Queen's sociologist Rob Beamish has suggested a contrasting hypothesis: to a considerable extent, small-town lacrosse organizers in Ontario and British Columbia were successful in resisting the monopolization and homogenization that deprived their hockey counterparts of any connection with the highest levels of the game.[17] Whatever the appropriate explanation, there is little justification for the dearth of popular histories for the game Parliament recognized in 1994 as Canada's 'national summer sport.'[18]

The scholarly work on Canadian sports that does exist has been written for the most part in university faculties of physical education and kinesiology. A promising start was made in the 1960s by Max Howell and his colleagues and graduate students at the University of Alberta. They set out to compile detailed chronologies – what Howell called 'first order studies' – of the athletic and institutional history of Canadian sports. Drawing heavily on newspapers, they plotted the major developments in a variety of sports and institutions. These studies recaptured much of what had been completely forgotten and have provided other researchers with useful entry points – names, accomplishments, dates, and sources.[19] But the work of the 'Alberta school' is deficient in several respects. Most accounts ignore class, gender, and ethnicity, offering what we might call a sporting version of the 'frontier thesis' – that people everywhere played together in a 'common love of sport.' They also tend to detach sports from their economic, political, and social context. Needless to say, others, notably Richard Gruneau, Ann Hall, Helen Lenskyj, and Alan Metcalfe, have challenged the notions of the 'democracy of sport' and the social autonomy of sporting development. They have shown that Canadian sports are significantly stratified at all levels, that both leaders and participants have been deeply affected by the economic and social structures within which they have lived, and that their relationships are replete with complex and contradictory social tensions.[20] Despite these promising beginnings, little of the historical work stimulated by the 'Alberta school' has been sustained, either at the University of Alberta or elsewhere. With a few important exceptions, the best social scientists labouring in the emerging field of 'sport studies' frame their work with sociology and political economy, not history.[21]

Most of what has been written tends to focus on two periods – the years between the mid-nineteenth century and the Great War, during which time sports were first formally organized, and the years since 1961, when the federal Fitness and Amateur Sport Act radically restructured opportunities and organization in the Olympic sports. But as this study shows, the 'making' of Canadian sports did not cease with the codification of rules and creation of governing organizations in the years before the First World War, nor did subsequent development follow a smooth and obvious progression. On the contrary, many popular ideas, activities, and teams of the 1910s did not survive the period, while others were seen and heard for the first time. The power relations that had characterized the years immediately prior to the war were completely transformed.

This volume is primarily a study of men and women who sought to control activity at the 'national' level rather than of the full totality of Canadian sports. Many others – athletes, coaches, referees, friends, fans, public commentators, investors, and patrons – contributed to the development of practice and meaning. Much local activity, especially in rural areas, was connected only distantly, if at all, to the national organizations. As many men played baseball as any other sport during the interwar years, for example, and many thought the World Series

'Canada's greatest "national" sporting event.' [22] Yet baseball was never effectively organized on a national basis and is not examined in this study. Football, another popular sport, is not analysed at length either, though Canadian football players were required to hold Amateur Athletic Union of Canada cards for much of the period and thus were affected by the debates over eligibility discussed in these pages. This book is thus only a beginning.

But the national organizations are a good place to start. They stimulated and steered many of the resources available for sports and contributed significantly to the expansion of opportunities. They enjoyed far more power than other Canadian cultural organizations of the period. Through their control of the rules and prestigious events and their countless interventions in the mass media, they shaped the dominant practices and coined the very language with which Canadians discussed what sports should mean. The major debates were conducted within or between them. With their iron control over eligibility, they determined just who could and who could not play in a broad spectrum of activities. To be sure, some sportspersons ignored them, and others openly resisted them. Their influence was far from complete. But they towered above the sporting landscape in the 1920s and 1930s. They left an indelible stamp on the Canadian sporting heritage.

1

The State of Play

The term 'sport' is used today in both broad and historically limited senses. In the first case, it refers to any form of competitive physical activity, without regard to place, period, rules, or meaning. Medieval jousting, Mayan ball games, Asian martial arts, and the World Cup of soccer are thus all considered 'sport.' But most scholars today prefer a more precise usage. They reject the naturalization of 'sport' as an unchanging, transhistorical, and universal cultural form performed and understood essentially the same way by all people in all societies. They argue instead that 'sports' – as a plurality – can be understood best as distinct creations of modernity, fashioned and continually refashioned in the revolutionizing conditions of industrial capitalist societies.

This conclusion has emerged from a number of comparative studies. Despite the well-orchestrated attempts by the International Olympic Committee and other appropriators of antiquity to claim continuity between the athletics of ancient Greece and modern sports, for example, most scholars now agree that the Greeks were unique in the classical world in their pursuit of competitive athletics and that the differences between the practices and ideology of the ancient games and those of today outweigh the similarities. Even by modern standards, classical athletics were extremely violent. The popular combative events were conducted with little concern for safety or fairness. There were no weight categories to equalize strength and size, no rounds, and no ring. Bouts were essentially fights to the finish, which is hardly surprising when we understand that they began as preparations for war. The modern Olympics are admired for their encouragement of participation for its own sake and personal growth through self-testing, but very few of the ancients held such ideals. Competitors prayed, 'Give me the wreath or give me death!' because victory alone brought glory. Placings other than first were rarely recorded, since defeat brought undying shame. Though the Greeks had the technology to measure records in the running, jumping, and throwing events, they rarely did so: performance for itself – pursuing 'personal best' despite one's placing – was meaningless to them. In fact, champions tried to intimidate their opponents into withdrawing so they could boast they had won without having to compete. There were no team events, because competitors did not want to share the glory of victory. No competitor would have congratulated an opponent for a fairly fought or outstanding triumph. Today's handshake would have seemed an act of cowardice.[1]

Scholars are equally careful to distinguish modern sports from the game forms of pre-modern Europe[2] and the physical recreations of indigenous and non-European peoples, such as the trials of strength and cooperative rituals of the northern Dene and Innu.[3] To be sure, sports have something in common with these other practices, but none of them can be fully understood if they are all assumed to be the same. While sports are conducted under the same rules throughout the entire world, other game forms were and are played under a bewildering variety of conditions. In the folk games of Europe played before the development of sports, for example, the rules were highly informal, depending entirely on unwritten custom and the bluster of the moment. Games such as 'football' may have enjoyed a common designation, but they were played in widely different ways from place to place. Moreover, there were usually no limits to the field of play and the number of players, no specialization in position or skill, and usually little distinction between players and spectators – all features that have come to define sports. There was no equivalent to the modern athlete's ideology of 'fairness,' or the fascination with measurable progress or 'records.' There were no sports bureaucracies to regulate the organization and conduct of play.[4]

Given the unique characteristics of modern sports, scholars have sought to investigate the complex dynamics by which they have been developed and elaborated – a process sometimes referred to as 'the sportization of game-contests' or the 'reconstruction of sports.'[5] The general view is that the making of modern sports began during the fractious industrialization of eighteenth- and nineteenth-century Britain. Enclosure of village commons and mechanization of wheat production removed thousands of small farmers and agricultural workers, the traditional players of folk games, from the countryside. In the burgeoning cities and towns, the tyranny of the 60-hour week, employer-initiated elimination of popular holidays, and repression of popular amusements all but eliminated folk games and active forms of popular recreation. These games, however, continued to be played in the elite, all-male 'public' schools such as Eton, Harrow, and Rugby.

In this crucible, pressured by parents from the rising capitalist class to reform the curriculum, headmasters and teachers gradually transformed what were once informal and often brawling, uncontrolled contests into regulated sports, with written rules, specialized tasks, an emphasis on skill and strategy, and an ideology of self-improvement. While sports had considerably less regimentation than classroom instruction and were celebrated in the vocabulary of 'play,' the public school innovators and organizers fully intended them to be educational. They hoped that the demands and discipline of game playing would prepare boys and young men for careers in business, government, colonial administration, and the military by instilling physical and mental 'toughness,' obedience to authority, and loyalty to class. The 'manly sports,' as the more vigorous activities were often called, were consciously promoted to extend and celebrate male power and privilege in the face of first-wave feminism.[6] By the mid-nineteenth century, public school graduates had taken this new approach to game playing to universities and private clubs and began to establish new associations to promote, conduct and regulate it. The 'character-building' ideology of sports, a form of social Darwinism romanticized as 'muscular Christianity,' was popularized by Thomas Hughes's best-selling *Tom Brown's Schooldays* and hundreds of imitators. Sports were quickly taken up by upper-class girls and women and working-class boys and men and spread to many parts of the world. In the United States and Canada, adaptation of British sports and the construction of indigenous ones began early in the nineteenth century. The process of diffusion has been tumultuous and complex, at one time or another involving evangelism, immigration, emulation, commodity production, and imperialism. Like the 'making' of sports, it continues to this day.[7]

The Making of Canadian Sports

The early inhabitants of what became Canada played all manner of games in the course of what were for the most part remarkably physically active lives. The peoples of the First Nations were accomplished runners, climbers, swimmers, and canoeists, and they enjoyed many games and tests of skill and strength.[8] The European explorers, entrepreneurs, and settlers brought their own amusements and tried the Native ones. By the nineteenth century, Euro-Canadians were engaging in a wide variety of athletic contests, though there was considerable difference in what was played. It was only males of the leisured gentry and the officers of the usually idle British garrisons who could devote the two or three days necessary to play a full innings of cricket, easily the most prestigious game of the colonial period. Upper-class women risked censure for being too physically active. Most other men and women were working too hard to have much leisure time, other than during holidays and special occasions such as harvest bees. In Lower Canada, the Anglo-Canadian elite tried to preserve the status and exclusive atmosphere of horse-racing for themselves by barring working-class *Canadiens* from attendance. Nevertheless, organized competitions steadily grew, particularly on the grounds of the taverns that dotted the rural crossroads and growing towns.[9]

While Canadians of every region and background engaged in these practices, it was a very narrow group – urban, middle-class males of British background – that succeeded in controlling the emergence of what became Canadian sports, steering adaptation of British sports to Canada and turning *their* favourite games into the sports everyone played. Montreal merchants meeting at Gilles Tavern in Montreal formed Canada's first sporting club, the Montreal Curling Club, in 1807, and Montrealers long dominated the development of curling. In the 1860s, Montreal dentist George Beers developed the modern sport of lacrosse – with a written set of rules, standardized equipment, and a governing National Lacrosse Association – from the Mohawk game of *tewaarathon*, which he had learned across the St Lawrence at Kahnawake. Montreal university and business men fashioned the sports of rugby football and ice hockey from European folk games and controlled the organizational development of track and field, golf, and competitive shooting. In the Maritimes and southern Ontario, others established rowing and baseball. The first organizers drew on their managerial and commercial backgrounds for the experience necessary to create clubs, constitutions, leagues, and schedules. Members of the upper class rarely played an active role. They rode their horses and played cricket, tennis, and golf among themselves, behind the trimmed hedges of their exclusive clubs.

Few of the new sports would be readily recognizable today. Baseball in Canada was first played with 11 players and four bases, and, very much like in cricket, one entire team batted before taking the field. In lacrosse, a team won when it scored three goals, whether it took six minutes, as once happened in a game between the Montreal Shamrocks and

Toronto, or six hours. Ice hockey was originally played by seven a side, and as they played the entire game without substitution, the pace was much more leisurely. An offside rule that prohibited forward passing, even in the defensive zone, made stickhandling, skating, and 'lifting' – arching long, clearing shots, with lots of 'hang time' – the premium skills of the game. Rugby football, played by 14, prohibited the forward pass as well. The ball was put in play from a scrum, and the flying wedge was the most popular means to score.[10]

Yet by the 1880s, the idea of sports that we take for granted today – competition governed by uniform, written rules (which specified field of play, number of players, duration of contest, permissible plays, and so on), ruling organizations, and 'national' championships – was widely accepted. Differences over rules, interpretations, meanings, and practices still had to be resolved, sometimes just before games were played, but increasingly within and among the new governing bodies. No one thought to ask the Mohawk what they thought about George Beers's new lacrosse rules, first published in 1860, so he was successful in imposing them on all who played. But in most other games, the accomplishment of uniform rules required considerable discussion, if not intense politics.

In these early struggles for control of sports, the most powerful people were usually the most influential. In baseball, most teams and leagues abandoned what was known as the 'Canadian game' for the 'New York' rules – essentially the format we know today – by the 1860s. In the strictly Canadian sports, it was the Montrealers – or, more precisely, the middle-class, English-speaking, male Montrealers from the ward of St Antoine – who made '*a* particular way of playing *the* way of playing.'[11] They enjoyed the advantages of strategic location and economic and cultural power. Long before they had the means to extend their activities across the full breadth of the new dominion, Montrealers established 'national' regulatory bodies in nine sports – cycling, track and field, rugby, ice hockey, skating, bowling, cricket, and water polo. Eight of these governing bodies were created by a single club, the Montreal Amateur Athletic Association (MAAA), formed in 1881.[12] They wanted to harness the sports they created to the National Policy economy in which they played a leading role and to the new project of 'nation-building' which they supported. They spread their sports wherever they could, encouraging other men of their class to adopt them. Many agreed to the Montrealers' rules so that they could join in the hunt for 'national bragging rights' in the ever more popular competitions. In ice hockey, the Haligonians were persuaded to abandon their faster, more open game of 'ricket' to facilitate competition with Montreal teams. Almost as soon as the new sports were established, they were taken up by women, children, and the working class, especially in the new cities and towns of the Canadian west. Further expansion occurred when 'progressive era' reformers actively promoted them in public playgrounds, businesses and factories, churches and service clubs. By the turn of the century, most Canadians were familiar with sports and accepted the same rules. In many local museums, the collections of formal team photographs date from this time.[13] Yet the politics of rule making continued. Complete agreement among all the governing bodies on the rules of ice hockey was not achieved until after the First World War; in football, it did not occur until after the Second World War.

Creation of sports was inextricably bound up with the transformations of work, leisure, household life, and notions of self and society that accompanied the expansion of capitalism. In North America, perhaps the most immediate stimuli were the rapid industrialization, urbanization, and western expansion of the late nineteenth century. Some historians even suggest that sports would have been impossible without the railway. Pre-railway travel was so time-consuming that even for the leisure class it was rarely undertaken just for games. In 1840, for example, it took a whole day to journey by stage from Toronto to Hamilton, and four days to Kingston. With the possibilities for intra- and inter-town competition opened up by the railway came the necessity for standard rules and a governing structure. Organizers took ready advantage of the expanding lines to promote the rules they favoured and to publicize events. The railway companies themselves promoted opportunities for players and spectators, which in turn stimulated the perfection of athletic skill and the interest of entrepreneurs.[14] As urban life came to be measured by the factory, office, and municipal clock, particularly after the rapid industrialization of the 1880s, the logic of industrial time gradually supplanted task as the measure of games' duration. It was about this time that the rules of lacrosse were changed to require the winning team to score the most goals within a fixed period.[15]

Mass production, marketing, and sale of equipment, especially following invention of the sewing machine, provided another essential ingredient. When players had to make their own balls, bats, and other implements by hand, it kept the numbers down and the quality of play uneven. Sporting goods companies not only manufactured the equipment, but promoted the games as commodities, publishing and distributing rulebooks, how-to-play manuals, and reverential biographies of successful athletes. In both Canada and the United States, the most ambitious individual in production, distribution, and marketing of sports was Albert Spalding, the player-entrepreneur who became the driving force behind Major League Baseball. Spalding's firm branched out into every sport imaginable. It sponsored American Olympic teams and even set up hockey leagues in Montreal to promote its brand of skates and sticks. Canadian manufacturers were active too. After James Naismith created basketball as a winter recreation for young men, the Harold Wilson Co., which produced balls and uniforms, freely distributed the rules. Large retailers such as Eaton's, Simpson's, and Woodward's advertised a full line of sporting goods in university and school yearbooks and the daily press.[16]

Steady immigration and increasing urban density provided both need and opportunity for sports. The population of Montreal tripled between 1861 and 1891, doubling the densities in all but the most affluent wards, compelling city dwellers to forge new relationships with each other and new arrangements for games and amusements. The pressure on vacant land led men to form private clubs and construct specialized playing areas, while urban taxes persuaded them to charge admission for watching. The rising populations made it easier to find a ready membership and paying spectators. But these forces did not by themselves ensure the success of sporting ventures. In 1890, after a decade of steady population and commercial growth in the city, the Toronto Athletic Club was formed by five well-established sports clubs and several prominent businessmen. Its lavish club-house, opened with great fanfare in 1894, was designed by the prominent architect E.J. Lennox and included the city's first indoor swimming pool, indoor tennis courts, a gymnasium, fencing, boxing, and billiard rooms, a Turkish bath, social facilities, and separate rooms for female members. There were 13 tennis courts, two bowling greens, and a running and cycling track on the grounds outside. But four years later, the club went bankrupt.

The psychic and ideological ambitions and anxieties unleashed by industrial capitalism fuelled the interest in sports as well. The separation of work time and leisure time, at least for men in the waged economy, encouraged them to make the most of those 'free' moments over which they had more control. The emergence of an urban working class, in the context of the emergence of meritocratic ideas, political struggles about the 'manhood' franchise, and the right to form trade unions, inflated the representational coin of competition. Games between the working-class Montreal Shamrocks and middle-class teams such as the Montreal and

Toronto Lacrosse clubs were always fiercely fought and closely followed. Class tensions also stimulated development of opportunities. While working-class struggles for the nine-hour day, a living wage, and the right to form trade unions were motivated primarily by the debilitating conditions of the shop floor and the harshness of urban life, workers were also interested in gaining time and spending power so that they and their children could take part in sports. Labour groups were in the forefront of public campaigns for parks and against Sunday restrictions on recreation. It was the Trades and Labour Congress of Canada that persuaded the dominion government to establish the statutory holiday of Labour Day in 1894. Middle-class concern about urban contagion and disease, class conflict, and homeless children led church leaders to agitate for sports in public playgrounds and business leaders to sponsor teams.

Gender uncertainties provided a further stimulus. As Varda Burstyn has suggested, the masculine addiction to sports can be understood in part as a creative attempt to compensate for the 'absent father' syndrome occasioned by the separation of work and home and to reassert and revalorize 'masculinity' amid the atomization of the bustling cities. One of the most supportive networks for sports in the late nineteenth century was the fraternal 'bachelor culture,' centred around taverns and poolhalls. (In 1901, the percentage of single adult males in the Canadian population was greater than at any time during the twentieth century.)[17] It is clear that there were tremendous synergies feeding the spectacular growth of sports.[18]

The various agencies of the Canadian state also contributed to the developing practice and meaning of sports, primarily through regulation of leisure. Governments declared public holidays, dedicated land for all manner of recreation, and bestowed prestige on what they sought to encourage, while they tried to eliminate what they deemed immoral and improper through temperance, sabbatarian, and criminal legislation. The Lord's Day Act of 1845 in Canada West (Ontario), largely adapted from British practice, prohibited 'skittles, foot-ball, racket or any other noisy game, to gamble with dice or otherwise, to run races on foot or on horseback, to go out fishing or hunting or shooting, or to bathe in any exposed situation in any water' on Sunday.[19] After Confederation, it became the law of Ontario. In 1868, Ottawa helped establish the Dominion of Canada Rifle Association and subsidized its competitions with public funds. Between 1868 and 1908, dominion assistance to rifle shooting exceeded $1.5 million.[20] In 1881, following a 'disgraceful, lewd prize fight' in Windsor, Parliament prohibited 'prize-fighting.' According to Justice Minister James McDonald, who introduced the legislation to the House of Commons, the ban was intended to 'vindicat(e) public morality and the peace of the people' by stamping out the rowdiness that was believed to accompany a highly publicized bout. The debates reveal little concern for the health and safety of combatants.[21] At the same time, governors general patronized the new middle-class male team sports of hockey, rugby, and lacrosse.[22]

Municipal governments were just as heavy-handed on the side of their friends. They provided parks and playing spaces, but just as often prohibited public use of traditional swimming holes and playing fields, usually at the instigation of entrepreneurs eager to sell admission to fenced-off areas of rivers and canals and private gymnasiums. Local governments also contributed to the growing representational status of athletes and teams, sponsoring banquets and rich prizes for athletes who brought home honour. Many cities assisted in the development of professional teams.[23] Such interventions, which reinforced and extended class-gender boundaries, were continually made, sought, and challenged in a complex politics.

Another site for the development of sports was the school. Private schools such as Toronto's Upper Canada College actively encouraged them. Once compulsory schooling was enacted, middle-class reformers tried to have state schools foster health, self-discipline, respect for authority, and a national 'community of feeling' through 'physical training.' Egerton Ryerson, the chief superintendent of Ontario education for much of its formative period, had been most impressed with the rigour of physical education in Prussia; instruction in Ontario emphasized gymnastics and military drill. The actual curricula sharply reinforced the gender division of labour. Since most girls were expected to graduate into domestic service, they were taught calisthenics, posture, and personal hygiene. Yet the children themselves much preferred the excitement of sports. Though public schools in Canada seldom taught them, both boys and girls played them during breaks and after classes.[24]

Perhaps the single most important factor contributing to the 'making of sports' was the celebrity given sports by mass-circulation newspapers and magazines. As early as Confederation, publishers and their employees promoted sports in their publications, initially to attract readers, then to sell male readers to advertisers. They often hired sportsmen and their friends to write about the events. H.J.P. Good, Canada's first full-time sportswriter, was a member of Toronto's Hanlan Club, formed in 1876 to put the young oarsman's career on a business-like basis.[25] Newspapers were among the first public voices to stress the representational character of athletes and teams, and they used the telegraph to give sports followers virtually instant results, even when they were not printing. In 1902, when the Toronto Wellingtons challenged the Winnipeg Victorias for the Stanley Cup in Winnipeg, Toronto's *Globe* gave fans a running account outside its King Street offices. Men from all classes and backgrounds stood in the cold to hear the brief wire play-by-play read out. It gave them a moment of shared interest. Newspapers gave even greater publicity to Canadians in international competition. In 1908, the first time a unified Canadian team was selected for the Olympics, several newspapers sponsored trials and the jingoistic publisher of the *Montreal Star*, Hugh Graham, publicly intervened against the American Amateur Athletic Union's challenge to marathoner Tom Longboat's amateur status. On the day of the big race, they broadcast mile-by-mile bulletins outside their offices and gave front-page coverage to the final results.[26] Recent U.S. studies reinforce the overwhelming importance of the mass media in the creation of sports.[27] It was no doubt because of their strategic position in the ideological marketing of sports that so many newspapermen became successful entrepreneurs. Byron 'Ban' Johnson, the American (Baseball) League president who led it to 'major league' status, started out as a sportswriter, as did Frank Calder, the first president of the National Hockey League.

Controlling the development of sports under such conditions was no easy task, but Canada's most powerful clubs and organizers strove to do so. By 1914, 20 volunteer-led governing bodies claimed 'national' jurisdiction in their respective sports, while the Amateur Athletic Union of Canada (AAU) organized track and field, gymnastics, handball, fencing, boxing, and wrestling (see Table 1.1). In addition, the Canadian Intercollegiate Athletic Union (CIAU), the Canadian Police Amateur Athletic Association (CPAAA), and the YMCA Athletic League conducted programs and championships in a range of sports for their members. In what was a uniquely Canadian arrangement, the CIAU, the CPAAA, and the YMCA, plus four national single-sport bodies, accepted the AAU's jurisdiction over amateurism.[28]

A group's assertion of national control in a sport brought it the right to organize participation in international competition. The first ventures by Canadians in other countries – in the 1840s in cricket, in the 1860s in rowing – were initiated by individuals and clubs, but with the establishment of national sport governing bodies in other industrializing countries (Table 1.2) and then international federations (Table 1.3), international

TABLE 1.1
Sports governing bodies claiming national status in Canada in 1914

Governing body	Year created
Dominion of Canada Rifle Association	1868
Canadian Association of Amateur Oarsmen	1880
Canadian Wheelmen's Association	1882
Amateur Athletic Union of Canada*	1884
Canadian Rugby Football Union	1887
Amateur Athletic Skating Association	1887
Canadian Cricket Association	1892
Royal Canadian Golf Association	1894
Canadian Lawn Tennis Association	1895
Canadian Canoe Association	1900
Canadian Snow Shoe Union	1900
Canadian Bowling Association	1901
Canadian Amateur Swimming Association	1909
Dominion Football (Soccer) Association	1912
Canadian Ladies Golf Union	1913
Canadian Squash Racquets Association	1913
Canadian Amateur Lacrosse Association†	1914
Canadian Amateur Hockey Association‡	1914

* The AAU began as the Amateur Athletic Association of Canada, formed in 1884. It was renamed the Canadian Amateur Athletic Union in 1898 and the Amateur Athletic Union of Canada in 1909. It governed track and field, gymnastics, handball, fencing, boxing, and wrestling.
† Preceded by the National Lacrosse Association (1867) and the Canadian Lacrosse Association (1887)
‡ Preceded by the Amateur Hockey Association of Canada (1886)

competition was brought under the governing bodies' monopoly. In each case, the international federation gave the national federation the sole right to send 'representative' athletes abroad. These developments, and the growth of international competitions, were encouraged by the modern Olympic Games, begun in 1896. At first, sending an official team into international competition was beyond many Canadian organizations' fledgling abilities. In 1893, when J. Astley Cooper invited the AAU to send a Canadian team to his proposed Pan-Britannic Games, its executive concluded, after circulating member clubs, that such an enterprise was premature.[29] Pressed by athletes and the press, the national organizations soon made the effort. In 1911, the AAU's team won the 'Festival of Empire' Games held to celebrate the coronation of George V.[30] By 1914, Canadians could identify with 'world' champions in rowing, figure skating, track and field, shooting, lacrosse, golf, soccer, and boxing.

TABLE 1.2
Creation of national sports bodies in selected countries

Sport	Year created			
	Britain	Germany	Sweden	United States
Cricket	1788			1878
Shooting	1860			1871
Soccer	1863	1900	1904	
Swimming	1869	1887	1904	1878
Rowing	1879	1883	1904	1872
Cycling	1878	1884	1900	1880
Lacrosse	1880			1879
Skating	1879	1888	1904	1888
Athletics	1880	1898	1895	1888
Lawn tennis	1888	1902	1906	1881
Ice hockey	1914			1896

SOURCE: Robert Glassford and Gerald Redmond, 'Physical Education and Sport in Modern Times,' in E.F. Zeigler, ed., *History of Physical Education and Sport* (Englewood Cliffs, NJ, 1979), 138–9

TABLE 1.3
Creation of international sports federations

Sports federation	Year created
Federation internationale de gymnastique	1881
Fédération internationale des sociétés d'aviron	1892
International Skating Union	1892
International Olympic Committee	1894
Confédération mondiale du sport de boules	1895
Fédération internationale amateur de cyclisme	1900
Fédération internationale de Football Association	1904
International Weightlifting Association	1905
International Yacht Racing Union	1907
Union internationale de tir	1907
Fédération internationale de natation amateur	1908
International Ice Hockey Federation	1908
Imperial Cricket Conference	1909
Fédération internationale de lutte amateur	1912
International Amateur Athletic Federation	1912
Fédération internationale d'escrime	1913
Fédération internationale de tennis	1913

Canadian sportsmen promoted their own sports abroad, too. Though McGill University's contribution to the development of American football was less than is frequently claimed, the modern international sports of lacrosse, ice hockey, curling, and competitive rifle shooting, and the winter carnival, were clearly Canadian – actually Montrealers' – innovations.[31] In 1876 and 1883, Beers took teams to the British Isles to 'utiliz(e) the great crowds gathered together to distribute information about the Dominion as a home and a field for the capitalist.' On both tours, the Canadians played an Aboriginal team from Kahnewake and beat them most of the time. Press reports stressed the superiority of the white side's 'scientific teamwork,' but the games may well have been staged to show the Euro-Canadians to maximum advantage. Both whites and Mohawks trounced the British clubs that had sprung up in the wake of the tours. In 1883, Beers distributed 500,000 copies of a special issue of the *Canadian Illustrated News* boosting immigration to Canada.[32] In 1910, when a team of hockey-playing Rhodes scholars at Oxford entered the European championship in Les Avants, Switzerland, they discovered that the English, German, and Swiss teams had been strengthened by fellow Canadians. The Canadians had 'ringers,' too: one Newfoundlander and one American. The Oxford Canadians held the European championship right up until the war.[33]

A Divided Terrain

While sporting activity was increasingly widespread, the nature of and access to opportunities continued to vary considerably. Only ice hockey and baseball were played by significant numbers all across Canada, and only baseball drew players and spectators from all classes. Americans have long claimed baseball as their own invention, but the 'summer game' has deep roots in Canada as well. In fact, Canadian players were so good during the late nineteenth century that the U.S. Congress was persuaded to keep them out through the Alien Contract Labour Act of 1885.[34] Climate, the local economy, age, class, gender, and ethnicity all influenced developments in sports. The best facilities, coaching, and competitions tended to be in the English-Canadian businessmen's clubs, universities, and YMCAs in the centres that had access to the surpluses from Canadian economic activity and where there were commercial and professional classes of sufficient size and wealth to invest in sports. For working-class and immigrant men, 'the most fundamental constraint on working class recreation ... was work itself.' They toiled long hours in exhausting, often unsafe conditions.[35] It would be wrong to assume that sports served as a ready unifier.

Yet First Nations, francophone, working-class, and immigrant men did find some time to participate, and some created organizations of their own. Native athletes were so accomplished in running, snowshoeing, and lacrosse that they were often excluded because they were too good; George Beers called them 'the best made men in the world.' In the 1870s, the most successful lacrosse team in Canada was the Montreal Shamrocks, whose players came from the skilled Irish-Catholic working class, though the organizers were lawyers and politicians such as Mayor James McShane. In 1895, the Young Jubilees hockey team from Dartmouth played the Halifax Eurekas for the 'Coloured Championship.' By the turn of the century, French-speaking Québécois played hockey and baseball on the streets and in classical colleges, while the Societé canadienne pour l'avancement du sport tried to stimulate a more scientific approach to training and competition. The society enjoyed the patronage of the governor general and the mayor of Montreal but soon disappeared for lack of funds.[36]

Many unions, from the respectable crafts of the American Federation of Labor (AFL) to the revolutionary International Workers of the World (IWW), had their regular summer picnics, where races, baseball, boxing, and wrestling (scheduled and otherwise) were accompanied by long lunches, conversation and courting, singing and dancing. The bonds forged by these activities were strengthened when working people were denounced by their 'betters' for engaging in them and for 'traipsing off' to velocipede and pedestrian races, prizefighting, travelling circuses, and cockfighting, on the Sabbath.[37] Non-British immigrants took up sports, too, often in their own social organizations, such as the Finnish club Yritys, formed in Toronto in 1906. In ice hockey, many teams were formed in the mining towns of the resource hinterland; in 1905, a team travelled all the way from Dawson City, Yukon, to Ottawa to challenge (unsuccessfully) for the Stanley Cup. Some of the fiercest rivalries in curling and baseball occurred between prairie towns.[38]

But on the whole, the best programs were located in middle-class men's organizations in the large, prosperous cities. Up until the First World War, few of the 'national' organizations extended beyond Montreal and southern Ontario. The Canadian Intercollegiate Athletic Union (CIAU) had only three active members – McGill, Queen's, and the University of Toronto. Up until 1908, track and field championships were always held in Montreal and no travel funds were available to help others attend. Of the 38 'national' track and field records standing at the outbreak of war, 27 were held by Toronto athletes and nine by Hamiltonians. Thirty-three record holders came from YMCAs.[39] Until 1909, the AAU was entirely controlled by Montreal and Toronto clubs. Veterinarian H.D. Johnson of Charlottetown was the first national officer to come from outside those two cities. He was elected in 1913, in the union's 29th year of operations.

Almost everywhere, sports were meant to be masculine, a training ground for those qualities of physical artistry and strength, courage and stamina, ingenuity and loyalty that gave men their claim to the greatest share of the social surplus. They were usually played in all-male institutions, and audiences were largely male as well. The 'sports page' was essentially the 'men's page.' In part, sports were promoted to sustain the mystique of male superiority at a time of first-wave feminism. At the same time, sports were taught as an antidote to the 'feminization' of young boys. The increasing separation of work and household left children to be reared by mothers and older sisters, while the establishment of compulsory schooling turned them over to female teachers (who could be hired at a fraction of what it cost for a man). In this environment, fathers, uncles, and civic leaders rushed to introduce sports to their sons and nephews lest they become 'sissified,' the way Theodore Roosevelt had to his weakly and asthmatic son, Theodore, Jr, the future American president. In the 1890s, churches and YMCAs began to offer sports as a way of reversing the exodus of young men from their services and programs.[40] The acclaimed equation of sport with manliness was so pervasive that it led constables and magistrates to equivocate with the law. 'I feel confident that it will be a long time before Parliament will think it wise to so hedge in young men and boys by legislation that all sports that are rough and strenuous or even dangerous must be given up. Virility in young men would soon be lessened and self-reliant manhood a thing of the past,' Judge Snider of Hamilton argued in his acquittal of two men who had been arrested for prizefighting.[41]

Organizers took no account of the needs and experiences of females and strove to maintain sports as 'male preserves.' They denied girls and women facilities and opportunities, ridiculed their attempts to participate in vigorous activity, and threatened them with the spectre of ill health and 'race suicide' when they did. Despite the abundant evidence of women working strenuously in agriculture, industry, and domestic service, many of these prohibitions were couched in the language of medicine and science. Helen Lenskyj calls it 'moral physiology.'[42] In 1914, the AAU rejected a proposal for female affiliation.[43] Working-class males generally shared these prejudices, even when females from their own class were involved, suggesting that sports helped men strengthen and extend cross-class masculine bonds. Economic and social conditions – long hours of physical and reproductive labour, less adequate diets, restrictive dress, and so on – also deterred many girls and women from participation.

Despite these obstacles, middle- and upper-class women in feminist organizations, social clubs, and the newly coeducational universities struggled to start events and clubs.[44] Their efforts were aided by the successful battle for dress reform and the fin-de-siècle fashion of the athletic 'Gibson girl,' the growing advocacy of some physical activity for women by progressive physical educators and doctors, and the invention of the 'safety bicycle,' which gave many women the chance to pursue physical activity for the first time.[45] To deflect male hostility, many women confined their activity to those sports such as croquet, figure skating, golf, and lawn tennis where the 'grace and bearing' expected of 'ladies' could be maintained, but they were not afraid of competition. As early as 1883, women held their own 'national' tennis championship in Toronto. Middle-class girls and women learned the game on the hundreds of church courts that were constructed at the time. After the turn of the century, university women and university-educated teachers led a growing number into the 'manly sports' of basketball and ice hockey, while younger girls played baseball and softball in the public playgrounds created by organizations such as the National Council of Women. In the Finnish and Swedish immigrant clubs, girls and women were actively involved in the annual gymnastics festivals. None of the games was played with or against men. The ideological constructions of the 'manly sports' and 'femininity' were too far apart to countenance it.

If Canadian sports were segregated by gender, they were also divided by ideology and organization. The men who created and promoted the new sports initially clothed them in the aristocratic mantle of British amateurism. The earliest 'amateur codes' restricted participation on the basis of class and race, reflecting the upper classes' desire to reproduce the social hierarchies of Victorian England and the British Empire and to maintain the primacy of sports as an expression of manly honour and elegant display. The definition used by the Montreal Pedestrian Club in 1873 stated: '[An amateur] is one who has never competed in any open competition or for public money, or for admission money, or with professionals for a prize, public money or admission money, nor has ever, at any period of his life taught or assisted in the pursuit of athletic exercises as a means of livelihood or is a *labourer or an Indian*' (emphasis added).[46]

But by the time the Amateur Athletic Association of Canada (AAA, predecessor of the AAU) was formed in 1884, the ideological landscape had shifted considerably. In an age of fierce industrial and commercial competition, the ethos of sports as a field of 'civilized' contest and achievement had begun to overtake the culture of sports as upper-class ostentation. Growing working-class political power, gradual acceptance of liberal-democratic ideas, and the celebrity of Native, Black, and working-class 'professional' athletes also made the ascriptive and racist provisions of the earlier codes difficult, if not impossible, to maintain. Perhaps most important, a growing segment of the middle class came to believe that sports would help civilize the lower orders. Along with others from the middle and working classes who established voluntary associations to promote public libraries, gardening clubs, and popular science lectures in the interests of purposeful leisure or 'rational recreation,' the middle-class amateurs hoped that sports would encourage good citizenship, social harmony, and nationalism. Participation 'for its own sake,' without the possibility of material reward, they believed, encouraged fair play and responsible dealings with others. [47] After Pierre de Coubertin made amateurism a condition of participation in his Olympic Games, the amateur leaders grafted his aspirations for international understanding and peace onto their ideology. These beliefs led them to eliminate from the rules of the new amateur federation the ascriptive provisions that hitherto had restricted sports to their own schools and clubs.

But the AAA retained the sanctions against the receipt of athletic income, even when it came from teaching or coaching, and the 'contamination rule,' which barred amateurs from the same field as professionals, even if no money were at stake. This approach mediated the tensions between the universalist ambition of 'rational recreation,' the possible embarrassment of losing to athletes from the lower orders, and the lingering desire for social isolation. It was a very 'cautious meritocracy.'[48] As a result, the amateur code still excluded many by circumstance, at least at the highest levels of competition, because it blocked one obvious means for working-class athletes to circumvent the inequalities of Canadian society: it required them to have the leisure to pursue sport on a systematic basis and the means to purchase club memberships, equipment, and travel to out-of-town competitions, while denying them the chance to earn the money to do so from their performances.

Amateurism was thus a complex blending of traditional upper-class and emerging middle-class views.

To be sure, some athletes and promoters earned a good deal of money from sports. As we have seen, the same industrial capitalist economy that facilitated 'reconstruction' of game contests enhanced the possibilities for production and sale of leisure-related commodities, services, and entertainments, in the process that Harry Braverman has called the 'universal market.'[49] As capitalism transformed work, urban space, and interpersonal relationships, entrepreneurs took over production of more and more of the means of everyday existence, including the material base and forms of culture. Sports entrepreneurs constructed rental facilities, manufactured equipment, established instructional programs, published inspirational and technical information, and staged and publicized contests. The advertisement of these commodities and services furthered the popularity and accessibility of sports and enabled a profit-seeking sector that emphasized professional spectacles to develop alongside amateur sports.

The production of athletic events as commercial entertainments has an uneven and unruly history. In the colonial period, tavern owners, enterprising non-commissioned officers, and itinerant promoters had staged prizefights, wrestling matches, and other exhibitions of strength, usually on the major holidays, as often as not along with cockfighting, bear-baiting and other 'blood sports.'[50] By Confederation, the growing popularity of sports allowed slightly more 'respectable' impresarios and enterprises – urban theatre owners, railway companies, and agricultural societies – to stage contests and exhibitions, not only in boxing and wrestling but in long-distance walking and running, rowing, swimming, and occasionally gymnastics. The highlight of the Confederation Day gala in Hamilton, for example, was a ten-mile relay race between two teams of native runners, featuring the legendary Deerfoot.[51] In the 1880s, the most sought-after attraction was the pedestrian or 'go-as-you-please' race, in which competitors walked or ran around a narrow indoor track, sometimes for as long as six days. In 1888, George Littlewood covered $623\frac{3}{4}$ miles in 142 hours, a record which lasted until 1986 and the revival of 'ultramarathoning' under infinitely better conditions. David Bennett's Canadian six-day record of $540\frac{3}{4}$ miles, set in 1891, still stands.[52] Throughout the decade, the 'peds' were much preferred by promoters to the more popular rowing races as a commercial proposition, because admission to the grounds could be controlled. The great sculling duels of the period were usually held over an out-and-back course of three miles. It was virtually impossible to fence off and police the whole 1½-mile stretch of water needed for the race. These regattas were often bonanzas for the railway companies, however.

Stake races, sponsored purses, and gambling on the outcome intensified popular interest and stimulated development of organization, measurement, and regulation. When Toronto's Ned Hanlan raced against – and trounced – Australian Edward Trickett on the Thames in London, England, in 1880, Canadians backed him with $42,000 in bets, while the Aussies put an estimated $100,000 on Trickett.[53] Throughout the nineteenth century, most commercial contests were one-time events, pitting two competitors against each other or involving very small fields. These had the advantage of small capital outlays and rarely required specialized facilities. The development of profitable entertainments from the newly codified team games proved more difficult, requiring cooperation of two or more clubs and larger and more specialized facilities.

One factor that retarded growth of commercial sports was the unsavoury reputation that surrounded most professional athletes and promoters. Cheating, fixed races, and gambling 'stings' were frequent, and even such icons of civic virtue as Hanlan engaged in questionable practices, such as dodging challenges until the conditions and purse were right, and were reduced to performing like circus clowns at exhibitions and fairs.[54] The brawls that frequently broke out among players and spectators during professional lacrosse matches evoked images of the blood sports and the violent, seemingly uncontrolled labouring-class masculinity of the pre-industrial era, which 'improvers' of all stripes sought to stamp out. It was largely because of the boorish behaviour of fans and the threat to public order that it was imagined to encourage that Parliament outlawed prize-fighting. Commercial leaders and the virtuous middle class also feared the absenteeism, drunkenness, and 'desecration' of the Sabbath that went hand in hand with professional sports. Creation of the AAA and other amateur governing bodies was one direct result. Amateur leaders felt that they needed to differentiate themselves from the debased professionals in order to win respectability for their activities and organizations.[55]

The Rising Tide of Professionalism

Yet amateur organizers increasingly faced conditions that tempted them to consider professionalism. Though their initial goals focused entirely on the benefits of sports to participants – even Pierre de Coubertin did not take spectators into account in his first plans for Olympic Games – their events often attracted audiences quite willing to pay. In the 1880s, the Montreal Shamrocks regularly attracted 8,000–9,000 fans a game. In 1896, when the average hourly wage was 15 cents, a box seat for a Stanley Cup game in Winnipeg between the Winnipeg Victorias and the Montreal Victorias – at the height of empire, the old queen's name was a favourite – cost \$12. Some athletes began to demand that they share in the proceeds. Another stimulus was the pressure to win. As the press and local boosters increased the representational status of athletes and teams, and as meritocratic and utilitarian ideas spread generally, 'winning' gradually replaced character building and fraternization as the primary goals of many organizations. If a town's reputation was on the line, then 'its team' had to have the best players. That eventually meant freeing players from their other jobs to enable them to practise, encouraging them to develop specialized skills, and 'importing' better players from outside the community.

These practices began in the United States, where amateurism held little sway, and came to Canada in the 1880s through the popularity of baseball, for which sport the border simply did not seem to exist. Moreover, the logic of professionalism was self-reinforcing. For those impatient to win, it was easier to import accomplished Americans than to nurture their own, which in turn retarded development of Canadian talent, which made imports still more attractive. By 1887, Toronto had an all-American team.[56] Organizing a fully professional league was extremely risky – with extremely short seasons, fluctuating revenues, and cut-throat competition, none of the early Canadian efforts lasted more than a few seasons – but the potential advantages for a single team were clear. Because athletes and organizers moved from one sport to another as the seasons changed, they took the professionalism with them. Some would object outright to the 'American idea – hiring athletes to play your games for you.' In 1888, the president of the Ottawa Lacrosse Club resigned over his executive's decision to 'import' several players rather than stay with its own. Some players refused to accept payment for their 'services.' But others were eager to be paid. Professionalism was unwittingly encouraged in Canadian rugby, hockey, and lacrosse by vice-regal patronage: while the Grey, Stanley, and Minto cups, respectively, were awarded for amateur competition, the prestige they offered persuaded some managers and community 'backers' to stack their teams with secretly paid 'ringers.' Amateur officials tried to stamp out professional-ism, but it was well established, if not always officially recognized, by the turn of the century. It was particularly strong in the mining towns of northern Ontario, such as Cobalt, Haileybury, and Timmins, and in the small towns of the prairies, where interest in sports was high, professionalism was felt necessary to gain a competitive edge, and there were few members of the middle class to oppose it.[57]

Until the late 1890s, most of those in a position to influence the development of Canadian sports adhered to amateurism. If the code prevented a few working-class athletes, itinerant professionals, and fast-buck artists from involvement in their activities, so much the better. But by the turn of the century, as more clubs tried to bolster their teams with imported stars, the AAA (renamed the Canadian Amateur Athletic Union, or CAAU, in 1898) was spending most of its time investigating alleged cases of professionalism. Some club leaders and officials felt that it would make more sense to accept the inevitability of professionalism and liberalize the rules. It was the heyday of the National Policy. Staple exports – fish, lumber and pulp, coal, iron, and other metals, and wheat – from the hinterlands and the prairies stimulated massive investments in infrastructural improvements and tariff-supported manufacturing in southern Ontario and around Montreal. In virtually every region, production soared and cities grew. In the industrial sector, the net value of annual output more than doubled from 1900 to 1910, from $214.5 million to $564.5 million. Between 1901 and 1911, the population of Vancouver and Winnipeg increased fourfold, while Ottawa, Montreal, and Toronto grew by 44, 67, and 82 per cent, respectively. Business and boosterism reigned, and creation of new ventures, corporate mergers, and projects of civic 'improvement' were the order of the day. In sports, teams proliferated, equipment manufacturing flourished, attendance climbed, and newspaper coverage intensified. It must have seemed to many that the ideology and practice of the capitalist market would quickly rout the restrictions of amateurism. More and more organizers were prepared to bankroll a team to make a run for a championship. It would have been impossible for the tiny town of Kenora to win the Stanley Cup in 1907 had it not been able to hire players from other parts of Canada.[58]

Yet not everyone in amateur sport was prepared to bend to the changing times. Many athletes and officials insisted that the rules be strictly enforced. As these differences became increasingly bitter, positions hardened. The CAAU became ungovernable. In 1905, the liberal forces won a brief victory, pushing through a motion 'not to enforce the penalties provided for in the event of amateurs competing with or against professionals' in lacrosse, thereby allowing clubs to pay some players. It was a step towards the sort of vertical integration of amateur and professional sport that had already occurred in American baseball and British soccer. But this concession angered so many amateur purists that at the very next meeting it was overturned. In response, several clubs walked out and created their own national body, the Amateur Athletic Federation (AAF), which would permit a limited amount of competition between pros and amateurs. Canadian sport was in a state of civil war.

During the next few years, Union and Federation leaders sniped at each other's athletes and stumped the country to win adherents, while athletes, sportwriters, and fans argued about the merits of each position. The split was at once ideological, practical, and regional. In a milieu in which ideals were prized, it pitted deeply held notions about 'order,' 'community,' and 'status' against the buying, selling, and uncertainty of the market. For the strict amateur, the idea of hiring an athlete to represent one's club was as repugnant as the idea of taking performance-enhancing drugs has been among Olympic circles in our own time: it undermined the sacred tenet of 'fair sport' and distorted the identifications between athletes and their followers. Many denounced 'pay for play' as a form of prostitution. For them, it debased sports and athletes by focusing on the outcome of the contest rather than on the character formation that it made possible. AAF supporters countered these arguments on a similar terrain; morality and remuneration were hardly incompatible, they contended, unless the AAU leaders, most of whom drew salaries or profits from employment or business, were admitting unethical behaviour at work. Fairness required that if amateur clubs were selling tickets, performers should get some of the proceeds.

The antagonists also understood that the amateur code significantly structured opportunity and the field of play. A less restrictive rule might afford more athletes the chance to make some money from sports, while enabling teams in smaller towns to purchase better players. But it also might reduce the opportunities for those deserving athletes not good enough to make a 'stacked' team and give the richest clubs and cities a long-term advantage. It would concentrate energies on production of champions rather than on provision of sports for all. These calculations were rarely omitted in the endless debates.

At the outset, it seemed that the liberal forces would win the day. It was not only shady promoters and small-town merchants who wanted to relax the rules, but some of the most powerful big-city clubs. The new federation was led by the influential Montreal Amateur Athletic Association (MAAA), whose directors had voted overwhelmingly – 250 to 12 – to allow amateurs to play with and against professionals. This decision would give the MAAA lacrosse team a better chance to retain the Minto Cup, whose trustees were not prepared to police players' eligibility. In 1906, the Stanley Cup trustees followed suit, declaring the challenge open to all comers. In the heady optimism and buoyant economy of the times, the AAF seemed to represent the wave of the future.

Yet adherents of strict amateurism were not prepared to give up without a fight. Their base was Toronto, where British loyalties were strong and the population was sufficiently large to ensure a vibrant sporting culture without athletes having to be imported from outside. It was the home of the 'Three Czars' – W.A. Hewitt, Francis Nelson, and John Ross Robertson – to whom the Ontario Hockey Association had given the power to enforce strict amateurism with an iron hand. W.A.'s son Foster has remembered that their fierce opposition kept professional hockey teams out of Toronto until 1913.[59] Another Toronto triumvirate – civil servant Norton Crow, police chief William Stark, and businessman James Merrick – led the CAAU. Crow, Stark, Merrick, and their supporters sought to win the 'amateur wars' by outflanking the AAF with a much broader base of support. They tried in particular to bring the often-neglected Maritimes and the new western provinces into the fold with the promise of a federal constitution and new, national programs. In 1908, to give substance to these promises, they took the prestigious CAAU track and field championships, which had always been held in Montreal, to Halifax.

The Union's campaign was pushed over the top by a disastrous tactical error on the part of the AAF. In 1907, at the invitation of Governor General Earl Grey, the feuding parties agreed to cooperate in the selection of a representative Olympic team for the London Games of 1908. But on the eve of the Games the following summer, the American AAU sought to have marathon runner Tom Longboat barred from the Games on the grounds that he was no longer an amateur. The CAAU staunchly defended Longboat as a member of the Canadian team, but AAF president Thomas Boyd supported the American protest. The Americans' appeal was denied, and Longboat raced, only to collapse at the 20-mile mark, just as he was overtaking the leaders. The report of the Canadian Olympic Committee indicated that he had been knocked out by a 'drug overdose,' though whether administered by friend or foe remains a mystery.[60]

Despite this disappointing result, the episode garnered the CAAU the potent Canadianism that the Olympic Games had aroused and fanned the anti-Americanism sparked by other conflicts, such as U.S. President Theodore Roosevelt's bullying treatment of Canada during the Alaska boundary dispute. Public opinion turned bitterly against the 'baseness and treachery' of the AAF. By the end of 1908, the CAAU had increased its membership to 1,200 clubs (from 36 in 1905) from all parts of Canada, while the AAF was reduced to its Montreal-Ottawa stronghold. The upstart federation was forced to capitulate. At the mediation of McGill professor Fred Tees, the winners agreed to a face-saving name change – the 'amalgamated' organization would become the Amateur Athletic Union of Canada (AAU) – but they insisted on and obtained a strict definition of amateurism.[61]

The Triumph of Amateurism and the 'Gospel of Order'

By upholding the sanctions against 'pay for play,' the men who rallied to the CAAU during the amateur wars hoped that a firm stand would reduce the instability produced by the cheating, misrepresentation, and frenzied bidding for players that accompanied the rapid growth of sport in the early twentieth century and preserve an emphasis on sport as 'rational recreation.' Don Morrow thinks that they were 'unrealistic' to do so, suggesting that in a capitalistic society it was vain and foolish even to think that they could block the ideology of professionalism. Alan Metcalfe concludes that 'nothing had been solved.'[62] But we must remember that the strict amateurs defined professionalism primarily as a moral issue, not a practical one. Their refusal to compromise resonated deeply with the dominant beliefs of their times. The conservative nationalism they espoused was 'the mainstream of Canadian opinion.'[63] Unlike Americans, with their founding myths of revolution, individual freedom, and unfettered competition, Canadians have always been more concerned with the orderly development of society and preservation of community traditions. The British North America Act of 1867 entrusted the dominion government with preserving 'peace, order and good government,' not ensuring 'life, liberty and the pursuit of happiness,' as in the American constitution. To be sure, there were always those, such as journalist Goldwin Smith, who admired the much more open and democratic American way, but in the years before the First World War they were in a small minority. The 'gospel of order' was one of the pillars of popular belief. It buttressed reverence for the family, the Christian faith, and the work ethic.[64] Ralph Conner was the most widely read English-Canadian novelist at the time. His Canadian characters, many of whom excelled in sports, 'espouse wholeheartedly a respect for legitimate authority and a recognition of the need for law and order within society.'[65] Rather than standing against the tide of professionalism, Crow, Merrick, Stark, and their supporters felt that they were raising dikes against it to protect what they took to be the fundamental values of Canadian society.[66]

Among the middle classes, it was not only the amateur sports leaders who sought to bring 'order out of chaos' during the destabilizing expansion of capitalism in the early years of the century by imposing and enforcing a system of restraint. Businessmen hoped to do so through protective tariffs; health advocates, through powers of quarantine and regulation; and women's and religious groups, through temperance restrictions. (Labour leaders sought it in collective agreements and employers' standards legislation, but that was not an example the amateur leaders wanted to encourage.) When Governor General Earl Grey established Music and Dramatic Competitions in Ottawa in 1907, the forerunner to the Dominion Drama Festival, he won popular support for his insistence that only amateurs could compete. Many others shared his unwillingness to entrust the challenge of creating an indigenous theatre to the 'crass' American and British professionals who toured the commercial houses.[67] Passage of the Lord's Day Act must have given the CAAUers further confidence. Sunday competition was also prohibited in the amateur code. In endorsing 'protection' of amateurism, the great majority of Canadian sportsmen were not unlike the English-Canadian voters who rejected the freer trade of Liberal 'reciprocity' in the dominion election of 1911. Unlike conservatives today, they understood that the market that liberals prized was neither 'free' nor 'neutral.' They sought to encourage the competitive spirit, but they did not want unrestrained competition. They were not prepared to relinquish their own control.

The CAAU's victory was a watershed, which continues to shape amateur and Olympic sports in Canada to this day. Though it did not bring all the leading sectors of Canadian sport back into the fold, it gave the Union unprecedented legitimacy and authority in the eyes of the sporting public and the stability, loyalty, and enthusiasm required for significant growth. The Union's new federal constitution, which gave voting power to provincial branches, allied members, and affiliates instead of to clubs, paved the way for expansion into the Maritimes, the hinterland of

Ontario, and new provinces of western Canada. Tensions between the goals of 'rational recreation' and pursuit of winning would continue to grow, but refusal to make any accommodation with professionalism ensured that voluntary participation and leadership would structure provision of opportunities. The amateur leaders were soon able to bring about creation of new governing bodies in lacrosse (the Canadian Amateur Lacrosse Association) and ice hockey (the Canadian Amateur Hockey Association) unashamedly devoted to amateurism. Though a few clubs continued to bend the rules, they 'never seriously threatened the hegemony of amateurism prior to World War One.'[68] In 1914, the AAU enjoyed a membership of 1,300 clubs and 100,000 registered athletes. No other organization could rival it in scope and influence.

The outpouring of Canadianism during the trials of the CAAU fired the 'nation-building' imagination of both leaders and members alike. In 1910, Norton Crow held discussions about the possibility of a pan-Canadian sports festival along the lines of today's Canada Games. Others dreamed about sports-focused physical education in the schools. Henceforth, the aspirations of Canadian amateurism and English-Canadian nationalism would ever be intertwined. The CAAU's victory also consolidated the shift in power from Montreal to southern Ontario that had begun in the 1890s, when the national bodies in lacrosse, rowing, and cycling established their offices there. While Montrealers would continue to be active, and sportsmen from other cities would work their way up to the highest positions of amateur leadership, the most powerful decision makers would be concentrated in southern Ontario. Toronton-ians controlled the Canadian Olympic Committee until after the Second World War.

Canadian Sports during the Great War

The war brought most activities abruptly to a halt. Many events were voluntarily cancelled. Despite elaborate preparations for its annual August track and field championships – they were to be held in Charlottetown in 1914 as part of Golden Jubilee celebrations of the conference that launched Confederation – the AAU immediately postponed them and urged its members to enlist in the armed forces. One of the first to do so was President Johnson, who encouraged 'every member [to] offer his services to help along the Empire's cause.' The Union would stage no events of its own for the duration. Neither would the YMCA Athletic League, the Canadian Police AAA, and most women's associations.[69]

Others went ahead with events scheduled for the fall of 1914 but held them as fund-raisers and then closed their doors. When it became clear that there would be no easy march to Berlin, more clubs and organizations followed suit. In 1915, following the terrifying gas attack at Ypres, the sinking of the *Lusitania*, and press reports of German atrocities, the Intercollegiate Rugby Union, the Alberta Amateur Athletic Union, the Alberta Hockey Association, and the Alberta Rugby Football League, among others, ceased activity. Still others were forced to cancel or curtail their activities when the army commandeered playing fields, gymnasiums, and arenas for training and accommodating troops and storing equipment. In Edmonton and Calgary, for example, the military took over the arenas, and the senior ice hockey teams had to suspend operations.[70]

Many teams disbanded because their officers and athletes had enlisted. In the Montreal Amateur Athletic Association, 965 men, or 30 per cent of the active membership, signed up in the first three months of the war. In the Vancouver Rowing Club, all but 26 of 187 active members volunteered. Norton Crow reported that enlistment was high from other clubs as well. In many communities, organizers and athletes formed 'sportsmen's battalions.' This prompt response to the call to arms should not be surprising. Men of British background were generally the first to enlist,[71] and they were overrepresented in Canadian sports. It was not only a mother country that was in danger, but the home of sports, whose heroic appeal deeply resonated with the call to national self-sacrifice and the glory of military prowess.

British loyalties were particularly strong among amateur leaders. In debates, they frequently appealed to 'the British principles of sport.' Events in the United Kingdom were regularly reported in the press and closely followed. British athletes were popular attractions while on tour, and those who immigrated were quickly adopted as 'Canadians' for national teams travelling abroad. Vice-regal representatives from Britain had donated the prizes for the best-known championships – the Stanley Cup for men's ice hockey, the Minto Cup for men's lacrosse, the Grey Cup for men's rugby football, the Connaught Cup for men's soccer, and the Lady Dufferin Cup for women's figure skating. It was the British Olympic Committee, through the offices of Governor General Earl Grey, that initiated creation of what became the Canadian Olympic Committee. The principal in this effort was Grey's secretary, veteran colonial administrator John Hanbury-Williams. In 1911, the AAU initiated his election as the first International Olympic Committee member for Canada, even though he had been posted to Scotland two years previously. Hanbury-Williams's nomination was an extension of another common practice: few Canadian organizations could afford to send representatives to international meetings in Europe, so the British delegate invariably was given Canada's vote.[72]

Many amateur leaders were caught up in that curious current of Canadian nationalism known as 'imperialism.'[73] On the one hand, they jealously guarded their autonomy, insisting on a 'made-in-Canada' amateur definition. In soccer, they refused to accept the 'Old Country' practice of pro-am competition, even though their refusal ultimately led to withdrawal of the Dominion Football Association from the AAU. On the other hand, they sought to strengthen Canadian institutions through creation of an imperial federation. In 1909, they proposed establishment of an Imperial Board to create common standards for international competition. In 1911, they enthusiastically agreed to contribute to an 'all-British team' at the 1912 Olympic Games. The idea was to assemble and train in London all athletes from the empire, who would then travel to Stockholm as a single group, though they would compete for their own countries and colonies. Neither of these proposals came to fruition, but that did not dampen the AAUers' interest. The Canadian Olympic Team still trained in London.[74] When the empire went to war, the Canadian AAUers felt that they should be there.

Playing sports had long been considered preparation for war. Certainly the popular literature of the day made much of the association.[75] Like other imperialists, some amateur leaders had campaigned for militarization of physical activity in the schools, through creation of cadet corps and strengthening of military drill in the schools. Many of the most ardent advocates of cadet training, such as Toronto school inspector J.L. Hughes, and university leaders Maurice Hutton and Nathaniel Burwash of the University of Toronto and Andrew MacPhail of McGill, were visible supporters of amateur sports.[76] To be sure, not everyone endorsed such schemes. In 1911, A.S. Lamb, McGill's Australian-born athletic director, along with church and labour groups, strenuously objected to implementation of the Strathcona Trust, which encouraged schools to adopt a curriculum of physical education heavy in military drill with the carrot of grants and prizes. The trust had been initiated by Wilfrid Laurier's minister of militia, Frederick Borden.[77] But once war was declared, most gave their full support.

On 14 October 1914, a 'Veteran' asked the *Calgary Herald*, 'What are the young men of Canada thinking about? Hundreds of able-bodied and husky young men could be found walking the streets or crowded around the bulletin boards of the local newspapers. What, reading the war news! Oh Lord no! watching the results of a baseball game. And yet the Empire is fighting for its very existence.' For the next four years, recruitment campaigns followed the same theme. 'Why don't they come?' headlined an appeal placed in the *Montreal Gazette* by the 148th Battalion and the McGill Canadian Officers' Training Corps. The ad showed a wounded soldier on the battlefront, imagining a packed stadium back in Canada. The subheadline read: 'Why be a spectator here when you should play a mans [sic] part in the real game overseas.'[78] Recruitment rallies were often held in conjunction with athletic events, where prominent sportsmen made an appeal. The widespread expectation that sportsmen be in khaki quickly cut off the revenues that fuelled 'under-the-table professionalism.' In the few leagues that continued, only those where it was advertised that the gate receipts were turned over to war charities were well attended.[79]

But while civilian activities were severely curtailed, sports thrived in the military. In 1916, for example, the only rugby football played in Canada was between battalions – the 180th, 205th, 207th, and 244th, from Toronto, Hamilton, Ottawa, and Montreal, respectively. Physical training directors and the YMCA secretaries attached to most units taught sports to promote overall fitness and morale. Sportsmen's battalions formed their own teams and went seeking competition. Lest any wrangling over a soldier's status disrupt these programs and undermine the overall effort, the AAU gave its blessing to the mixing of amateurs and professionals – as long as they were in uniform. It also conferred the status of 'Canadian championships' on major events. Such dispensation would have been unthinkable in peacetime.[80]

Most competitions were held completely under military auspices, but several battalions while in Canada competed in civilian leagues, keeping them alive. Without a team from the 228th, for example, the professional National Hockey Association might well have folded in the winter of 1916–17. There were only three other teams. A winning team could bring honour, wagers, and spectator revenue to a unit, so commanders recruited and traded athlete-soldiers as ruthlessly as experienced sports managers. Conn Smythe later recollected that his 40th Battery team took almost $7,000 in gate receipts and wager winnings with it to Europe.[81] When the Canadians reached Europe, the best athletes were often matched against Allied teams, sometimes within a few miles of the front. In a race near Vimy Ridge in 1917, for example, Native Canadian Olympians Tom Longboat and Joe Keeper combined to win Canada the inter-Allied cross-country championship. The popular Longboat was frequently transferred, usually for sporting reasons. By war's end, he had served in seven units. Sports were also an essential part of the rehabilitation programs for wounded soldiers developed by R. Tait McKenzie, the Canadian-born and McGill-educated physical educator and surgeon who had become the director of physical education at the University of Pennsylvania. Soon after McKenzie enlisted, the British Army discovered that he was the author of the primary textbook on rehabilitation that it was using and put him in charge of the entire program.[82]

Continuities and Conflicts

These programs and events ensured that sports would continue to have a large following after the war, despite the tremendous loss of life among athletes and organizers and the disruption of so many activities. In fact, the war may well have strengthened the hold of sports on many Canadians. The army gave more men opportunities to participate than the amateur clubs had ever done. The élan of athletes performing in competitions behind the front line 'served to compensate for a sense of historic loss and disempowerment' emanating from the mindless slaughter in the trenches.[83] Certainly, a number of veterans' organizations were inspired to conduct programs for themselves and others long after the war. The high rates of enlistment for athletes and the many reports of their bravery in the field, the general popularity of the military events, and the successful use of sports in rehabilitation seemed to confirm the utilitarian claims so frequently made by AAU leaders. While there were critics of individual athletes and organizations, no modern-day Aristotle was heard to complain that athletes as a group were too pampered to fight an arduous campaign.[84] They became the source of considerable pride to Canadian troops at inter-Allied competitions. The memory of these competitions, along with the growing belief that Canada should play an independent role in foreign affairs, strengthened interest in Canadian Olympic athletes after the war.

The broader changes brought about by the war also improved conditions for sports. Mobilization accelerated the movement of young men and women to the cities and towns and increased the membership base for clubs of all kind. Some activity actually resumed with introduction of conscription in 1917 because it 'reliev[ed] the individual of any personal responsibility for the successful prosecution' of the war.[85] With the Armistice, startup began in earnest. Toronto high schools announced resumption of their ice hockey league the following day. Not even fear of a renewed influenza epidemic, which forced a ban on all cultural activities during the last two weeks of October 1918, could discourage them. In anticipation of the war's conclusion, those officers of the AAU still in Canada formed a 'reconstruction committee' to plan the return to normality. Despite four years of inactivity, the affairs of the Union were quickly back in full swing.

The AAUers would soon face new challenges from the sports entrepreneurs. The war had further accelerated penetration by the 'universal market' and interest in purchased entertainments such as spectator sports, especially in ice hockey, football, and lacrosse, where the representational status of teams was high. Henceforth, these battles would be fought out not only within the Union, but between it and openly professional organizations such as the National Hockey League, formed in 1917. The AAU's victory drove those organizers and athletes who embraced market forces into a much more aggressive commercialism than might have been the case if amateurs and professionals had been allowed to play alongside each other and produced devastating consequences for their pan-Canadian development. Though the AAU repeatedly lobbied the dominion for assistance, it was the NHL that gained the most from state intervention.

Other conflicts of purpose and meaning would intensify as well. Suffrage victories and the greatly increased participation of women in the wartime labour force validated feminist demands for access to traditionally male-exclusive spheres, including sports. But mothers, teachers, and women's leaders were far from united about the kind of sports they wanted their daughters to take up. At the same time, the trauma of the trenches; loss of the tavern, a traditional male bastion, to prohibition; and the uncertainties of demobilization and the postwar recession served to sharpen the importance of sports as male culture. At any moment, the sparks of gender politics might touch off a full-scale battle.

Regional and class conflict was hardly new either, but it also seemed to increase during the war and its aftermath. The uneven development of the Canadian economy, with its frequent cycles of boom and bust, accentuated the differences among regions and occupational groups, particularly in the Maritimes and the prairie provinces. These inequalities were exacerbated even further by the great crisis of capitalist speculation and overproduction of the 1920s. The ensuing Depression took a particularly heavy toll on the unskilled and the unemployed. The tasks of social development were further complicated by the steady immigration and out-migration of the period. During the 1920s, 1.2 million people came to Canada, while almost a million left, mostly to the United States. In this context, new organizations were formed to advance the interests of subordinate and marginal regions and groups. Though the workers' uprising that erupted in strikes all across Canada in the immediate aftermath of war was soon quelled, international developments in the socialist world led to creation of a new party that would put sports on its organizing agenda.

These challenges and the bitterness created by underlying inequalities would weigh heavily on sports development between the world wars, greatly complicating the AAU's ambition to build a unified national movement.

2

'The Making of Men'

Plenty of room for dives and dens (glitter and glare and sin)
Plenty of room for prison pens (gather the criminals in),
Plenty of room for jails and courts (willing enough to pay!),
But never a place for the lads to race (no, never a place to play).

Plenty of room for shops and stores (mammon must have the best!),
Plenty of room for the running sores (that rot in the city's breast!),
Plenty of room for the lures that lead the hearts of youth astray,
But never a cent on a playground spent (no, never a place to play!).

Plenty of room for schools and halls (plenty of room for art),
Plenty of room for teas and balls, platform, stage and mart.
Proud is the city – she finds a place for many a fad today,
But she's more than blind if she fails to find a place for the boys to play.

Give them a chance for innocent sport, give them a chance for fun;
Better a playground plot than a court and jail (when harm is done),
Give them a chance – if you stint them now, tomorrow you will have to pay
A larger bill for a darker ill, so give them a chance to play![1]

Dennis McCarty, *The Playground*, 3 June 1909

Humans have organized sports for excitement, friendship, profit, and prestige, and loyalties of place and class. But in the years immediately following the Great War, it was the contribution that sports could make to the purposeful education of boys and men that mattered most to the middle-class patriarchs of the Amateur Athletic Union of Canada (AAU). Thomas Boyd of Winnipeg made that clear by his ardent recital of

McCarty's plea for 'rational recreation,' quoted above, at the close of his presidential address in 1919. Ever since creation of the federation in 1884, the amateur leaders had tried to harness the sports they controlled to the tasks of moral uplift, male discipline, and nation-building. The Great War sharpened these ambitions and gave these leaders new confidence. 'The value of athletics to the Army has been recognized more than at any time in the world's history,' Boyd told delegates to the 1919 meeting – the first in five years – at the Chateau Laurier Hotel in Ottawa. 'It is a source of gratification to know,' he continued with swelling pride, 'that among the first to enlist were the members of many athletic organizations affiliated with our Union, who with their training had learned team play and obedience to command – two of the foremost essentials of any Army. The fostering of games and competitions had a splendid effect on the morale and spirits of our men.'

Boyd and his colleagues were convinced that sports could play an even more beneficial role in peacetime, not only to facilitate the soldiers' return to civilian life but to lead Canada to a magnificient destiny. They were swept along by the spirit of 'reconstruction' that sprang up in many countries out of the promises, disruptions, traumas, and transformations of the war. While proposals for 'reconstruction' covered a broad swath, ranging from the religious to the economic, advocates usually held two goals in common – prevention of future conflict by creation of new international organizations such as the League of Nations, and revitalization of national life through articulation of new values and selfless devotion to 'service.' In Canada, reconstruction was accompanied by zealous nationalism. In governments, churches, and universities, men and women eagerly planned new activities and reorganized existing ones in the effort to make their institutions worthy of the goals and sacrifices of the war. The Methodist General Conference approved a report of its Committee on Social Services and Evangelism calling for 'nothing less than a transference of the whole economic life from a basis of competition and profits to one of co-operation and service.' At McGill, the newly appointed principal, General Arthur Currie, steered the faculty toward projects that would 'make Canada a front-ranking industrial nation.' One of these initiatives was a far-reaching plan for sociological investigation into every major aspect of Canadian life.[2]

The AAU's 'reconstruction committee' – Thomas Boyd, secretary Norton Crow, past president James Merrick, headmaster Bruce Mac-Donald of St Andrew's College (Aurora, Ontario), and sportswriters Thomas Nelson and W.A. Hewitt – began to meet at the University Club in Toronto in the summer of 1918. Its thinking was dominated by the developmental and regulatory ambitions of 'rational recreation.' Members sought to promote the use value of sports, not their exchange value. They had always believed that sports built health and manly character, what they called 'the making of men.' Muscles and masculine mettle were forged in the engrossing exertions and challenges of football and track, discipline and respect for authority via firm and even-handed administration of rules. With the war almost won, they were convinced that the rapid spread of supervised sports could inject strength, resourcefulness, and social discipline into a war-weary population. Sports would counter the 'negative recreation' of idleness and delinquency among boys and unemployed veterans. Such sentiments had inspired earlier efforts to introduce sports in the churches, voluntary organizations, banks, and businesses, but now they would extend to 'all' – that is, all males. (As the next chapter shows, the AAUers had to be pushed into assisting girls and women.) These endeavours would complement other projects of nationalism and 'service' being planned for the postwar recovery by the Boy Scouts, the YMCAs, and a broad array of health reformers, social workers, and moralist clergy. Rick Gruneau and David Whitson call the amateur leaders 'moral entrepreneurs.'[3]

If the AAUers experienced sports as pleasure, they did not admit it in public. It was the physical, mental, and social discipline that sports demanded which they felt Canada needed most during the trials and challenges of the aftermath of war. 'To strengthen the body is to improve the vehicle of almost all our activity, and to strengthen the bodies of a nation is to strengthen that nation,' Henry Roxborough promised in an article, 'What Is Sport Worth to Canada?,' in *Maclean's*.[4] Properly conducted sports also honed the mind, cultivated leadership, taught sound morals and social idealism, and undermined racial and religious prejudice, he contended. A Toronto hardware clerk, Roxborough served tirelessly on amateur committees. During the 1920s, he took up writing as a second hobby and quickly became an influential public voice of the AAU, extolling the virtues of amateur sports in such magazines as *Canadian Magazine, Liberty, Maclean's*, and *National Home Monthly*.

To ensure realization of their goals, amateur leaders stressed the process of playing sports, not the score or the spectacle. 'The guiding principle [should be] "the game first and victory second," ' Bruce MacDonald of Toronto, who succeeded Boyd as president, told delegates to the AAU's 1920 annual meeting. MacDonald and his colleagues also wanted 'fewer people in the stands and more on the field of play.'[5] 'It is not the primary function of an amateur organization to entertain the public. The first, last and only principle we are interested in is the encouraging of "Play for play's sake,"' William Findlay of Montreal, who became president in 1924, emphasized. Nothing could be left to chance. 'The element of supervision is absolutely essential, and the importance of encouraging the playing of games without any evasions of the rules is more far reaching in later years of the individual's life than one would superficially suspect,' Findlay sternly declared.[6]

The necessary instruction and supervision were provided by uniform rules, a trusted cadre of officials, and a national system of registration. Every athlete had to sign an annual declaration of allegiance to amateurism, carry an up-to-date amateur card, and register for every competition. If the athlete sought to compete in another branch, he had to register that too. Out-of-country competition required a special permit. Critics of modern society have insightfully explored the connection between the embodiment of political and ideological controls and the surveillance, measurement, and punishment conducted by such compulsory institutions as the public school.[7] The AAUers would have found themselves at home with this analysis. The developmental/regulatory regime they established had much the same purpose and character.

Previously, the AAUers had concentrated their efforts on member clubs and organizations, an understandable priority, given that they were volunteers with scarce time and resources. But their 'national duty' led them to plan the broad extension of the pedagogy of sports. They envisioned a massive increase in facilities and programs all across Canada. They wanted parks, playgrounds, gymnasiums, indoor and outdoor swimming pools, athletic fields, and ice rinks available to everyone, especially those in rural communities, constructed and operated by a dominion ministry of sports. In all these facilities, they sought supervised programs, planned and conducted by their own associations in conjunction with provincial and municipal governments, churches, and social service organizations. Teachers, community leaders, and parents would be trained to assist through workshops and clinics and a broad program of propaganda, with 'how to play' guidebooks, newsletters, and instructional photographs and films. The mass media would cooperate by devoting special coverage to the campaign.

As an urgent priority, physical education and supervised recreation would be offered as part of the curriculum of every educational institution in the country, from the common school to the university. Such a regimen would keep the population not only healthy and active, they insisted, but out of the distracting clutches of commercial culture. 'The amusement thus afforded will be vastly more beneficial to the citizens and the state than the continuance of picture shows and entertainments of a similar nature. There is no doubt that an athletic people will be saner people for having made such use of its leisure hours,' MacDonald counselled. Earnestness was never in short supply.

These were heroic, if not utopian dreams. The reconstruction committee's facility plan alone would have increased the outlay for sports many times over. The Union had few resources of its own other than the energy and dedication of its volunteers. Most of its limited revenues came from members' dues. Even if many more people were attracted by the AAU's missionary spirit, it is not likely that they could have bankrolled the cost of carrying it out. Nor were governments eager to step in. Though the AAU delegation to Ottawa was politely received, it came away empty-handed. The modest attempts of the coalition Union government at reconstruction focused on the medical treatment, re-employment, and agricultural settlement of soldiers, not on sports. Taxpayers seemed just as reluctant. In Toronto, despite enthusiastic endorsement by the city's board of control, electors rejected a proposal for a new municipal 'Soldier's Memorial Stadium.'[8] In the schools, if physical activity were offered at all, it was via the Strathcona Trust system of calisthenics and marching drills. Sports were, for the most part, played only after school. Some teachers organized practices and interschool competitions, but their leadership was characterized more by enthusiasm than by knowledge of the rules or expertise.[9]

While the AAUers preached sports for all, their executive came almost exclusively from the male, English-speaking middle class. Thomas Boyd sold printing services and sat on Winnipeg city council. A prominent Orangeman, he had been active in cycling, swimming, and snowshoeing and had led the campaign for public playgrounds in that city. Norton Crow, perhaps the most visionary of the amateur leaders, had been an outstanding baseball player and speedskater for Toronto's Central Y before moving into volunteer sports administration. He worked as a financial analyst in the Ontario treasury department in Toronto. Bruce MacDonald was a Presbyterian minister as well as principal of St Andrew's. He represented the University of Toronto Athletic Association on the Canadian Intercollegiate Athletic Union (CIAU). Of the 30 others elected to national office during the interwar years and for whom biographical information is available, eight were public servants, six worked at universities, three were practising lawyers, and one was an accountant for the Canadian Pacific Railway. There were 12 small businessmen: four merchants, two publishers of small-town newspapers, two customs brokers, a butcher, a roofer, a manager of a correspondence school, and a manager of a cinema. Eight of the 33 amateur leaders held municipal office. In the key position of president, there were four professors and four lawyers (including one judge) among the 12 who served during the interwar period. Only one francophone was ever elected to national office. He was P.G. Majeau, representing the Canadian Snow Shoe Union, one of eight vice-presidents in 1926. The 'nation' that the AAUers sought to strengthen was unilingual. For the most part, 'Quebec' meant anglophone Montrealers.

Theirs was the advocacy of satisfied alumni. All of them had been athletes themselves and had benefited from the experience. Most of them still spent many weekends officiating at games and meets. First and foremost, they believed in sports *for themselves and their class.* As intellectual workers and self-employed professionals, they lived by their wits and their knowledge of the social order and its proprieties. To get ahead, a man needed the good health, self-knowledge, broadened horizons (through travel and new experiences), and lifelong contacts thought to result from sports. As admirers of the occupants of economic and political power, but often beholden to them, they had a great appreciation for civility and 'fair play' in interpersonal relations, even if they did not always practise them themselves. Like thousands of other middle-class men and women who sustained other voluntary associations, they contributed to the vast network of councils and committees that constituted amateur sports in order to gain community status, enjoy opportunities for fraternal 'bonding,' and insert their values into an ever-more popular sphere of Canadian life.

Most of the AAUers were conservative in outlook. Their sympathies for business were pronounced. Past president Merrick, the first Canadian to be appointed to the International Olympic Committee, was Ontario's most notorious union-buster. A lawyer, he acted as secretary for the Employers' Association, which sought to establish the right to 'free labour,' often resorting to nativist attacks against the 'control of foreign (union) officers.' In 1919, his refusal to negotiate with the Metal Trades Council precipitated the short-lived Toronto general strike.[10] Only two members of the national leadership were associated with organized labour – B.W. Bellamy, who kept up his membership in the International Typographers' Union while owning and editing the Wetaskiwin *Times,* and S.H. Wilson, a member of the Amalgamated Engineers who was elected to Port Arthur City Council in 1920 as a member of the Labour party.

Most AAUers held views similar to Merrick's. Like other proponents of 'rational recreation' and 'moral purity,' they hoped that sports would instill the work ethic, respect for authority, and loyalty to Canada as a British nation in the alien and dangerous elements in society, immigrants, and the working class. 'A nation that loves sport cannot revolt,' Henry Roxborough assured his readers.[11] When the Canadian National Railways (CNR) began to organize employee recreation programs in the late 1920s, as part of the North America–wide experiment in 'welfare capitalism,' the AAU immediately created a standing committee on industrial recreation to help other companies get started. CNR recreation director W.H. Kilby was appointed committee chair.[12] Social obedience, labour discipline, and company loyalty could be inculcated amid the joys and excitement of a well-played game. But apart from the large employers, only the state had the resources and leverage to extend these activities significantly. Surely governments would see the logic.

The AAUers' approach to national regeneration was strongly supported by their three most loyal allied bodies – the CIAU, the Canadian Police AAA, and the YMCA. Each of these organizations had long been in the business of offering 'improving' recreation. Many police clubs were formed to combat juvenile delinquency and raise funds for charity, though the emphasis was increasingly on the forces' own well-publicized teams. The Y began to offer athletic facilities and programs in the 1890s, as a means of strengthening its mission of secular Christian proselytizing. Some of its programs differed little from those of ordinary sports clubs. The three Toronto branches – Broadview, Central, and West End – dominated national competitions for many years. Yet in the eyes of Y leaders who attended AAU meetings, sports programs were intended to enhance the organization's overall moral and spiritual values, not just bring back trophies, and staff and volunteers were directed accordingly. The four universities that comprised the active membership of the CIAU – McGill, Queen's, Toronto, and Western, which joined in 1929 – were also athletic powers, winning frequent national honours against all comers and earning considerable revenue from the sale of tickets to their games. But unlike most of their American counterparts, which openly hired athletes to compete for them, to the frequent neglect of any education, the central Canadian universities regarded their athletic programs as an adjunct to demanding higher education.[13] The Ontario universities have remained stalwart defenders of amateurism to this very day.

The Canadian Parliament of Sport

The AAU felt that a national system of order and control was indispensable to its civilizing mission. From its inception in 1884 (as the Amateur Athletic Association), each generation of leaders sought to extend its jurisdiction over more and more sports and regions, so that all Canadian sportsmen enjoyed the benefits of amateurism and adhered to its precepts. There was a practical dimension to this ambition: most athletes played several sports and usually did so in the colours of a single association such as the Montreal Amateur Athletic Association (MAAA). For example, the future railway- and castle-builder Henry Pellatt, who won the first national one-mile championship in 1878, ran and played for the Toronto Lacrosse Club. If an athlete had to register afresh each time he changed sports, there would have been endless confusion and bureaucratic duplication. To this end, the AAA gradually increased the number of sports it governed directly. In sports outside its jurisdiction, it sought working agreements, or 'alliances,' with the respective governing bodies, on the basis of adherence to a common code of eligibility. The AAA was the first such amateur federation in the world. The Americans would follow its example four years later. Most others, such as the British and Australians, would never try, feeling unification of sports through a single body too difficult to achieve.[14]

For most of its first three decades, the AAA/CAAU/AAU made little headway outside the Montreal–Hamilton corridor. While amateur sports thrived in the Maritimes, and new clubs sprang up in the western provinces with every new spur line, the 'national' body had little communication with them. But during the 'amateur war' of 1906–9, protectors of strict amateurism brought many of these clubs into its ranks with the promise of a genuine federation. Once they routed their opponents, they made every effort to provide such a system. The original constitution had been a virtual 'legislative union,' with the majority of votes held directly by clubs, an arrangement that all but guaranteed the domination of Toronto and Montreal. So the AAUers abolished it, setting up instead representation by provincial branches. Voting was weighted by branch membership, so it still favoured central Canada, but the 1909 constitution did give the regions greater voice and formal recognition. Allied bodies, such as the YMCA, continued to vote as single entities.[15]

The victorious Union leadership – essentially Crow, MacDonald, Merrick, and Fred Tees of McGill – brought men from the regions into national office, scheduled events outside Toronto and Montreal, and negotiated new alliances with the independent sports bodies. In 1913, it helped create sympathetic new organizations in hockey and lacrosse – the Canadian Amateur Hockey Association and the Canadian Amateur Lacrosse Association respectively – and brought them into the fold. It accelerated and expanded on these policies after the war.

In the early 1920s, flush with the spirit of nation-building and representative democracy stimulated by the war, the AAUers elevated their annual general meeting into 'the Canadian Parliament of Sport.' If the vast and far-flung activities of sports were to serve the national interest, these men understood, then they should be planned, carefully coordinated, and strictly supervised under the Union's banner in a manner that was visible to all. The 'Parliament' would enable the leaders to broaden the coalition of men who held to the 'improving' view of amateurism, thus extending their control over more aspects of Canadian sport. Moreover, the sound, orderly, and responsible governance of sports would maintain public confidence and win over government support. Amateur sport could not afford an embarrassing scandal like the Chicago White Sox betting fix of the 1919 World Series. The presence together of so many distinguished and public-spirited men would strengthen the image of the movement. 'Parliament' thus brought elected representatives from every region and sport to meet, debate, and develop policies. There was a broad hope that the process would 'make no mean contribution to the tremendous problem of unifying a wide national heritage, to promote common bonds of sentiment from coast to coast,' and enable the leaders to speak with a single voice.[16]

Apart from the churches, few Canadian voluntary organizations had established a national public presence at this time. In fact, at war's end, other than the dominion government, the national political parties, and the Canadian Pacific Railway (CPR), there were few institutions of any kind that sought to link together Canadians from one end of the country to the other in common purpose. The Canadian Manufacturers' Association, the Canadian Medical Association, and the National Council of Women, for example, had just begun to branch out from a central Canadian base. In the arts and letters, groups of painters and writers were just beginning to address the challenge of 'inventing' Canada in cultural terms. 'After 1919,' Arthur Lismer recalled, 'most creative people began to have a guilty feeling that Canada was as yet unwritten, unpainted, unsung. In 1920 [the year of the Group of Seven's first exhibit], there was a job to be done.' *Manitoba Free Press* publisher John Dafoe told the Canadian Authors Association in 1923: 'National Consciousness doesn't happen. [It] must be encouraged. It is a product of vision, imagination, and courage.' Such sentiments inspired creation of a number of new national voluntary associations during the 1920s.[17]

The AAU tried to lead the way. It was one of the first bodies to direct its ongoing activities to the task of knitting together a common Canadian identity. The three-day 'Parliament' took place in a different city and region every fall, usually in a major railway hotel. Between 1919 and 1939, it was held in 12 cities, from Halifax to Vancouver. Wherever they met, the AAUers used their presence to animate the local scene and wave the flag. They held their 1926 session in Saint John, New Brunswick, for example, for the explicit purpose of reviving the moribund and virtually bankrupt Maritimes association – a casualty of the strapped economy and years of neglect. To this end, they recruited new leaders, offered them assistance, and 'pumped them up' at the meeting. The effort paid off only partially, however, and the Maritimes branch would limp along for years to come.

In the years that followed, preoccupation with governance, and jockeying for power within the multi-layered amateur organizations, became defining characteristics of the movement. For many volunteers, the formal meetings, the elaborate public functions, and the endless lobbying and logrolling behind the scenes took on a greater importance than provision of opportunity for sports. For anyone who aspired to positions of leadership, these activities consumed a great deal of time and energy. Nevertheless, the emphasis on governance intensified the Union's commitment to 'service.' The national sessions were opened with great ceremony and civic ambition by public officials. In 1927, in Edmonton, for example, Prime Minister William Lyon Mackenzie King and Alberta's premier, John Brownlee, 'stressed the relationship of competitive athletics to the spirit of brotherhood and National Unity' and urged delegates to put local matters aside in the national interest.[18]

In this heady spirit, delegates dealt with not only the nitty-gritty of officers' reports, eligibility, rules, and records but also social and material conditions for sports and the welfare of humankind. Throughout the 1920s, for example, they strove repeatedly to obtain extensions of daylight saving time, lower train fares, and reduced amusement taxes. In the early 1930s, as the world began to re-arm in earnest, they called on 'all play, athletic and sporting bodies throughout the world to join in a protest

TABLE 2.1
The Canadian Parliament of Sport, 1919–39

Organization	Dates of participation
Amateur Athletic Union of Canada (AAU)	1919–
Canadian Association of Amateur Oarsmen	1919–
Canadian Intercollegiate Athletic Union (CIAU)	1919–
Canadian Police Amateur Athletic Association (CPAAA)	1919–
Canadian Snow Shoe Union	1919–
Canadian Amateur Hockey Association (CAHA)	1919–37
Canadian Amateur Lacrosse Association (CALA)	1919–37
Canadian Amateur Swimming Association	1919–23
Canadian Wheelman's Association	1919–32
YMCA Athletic League	1919–
Amateur Skating Association of Canada	1920–37
Dominion Football Association	1923–32
Women's Amateur Athletic Federation (WAAF)	1928–
Canadian Amateur Basketball Association (CABA)	1930–37
Canadian Secondary Schools Athletic Association	1933–
Canadian Amateur Ski Association	1934–

NOTES: The Canadian Rugby Union (CRU), though not formally aligned, required its members to hold valid AAU cards until the late 1930s, so that football players were subject to AAU discipline. The CRU could usually count on men who held offices in other associations to voice its views at the annual parliament.
   In 1931, the Newfoundland Amateur Athletic Association entered an alliance with the AAU and began to participate in the annual sessions.

against war as a settlement of international differences.' After each session, these deliberations and all reports and votes were carefully transcribed, printed, and distributed in bound volumes, so that those who could not attend could discuss them during the winter.

As Table 2.1 indicates, most of the major national bodies participated in the annual forum through an article of alliance or working agreement with the Union. Only the cricket, golf, lawn and table tennis, squash, and archery associations had no dealings with it. Though delegates regularly complained about the high cost of rail fares, most branches and allied bodies were generally represented. Even associations that had fallen behind in their dues were usually allowed voice and vote, as paid-up members regularly waived the constitutional clause suspending them so as to ensure wide representation.

The 'parliaments' seemed to stimulate a broader cross-section of backgrounds in the leadership as well. Prior to the war, virtually every Union official came from either Montreal or Toronto, but during the interwar years, only 14 of 41 national officers were elected from those cities. Eight came from Winnipeg, including four presidents. Though the leadership group kept tight reins over the nomination process, like their cabinet-making counterparts on Parliament Hill, they tried to balance the slates of officers they presented for election. No president served more than two one-year terms. Four came principally from hockey, three from football, and two from track and field, while others worked their way up through baseball, cycling, boxing, and rowing.

To be sure, we are much more sensitive to issues of diversity today and expect other constituencies to be included in decision-making bodies. For example, the Canadian Sport Council is committed constitutionally to gender equity and enfranchisement of athletes and coaches and includes representatives of the First Nations and from the provincial and local authorities that provide facilities and programs.

But the AAUers were concerned less about recognizing diversity than with overcoming it. For the times, they did as well as most middle-class organizations in broadening their leadership.[19] Certainly, the press deemed them representative and worthy of respect. Newspapers reported extensively on debates and decisions and published formal photographs of the delegates, and columnists admired them for their hard work. 'The men here from the several provinces showed a determined desire to meet and settle problems,' M.J. Shea told readers of the *Manitoba Free Press*. 'There was no sign of lack of courage in facing issues. Industry was the keynote of the meetings and long sessions were the rule ... The results achieved should prove of outstanding merit.'[20]

The Amateur Code

Norton Crow called the amateur code the 'bedrock' of the Union. It bound 'the making of men' to the broader project of nation-building. In 1919, the code stated:

An Amateur is one who has never
A. 1. Entered or competed in any athletic competition for a staked bet, moneys, private or public, or gate receipts.
    2. Taught or assisted in the pursuit of any athletic exercise or sport as a means of livelihood.
    3. Received any bonus or payment in lieu of loss of time while playing as a member of any club, or any consideration whatever for any services as an athlete, except actual travelling or hotel expenses.

4. Sold or pledged his prizes.

5. Promoted an athletic competition for personal gain.

Note: An athlete guilty of any of the above offences can never be reinstated.

B. An athlete who has competed with or against a professional for a prize or where gate receipts are charged ... or has entered in any competition under a name other than his own, shall be ineligible for registration and competition as an amateur.

Note: Such an athlete may be eligible for reinstatement.

C. All others shall be considered eligible for registration and competition in the Union and its affiliated bodies.[21]

These harsh strictures were enforced by an iron, often arbitrary hand. The responsible committees investigated allegations and recommended penalties without any obligation to hear the accused's side of the story. In 1921, a proposal to provide those facing discipline with the basics of 'natural justice' – the right to defend oneself in an impartial hearing – failed for want of a seconder. Some athletes learned from the newspapers that they had lost their right to compete, sometimes on the basis of unfounded rumours or press reports. Even in cases where public controversy or the interventions of a powerful club forced the authorities to hold a hearing, the onus was on the athlete to prove innocence, the very opposite of what was expected in the justice system.

Yet this approach was supported by an elaborate and widely accepted moral economy. It began with the essential developmental/regulatory calculation of 'rational recreation.' If sports were professionalized, amateurs believed, the athlete would focus so narrowly on pursuit of victory that he would lose sight of the educational and social purposes of participation. 'Professionalism is not largely concerned with the purpose of play, the building of character, the development of physique, the challenge of courage,' Henry Roxborough explained. 'It has no place for those who want to play but lack ability. It weakens [the] amateur clubs whose ideals are to emphasize that the game is the thing and not the reward.'[22] Advocates feared that after a brief career in sports, the professional athlete would be left without an occupation or trade – the worst middle-class nightmare, downward mobility. The popular press provided ample justification. In an article entitled 'Does Sport Pay a Dividend?,' journalist Leslie Roberts advised parents to 'keep your boy out of professional hockey, baseball and all the money sports, unless you want to see him earn easy money for a few years and find himself, at thirty, jobless and drifting around the fringes of the Big Time, looking for a job driving pegs.'[23]

The code was also linked to the ideal of 'fair play' between competitors and teams. By prohibiting every imaginable form of benefit or inducement, the rules were intended to discourage development of a 'players' market' and the hated practice of 'ringers' – getting somebody else to play your games for you. They were intended to deny individual competitors the advantage of a sport-related job where they could practise their skills. Athletes and coaches who broke or circumvented the rules were condemned as 'cheaters.' It was a matter of honour. Men who 'enlisted under one flag and then fought under another' could never be depended on to play fair in sport or in life.[24]

Many of the amateur leaders believed that without the code it would have been impossible to develop sports evenly across the country. If athletes could sign with the highest bidder, or have the incentive of money prizes, the good ones would never stay long enough in the poorer or less populous places such as the Maritimes and give them something to cheer about. Certainly, promoters of professional sports took little interest in the tasks of athletic and social development. 'Not many industries can secure raw material without paying for it, but professional sport does ... It raids amateur teams with little consideration,' John Jackson, a Lethbridge judge, complained in his 1922 presidential address. Remuneration ran counter to the amateurs' own strong commitment to volunteerism. It was not that anyone was squeezing profits out of the athletes they supervised; coaches and officials were expected to be amateur, too. Most of them put in long hours and paid their own expenses in what they believed was a community service. Most clubs had difficulty in staying afloat. From this perspective, it was unseemly that anyone should be paid, least of all the athletes who were the primary beneficiaries of the educational, social, and moral training sports provided.

There was one further justification. If Canadians were to compete overseas, the AAU had to ensure that they met the equally strict international eligibility standard. 'Don't let Canada get out of step with the rest of the world,' Olympic Chair Patrick Mulqueen warned during one debate in 1925. 'Canada cannot have a different amateur definition and expect to go abroad and compete, because they are not going to accept us.'[25] Observers agreed. 'A pretty rigid line of demarcation has been maintained between the amateur and the professional, and for good reason – namely, fair play to the amateur athletic sport,' the *Ottawa Journal* weighed in supportively. 'The rest of the world is not going to depart from that to please Canada, even if a majority of Canadian athletes wish to, which we doubt.'[26]

Defended in these terms, the amateur 'code of honour' commanded fierce loyalty, and anyone who betrayed it could expect immediate banishment. 'Once a pro, always a pro' was the dictum, and outright pros were barred for life with little sympathy. 'The professional [who] sells his wares is concerned only with the money involved, and is content to allow himself to be speculated in, to be bought and sold as cattle,' national secretary A.S. Lamb, an Australian-born professor of physical education at McGill, wrote in his 1926 report. 'Their only idea of victory is to win at any price – unless it is better worth their while to lose – at a price. What should they know of the true sportsman?' In virtually a Gresham's law of sport, Lamb and others feared that a single 'professional' could ruin the experience for others.[27] Professionals were not only denied entry to amateur competitions, but in what was known as the 'contamination rule' amateurs were prohibited from playing against them – even in exhibitions.

The allegiance that amateurism commanded can also be illustrated by the rarity with which the Union granted exceptions to the rules. In 1916, it decided to allow amateurs in uniform to compete against enlisted professionals in the interests of recruitment and wartime training. But once the war was won, it was not prepared to welcome those professional athletes back into the fold. A majority voted down two proposals to reinstate professional veterans. They relented only when western delegates, armed with a stack of telegrams from their colleagues back home, threatened to secede from the Union and form their own, rival body. To avoid the split, the Union gave the western branches 'the whitewash' on a limited basis. In the compromise, veterans in the four western provinces who had not resumed professional sport were given three months to apply for reinstatement. Pardon was not automatic, however, and the branches were allowed to reinstate only men with 'merited cases.'[28]

There was no exception for physical education teachers, playground leaders, swimming instructors, YMCA physical directors, and those in training for these positions – a vestige of the earlier class prejudice against persons engaged in physical labour. Presumably men in these categories shared the same aims as the AAU, yet they were required to join as 'non-competing amateurs.' If they wanted to play with their pupils, they could do so only on an exhibition basis. In 1923, part-time instructors, such as summer playground leaders, were allowed to resume competition ten days after their employment concluded, but this concession did little for those in the summer sports. In 1931, full-time instructors were given the right to apply for playing privileges one year after their employment ceased. The Canadian AAU was one of the last jurisdictions in the world to retain this rule. One of those excluded was Em Orlick, an outstanding gymnast who worked his way through high school and university by supervising Hamilton playgrounds and teaching at the Y. He has estimated that 'Canada was seriously handicapped by eliminating thousands of athletes in all sports, who had they been in any other country in the world, would have been active competitors.'[29]

In 1926, the AAU prohibited athletes from receiving travelling expenses for more than 21 days a year (except for the Olympic Games). Even monetary prizes at church picnics were prohibited. Those who broke these rules, no matter how slight the infraction, were quickly suspended. In 1926, for example, William B. Anthony of Brampton played ten minutes of lacrosse on a professional team, without payment, and was declared a professional. In 1930, ten Winnipeg hockey players were suspended for participating in an exhibition game in which one of the opposing players was a professional. Though the Union did not publish statistics on suspensions, which were a responsibility of branches and allied bodies, some idea about numbers can be gleaned from the annual applications for reinstatement. Athletes who had violated the 'contamination' rule could apply for reinstatement. In each year 1927–30, 61, 44, 25, and 84 athletes, respectively, applied for reinstatement, most of them from western Canada.

Enforcement was ensured by the monopolies that the AAU and its allied bodies enjoyed by virtue of their membership in the international federations and the Olympics. They guaranteed adherence throughout the system. Anyone could play in a sandlot or a company league without an amateur card, but if he wanted to compete in any championship worthy of the name, he had to join an association. The same was true for teams and leagues. In 1919, the hockey men of Sudbury were invited to join the newly created Northern Ontario Hockey Association, but so great was the allure of the AAU-affiliated Ontario Hockey Association that they refused until the NOHA joined the OHA. Even those who stayed outside the OHA were nevertheless drawn to its rules.[30] Amateurism was thus a system of tremendous power, with tentacles into every corner of Canadian sport.

To be sure, not every member accepted the code in its entirety. Considerable time was taken up at the annual 'parliaments' with attempts to amend the rules. Western Canadian representatives repeatedly sought several forms of liberalization. The Saskatchewan branch wanted permission for a pro in one sport to register and play as an amateur in another. (This became known as the 'Saskatchewan amendment.') Alberta sought permission for amateurs to play on the same teams as professionals in baseball and football (the 'Alberta amendment'). Throughout the interwar period, the short seasons rarely overlapped, and top athletes were accustomed to playing several sports over the course of the year. Lionel Conacher, who played baseball, football, and hockey, and boxed and wrestled – all professionally – is the best-known example, but there are many more. Conn Smythe signed Syl Apps for the Maple Leaf hockey team after watching him play football. Apps also won a gold medal in pole vaulting in the 1934 Empire Games in London, England. Olympic track champion Fanny 'Bobbie' Rosenfeld starred in basketball, baseball, and hockey. Most hockey players turned to either lacrosse or baseball in summer. Narrow specialization did not become widespread until well after the Second World War.

In the small towns of the prairies, where good players were always hard to come by, a professional athlete returning home for the off-season in his sport was a valued asset. Without a rule change, his presence created a tremendous problem for the ambitious young amateur, as R.S. Stronach of Banff explained to the 1927 annual meeting: 'Canada is a vast country and what is suitable for conditions in the east might not be suitable for the west ... The main problem we are trying to cope with is the college boy who during the winter takes part in hockey as an out and out amateur, and then goes back home to some small town and they may have a man who has been a professional baseball player resident there (or he is an old pro from hockey or lacrosse). He has a local team backed up by the residents and great pressure is brought to bear on the boy to play on the team. He is in the position of losing his amateur standing for supporting his home team.'[31]

Westerners also sought to legalize 'broken-time' payments – financial compensation for earnings lost when athletes had to take time off work to compete. They argued that strict amateurism discriminated against those from the regions, who had to travel further and more frequently for national competitions, and against hourly waged athletes, who were not as likely as salaried workers to be paid while away.

But such proposals were regularly defeated by wide margins. The advocates of uncompromising amateurism could count on the power of numbers, long-standing personal friendships, and public opinion. The votes usually came from the Maritimes, Ontario, the CIAU, the CPAAA, the YMCA, and the Canadian Association of Amateur Oarsmen – the branches and allied bodies that had undone the more liberal Amateur Athletic Federation of Canada in the pre-war period.

Such stringency seems like zealotry today, but we must remember the context. The overwhelming majority of athletes, even among the most successful, accepted these rules, either because they believed in them or because they were deterred by the penalties. Art Keay, who raced against Paavo Nurmi in the 1928 Olympics told me that he was 'proud to be an amateur athlete.' Rower Bill Thoburn, who competed in the Los Angeles Olympics in 1932, recently told an interviewer: 'I never accepted money for winning anything even though I was several times offered it [in other sports]. What put me off that was reading about Jim Thorpe being [forced to return his Olympic gold medals in 1912] because he had played in a semi-pro baseball team.'[32] One of the best hockey teams of the 1920s was the Toronto Granites. 'The Granites could beat the Leafs on their lunch-hour,' Ted Reeve, a football and lacrosse star who wrote a sports column in the *Telegram* for almost 50 years, once told me. 'All of them were invited to turn pro, but only one or two of them did. They were far more interested in their careers as lawyers and stockbrokers.' The same was true for many other teams of the 1920s.

Of course, rumours persisted that some athletes and teams were paid 'under the table.' But when *Toronto Star* sports editor Lou Marsh investigated several widely believed allegations of athletes 'on the take,' he found them adhering to both the letter and the spirit of the code. He also reported that by establishing residence rules and requiring clubs to submit annual, audited financial statements, amateur bodies such as the Ontario Hockey Association had made 'it more difficult than ever for the cheaters.' Estimating that the total number of rule breakers in all categories amounted to less than two per cent of all registered athletes, he concluded that the abuses of professionalism were quite controllable. Marsh favoured 'broken-time' payments and pro-am 'mingling,' but he recommended that the rule against outright payment be strictly enforced and that the AAU be given sweeping powers to catch the rule-breakers.[33]

Other community-based sports organizations set and enforced similar conditions. In the popular church baseball and basketball leagues, for example, players who did not attend Sunday services were expelled.[34] During the 1920s, the AAU leadership faced many more calls for tighter enforcement than it did for liberalization. While a few leaders – Findlay, for instance – feared that the effort to stamp out professionalism sometimes led to 'too much legislation,'[35] most were convinced that the public expected them to maintain and enforce the strict code. 'I see nothing to be gained whatever by easing up on our amateur requirements,' Winnipeg lawyer James Morkin argued in 1926, 'but [if] amateur sport [is] clouded with veiled professionalism, the public today, whom we have always found ready and willing to make us donations, and to attend our different amateur meets ... will turn their backs on us.'[36] Certainly the elected officials who opened the amateur 'parliaments' gave amateur leaders no reason to believe that they were out of step with public opinion. Mayor Ralph Webb of Winnipeg told delegates to the 1931 session that 'everyone trusts and believes and hopes that very little will be done to change the basic principles of amateur sport. Amateur sportsmen are the best citizens that any community or city or country can have.' Most press commentary confirmed this view. Frederick Wilson, sports editor on Toronto's *Globe*, advised delegates that the code 'ought to be strengthened, not weakened. These conspirators have never been made to suffer for their misdeeds enough.'[37] The *Edmonton Journal* told them that 'the AAU has discharged a most useful function in promoting good sportsmanship and safeguarding [athletics] from demoralizing tendencies.'[38]

Up until the early 1930s, amateurism was a system that worked, at least for the class that championed it. In fact, it virtually guaranteed the dream of middle-class masculinity – it placed an effective limit on the amount of time and energy the top athletes had to devote to training, enabling them to prepare simultaneously for a post-sport profession. Urban middle-class males could thus prosper in sport *and* career. During the 1920s, the athletes who embraced amateurism captured every honour they sought. University football and hockey men won Allan and Grey cups, respectively, and went on to distinguished careers in law and business. Doctors, teachers, and civil servants brought home gold from the Olympics. At the same time, by regulating the labour market, amateurism enabled clubs from every part of the country to take part, thus facilitating development and strengthening of a national sports system. The rules discouraged working-class athletes with little time or means, especially at the highest levels of competition, leaving the field clear for university students and members of private clubs to win the prizes while legitimating the system as 'fair' and 'just.'

Much of the same ideological structure supports the pan-Canadian system in the Olympic sports today, refashioned as the fight against 'performance-enhancing drugs.' Perhaps the parallel will explain some of the earlier passion for amateurism. Like the prohibition against remuneration, the Olympic anti-doping protocol enforces a regime that is far stricter than the standards of personal conduct in other spheres of activity. While businessmen, musicians, university students, and professional athletes resort to all manner of performance-enhancing aids without qualms or comment, Olympic athletes are proscribed from using more than 300 legal drugs and medicines, many of which have no demonstrable effect on performance. Rule-breakers such as Ben Johnson, who tested positive for steroid use after his world-record–shattering run at the Seoul Olympics in 1988, are demonized as 'cheaters' and suspended for long terms, even life, and receive little sympathy. The Olympic drug protocol is defended in the interests of athletes' health and a 'level playing field.'

Like amateurism, the Olympic drug protocol has its detractors. Critics argue (quite rightly, in my opinion) that the prohibition deals only with the symptoms and that the protocol can do very little to create a 'level playing field' when widespread inequality distorts access to other resources, such as specialized facilities and coaching. At a time of shrinking budgets, the protocol has created an enormous, expensive-to-maintain bureaucracy of testers and judges. Yet during the long debate since Mr Justice Dubin's inquiry into drug use in sports (1988–90) these doubts have had very little effect on the leaders of the pan-Canadian organizations, most of whom continue to come from the middle class. The system of policing against drugs was reaffirmed by a large majority of athletes, coaches, and officials in every forum held on the issue, and the critics were silenced. In my view, the reason for this outcome is the lingering grasp of the amateur ideal. There continues to be strong support for the developmental aspiration – sports should be primarily about personal growth and the expansion of cultural horizons – which would have to be abandoned or significantly recast if free rein were given to the medicine cabinet in the quest for better performance. (This is why I support the ban against drugs.) The prohibition also resonates deeply with the desire that sports constitute a system of rules and 'fair play' – a contemporary version of the 'gospel of order.' Canada has one of the world's most rigorous systems for guarding against performance-enhancing drugs, just as it did for protecting amateurism. The one is a direct legacy of the other.[39]

The Turn to High Performance

While the AAU leadership held fast to the pole of amateurism during the 1920s, it shifted direction in another important respect: it gradually moved away from the goals of 'rational recreation' – the civilizing pedagogy of sports participation and sport for all – to concentrate on winning Olympic and other major honours. The change occurred almost imperceptibly. It was rarely debated explicitly, because the AAU had always been concerned with top athletes and the 'improving' discourse remained much the same. The AAUers continued to encourage the 'making of men' in the interests of Canadian greatness. But by the end of the 1920s, the goal of supervised sports for all was forgotten for all practical purposes. The AAUers devoted their energies instead to the challenge of creating inspirational champions. As Henry Roxborough explained about the Olympics: 'In every land there are schoolboys of ability who would cease training after a local success if it were not for the fact that they visualize the honor of representing their country at these great international contests. Prior to the Olympiad year all sports experience feverish activity; entry lists are large, competitions are numerous and there is a readily visible growth in all lines of physical development. And when a nation produces an Olympic champion, the inspiration encourages thousands of lads to emulate the achievement.'[40]

There were several reasons for the AAU's shift in focus. Failure to persuade governments to embark on a broad program of grass-roots recreation was no doubt an important factor, as was the growing preoccupation of the media with the representational status of athletes. In part, the shift was a case of unintended consequences. The practical task of policing amateurism led the AAU to focus much of its energy on the best athletes, who were most suspected of straying from it. But the turn to high performance was also an expression of the amateurs' proud commitment to Canadian nationalism. To ensure that the status and community pride of 'national champion' were deservedly won, and Canada was fittingly represented in international competitions, the AAUers felt that they had to strengthen the institution of the Canadian championship and the preparation of national Canadian teams competing abroad. Their dream, first articulated by Norton Crow in 1910 and reiterated throughout the period, was to stage Canadian Olympics, in which national championships in all the amateur sports would be held every four years in a different city. Such games would excite at home the enthusiasm for amateur sport that the Olympics created within the world.

In the first years after the Great War, strengthening the national championship was another formidable task. Few Canadian championships in any sport were truly representative of the sporting activity of the entire country. The time and cost of transcontinental train travel prevented many athletes from competing outside their region. It took four days to go from Vancouver to Toronto and another day or two to recover from the trip. The amateur code prohibited compensation for days lost from work, and many employers simply refused to grant the time off. If athletes had the time, the rules allowed reimbursement for the ticket and other expenses, but in the recession that immediately followed the Armistice very few clubs could afford to subsidize them. Most athletes had to raise their own cash. The Union was financially strapped as well, and in no position to help. In 1922, to stay afloat itself, it had to give up its rented Toronto office, forcing secretary Crow to work out of his home (the period is still referred to as the 'kitchen table era' as a consequence of this widespread practice). The problems were less acute in basketball, football, ice hockey, and lacrosse, where regional playoffs were held and only one or two teams had to cover great distances for the final. Gate receipts could often offset expenses, and community interest encouraged employers to give athletes the time off. But in the individual sports such as swimming, track and field, and wrestling, with a number of events and limited revenue possibilities, only a fraction of the eligible athletes ever made it to the championships. As a result, most national 'titleholders' came from the region where the event was held, while those who had to stay home wondered bitterly if they could have won.

Nevertheless, the AAU ceaselessly struggled to improve the representation, quality, and stature of these annual competitions, so that every athlete in the country could have the chance to vie for national honours. It had to rely on provincial branches and local clubs to apply for and conduct events, so there was a limit to what it could achieve, but it tried to spread the championships by rotating them among the regions and to arrange travel subsidies for top athletes. To make the championships more attractive to competitors and to ensure that the prestige of a national title stayed in Canada, it closed the events to foreigners.[41] These efforts met with mixed results, but the AAUers did manage a much broader allocation of events than their predecessors.

Between 1920 and 1939, 17 championships in track and field were held in nine different cities, from Halifax to Banff. (In this latter case, the AAU tried to make it a tourist event, persuading the CPR to take out a carload of stars from the central provinces.) Twenty championships in boxing took place in eight cities, though Winnipeg had six of them and Montreal five. Twenty wrestling championships were held in seven centres, with Winnipeg staging six and Toronto five. The gentleman's agreement that permitted regional rotation broke down only once, over the Olympic Track and Field Trials, which were usually held in conjunction with the national championships. In 1930, it was understood that the 1932 Trials would be awarded to Vancouver, but at the 1931 annual general meeting the eastern majority gave the event to Hamilton, site of the 1928 Trials and the 1930 Empire Games, ostensibly because a promised new stadium had not been built in Vancouver.[42]

The AAU had a much harder time finding willing organizers in the other sports under its jurisdiction. Except for two years in Winnipeg, the fencing championships rotated between Toronto and Montreal. The gymnastics finals, begun in 1923, were held under the auspices of the Canadian National Exhibition in Toronto for 12 consecutive years. It was only after the CNE declined to host them in 1935 that sponsors were found in Montreal (in 1937) and Vancouver (in 1939). With few exceptions, the championships in tug-of-war (13), handball (six), weightlifting (three), and quoits (one) were strictly Toronto events.

Broad participation in the championships was always difficult to achieve. In 1922, when the national track and field championships were held in Calgary, the Ontario branch scheduled its provincial finals for the same day. Largely as a result, only two athletes from east of the Manitoba border competed. The boxing championships were also held in Calgary that year. Expecting a strong national turnout, the organizers restricted entries from Alberta, only to have many out-of-province athletes scratch at the last minute, forcing them to cancel many bouts. They lost a good deal of money as a result.[43] Last-minute withdrawals became a frequent complaint, especially when the championships were held in the west.

In response, the Union prohibited all other competitions within two weeks of the national contest, but the new rule did little to enlarge representation. Even when berths on international teams were at stake, few championships drew many competitors from outside the region where they were held. The two-week ban was repealed when it became clear that it had little effect.[44] The experiment with closed championships met a similar fate. Organizers felt that the presence of American (and occasionally British) stars added to the attractiveness of the event. The provision was replaced by a distinction between 'open' and 'native' national records. In 1937, the AAU tried to increase the numbers trying out for the Empire Games by staging four regional events instead of a single championship and Trials. The track and field committee declared the experiment a qualified success, but the Second World War broke out before it could be tried again.

Another factor that encouraged the turn to high performance was the evolution of the Olympic Games, founded by Pierre de Coubertin, into an arena of proxy nation-state competition. It was not Coubertin's intention that his Games would take this course. He wanted them to demonstrate the educational benefits of athletic striving and stimulate a new sense of international understanding. While he welcomed the pride that spectators and followers took in successful athletes from their countries, he sought to discourage the chauvinism that resulted from an exaggerated reading of representational status. Initially, competitors entered the Games on an individual basis. Gradually flags and national anthems were brought into the ceremonies, and after 1908 national Olympic committees were given the responsibility of assembling teams, but Coubertin still tried to discourage the idea that the Games pitted nations against each other, forbidding officials from calculating team scores.

The First World War, however, intensified national identifications, not only in Canada but around the world. The postwar growth of teams and leagues in many countries, accompanied by the explosion of sports coverage in the press, in newsreels, and over the new medium of radio, increased the representational status of sports. National Olympic leaders came under great pressure to compete with success. In the United States, the U.S. Olympic Association had no trouble persuading General Douglas MacArthur to take a leave of absence to lead 'America's athletic army' into the 1928 Olympics. In the International Olympic Committee (IOC) and the international federations, technical considerations emanating from the competitions came to take precedence over Coubertin's educational and intercultural aspirations. These developments brought Coubertin 'to the painful conclusion that the IOC was neglecting its mission of reflection' and that the Games were eclipsing the Olympics' broader purpose. In 1925, he resigned the IOC presidency.[45]

In the years immediately following the war, when the AAU had given priority to the aims of youth development, the Canadian Olympic Committee stressed the developmental aspects of participation. 'All peaceful international contacts are good and the competitors who go overseas receive a liberal education and a broader vision,' outlined James Merrick, who became the first Canadian to be appointed to the IOC in 1921.[46] But as the status of the Olympics increased, getting to the podium began to be more important than promoting intercultural understanding. The 1924 Olympics in Paris proved a turning point. The AAU sent its largest team ever, but it returned almost empty-handed. Rowing eights from the University of Toronto, fours without cox from the Vancouver Rowing Club, and the shooting team finished second, while Toronto welterweight boxer Doug Lewis clinched a bronze. But the rest of the 86-man team returned with little but 'might have beens' and complaints about the Paris prices. It was the first time Canada had not won a single gold medal, and its worst-ever overall result. Henry Roxborough and others began to ask whether the $52,000 expenditure 'was justified by the results.'[47]

In an effort to identity and eradicate weaknesses, Norton Crow prepared a statistical analysis of the results. Others began to argue for the concentration of resources on a much smaller team. Canada should send only those athletes with a chance to place in the medals, they felt. Though dollars were few, they all agreed that earlier recruitment and better training were essential. 'Natural ability is no longer enough,' Crow pointed out.[48] To encourage young men to raise their sights, the AAU started regional and national schoolboy championships, a national incentive award scheme, and a plan to keep the best high schoolers active after graduation. Because few athletes had the advantage of regular coaching, the AAU sent Olympic coach Walter Knox and other experts into schools and rural areas. It tried to establish regional equipment banks and a national library of technical materials. It raised enough money to enable the Olympic Committee to subsidize some athletes' travel to the Trials and to conduct two extensive training camps for those who made the team.

The AAUers made a point of tying these new programs to their broader goals of nation-building. In 1927, the Olympic Committee put a damper on the time-honoured practice of Canadian athletes moving to the United States for training, competition, and under-the-table inducements, only to return to claim Canadian honours at championships and selection trials. Henceforth, those continuously residing outside the country for more than five years would be ineligible to represent Canada internationally. 'There is not much glory in winning with men who were not Canadian born or who were not domiciled in Canada or whose experience will not be used to develop or inspire other Canadians after the Games are over,' Roxborough explained in *Maclean's*. Instead, the Union would redouble its efforts to help the 'many Canadian boys permanently located in Canada eager to make the trip.'[49]

In the 1920s, a decade when almost a million Canadians emigrated to the United States, often in search of work, the new rule was a risky move. With the growing financial carrots of American 'athletic scholarships,' the exodus of talent was considerable. Canadians harboured few scruples about taking credit for the achievements of native-born authors, painters, and film stars who trained or settled in Europe or the United States,[50] so there was little reason to fear that they would object to American-based stars representing them in sports. The policy would have disqualified the only track and field champion Canada claimed at the Antwerp Olympics in 1920, 110-metre hurdler Earl Thomson, and it was almost sure to cost Canada a medal in the forthcoming Olympics in Amsterdam. The pre-Games favourite for the prestigious 100-metre dash was Cyril Coaffee, a Winnipeger who had been lured to the Illinois Athletic Club shortly after he had equalled the world record in the 100 yards in 1922. Coaffee competed for Canada in the 1920 and 1924 Olympics and had returned every year to win the national championship. Despite his Chicago address, he remained very popular. In Paris, he was chosen captain of the Olympic team.

Hoping to embarrass the selectors into reconsideration, Coaffee attended the 1928 Canadian Championships and Olympic Trials in Hamilton anyway, racing in his Canadian Olympic uniform. But he pulled up lame in the final and was quickly forgotten. The new national champion in the 100 metres that day was an unknown Vancouver teenager, Percy Williams. The slender, taciturn Williams did not stay unnoticed very long. Three weeks later in Amsterdam, to the surprise of almost everyone but his personal coach, Bob Granger, he outsprinted the fastest in the world to win *two* golds – in the 100 and 200 metres – and become the celebrity of the Games, besieged by the press and instant fans. His electrifying jump finish, with the maple leaf emblazoned on his chest, was replayed on newsreels around the world. General MacArthur grudgingly admitted that the Canadian champion was the 'greatest sprinter the world had ever seen.' Williams's teammates won another 12 medals in five sports, earning Canada ninth place among 40 nations, and first if points were weighted on the basis of events entered. Prime Minister Mackenzie King cabled that they had brought the country a 'splendid victory.' The outpouring of national rejoicing seemed to vindicate all of the amateur leaders' new emphasis on high performance. If sport for all was beyond their powers, they could certainly contribute significantly to Canadian unity through the elite of Olympic sports.[51]

But the growing preoccupation with winning provoked a bitter public dispute, which revealed some of the contradictions between the developmental ideal of 'play for play's sake' and the single-minded pursuit of medals. At the 1928 Olympics in Amsterdam, Fanny 'Bobbie' Rosenfeld of Toronto was declared second after an extremely close finish. The judges did not have the benefit of a 'photo finish.' The manager of the women's team, Alexandrine Gibb, supported by Pat Mulqueen and M.M. Robinson of the Canadian Olympic Committee, sought to lodge an official protest, but she was prevented from doing so by A.S. Lamb, the AAU's president and chef de mission of the Olympic team. Lamb felt the protest a regretable slight on the judges and a repudiation of the intercultural goals of the Games. 'The whole programme of activity is not worth-while unless there is the right attitude of tolerance, sympathy and forbearance, ... unless we enter with a spirit of what we can give rather than what we can get,' he later wrote. The resulting brouhaha was front-page news. Despite Lamb's eloquent defence of 'moral and social values,' he got the worst of it, in both the press and in 'the battle of Port Arthur,' as the post-mortem at the annual 'parliament' four months later came to be called. Because the 'cause is being jeopardized by very undesirable actions and publicity,' he did not seek a second term. He was the only president during the entire period not to be re-elected.

The AAUers' growing athletic ambitions, their hopes for nation-building, and the example of Canada taking an independent place in the League of Nations impelled them to seek a leading role in Olympic governance. They strongly supported the proposal by European bob-sleigh and skiing enthusiasts for a separate Winter Games every four years, offering to hold them on a regular rotation with France, Norway, and Sweden.[52] In 1926, after years of debate, the IOC agreed and retroactively named the 1924 Chamonix International Winter Sports Week the First Olympic Winter Games. The Canadian leaders also initiated the idea of 'demonstration' events in the Olympic and Winter Olympic Games. For many years the practice gave host countries the chance to stimulate domestic and international development in sports not already on the program. At the Calgary Winter Olympics in 1988, for example, demonstration events were staged in curling, freestyle skiing, short-track speed skating, and downhill skiing for persons with disabilities. (The option was discontinued in 1992 because of the costly 'gigantism' of the Games.)

The AAUers' most significant international achievement, the British Empire Games, also grew out of their desire to make Canada a nation of influence through sports. Of the two prominent variants of English-Canadian nationalism held during the interwar period – 'imperialism' and a liberal nationalism that sought to break the remaining ties with

Britain – they ardently held to the former. They sought an independent Canada, too, but within a federation of countries from the British Empire. They had always regarded sporting competition with Britain and the other dominions as on a plane above other international competition. It was 'within the family,' so they felt that they could trust their opponents to be fair. Whenever hard done by international judging, as happened frequently in boxing, wrestling, and fencing, they discussed substituting purely British Empire competitions in these sports for Olympic ones.[53] At the same time, they were as ready as Conservative leader Arthur Meighen to follow the British into a fray. Despite considerable opposition to the 1936 Olympic Games in Nazi Germany, when the British Olympic Association decided to send a team the Canadian AAU simply voted to do the same. There was no further discussion.[54]

The idea of permanent Empire Games was not originally the AAU's. Credit usually goes to Sir Astley Cooper, who proposed it to *The Times* in 1891. The 1911 Festival of Empire and the inter-Allied competitions of the war also served as precedent. But the Canadians kept the concept alive, perhaps reminded by the bite that the bill for insuring the solid silver Lord Lonsdale Cup, which they had won in 1911, took out of their meagre budget. In 1924, Norton Crow, ever the source of new projects, recommended 'the advisability of taking the initiative in an All–British Empire Games, to be held between the Olympic Games.' Four years later, during the Amsterdam Olympics, sportswriter M.M. Robinson, manager of the Canadian track team, raised the idea with his Australian, British, New Zealand, and South African counterparts, offering his home town of Hamilton as the site for the first Games in 1930. Robinson had obtained the city's promise to build new facilities, pay for visiting athletes' and officials' meals and accommodation, and assume any overall loss in the operations; as well, Hamiltonians had already begun to pay two dollars each to become 'boosters' of the Games. The others agreed to recommend it on a trial basis to their respective governing bodies, which accepted. In 1929, the British Olympic Committee tried to scuttle the whole plan, contending that the necessary fund-raising would seriously interfere with its appeal for the 1932 Los Angeles Olympic team. Robinson immediately travelled to London to reassure the timid, promising them travel subsidies if they would still send a team. This second round of negotiation cost Hamilton $30,000 in travel grants, but everyone agreed to attend.[55]

The Games unleashed an outpouring of imperialist sentiment. Longtime Canadian advocates of a close British connection, such as Sir Max

Aitken (later Lord Beaverbrook), Sir George McLaren Brown, Sir Ian Colquhoun, Sir Arthur Currie, Sir Robert Falconer, and Sir Campbell Stuart, readily lent their names to the undertaking, while Sir Edward Beatty, president of the Canadian Pacific Railway, agreed to chair the organizing committee. In *Maclean's*, Henry Roxborough abandoned all thoughts of medals in his excitement about the prospects of uniting 'the red-coloured lands':

Today the British Empire is held together by sentiment rather than force; and whatever develops friendships will stimulate that understanding and goodwill. Therefore, an assemblage of the best athletes in the Empire will not only strengthen national pride, but should develop social ties that will tend to seal more strongly the bonds of Empire ...

The games should certainly turn the searchlight of publicity on the athletic prowess of the British Empire ... An even more desireable consequence will be the unifying of the sporting organizations of the Empire. Under conditions existing in international competition the motherland and each dominion is considered apart; the victories of each are tabulated separately; when one unit voices an opinion, that expression does not receive the same consideration as would the decision of an Imperial athletic federation ... It is not too much to hope that [the Games] will go far towards crystallizing Empire sportsmanship into one coherent whole.[56]

Athletically, socially, and financially, the Games were a great success. Three hundred athletes from ten 'nations' – Australia, Bermuda, British Guiana, Canada, England, New Zealand, Newfoundland, Northern Ireland, Scotland, and South Africa – competed in 59 events in six sports. The Canadian team gave its fans in the packed stands plenty to cheer about. Percy Williams won a stirring 100 yards with his trademark finish, and his teammates took away another 18 track and field medals. Led by diver Alf Phillips, who won both the springboard and the platform events, the swimmers and divers took 11 medals. The wrestlers won every weight classification. Canadians also scored well in the other sports – bowling, boxing, and rowing – and only narrowly lost the overall point championship to England.

The competition was as friendly as predicted. 'True, perfect harmony reigned all the time,' M.M. Robinson reported later. 'There was a spirit about the competitions that certainly has never yet, to my knowledge, been found in Olympic competitions. There was a great friendliness and it did not matter really with the competitors who won. There was just as much acclaim for the chap from New Zealand who won.' The Games brought Hamilton a new pool, a new rowing course (in the Dundas basin), $9,000 in new equipment, and a good deal of civic pride. Newspapers across the world praised the organization, carried out entirely by volunteers. Revenues exceeded expectations, so the organizing committee was able to return $15,000 of its $19,000 city grant. Most of the revenue came from ticket and concession sales and program advertising. The dominion government also provided $5,000. The total operating budget was $97,973.[57]

Hamilton's success persuaded the empire's sports leaders to put the Games on a permanent footing. While they were in Hamilton, they created a governing body for the Games, the British Empire Games Federation, and agreed on a draft constitution to submit to their bodies back home. They also awarded the next Games to Johannesburg. The South Africans promptly made it clear that black athletes would not be welcome. In 1931, the American AAU had capitulated to a similar prohibition, agreeing that sprinter Eddie Tolan should not race against white athletes during a tour by the American team, but the Canadians (and several other countries) refused to accept the exclusion, forcing the new Federation to transfer the 1934 Games to London. It was the first blow in the long international campaign to eradicate official racism and apartheid from South African sport.[58] The Australians were so enthused by their experience in Hamilton that they established a quadrennial Empire Schoolboy's (track and field) Games, to begin in 1934 in Melbourne in conjunction with that city's centenary celebrations. In 1938, they held the Empire Games in Sydney.

The Empire Games thus gave further stimulus to high performance, especially in the individual and largely non-commercial amateur sports within Canada. (To date, there have not been any team sports in these Games, renamed the Commonwealth Games in 1966; netball will be included for the first time in 1998.) Though branches of the Canadian AAU complained about the costs of sending athletes to the Empire Trials, the lure of the trip abroad and Empire honours encouraged many more competitors to do so, with the result that there were hotly contested provincial events and a more representative national championship every two years, instead of every fourth (Olympic) year as previously. The Empire Games (and the associated schoolboy competition) also gave the amateur movement another boosterish front-page story. If the Second World War had not intervened, they would have been staged in Montreal in 1942.[59]

But there were limits to the AAU's ability to recruit and train athletic ability. Despite the effort to improve coaching, the amateur leaders were not able to increase the number of coaches significantly, nor systematically update their technical knowledge. Elsewhere, especially in American universities and German clubs, use of full-time, 'professional' coaching and physiological, pharmacological, and psychological research into performance were on the increase, the latter stimulated by the push for 'all-out' efforts during the Great War. Yale rowing crews that won gold at the 1920 and 1924 Olympics were aided by high-fat and -carbohydrate diets pioneered by university medical researchers, when conventional athletic wisdom advised that the athlete's best nutrition came from the protein of steak. Others tried to boost performance by ultraviolet radiation, adrenalin injections, and caffeine. (Scientific debate on the ethics of sports 'doping' first became heated during the 1920s.)[60]

By comparison, few Canadian athletes had coaches at all. Those available were volunteers who came out to the pool or gym in their spare time. Many were former athletes who could transmit the lessons of their own experiences but had little connection to the new 'sport sciences.' As a result, it was not uncommon for Canadian champions to discover new techniques at international competitions. American Johnny Weismuller taught Toronto breast-stroker Jack Aubin how to gain 'a couple of feet' on his turn in the practice pool in Amsterdam immediately prior to the 1928 Olympics, where both were competitors. But such last-minute instruction was often more disconcerting than helpful. Canadians rarely had the most advanced equipment either. Aubin raced in a cotton tank suit that held the water, while Weismuller and his teammates wore lighter, water-resistant silk. At the 1932 Winter Olympics in Lake Placid, Howard Bagguley, who competed in the nordic combined event, got his first pair of good jump bindings just a day before his event, by trading his maple leaf crest to a Norwegian competitor. In 1936, the highly rated eights from the Leander Rowing Club in Hamilton, bronze medal winners in Los Angeles, could not afford to send their own shell to Berlin, so they had one made in Germany. 'It was a big, bloody barge. The boat was belly heavy and there was no running it,' cox George 'Shorty' McDonald remembered. The frustrated crew did not get out of the heats.[61]

'Universal Registration' and the Depression

By the late 1920s, the Union was at the height of its power. The rightfulness of amateurism as the basis for sporting morality and

governance was widely recognized, its contribution to national development universally praised. The AAU enjoyed the allegiance of virtually
every major sporting body in the country. Through its far-flung networks,
it provided responsible supervision to thousands of boys and men in
healthy, satisfying participation and brought joy and pride to thousands
more in the stands. In the affiliated associations – for instance, the
Canadian Amateur Hockey Association and the Canadian Amateur
Swimming Association – and in the sports that it controlled directly, the
national championships were highly competitive and widely followed. As
the results from the Winter Olympics at St Moritz, where the Canadian
hockey team rolled over the opposition by a total score of 38–0, and the
Olympic Games in Amsterdam clearly indicated, Canadians had to be
counted among the best athletes in the world. To be sure, the Union
faced the same difficult sectional tensions that divided the country in
other ways. Professional sport was growing in popularity and legitimacy,
fuelled by the spectacular growth of commercial entertainment in the
postwar industrial boom. The growing popularity of the 'athletic
scholarship' in U.S. universities gave new respectability to the idea of
selling one's athletic labour. But if the amateur leaders were troubled by
these developments, they gave little indication. On the contrary, they
moved to tighten their control by implementing a system of 'universal
registration.'

The dream of 'universal registration' had sprung from the highly
centralized origins of the Union. All athletes had had to sign an identical
pledge of loyalty to amateurism, and they received an identical membership card, whether they competed in boxing, track and field, or fencing.
The system had worked because the Union had directly controlled
participation in these sports. But as other sports bodies developed, they
created their own definitions of amateurism, their own systems of
registration, and their own membership cards. When the leaders of the
new federated Union had approached them about affiliating in the early
1910s, most of them had held out for a measure of autonomy. In some
cases, there were different definitions of eligibility. The Canadian
Wheelmen's Association wanted to oversee both amateur and professional
cycling. The Dominion Football (soccer) Association sought to follow the
'Old Country' practice of allowing pros and amateurs to play on the same
field. In each case, a compromise had to be found before an article of
alliance could be signed.[62] Other associations wanted to retain responsibility for issuing cards, collecting fees, and policing the code. The resulting
pattern of alliances gave the AAU the power to define amateurism in

broad outline but left the affiliated body in charge of the specifics, including day-to-day administration. The allied bodies had some opportunity to adapt the terms of eligibility to sport-specific conditions and a healthy measure of discretion in enforcement. The effective basis of the federation was that each of the Union and affiliated bodies agreed to respect each other's cards.

In 1925, Norton Crow suddenly retired, ill and pressed by his duties at the Ontario treasury. He died four years later at 53, a terrible loss to the amateur movement. Crow's responsibilities were assumed by the arch-conservative Lamb. Lamb and other hard-liners were unhappy about the measure of decentralization and sought to develop a single, unified system of 'universal registration.' They wanted every athlete in Canada to sign the same declaration and carry an identical card, in a system that would be completely administered and enforced by the Union. It would not only strengthen adherence to amateurism, and simplify administration, they thought, but bring the Union increased dues. At the 1927 annual meeting in Edmonton, Lamb was elected president, and he and his allies were successful in pushing through 'universal registration' in principle. Implementation would occur through renegotiated articles of alliance. The single registration fee would be shared among the allied body and the provincial and national AAUs. It would bring about 'a major change in procedure in the whole realm of the Canadian body,' legislation chair J.H. Crocker of the YMCA declared.

But when implementation actually began in 1931, conditions could not have been worse. The terrible economic hardships of the Depression put an enormous strain on sports administration. For the amateur leaders the 1930s brought great contradictions and swings of emotions. On the one hand, local participation in many sports increased, in part because it helped people fill the time in an enjoyable, social way for very little money, and in part because it gave them a sense of achievement at a time when there was little room for optimism. Most of the leaders and those older athletes who were well established in their careers kept their jobs. For civil servants and others with fixed incomes, the widespread deflation may actually have improved their standards of living.[63] On the other hand, the Depression intensified public expectations while leaving the amateur bodies with few resources with which to respond. Membership receipts fell off, as the growing number of unemployed could no longer afford to register. In the individual sports especially, sponsorships and gate receipts dried up as well. As a result, the Union was forced to cancel the travelling coaches and national training camps, suspend publication of its monthy magazine, the *Canadian Athlete*, and shelve other planned initiatives indefinitely. It became even further isolated from the grass roots of sports development.

The AAU had no money to help the top athletes either, forcing some of them to 'ride the rods' to trials and championships. In 1932, even though the Olympic Games were just a train ride away in Los Angeles, the Canadian Olympic Committee raised so little for the team that all the athletes and officials were required to help pay for their participation. Boxing bantamweight Horace 'Lefty' Gwynne scored a pleasingly easy victory over the German favourite, and the team brought back a record 15 medals, including ten in track and field. But in other events, despite smaller fields occasioned by the high costs of travel, the Canadian-trained athletes frequently found themselves outclassed. To the AAUers' chagrin, every individual male Canadian medallist in track and field, including gold-medal high jumper Duncan McNaughton, received his training at an American university. They were just as cash-strapped in 1934 for the Empire Games and in 1936 for the Berlin Olympics, and they were forced to ask most athletes and all team officials to pay their own way. Some of those who did make the trips were so hungry when they assembled for departure that they ate themselves out of condition on the 'three square meals' they got as members of national teams.[64]

The Depression irreparably damaged the material and ideological conditions on which amateurism was based, especially among athletes. Young men were the most heavily hit by the massive lay-offs resulting from collapse of commodity prices and the downward spiral of investment, consumption, and production that followed the Great Crash of 1929. In 1932 and 1933, 26 per cent of the non-agricultural workforce in Canada – more than 600,000 workers – could not find jobs. Most of them were men under the age of 30. The situation forced many to find an income anywhere they could. Under these devastating conditions, the 'honour' of abiding by the amateur code became a luxury many could not afford. Few athletes in sports such as track and field, gymnastics, and swimming would ever have the chance to consider making money from their efforts. But in such team sports as hockey, baseball, football, and lacrosse, the desire of local and regional boosters to 'maintain the community' in the face of economic and social adversity further elevated the importance of representational teams, giving the top athletes in those sports some bargaining power.

It is not clear if there was a widespread increase in the number of players who were paid under the table in the early years of the Depression. Estimates vary considerably.[65] My own research leads me to believe that few players were receiving payments until the latter part of the decade. For example, Art Rice-Jones – who played goal for hockey teams in Fort William, Winnipeg, and Calgary, including the Winnipeg Monarchs squad that won the World Championship in 1935 – told me that despite all the press reports that he and his teammates were well paid, he never received anything more than expenses. 'Under the table! Don't make me laugh – that was the Depression. Whenever and wherever I played, I always had a job to get my money. We didn't even get "broken-time payments!" '[66] But certainly there was a marked rise in the number of athletes who exchanged their athletic skills for employment or other benefits. Rice-Jones and players like him were given work by local boosters to keep them in town. The Olympic boxer 'Lefty' Gwynne, and runners Johnny Miles, Bill Fritz, and Scotty Rankine, took advantage of award presentations and civic receptions to ask for work. Miles gained a foreman's position at International Harvester, where he had worked sporadically up until then. Fritz, who could no longer afford to continue his engineering studies at Queen's, moved to Toronto when the West End Y found him a position on the anti-freeze canning line at the Canadian National Carbon Co. But the others were unsuccessful. When Gwynne, the Olympic champion, 'asked the mayor [of Toronto] to get me a job, he nearly dropped dead.'[67] Athletes bartered their talents for other benefits too. Football star Bert Gibb held out for a new bicycle tire before he would practice with the Hamilton Tigers. Another player would not play until the club gave him a cellar of coal.

In the case of 'company' teams sponsored for advertising and goodwill, the high levels of unemployment gave employers new bargaining power. The competition for positions became so great that firms were able to get good players for their teams without financial inducement, simply by offering them a job. 'You got your job because you were good at sports, but you always had to work,' confirmed W.E. 'Stuffy' Richards, who gained four jobs in Toronto in the 1930s because of his soccer goal-tending abilities. 'There were lots who did that, and we put in a full shift like everybody else. Sure, it helped us get a job, but if you couldn't do it, or slacked off, you were gone no matter how good you were on the field. I was laid off at Lever Brothers, even though I was the star of the team.'[68] Trading on their sporting skills was a violation of the spirit of amateurism, yet in the circumstances it did not seem so shameful to the athletes involved. More athletes than ever before found themselves doing so in order to keep body and soul together.

The pressures that encouraged these practices had been building for years. During the 1920s, professional sport rapidly acquired more respectability as a whole new galaxy of stars, lionized by the commercial media, descended on the hearts and minds of Canadians. The centre of these developments was the United States, but Canadians were kept well informed by their own newspapers and radio stations. It was in these years, for example, that the renowned Canadian sports photographers Mat and Lou Turofsky began driving to American events to telegraph shots of the action back to Canadian newspapers.[69] Boxing was legalized in most jurisdictions after the Great War, and millions followed the bouts of Jack Dempsey, Benny Leonard, and Gene Tunney. Baseball-loving fans idolized Babe Ruth.

These more favourable conditions enabled Canadian entrepreneurs to expand their base of operations. In 1926, amusement king Sol Solmon persuaded the Toronto Harbour Commissioners, a public body, to build him a stadium for his International League Toronto Maple (baseball) Leafs on seven acres of centrally located waterfront land and Conn Smythe talked several prominent Toronto businessmen into helping him buy the National Hockey League's St Patrick's franchise. It was not so disgraceful to be associated with professional sports anymore. On the contrary, turning pro brought celebrity and the attention of powerful men.

Unwittingly, the AAU's increased emphasis on high performance narrowed the ideological distance between amateurism and professionalism. During the countless debates about the merits of the different approaches, promoters and professional athletes alike had pitched customers with three interrelated appeals: they promised (1) a representative identity and (2) exciting entertainment, performed (3) at the highest level of athletic skill. By comparison, the amateurs had traditionally promised the personal rewards of education, fitness, and the excitement of playing and the opportunity to contribute altruistically to the tasks of nation-building. But as they focused more on recruitment and training of highly skilled national teams, the inspiration offered by Olympic and Empire Games champions, and collection of gate receipts, the image of cultural production they presented began to converge with that of the professional promoters. It became accepted for amateurs as well as professionals to trade on their athletic talent. Significant differences remained, to be sure. Few amateur clubs treated their players as harshly as the pros. But it must have been harder for a young hockey player readily to tell the difference.

The onset of the Depression marked a turning point. The sanctity of amateurism had been slowly eroding during the 1920s, but the process was dramatically accelerated by the mass unemployment of the 1930s. It was the beginning of the end of amateur hegemony. Consider signings in the NHL. In the mid-1920s, only two members of the Allan Cup and Olympic-champion Toronto Granites, Reg 'Hooley' Smith and Dunc Munro, turned pro. 'All of the [NHL] teams had been after Harry Watson, but this great player elected to remain an amateur and rejected all proposals.'[70] Only Lorne Chabot from the Port Arthur Bearcats, which won the Allan Cup in 1925, left his team to sign with the pros. Captain Gord Wilson and winger Wilf L'Heureux stayed on to lead Port Arthur to two more cups, in 1926 and 1929. But in 1931, the entire Allan Cup–winning team from Montreal signed with the NHL's Montreal Maroons. The following year, Hugh Plaxton, captain of the 1928 Varsity Grads, which followed the Granites to Allan Cup and Olympic titles, signed with the Maroons, despite his newly minted law degree. Conditions were changing rapidly, and, with them, many people's beliefs. The shift would enormously complicate the tasks of governing the Union.

In the first years of the crisis, the old majorities stood firm. In 1930 in Vancouver, a special committee on amateurism composed of W.H. Kilby, director of the CNR Recreation League, past president John Jackson of Alberta, and Bill Fry of the Canadian Amateur Hockey Association (CAHA) recommended against any change in the code that would jeopardize Canadian chances in international competition. The recommendation was overwhelmingly accepted. A BC motion calling for reinstatement of professionals after three years was immediately withdrawn. Prior to the meeting, both the Ontario Hockey Association and the Canadian Association of Amateur Oarsmen publicly announced their determination to defeat it.[71] In 1931, delegates to the annual 'Parliament' in Winnipeg overwhelmingly reiterated the importance of 'universal registration' and unanimously defeated a Maritimes motion endorsing 'broken time' payments – no one from the Atlantic provinces had been able to attend the meetings. Even the region's proxy, Fred Marples of Winnipeg, voted against the resolution.[72] In 1932 in Ottawa, delegates gave a one-year hoist to a Saskatchewan proposal to allow pros in one sport to register as amateurs in another. Immediately before the meeting, President James Morkin of Winnipeg, widely regarded as a supporter of a more flexible rule, announced that he would oppose the Saskatchewan resolution.[73]

But even in the rarefied circles of the AAU leadership, views were slowly changing. The Kilby committee of 1930 prepared the ground for subsequent liberalization. In the preamble to its long report, it recognized the winds of change: 'Those who think there should be a change to meet modern conditions are growing greater in number all the time. This, we feel, is not due so much to the desire to lower the standard as to the knowledge that we must endeavour to meet changed conditions in the world, where gate receipts and championships play such an important part.' In response to the new conditions, the Kilby committee completely abandoned moral condemnation of professionalism, recognizing that it 'has entered into sport in a large way and no blame can be attached to a young man who openly becomes a professional, especially where his income would be much larger as an athlete than as an artisan ... The man who has to earn his daily bread may have just as true a love for sport as the person who has the leisure and the means to participate in games.' Committee members admitted that their own 'contamination' rule was contributing to the problem: 'It is possible [that some athletes] may be professional only because of the present codification of amateurism ... In living up to a strict interpretation of our rules we seriously handicap those who are desirous of being true amateurs. This particularly applies to the more sparsely settled portions of our country, where, if even a few are stricken off the roll as amateurs, the remaining few are not enough in numbers to carry on ... Then again, when a player is automatically suspended by playing with or against a professional, the opportunity for taking part in games in which skilled persons take part is greatly lessened. In several large portions of Canada, sport is practically at a standstill because amateurs cannot play against a professional team.'[74]

The immediate effect of this reasoning was recommendation of a limited form of 'intermingling' – namely, that amateur teams be allowed to play charity matches *against* professional teams at the discretion of local branches and allied bodies. (The committee rejected the idea of amateurs and professionals playing *with* each other on the same teams.) The proposal was accepted, by a vote of 90 to 30 that was widely regarded as a victory for John Jackson and the persistence of Alberta spokesmen.

The Kilby report permanently changed the terms of debate. It cast aside the moralism of previous years, and thereafter the majority positions became increasingly pragmatic. When Jim Morkin decided against the Saskatchewan proposal to permit pros in one sport to play amateur in another, it was because he objected not to contamination but to the 'complications.' 'If the Union votes to this drastic step,' he told the press, 'it will mean the wrecking of many of the powerful allied bodies [and make] the choosing of our Olympic teams a difficult matter.'[75]

The first major break in the strict amateur coalition came at the annual 'parliament' in Winnipeg in 1933. Several traditionalists began to abandon their time-honoured positions and to canvass openly for changes. The main item of discussion was the report commissioned in response to the Saskatchewan resolution of the previous year. Written by A.S. Lamb, the report was an impassioned defence of the status quo: 'We have obligations in this time of national crisis such as never before ... The problems [of intense competition, the desire to win, and gate receipts] cannot be solved by legalizing offences which now exist. Incapable, dishonest and incompetent officials must be replaced, the tradition of amateurism in its strictest sense must be perpetuated and public opinion must be reassured.' But even Lamb had to acknowledge that the Union had to take public opinion into account. He urged it to 'reaffirm its faith ... [and] to enlist the cooperation of competitors, officials, and the general public in discouraging practices which are not directed to [the promotion of] health, character and citizenship.' The document was signed by President Howard Crocker, Secretary John Leslie, and John Hamilton of Saskatchewan, immediate past president of the CAHA.[76]

In other years, the report would have been quickly approved. But in 1933, few delegates were prepared to listen. The Depression had drastically altered the conditions in which they conducted their activities, widening differences between sports and regions. 'Universal registration' had significantly increased the political weight on the Union, by giving it sole responsibility for eligibility, and it could no longer be supported. When a Saskatchewan delegate proposed an amendment to give the allied bodies in the team sports the right to make their own rules with respect to professional-amateur contacts, the Canadian Olympic Committee's chair, Pat Mulqueen of Toronto, long a leader of the traditionalists, rose to support it: 'I do not believe in the Saskatchewan resolution, I think it would be a tremendous mistake if it were carried, but now I will put myself right: I believe that ... this organization should permit the governing bodies in team sports to use their best judgement as to whether they allow two or three or a limited number, say, two professionals to play on these amateur clubs.'

When President Crocker immediately stepped in to declare the Saskatchewan amendment a separate motion (thus enabling the meeting to approve the Lamb report), Mulqueen quickly seconded him. When it came back from the resolutions committee late that evening, two Ontario delegates tried to have the discussion put off but were voted down. The old guard managed to muster enough votes to defeat it, but several prominent allies, including Secretary John Leslie and past president Morkin, stood in the opposing camp. A few minutes later, Mulqueen, Leslie, and Morkin supported a surprise resolution from Vice-president Bill Fry calling for unconditional reinstatement of professionals after three years. This time they were successful. After another long debate, the weary delegates approved the move on condition that no athlete would be reinstated more than once. They also gave the allied bodies the right to allow professional tryouts without penalty.

The new state of affairs satisfied no one. Sydney Halter, secretary of the Manitoba branch, slammed the Lamb report, which the meeting also passed, as 'a masterful piece of graceful evasion.' He told the press that he 'had hoped for something more toward allowing pro-am competition.'[77] Traditionalists were equally upset. Charles Higginbottom, the Central Ontario president who had tried to postpone consideration, bitterly opposed the revisions, warning that 'everybody [will] be so sick of the mess that they [will] want to get back to the present code before the year is out.'[78] Henry Roxborough, a member of the Lamb committee, lambasted his old friends Mulqueen and Fry in *Maclean's*: 'When men occupying positions of prominence in amateur sporting fraternities not only support resolutions contrary to the spirit of amateurism but also publicly chide the association in which they hold office, then how can anyone reasonably expect the humbler executives, the players, or the public to show any enthusiasm for the amateur ideals?'[79]

At the following year's annual meeting in Toronto, no further changes were made. Perhaps the new reinstatement rule – 153 former pros were allowed back that year – relieved some of the pressure. Perhaps those who had compromised decided to go no further. Delegates voted down without debate a BC proposal to permit unlimited pro-am contact. Their major concern was the rapid increase in the number of American 'imports' playing amateur rugby. At the urging of Central Ontario's Higginbottom, they passed a strongly worded resolution condemning the practice.[80]

Still the winds of change continued to blow. In 1935, eight branches and allied bodies submitted motions calling for amateur amendments to the annual meeting in Halifax. Bill Fry, the president, thought 'some of the[m] so radical as to seriously affect the vital amateur principles for which this Union has stood for 60 years.'[81] Branches from British Columbia, Alberta, Thunder Bay, and the Maritimes all called for a large measure of open competition, based on what they called 'the British principles of sport' – the practice of some British federations of allowing amateurs to play alongside and against pros without penalty. Opponents replied that in other sports, such as rowing and rugby, British rules were much more stringent than the Canadian.[82] Central Ontario, one of the staunchest defenders of strict amateurism, called on the AAU to register both amateurs and professionals during a one-year trial. Though this move was intended 'to expose the athletes receiving [illegal] compensation for their services and to restore the confidence formerly existing among those who participate in the games for the pleasure of playing,'[83] it had the unintended effect of strengthening pressures for revision. Most significant, the allied bodies governing the three most widely played team sports in the Union – the CAHA, the Canadian Amateur Basketball Association (CABA), and the Canadian Amateur Lacrosse Association (CALA) – joined the voices for change. The CAHA had traditionally been a pillar of strict amateurism. Two years previously, the CALA had condemned efforts to allow 'mingling' of professionals and amateurs. Now both bodies wanted a new definition altogether.

The urgent appeals for pragmatic accommodation with professionalism, especially but not exclusively in the team sports, reflected the increasingly desperate circumstances of most amateur organizations and the further gains that professional sport had made in the early years of the Depression. If by the late 1920s professional sport had outgrown its earlier, disreputable associations, by the mid-1930s it had become enormously popular. This was particularly the case in hockey, where the spectacular success of the 'Hockey Night in Canada' radio show made the Toronto Maple Leafs a household habit. But the glow of 'professionalism' extended to activities such as wrestling, where even admirers admitted that the contests were faked. In 1931, for example, Henry Roxborough told his *Maclean's* readers that 'the once maligned sport of wrestling [has won] an astonishingly wide popular favor ... The game has made good because the organizing was sound and the matching skilful; because the athletes and managers sacredly kept promises, and principally because showmanship has been added in large doses to wrestling ability.'[84]

Hard times drew amateurs and professionals closer together. Gate- and victory-conscious amateur organizers sought the popularity and athletic challenge of successful professional teams (and recently retired pros) to enhance their own revenues and the experience of their teams. Sports entrepreneurs frequently sought to exploit the fresh talents of amateurs, and they had revenue to offer (and could disrupt amateur activities through aggressive raiding campaigns). In hockey, the NHL sought unrestricted access to the stars of the CAHA's far-flung leagues and the adherence of the amateur organization to its rules (so that players would learn the game the NHL way). It obtained such an agreement in 1936, in exchange for promising not to buy away more than one player per team per season. In wrestling, promoters wanted to include amateur bouts on their professional cards and offered payments to the AAU bodies in return.[85]

But perhaps the most compelling consideration was the spectre of 'a vast army of athletes now participat[ing] in amateur sport to whom living conditions constitute a struggle,' as Sydney Halter put it repeatedly: 'Time has completely changed the situation. As a result of war debts, depression years and many other matters, nations have become impoverished ... Many there are competing in Amateur Sport to whom every penny of their income is desperately needed. Can it be logically argued that a boy whose small income is the sole support of an otherwise unemployed family, whose absence from work for a short period to participate in an amateur athletic engagement will entail a loss of earnings, which might occasion a shortage of food or shelter for his family is none the less "playing the game for its own sake" should he request only that the amount of earnings he lost be repaid to him?'[86]

In 1935, the Winnipeg football team of which Halter was treasurer began to pay of some of its players, including American 'import' Fritz Hanson, who led it to the Grey Cup. To avoid hypocrisy, Halter quietly stopped the practice of having team members get AAU cards. Within a year, his example was widely followed across the west. Though the Canadian Rugby Union continued to maintain the amateur rule on its books, it no longer pressed for enforcement, turning to residence requirements as a way of monitoring eligibility.[87]

Amateurism in Retreat

As AAU delegates assembled in Halifax for the 1935 'Parliament,' the press was as divided as they were. Toronto's *Globe* continued to advocate tough enforcement of the existing rulebook, scoring President Fry for procrastinating in the investigation of an alleged professional football player,[88] but the *Halifax Herald*, perhaps basking in the success of the Maritimes hockey loop, where players were brought in from all over the country, ridiculed them for their resistance to change: 'Does any delegate to this particular convention imagine that such sports as organized senior hockey and baseball are conducted on a strictly amateur basis in this country today? *If he does, then he is just about the only person in this country who does think so*. Isn't it about time, therefore, that those who legislate for and administer Canadian "amateurism" stepped right out in the open and faced this question squarely – and effectively? As matters stand at present, the situation is shot with hypocrisy. And that, most certainly is not a desirable or healthy situation. Few Canadians can afford in senior league schedules to be amateurs in the old accepted sense of the term.'[89]

The debate on the code took up an entire session. By general agreement, the several motions were combined into three alternatives:

- that one professional player be allowed to play on an amateur team in another form of sport in which he is not a professional
- that any number of professionals be allowed to do this, subject to the ruling of the respective allied body
- that professionals be allowed to play with and against amateurs without restriction.

But while the traditionalists, led by A.S. Lamb, stood firm, the reformers were divided. When the votes were taken, all three proposals were defeated by wide margins. Only Alberta and Thunder Bay voted for all three. The following day Lamb pushed through a motion that 'admitted that there was deceit, dishonesty, and hypocrisy in some forms of amateur sport' and called on all bodies to 'eliminate these evils.' The press could not agree, either. The editorial page of the *Halifax Herald* endorsed prosecution of amateur 'perjurers ... promptly, fearlessly, and effectively,' while the sports page condemned the Union for 'not meeting ITS responsibility man-fashion and legislating in accordance with the conditions and the demands of 1935.'[90]

Stung by their defeat in Halifax and what they thought was betrayal by President Bill Fry, a former president of their own association, CAHA leaders refused to drop the issue. At their annual meeting in Toronto the following spring, they unilaterally redefined an 'amateur' for themselves on the basis of the following four points:

1. Hockey players may capitalize on their ability as hockey players for the purpose of obtaining legitimate employment.
2. Hockey players may accept from their clubs or employers payment for time lost from work while competing for amateur clubs (i.e. "broken-time").
3. Amateur hockey teams may play exhibition games against professional teams under such conditions as may be laid down by the individual branches of the CAHA.

4. Professionals in other branches of sport may be permitted to play on amateur hockey teams.[91]

In dismissing the argument that the new rules would render Canadians ineligible for international competition, CAHA spokemen replied: 'It is [our] business to legislate for the good of hockey in Canada, and ... international competitions are at best only a secondary consideration. [The CAHA] would argue further that Canada has a right to bring forward changes in the rules for Olympic and international competition ... The principle which the CAHA wishes to follow is that in Canadian hockey the facts and realities of the situation should be faced fairly and honestly, and that open and above-board legislation should be framed to meet them.'[92] When the AAU voted down all four points at the 1936 annual meeting in Regina, the CAHA announced its disaffiliation. The CALA and the CABA soon followed suit, though in the latter's case the reasons were more complicated. The basketball association was upset primarily because the AAU had recognized the Canadian Secondary Schools' Athletic Association, which tried to prevent high-school players in some provinces from playing in CABA leagues.

In response to the shock of the hockey men's departure, the remaining AAU members elected another former CAHA president, John Hamilton of Regina, to the presidency, in hopes that he could negotiate their return. Hamilton proposed that the voting rules be altered to give the allied bodies in the team sports effective control over issues directly affecting them. Other members sought a more flexible eligibility rule to woo the team sports back. In 1937, Vice-president Sydney Halter of Winnipeg proposed that the Union allow its constituent bodies to employ whatever definition had been established by their respective international federations even if that definition was more liberal than its own: 'That year I carefully checked the amateur definitions of each international sport, and found, to my surprise, that the amateur definition in the rule book of the AAU of Canada was word for word with the amateur defini-tion of the international track and field association, and while the "amateur" definition of all other international sports was to some extent similar, yet each had its own definition; and here was the AAU of Canada, which was the representative in Canada of each of the other sports organizations maintaining the definition of one of the affiliates against those of all the others.'[93]

Halter's motion won over the majority, 89–53, but it fell six votes short of the two-thirds necessary for a change in the code. Curiously, Alberta,

British Columbia, and the Maritimes, frequent advocates of liberalization, refused to support it. Immediately after the meeting, however, some of the 'old guard,' led by Pat Mulqueen, took Halter aside and told him that they had made a mistake and promised to vote for it the following year. They were good to their word. In 1938 in Fort William, the motion passed without debate. Halter was then elected president.

Halter's astute leadership averted another amateur war. The CAHA did not proceed with creation of a National Sports Federation to rival the AAU, as it had threatened, nor did the Union take reprisals against the departing associations. The CAHA also decided not to implement its 'fourth point' – to allow professionals in one sport to compete as amateurs in another – which would have got Canadian hockey players in Olympic tournaments into trouble with the International Olympic Committee (IOC). After Fry's departure, cordial relations were quickly re-established. CAHA representatives continued to sit on the AAU's Olympic Committee. In 1939, the CAHA gave the AAU a grant of $300 (which represented 16 per cent of revenue that year) in recognition of their 'common interest ... in the furtherance of amateur sport in Canada.'[94] There was even hope that the CAHA, the CALA, and the CABA would return. That year, the amateurs' 'Parliament' gave its allied bodies an effective veto over any changes affecting their rules. But the team-sport associations never affiliated again. The desire for independence was too great. Though Hardy, principal author of the 'four points,' tried to get the CAHA to reaffiliate, his colleagues on the executive outvoted him. Perhaps they felt that their new relationship with the NHL would be jeopardized. At the very time the CAHA was discussing reaffiliation, NHL President Frank Calder proposed establishment of a single governing body for both professional and amateur hockey. He had been invited to address the golden jubilee banquet of the Ontario Hockey Association, once one of the fiercest opponents of 'intermingling' in Canadian sport.[95]

'Universal registration' – the ideal of a single eligibility code for all affiliated sports, administered through a common registration card and centrally enforced – was thus a near-fatal mistake for the AAU. It greatly increased the Union's political vulnerability at a time of rapid, unsettling change, because it – and not the allied body – became the target when there was a challenge to the code or a ruling was unpopular. When delegates to the CAHA's annual meeting complained about the registration system, for example, Bill Fry got nowhere when he told them, 'It isn't my Union; it's your Union.'[96] If the CAHA had still been free to determine and administer its own amateur definition, it might well have stayed in the fold. The leadership's view of Canada also contributed to the divorce: its vision of a homogeneous, English-speaking 'nation' did not leave much room for diversity. It prevented the Union from welcoming French Canadians and non-British immigrants into the leadership and led it to turn a deaf ear to the appeals for some recognition of regional differences.

Sports were ready vehicles for the expression of other forms of identity, especially for people in the Maritimes, the resource hinterland of Ontario, and western provinces who felt exploited and slighted by the National Policy economy and the political clout of Ontario and Quebec. It was invariably men from those regions who first found that amateurism constrained their ability to compete. In hockey, it was the Maritimes and northern Ontario amateur teams that first began to pay players in a significant way. In football, western teams most strenuously pushed for importation of Americans and American rules, such as downfield blocking and the forward pass. They came from the same middle-class background as their counterparts from southern Ontario and Montreal, but the greater difficulty they faced in fielding winning teams made them more pragmatic. 'Universal registration' greatly reduced the amount of difference that the AAU was able to tolerate and, in so doing, destroyed it as a broadly representative federation.

In the CAHA, acceptance of 'broken time' greatly strengthened the senior leagues in their struggle with the NHL for players and fans. In practice, it meant that players could be openly paid without reprisal. The new rule simply stated that 'an amateur hockey player is one who has not engaged in, or is not engaged in, organized professional hockey.' Players could stay with the teams they wanted, live close to friends and families, and get started in business or a career. Most of all, they could get paid without all the attendant risks of trying for the NHL. By the late 1930s, some CAHA players made as much as the pros. In 1938, Canadiens' owner Ernest Savard complained that the Montreal Royals were making *more* than he was paying his outright pros. 'It is an open secret that the practical operators of the NHL are not completely sold on [the CAHA's decision to allow players to be paid],' observed Ralph Allen in *Maclean's* in 1940. 'It was unfair competition, that's what it was.'[97] The new rule gave the CAHA the chance to develop the community-based, not-for-profit variant of professionalism found in British soccer. In football, development of open professionalism took longer. Its adoption was complicated by bitter simultaneous debates about passing and blocking rules and use of American-trained players. But after the Second World War, the community-based professional approach, which Halter had legitimated with the Winnipeg team, provided the basis for the Canadian Football League, established in 1958. Not surprisingly, Halter became its first commissioner.[98]

But self-determination also led to a wide variety of eligibility criteria, resulting in great confusion for athletes seeking to compete in several sports. The chastened AAU no longer tried to coordinate eligibility in all Canadian sports. By 1949, Canada had 35 amateur definitions in force, and 'simplification, unification, and honesty' became goals once again.[99] The Halter revision did not end strict amateurism. In the seven sports that the AAU directly controlled, it continued for another 30 years to prohibit 'broken time' payments, 'mingling,' and 'capitalizing on [one's] athletic fame,' in keeping with its international obligations in those sports, though some provisions, such as the sanction against teaching physical education, were less frequently enforced. The strict definition prevailed until 1974, when the IOC dropped the word 'amateur' and the prohibition against 'broken time' from its eligibility code. In 1983, the IOC adopted its own version of the Halter revision, giving each international federation virtually unlimited discretion to determine who can compete in its sport in the Olympic Games, which paved the way for the relatively unrestricted professionalism of today.

Withdrawal of the team sports was a serious blow to the AAU in many ways. It decimated the Union's revenues, most of which came from direct and indirect fees. In 1936, the year of the split, the Union boasted 18,408 paid-up senior members. Two years later, membership had fallen to just 1,852. Revenue dropped from $3,083.19 in 1936 to $1,197.60 in 1938.[100] Though membership bounced back to 2,753 the following year, revenues could not cover the costs of selecting and sending schoolboy and British Empire Games teams to Sydney, forcing the AAU to cancel its most prestigious event, the Dominion Track and Field Championships. The split also cost it a large pool of talented men for its committees and greatly reduced the constituency – and the legitimacy – of its annual gathering. Henceforth the 'Canadian Parliament of Sport' was known simply as the annual meeting. While the Union's activities continued to make headlines, and it continued to enjoy the hospitality and plaudits of public officials, a new generation of sportswriters that idolized the pros, led by Andy Lytle of the *Toronto Star*, taunted it about its anti-market ideas. The hegemony of amateur sport was over. In hockey, as Ralph Allen wryly commented, the story could be told in three lines:

'1930 What is an Amateur? / 1935 Why is an Amateur? / 1940 Where is an Amateur?'[101]

When the dominion government declared war on Germany, the AAU quickly brought its activities to a halt, as it had a generation earlier, and gave its full support to Canada's fighting forces. For veterans such as Crocker, Jackson, Lamb, and Mulqueen, who had enjoyed the heady successes of the 1920s, only to be plunged into the protracted crises of the Depression, it might well have come as a relief, like the break that athletes and teams took after a long, tumultuous season.

Despite the tremendous loss of power, the AAUers were not without accomplishment during the interwar period. They managed to add significantly to the framework for pan-Canadian sport. In 1919, sports were played in every part of the country, but there were few solid links between the nodes of activity. Few athletes living outside the Montreal region and southern Ontario had much of a chance to compete for 'national' honours. But through shrewd promotion of the 'Canadian Parliament of Sport,' careful recruitment of officers, and judicious placing of national championships, the amateur leaders effectively united the west with central Canadian sports circles and maintained a semblance of relations with the impoverished, alienated Maritimes. Distances and scarcity of funds made communication difficult at all times. The organizers travelled by train whenever they could, but for the most part they had to rely on the mails and the telegraph.

Certainly the Union's 'nation-building' suffered from the familiar myopia of English-Canadian nationalism. Few French-Canadian, First Nations, immigrant, and working-class sports groups were included. The AAUers had few ideas about how to involve girls and women. The prohibition against physical educators prevented many others from realizing their athletic ambitions. In their arbitrary suspensions, the amateur tribunals were appallingly indifferent to athletes' rights. Moreover, during the Depression, at a time when there was greater need for the grass-roots development of sports that it had once so passionately demanded, the AAU was so preoccupied with the Olympics that it had nothing to give. These were all serious failings. But by struggling to include every region and association, striving for 'made-in-Canada' training programs, and emphasizing a spirit of public-mindedness and 'fair play,' the AAU helped establish the idea that sports were inseparable from responsible citizenship. It was a platform from which subsequent generations, including all those groups left out, could build.

For those who managed to participate, amateur sports provided an enjoyable means of masculine self-definition and a complement to an active, productive life. Though attention was increasingly focused on the technical requirements of training and the strategic and tactical aspects of competition, the discourse of 'rational recreation' was sufficiently strong to allow for simultaneous pursuit of academic study, professional careers, and other avocations – i.e., a masculinity characterized by education, culture, and autonomy, among those who had the means. In his survey of the major team sports in 1931, Leslie Roberts found that only footballers 'landed on their feet' after they retired. Because 'football's spirit is amateur down to the last man, it does not interfere greatly with his efforts to obtain a foothold in the ordinary world outside the stadium walls ... It will help, not injure his chance to be a judge or a financier, by making a man out of him.'[102] Canadian football retained that atmosphere for many years.

I remember much the same when I was an amateur runner in the 1950s and 1960s. Clubs emphasized the pleasures of competition, travel, and fraternizing with athletes from other clubs and countries. As most coaches and officials were volunteers, athletes were able to conduct their activities with a considerable amount of autonomy. Those who could afford it led well-rounded lives. We should not romanticize the 'kitchen-table era' of volunteer sports administration, but it did provide many rewarding opportunities for those involved.

The amateur movement gave many other people a measure of pride in that larger, often ambiguous entity called Canada. In 1939, Vincent Massey, Canadian high commissioner to Britain, boasted in a letter to W.L. Mackenzie King about a recent string of victories by Canadian amateur athletes in England. To make sure the unathletic prime minister got the point, he wrote a postscript by hand: 'This may seem a relatively unimportant sphere of activity, but it has its place in international relations.'[103] Canadian athletes did not win so frequently in international competitions that anyone could suggest, as Mark Dyerson has done for the United States, that they 'confirm[ed] their nation's exceptionalism in Olympic stadiums.'[104] But the enthusiastic, patriotic, and charmingly naive young men and women who wore the maple leaf in the growing international competitions of the period gave Canadians lots to cheer about. Few of them exhibited the extroverted personalities that would land American swimmers Buster Crabbe and Johnny Weismuller Hollywood film contracts. The much-celebrated Percy Williams was unbearably shy. But people flocked to their performances and tied their hopes to them all the same. During those special competitions such as the Olympics and the Empire Games, when newspapers and radio dissected how Canada fared against other nations, the amateur athletes gave ready demonstration of that 'virile and united Canadian spirit' which other organizations – the Canadian Clubs, the Canadian Authors Association, and the Group of Seven, for instance – sought to foster through education, literary and artistic expression and creation of national symbols and heroes.[105] In 1928, when Williams and his teammates returned from Amsterdam, they were met by large crowds and fêted in every city where they stopped for the recognition and honour that they had brought Canada. On the dais in Montreal, the French-Canadian nationalist Mayor Camilien Houde asked Williams to spurn the many offers of 'athletic scholarships' from American universities so that he could continue to inspire Canadian youth. 'You have advertised the nation of Canada to the entire world. Don't take it away from us,' he said. Williams and his 'sweetheart-like mother who was there with him' promised to stay in Canada. According to the *Toronto Star*, that response touched off a cheer 'like a blood bond of brothers.'[106]

3

'Girls' Sports Run by Girls'

The First World War seemed to herald a bright future for women. The senseless slaughter at the front, the ignominious botch-ups of the high command, the scandalous profiteering of wartime suppliers, and the divisive dominion election of 1917 all appeared to undermine traditional authority, which everywhere was male. The unstinting contributions of female nurses, munitions and agricultural workers, and volunteers to the war effort and the successful female-led prohibition and suffrage campaigns suggested to many that the doors to women's full participation in society could no longer be kept shut. It was not only feminists such as Nellie McClung and Emily Murphy who prophesied better days to come. 'The woman who is receiving her education today is fortunate, for she is living in a period when the old order of things is passing away and a new era is at hand,' Col. George S. Nasmith told the graduating class of the Margaret Eaton School of Literature and Expression, the well-connected Toronto private school for female drama, dance, and physical education teachers, in 1918. He held out to them the prospect of distinguished careers in public service.[1]

Much of the optimism of the immediate postwar years quickly faded. Masculine authority, which had never disappeared, was quickly re-asserted, and Canadian women did not experience the dawning of a 'new day' in the major decisions and activities in their lives.[2] But many young women took up the challenge none the less. They stayed in school longer, enrolled in colleges and universities and entered the workforce in greater numbers than ever before. A few tried to crack the male monopolies in politics and the professions. They travelled on their own, climbed mountains, and embarked on all sorts of adventures rarely attempted previously by members of their gender. And they were quick to win new honours for themselves in the staunchly male bastion of sports.

Largely because of the dramatic Canadian victories in the first international competitions for women, some historians have dubbed the 1920s 'the Golden Age of Women's Sport.'[3] By whatever measure employed, it was a decade of remarkable advances. Prior to the war, women's participation in sports was well established, but it was highly uneven and received little coverage in the press. The best opportunities were in high schools and in smaller centres and towns. Tennis was the most popular community sport, as schools and churches provided courts free of charge. My great aunt Katherine Robbins regularly played at her church in Yarmouth, Nova Scotia, in the mid-1890s, before journeying to China to teach in an Anglican mission. In the big cities, opportunities were much more restricted. In Montreal, the increase in participation that occurred immediately prior to the war was limited to the upper class. In Toronto, Ada Mackenzie remembered, sports were out of reach unless your father was a member of a private club.[4] When university women ventured into the traditional 'manly sports' of track and field and team games such as ice hockey and baseball, they faced condemnation and ridicule. Virtually all competition was conducted on a sex-segregated basis. The University of Toronto refused to allow the women's athletic association to grant the prestigious letter award to its athletes, on the grounds that females 'could not display the same prowess as men.'[5]

But by the early 1920s, participation had grown to the point that girls and young women of all classes engaged in sports, not only in towns and villages but in staid Toronto and other big cities. Though their activity was frequently termed an 'invasion,'[6] suggesting both the boundary they had crossed and the resistance they would encounter, there were very few sports women did not attempt. They excelled at swimming, track and field, and the team sports of basketball, ice hockey, and softball. A few even competed against men. In 1928, inspired by US marathoner Gertrude Edele, who swam the English Channel in record time just two years earlier, women won eight of the first 11 prizes in the Halifax five-mile swim championship. There were 16 men in the race. The famed Edmonton Grads practised regularly against male basketball teams and won seven of nine games against them. The Preston Rivulettes played hockey against men's teams. Toronto lawyer James 'Hud' Stewart, who competed in the 1932 Olympics and founded the University of Toronto Sports Hall of Fame, says that Fanny 'Bobbie' Rosenfeld was the greatest hockey player, male or female, of the period. Others such as Marion

Hilliard and Hilda Ranscombe were reputed to be as good. Astute commentators noticed that female performances were improving faster than those of the males and began to speculate on the day when women could compete on a par with men in most sports.[7]

Women also undertook ambitious physical challenges away from the formal contests of sports. In 1926, four decades before completion of the Trans-Canada Highway, my aunt Dora Easto and her friend Frances 'Frankie' Routledge pedalled from Toronto to Vancouver on single-speed bicycles, sleeping in a small tent and cooking on the utensils they carried with them. They were frequently held up by the 'gumbo' on prairie roads after a heavy rain. Delays and all, it took them two months. Whenever I have asked her about their accomplishment, Dora's attitude is always 'no big deal.' Other women of her generation went on similar adventures, she tells me. Certainly women did not stop cycling after 'the cycling craze' of the 1890s ended, though the media eventually lost interest in the novelty of their participation. Women also covered great distances on foot (including skis and snowshoes) and horseback and by canoe, kayak, and sailboat, for challenge and recreation. They swam large bodies of water and climbed some of the highest mountains.

In western Canada, the explorations of Mary Schaffer and Mary Vaux helped open up what are now the national parks of Banff and Jasper to hiking and wilderness camping. It was only at the nationalist insistence of Winnipeg journalist Elizabeth Parker that the Alpine Club of Canada was formed in 1906 – the leading male mountaineers were prepared to become a Canadian branch of the American organization. By the First World War, half the members were women. Of 638 'first ascents' recorded in the national parks between 1885 and 1950, women participated in the climbing parties of 159 of them and were given credit for leading 59 of them. Englishwoman Katie Gardiner, who did not begin climbing in Canada until she was 42, made 33 of the individual ascents. In the 1920s, local Alberta and BC women – Agnes Truxler and her sister Mona Matheson, for example – began to work as licensed trail guides.

Canadian women were also active in the non-competitive gymnastics of such organizations as the Women's League of Health and Beauty.[8]

But it was women's athletic performances that won the loyalty of spectators and regular coverage in the mass media. In Toronto, the amateur women's softball leagues at Toronto's Sunnyside Stadium drew regular crowds of several thousand. In several years, as we see below, their total attendance[9] was greater than that enjoyed by professional men's baseball, played two miles away at Maple Leaf Stadium.

In basketball, the Edmonton Grads drew record crowds wherever they played. In 1926, when they competed against the Toronto Lakesides for the national championship in Toronto's Arena Gardens, the series drew 'the largest crowd ever to see a basketball game in the city.' In 1929 in Edmonton, audiences of 4,495 and 6,500 watched them play the Chicago Taylor-Trunks for the Underwood Trophy, prompting one columnist to write that 'it was reminiscent of the days when western hockey was hockey.' In another four-game series, they drew 28,000.[10]

A number of sportswomen actively contributed to the popularity of their sisters, obtaining and delivering live radio broadcasts of events and writing publicity releases and regular reports for the press. Mabel Ray began writing for Toronto newspapers in the mid-1920s. Alexandrine Gibb (*Toronto Star*), Phyllis Griffiths (*Toronto Telegram*), Bobbie Rosenfeld (*Globe*), and Myrtle Cook (*Montreal Star*) followed her to become daily columnists, ensuring regular and sympathetic coverage of happenings and debates. Gladys Gigg Ross, who used the byline 'ABC' in North Bay's *Capitol News*, Patricia Page (*Edmonton Journal*), Lillian 'Jimmie' Coo (*Winnipeg Free Press*), and Ruth Wilson (*Vancouver Sun*) reported on the major women's events. All these women had been successful athletes, and many of them served as coaches, administrators, and referees. It could be argued that the media image of the female athlete – young, confident, vigorous – was the most enduring model of active woman-hood during the entire period. Long after the rebellious 'flapper' had given over to the coquettish 'moppet,' the athlete continued to demonstrate that a woman could push back the conventional limits of her world.

A few sportswomen, whose efforts have received much less attention, also tried to influence the nature of sporting opportunities for their gender. They lobbied for facilities, fought for positions of leadership in the men's clubs, and started independent women's clubs and governing bodies. In the most ambitious of these endeavours, a small group of Torontonians – several of them active athletes – set out in 1925 to create a national amateur governing federation for women's sports on the model of the Amateur Athletic Union of Canada (AAU). At the time, there was but one national sports body controlled by women – the Canadian Ladies Golf Union, formed in 1913.[11] Within a few years, the organization formed in 1925 – the Women's Amateur Athletic Federation of Canada (WAAF) – brought a uniform system of administration and health inspection to seven sports, with branches in every region of the country.

The Rise of Women's Sport

The increase in female sporting participation that has been associated with the 1920s actually began well before the war. The first hockey teams sprang up in the last years of the nineteenth century. Soon afterwards, a major stimulus came from the public and private high schools, which began to hire women to teach games to girls. As teachers became more experienced, their pupils became more skilled, and some went on to organize teams and leagues for themselves.

The war was a period of rapid growth. Though no high-school yearbooks were published between 1915 and 1920, the first peacetime editions indicate that the number of girls' events and the quality of play rose steadily during the interval. The elementary schools were quick to follow. In 1913, the Ontario Department of Education gave schools permission to teach sports to girls as part of the compulsory physical education curriculum. Previously, they could conduct only formal calisthenics and marching drill. In Toronto, this led to creation of a city-wide girls' (elementary school) athletic association in 1917. The same pattern occurred elsewhere. In Edmonton, the basketball team that became the 'Grads' began playing together at John A. McDougall School during the winter of 1914–15. It continued throughout the war. Other teams started up about the same time; the first Alberta championship was held in 1915.[12]

It was the generation which learned sports in schools prior to and during the war that lined up for and sought to govern the new adult leagues and competitions in the community when peace came. Ann Clark, who became WAAF national president in 1936, got her start in Vancouver schools in 1916. Frances Watson, who played basketball throughout the 1920s and 1930s, before becoming a coach and then Ladies Ontario Basketball Association president, learned the game in her Perth, Ontario, elementary school in 1913. Most of these women were the first females in their families to play sports. Gladys Gigg Ross played, coached, refereed, and wrote about sport in North Bay before becoming president of the Provincial Ladies Softball Union (of Ontario). 'No one older than me in the Bay took part in sports,' she told me. Doris Butwell Craig, a high school track champion who starred in basketball and softball for the Lakeside Ladies Athletic Club of Toronto, remembered that her sister Laura, who was 14 years older, could not understand her love for sports and was frequently critical of it. 'She was just of another era,' Doris explained.[13]

The schools' encouragement of sports grew in response to a new appreciation of physical education for girls and a significant improvement in instructional resources. In the nineteenth century, most medical and educational authorities held that physical activity was harmful, claiming that it drained vital energy from a girl's reproductive organs, thereby rendering her unfit for the destined task of motherhood. But the success of American, British, and Canadian girls' private schools, which gave their charges a regular diet of games and gymnastics and turned them out healthier than when they were first admitted; the popular fashion of the energetic 'Gibson Girl'; and widespread participation by women in the 'cycling craze' of the 1890s undermined these restrictions. Growing desire for fitter populations encouraged reconsideration. Gradually, those who advocated cautious provision of physical activity won acceptance for their views. The subject would be taught on a sex-segregated basis, in a much less vigorous fashion than for boys, to prepare girls for 'healthy motherhood.' There was far from unanimity about the content, but it was encouraged. By the 1920s, YWCAs, employee fitness programs, and public health campaigns took up the same themes for young working women.[14]

In the course of these changes, organizers began developing special rules to reduce the stress they feared sports might place on females. In 1898, a conference of American physical educators modified the rules of basketball to cut down the amount of running and body contact in the female game. At this time, both men and women played nine players a side. Under women's rules, the court was divided into three, and only three players per team were allowed in each of the three zones. A player could not leave her zone. Publicized by the sporting goods manufacturer, the 'Spalding rules' were quickly taken up in Ontario.[15]

At the same time, a greater effort was made to prepare women to teach girls 'physical culture' and sports. Two developments were crucial. Normal school preparation was strengthened and special diploma programs were established, at the University of Toronto in 1900, at the Margaret Eaton School in Toronto in 1906, and at Montreal's McGill University in 1912. Graduates of these courses provided skilled instruction and female role models wherever they were employed. The establishment of the Strathcona Trust in 1909 to increase military readiness and social discipline gave national stimulus to the subject area itself. The syllabus, a reprint of the 1906 British manual for state elementary schools, stressed rote gymnastics and marching drill and encouraged rifle practice for boys. Though teachers' organizations and prominent physical educators were critical of its military cast, every province soon adopted it. The trust facilitated implementation with free instructional handbooks and prizes. Some scholars suggest that it was the most widely taught curriculum in Canadian educational history.[16]

While the trust emphasized male activities – teachers were encouraged to devote 50 per cent of the time to military drill and rifle practice – it did stipulate instruction for girls, validating their participation in organized physical activity. As in Ontario, it became the foundation on which sports could be introduced. Other practices contributed to this development. Encouragement of female attendance at highly publicized male sporting events facilitated their entry and introduced them to the rules. Suffrage agitation and other feminist campaigns provided arguments for inclusion of females in other social spheres, while wartime necessity demonstrated that it was possible. Some schools even formed female rifle corps. By the Armistice, there remained little room to argue that sports should be off limits for women. During the next two decades, female attendance in high school increased by one-third, from 27 to 37 percent of the age cohort, enabling many more to learn to play.[17]

School-trained athletes gradually found – and created – new competitive opportunities for themselves in the community. Municipal playgrounds were often a stepping stone, providing further competition in a supervised, publicly approved setting. In Toronto, inter-playground competition for girls was well under way before the end of the war.[18] In the 1920s, growth of university sports for women, during a decade when female enrolment more than doubled, added considerably to the cadre of high-school coaches. According to Helen Gurney, who attended school in Toronto, 'the influence of [university grads who had played intercollegiate sports] on high school sports for girls was most noticeable in this period.'[19] Churches, YMCAs and YWCAs, and some men's sporting clubs began to organize events for older girls and adult women. Major employers of women, such as Eaton's and the Western Clock Co. in Peterborough, opened elaborate recreational facilities, organized formal programs, and sponsored company teams for their workers. They helped draw women from different departments of these vast enterprises into a 'specially bonded' female community.[20] But just as often, women set up things on their own. Toronto's first softball league was organized by Mabel Ray, with six of her 'tomboy' friends, during the war. They had to chip in to buy their first ball and bat, and during their first season they played boy's teams, charging spectators one dollar to watch. It was only in their second season that they were able to recruit enough women to form three other teams and a league.[21]

More permissive dress codes allowed athletes to discard bulky dresses and bloomers for shorts and T-shirts, greatly increasing their mobility and their enjoyment of the games. This process is most dramatically illustrated in the team photographs that became a staple of school and university yearbooks and company publications at this time. Of course, adoption of more streamlined uniforms often provoked moral censure. The Edmonton Grads switched to shorts in 1923 but, fearing criticism at home, wore them only on the road that season. Hamilton sprinter Audrey Dearnley McLaughlin remembered 'how shocked the people in Fergus [Ontario] were to see our short shorts' a decade later. In 1937, the University of Toronto swim team was blasted in the city newspapers for proposing to wear a skirtless swim suit. The university forced it to accept a suit with an inside apron. But whenever they could, women opted for more comfortable and efficient sportswear. Many marathon swimmers competed in only axle grease (to protect them from the cold). A photo from the start of the 1935 CNE five-mile swim shows the swimmers diving into the lake with their suits rolled down to their waists, presumably to make it easier to remove them once they hit the water. The practice did not seem to provoke commentary, and the world did not fall apart.[22]

Newspapers, which were essential to the growth of men's sport, began to support women's sports, too. They reported creation of new clubs and leagues, details of competitions, and news of women's sporting activities in other countries, which were also on the upswing. Female sporting activities and accomplishments were also featured in the daily photo page of happenings around the globe that many big-city presses published. In 1922, 'Women as Athletes' became an entry in the *Reader's Guide to Periodical Literature*. Though patronizing by the standards of today, this coverage reinforced the new interest in Canada.

The most rapid growth during the 1920s seems to have occurred in basketball. According to Margaret Lord, the long-time leader from Hamilton, it was the sport of entry for most girls. Creation of teams, leagues, and governing bodies began in the last years of the war and continued throughout the next decade, in virtually every region of the country. In 1919, when the Ladies Ontario Basketball Association was formed, four teams entered the provincial playdowns – from Hamilton, London, Stratford, and Toronto. The following year, Guelph, Peterborough, St Catharines, St Thomas, and Woodstock fielded teams, while Stratford dropped out. In 1922, Stratford returned and Niagara Falls and St Mary's joined what had become a two-division league. Most cities had 'feeder' teams playing a notch below these 'representative' teams. In

Toronto, for example, there were as many as 25 teams in different leagues. In 1931, there were 21 teams in three Montreal leagues, and a six-team league in Edmonton. The game also flourished in Halifax, Saint John, Ottawa, Calgary, Vancouver, and Victoria.[23]

Basketball quickly became organized on a national basis. The first national championship was held in 1922, the same year as the first men's championship. The Edmonton Grads travelled to London, Ontario, to play the home-town Shamrocks. The Shamrocks won the first game, played under the five-a-side 'boys' rules,' 21–8. But the Grads won the second, under the six-player Spalding rules, 41–8, and took the series on overall points. The second game was refereed by the Grads' coach, Percy Page, because he was the only one who knew enough about 'girls' rules.' Henceforth, all Canadian championships were played under 'boys' rules.' The Grads' remarkable record – 404 victories in 424 games, several won by a single point; 17 consecutive Canadian titles; 17 North American championships; and four Women's Olympic championships – has obscured the extent of participation and the abilities of other teams. Though many stuck with a version of 'girls' rules,' thereby eliminating themselves from the quest for national honours, there were always good men's-rules teams to give the Grads a challenge. In 17 interwar championship series, the Grads faced nine clubs from five cities. In 1930, when other commitments forced them to decline the invitation to represent Canada in the Women's World Games in Prague, the University of British Columbia's team stepped in and won the title.[24]

Ice hockey was also a popular winter team sport for women. The first recorded game was played in Ottawa in 1891 by two unidentified teams, and newspapers reported women's games in other parts of Canada throughout the decade. When Mabel Ray and her friends organized Toronto's first women's team, the Wellingtons, in 1902, they knew of teams in Hamilton, Markham, and Waterloo. The best records are available for university and high-school teams, which began playing soon after 1900. When the Ontario Ladies Hockey Association (OLHA) was created in 1922, 20 senior clubs sent representatives to the inaugural meeting in Toronto while another ten sent in applications for membership. Fights, stitches, and male ridicule were not uncommon, so the game had a 'reputation' and many respectable girls and women avoided it. According to Ray, the Wellingtons 'were looked on as a crowd of "roughnecks." ' Ann Spalding, who became a WAAF vice-president, was told by her mother to stay away from 'the rough girls who played hockey.' In 1925, the University of Toronto's hockey team, reigning

OLHA champions, dropped out of the league because of 'certain unsatisfactory aspects of the competition.' The University re-entered the league in 1935–6 but withdrew again a year later because 'the players did not like the type of competition.'

But among factory workers, department store clerks, and secretaries, hockey had a wide following, especially in small towns. Teams from the Maritimes, Montreal, southern Ontario, and the prairies challenged for the Lady Bessborough Trophy, emblematic of the national championship, established in 1935. Like basketball, ice hockey produced its legendary team. During the 1930s, the Preston Rivulettes won all but two of their 350 games. One of the losses, to a Calgary team, occurred after a three-day train trip. The Rivulettes took the Ontario title ten times, the eastern Canadian championships six times, and the Lady Bessborough Trophy six times. The best teams could always draw a crowd. In 1935, when the Rivulettes defeated Winnipeg for the first national title, they drew the largest crowd ever to attend the Galt Arena – 6,000 for the two-game series. In 1939, the Toronto Ladies and the Montreal Royals played to 21,000 spectators in a five-game barnstorming tour of the northern United States.[25]

Despite the popularity of field hockey in the private schools and the *Girls' Own* sports literature available from Britain, except in British Columbia the grass game was rarely played in the universities or the community at large.[26] The same was true of lacrosse. Teachers may have learned it, as Joyce Plumptre Tyrrell did at the McGill School of Physical Education in the early 1920s, but they were only rarely called on to conduct it.[27]

Softball was the favourite summer sport. The rules were identical to the men's, except that the pitcher's toe-line was closer to the plate, the base paths were shorter, and a batter was automatically out on a dropped third strike. Helen Lenskyj has suggested that softball became readily acceptable for women because body contact was limited, but Helen Gurney contends that 'Lenskyj obviously never saw the women play at Sunnyside – they slid into bases in bare legs and shorts on pretty rough ground. I broke an arm this way when I was in Grade 12.' Other veterans say the same. Only the catcher and first basewoman could use mitts, and players frequently suffered broken fingers from line drives. Gladys Gigg Ross has crooked fingers on both hands from playing the game. Abrasions and bruises from sliding on rough ground were also common.[28]

None the less, after the war, teams and leagues sprang up in every part of Canada. Though there was little interregional competition – the best

TABLE 3.1
Attendance and gross revenues at Sunnyside and Maple Leaf stadiums, 1924–39

	Sunnyside Stadium		Maple Leaf Stadium	
	Attendance	Gross revenue	Attendance	Gross revenue
1924	114,000			
1925		$13,071.13		
1926		18,926.29	294,514	$193,224.07
1927	149,088	20,650.74	127,890	98,823.74
1928	115,587	20,102.45	215,724	166,975.23
1929	147,112	22,269.90	163,988	119,642.14
1930	135,000	21,493.90	122,385	86,746.48
1931	47,418	8,238.20	102,589	68,585.10
1932	80,112	14,379.22	49,960	31,604.62
1933	68,389	12,059.70	110,810	63,079.88
1934	49,934	8,427.74	211,670	140,824.83
1935	52,841	8,469.00		
1936	50,228	8,071.80		
1937	49,324	8,278.91	183,962	103,965.91
1938	71,558	11,736.10	165,037	82,711.18
1939	65,970	13,677.35	178,351	92,685.34

SOURCE: Toronto Harbour Commission Archives, RG 3/3, Sunnyside Stadium records

teams sought challenges across the border instead – the sport was highly organized and enjoyed a great following. Some of the best players were lured away to semi-professional and professional teams in the United States. Ten per cent of players in the All-American Girls Professional Baseball League, which Philip Wrigley operated in the U.S. midwest during the Second World War, came from softball leagues in Canada. Half of the Canadians, including the only one who was briefly allowed to manage a team, Mary 'Bonnie' Baker, came from Saskatchewan.[29]

The revenues enjoyed by the Toronto Sunnyside leagues were perhaps not representative, because they played next to a popular amusement park, but their pattern (see Table 3.1) is illustrative of growth in many centres. The Toronto Ladies Major Softball League, with teams representing the Toronto Ladies Athletic Club, Humber Bays, Karry's Recreation Club (a bowling and billiards hall), and the papermaker Hinde and Dauch, was formed in the early 1920s. In 1923, it obtained permission to play two evenings a week on a rudimentary diamond – it had no backscreen, bleachers, or changing rooms – just west of Sunnyside Beach, on lakefront land owned by the Toronto Harbour Commission (THC).

The first season was so successful that the league installed a screen, obtained three nights a week for 1924, and expanded itself to eight teams. Another league, the Sunnyside Ladies, got two nights per week. There was park bench seating for about 600, but the games proved so popular that most fans had to stand. Six thousand attended the opener, and crowds remained high all season. During one August game attended by the Brotherhood of Locomotive Engineers, rows of standing fans completely encircled the diamond and passersby were pushed onto the adjacent Lakeshore Boulevard. The parking lot across the street was filled to capacity. An internal THC memo after another game reported that spectators stood on a nearby bridge and the King Street elevation 100 metres away. The league's estimated attendance for the season was 152,000 for 36 games, including 16 exhibitions. The Sunnyside Ladies drew an estimated 65,000 to 32 games.[30]

During the first two seasons, the clubs simply passed the hat to meet expenses. In 1925, they persuaded the THC to erect bleachers and charge admission. In return, the commission required them to sign a detailed contract, specifying ticket prices and revenue sharing for each type of game played (league, intercity, doubleheaders, and playoffs) and each party's responsibility for expenses. In 1927, with paid attendance of 149,088, women's softball grossed $20,650.74, with the THC taking $7,462.76 and the leagues splitting $13,187.98. In 1928, attendance was 115,587, and the gross $20,102.45, with the commission receiving $7,462.76 and the leagues, $12,639.69. Women's softball was strictly amateur, so neither players nor coaches could be paid, but the gates enabled teams to buy flashy uniforms and good equipment and pay most travel expenses. These were gravy days. Phyllis Griffiths, the *Toronto Telegram*'s sports columnist, wrote that the leagues were 'run like pro hockey.' Alexandrine Gibb at the *Toronto Star* suggested that the expense bill included 'schooling, piano lessons, perfume, stockings, taxicabs – bills even for bringing mother to Toronto from the country.'[31]

Attendance fell off drastically in 1931 – in part because of the depression, in part because of a struggle for control of access to the stadium – but women's softball still drew more than any rival attraction, such as men's softball and lacrosse, both of which were tried. In 1932, crowds picked up again. Though not as lucrative as the other Sunnyside amusements, the facility brought the heavily indebted THC a bit of revenue most years of the Depression. Phyllis Griffiths and Ted Reeve thought the rent excessive. It was also discriminatory. The THC took 50 per cent of the Sunnyside gate at league games and 25 per cent of playoff receipts – an

effective overall rate of 40 percent – while it charged the men's professional baseball club only 8 per cent at Maple Leaf Stadium. The
revenue-hungry commission continually made improvements to the
stadium in order to make the women's game more attractive to customers. It installed lights in 1930, dressing rooms in 1933, and radio
equipment in 1938. In 1939, with attendance rising, it rebuilt the stadium
completely and began to push the leagues about improving the balance
between teams.[32] No other women's league has left such detailed records,
but most of them stayed popular throughout the Depression. In
Winnipeg, 'women's softball would get crowds of 2,000 under the lights
at Osborne Stadium for many years.'[33]

Canadian women competed in a number of individual sports as well.
Upper-class women continued to play golf and tennis and 'fancy skate'
in winter. In the late 1920s, encouraged by the society pages, they began
to take up badminton, which was soon being taught in many high
schools. In 1939, Dorothy McKenzie Walton became the world's amateur
champion.[34] As almost every community had an outdoor rink, a playing
field, and a swimming hole, and most cities had developed public
facilities, middle- and working-class girls and women began to compete
in speedskating, track and field, and swimming. Many of them excelled.
Lela Brooks Potter, the first female member of Toronto's Old Orchard
Skating Club, set six world speedskating records and was the first
allround world's champion in 1926. On the track, Myrtle Cook, Rosa
Grosse, and Fanny 'Bobbie' Rosenfeld each broke the world's record for
the 100-yard dash. Canadian teams distinguished themselves in the
Women's World Games, the Olympics, and the British Empire Games. In
the pool, Phyllis Dewar, daughter of a CPR conductor from Moose Jaw,
won four gold medals at the 1934 Empire Games in London.

    The Canadian National Exhibition (CNE) in Toronto was a major site
of competition in both sports, often paying the fares of the best Canadian
and American athletes to ensure their attendance. In 1927, after
Toronto's George Young won the professional swim across California's
Catalina Channel, the CNE held an open professional race along the
lakefront for prizes totalling $50,000. Thirty women, including five of the
featured favourites, lined up for the start, alongside 229 men. Only three
competitors, all men, finished the 15-mile course in the frigid, 8°C water.
In 1928, the CNE created a separate race for women, with $15,000 in
prizes (the men got $35,000). Such races, along with a full amateur
program, gave female swimmers pages of publicity for many years.[35]

Like their male counterparts, many of these athletes competed in more than one sport. Bobbie Rosenfeld was the most versatile, starring in basketball, softball, ice hockey, tennis, and several events in track and field, but many other women spread their talents almost as widely. Jane Bell and Ethel Smith, who teamed with Rosenfeld and Myrtle Cook to win the sprint relay in the 1928 Olympics in Amsterdam, were accomplished basketball and softball players. Nora Gordon, who led Toronto Lakesides to the eastern Canadian basketball championship and pitched for them in softball, was one of the best equestrians. Geraldine Mackie, a North American speedskating champion, spent her summers playing at Sunnyside. There were few sports women did not attempt. In addition to those already mentioned, women competed in billiards, bowling, canoeing, cycling, football, gymnastics, race walking, rodeo riding, rowing, skiing, soccer, speedboat racing, and wrestling.[36] To be sure, the pattern of participation was not everywhere the same. According to Gladys Gigg Ross, 'basketball never took off in the north.'

Unlike their male counterparts, who usually basked in uncritical public acclaim, the female athletes faced the constant pressure of social questioning. It came from parents, older siblings, teachers, and public figures, and it focused on the nature of their contacts with men, the propriety of dress, competition, and travel, and the health risks involved. It was expressed in the incredulous praise, heterosexual expectation, and sexist commentary of the sports pages, the formal inquiries of public bodies, and the outright condemnation of moral authorities such as Olympic President Pierre de Coubertin and the pope. These concerns were signalled by the expectation that female athletes be 'feminine' and that their participation in sport not undermine their adherence to the traditional sexual division of labour or loosen their morals.

No doubt, many would-be athletes were thereby prevented or discouraged from taking part. In 1928, Gertrude Phinney resigned from the Canadian Olympic team at the request of her father, who feared 'irreparable harm' should she participate. Those who did engage in sports remember the doubts and contradictory expectations of elders, parents, and friends. 'Girls weren't supposed to go into sports – my mother didn't like the idea at all,' Audrey Dearnley McLaughlin has recounted. Of course, there were often class, religious, and ethnic differences in expectations. Young, employed, working-class women seemed to suffer from – or accept – fewer restrictions, while middle-class women were burdened with class fears about loss of respectability.

Gladys Gigg Ross, who came from a working-class family in North Bay, remembers being encouraged by 'men who never would allow their daughters to do what I was doing.' It may have been acceptable for girls to play in school, where there was little public scrutiny, but many middle-class parents drew the line at community events and teams. Such was the case of an Anglican priest who prohibited his daughter, one of Gigg's school teammates, from participating in playground track and field and softball during the summer. In 1930, Gigg competed against Olympic high-jump champion Ethel Catherwood in an exhibition, wearing a loose-fitting tunic. The next day, a Sunday, the minister stopped by her house to give her his old university track shorts – 'I know you can do better with these, Gladys,' he said – but he still did not allow his own daughter to take part.[37]

'Girls' Sports Run by Girls'

Outside schools and universities, leadership, facilities, and financial support for the new women's sports came from several sources. In the first place, women such as Mabel Ray formed teams and leagues themselves, raising the necessary funds by ticket sales and special events such as the popular 'minstrel show' that Ray produced, in which she and other women donned costumes and blackface and sang and danced like vaudeville stars. Organizational support came as well from existing men's sports clubs, churches and youth organizations, large and small businesses, and sports entrepreneurs. In Hamilton, for example, the women's section of the Olympic Club was created when the men's executive invited Margaret Lord, then secretary of the city's basketball league, to bring female athletes into the club. In many centres, both Protestant and Catholic churches organized teams in women's basketball and softball, but the YWCAs were often reluctant to do so, particularly in Toronto and Halifax. The YMCA was much more likely to make its facilities available to women's events.[38]

Many companies started teams and leagues to give their female employees recreation. They were not indifferent to the added benefits of publicity. The first hockey team in Preston, Ontario, was started and managed by Dolph Hurlbut of Hurlbut Shoes. The Sunnyside softball leagues were started by M.H. McArthur of Hinde and Dauche and William J. D'Alesandro of the Seiberling Rubber Co. of Canada. Both companies became well known through their sponsored teams. The best players were usually recruited. Fanny 'Bobbie' Rosenfeld, a Jewish immigrant from Russia who grew up in Barrie, was induced to Toronto

in 1922 by the Patterson candy company, which promised her a job and
the opportunity to play for top teams. Rosenfeld played hockey,
basketball, and softball and competed in track and field. She scored all
six goals when the Pats won the two-game, total-goal, provincial hockey
final 6–0 in 1926 against the Ottawa Rowing Club. Patterson's major
competitor, the Planters Nut and Chocolate Co., soon copied it. The
most flamboyant sponsor of women's teams was Teddy Oke, a Toronto
hockey star and mining promoter. In the late 1920s, Oke tried to build
a power-house in his Parkdale Ladies Athletic Club. Until he went broke
in the stock market crash of 1929, he lured top athletes away from other
clubs with tuition fees, jobs, clothes, and unlimited expenses. The Ladies
Ontario Basketball Association fought back by establishing a strict anti-
transfer rule and, when that was ignored, suspending the Parkdale club.
Oke took them to court, but to no avail.[39]

Most sportswomen felt that they should administer their own activity as
much as possible. In 1921, the Toronto Ladies Club was formed as an
exclusively women's organization, with teams in several sports coached and
managed by women. It refused all offers of sponsorship, choosing instead
to raise funds through its own activities under the slogan 'Girls' sports run
by girls,' coined by founding member Alexandrine Gibb. A good basketball player, Gibb also helped found the Ladies Ontario Basketball Association (LOBA), which was infused with much the same spirit. An all-
female slate of officers was elected, with Lady Beck, Sir Adam Beck's wife,
chosen honorary president. She tossed up the first ball at the first game
between London and Hamilton. The association played with 'boys' rules.'[40]

Even where males continued to be involved as coaches, managers, and
referees, women sought to control the governing bodies. The Ontario
Ladies Hockey Association (OLHA), formed in 1922, began with a male
president, but the women soon relegated the men to the position of
'advisers.' In 1925, all the officers were female. The pattern was the same
in the Ontario Women's Softball Association (OWSA). The principal
organizer, Mabel Ray, invited national AAU secretary A.S. Lamb to chair
the founding meeting, in 1925, as an impartial 'outsider,' but she
ensured that the first slate of elected officers was female. The new
constitution denied males the right to 'take part' in meetings, though
they retained their right to vote. After a long debate, the 40 delegates at
the founding meeting decided to call themselves 'Women' instead of
'Ladies.' At their first annual banquet, President Edith Anderson of
Ottawa boasted that those in attendance were 'female players, female
officers, and female speakers.'[41]

The early organizers 'felt that the men weren't particularly interested in promoting girls' sport,' Margaret Lord explained. 'You didn't get too much encouragement in those days, there weren't a great many female doctors and lawyers – you were a teacher or a nurse and that's about it. The general opinion was that girls who got involved in sports were not feminine. They thought they could do something for other women and get a voice if they controlled the governing body. They wouldn't even have a voice if they stayed under the umbrella of the men.' Lord also suggested that the desire for friendships with other women led the organizers to keep men at bay: 'They were anxious to meet other women who were interested in the same thing. They didn't sit down and work out a philosophy. Friends were doing this and we could enjoy their company if we stayed in as organizers. It was also nice to travel back and forth to events and meetings. In my case, I loved sports and the people I met but I wasn't a very good athlete. I realized that if I was going to keep involved, I had to do it in another way.'[42]

Though it is masked by their demure, genteel expressions in official photographs, the early female organizers were able, resourceful, and determined. They worked extremely hard, arranging schedules, hiring officials, arbitrating disputes, and publicizing events in the little time they had after work and, in some cases, child-rearing and familial responsibilities. They met frequently, usually long into the night, cadging rides and billetting with each other to do so. Ann Spalding remembers travelling from Preston to Toronto on a transport truck, staying over with a friend on the softball executive. Irene Moore McInnis from Thorold, who was president of the Ontario WAAF branch, did the same, often with the same friend, Hilda Thomas, whose mother ran a boarding-house on Toronto's Hallam Avenue. Women such as Thomas were integral to the developing women's sports networks. They not only provided a meeting place and beds for out-of-towners but made careful records of addresses, birthdays, and friends and spouses and kept everyone in touch. For those active in the leadership during the Depression, her house was their 'home away from home.'

Most of the female sports leaders were active athletes. Ray played softball and hockey throughout the 1920s, while taking on increasing responsibility for administration of women's sports. The first LOBA executive was composed entirely of players. One of them, Toronto's Rosa Grosse, combined administration with vigorous competition for another ten years. In 1925, the president and secretary of the OLHA were basketball stars Janet Allen and Bobbie Rosenfeld, respectively. Many of the women's leaders were extremely young. Gladys Gigg Ross became secretary of the Northern Ontario Women's Softball Association at 14. Ann Spalding became president of the Provincial Women's Softball Union, formed out of the OWSA in 1931, at 17. Margaret Lord was 18 when she joined the LOBA executive and 28 when she managed her first Olympic Team.

Few of these leaders had gone beyond high school. Those who were employed usually held menial or secretarial positions, with few occupational resources to tap for sport. Gladys Gigg Ross worked for ten years in a laundry. At the time they were first elected to head their provincial associations, Alex Gibb and Janet Allen were secretaries and Ann Spalding a ticket seller in a cinema. In status, age, and experience, let alone gender, they were much the junior of the men who coached and managed women's teams and controlled the established organizations in men's sports. For much of this period, for example, the AAU's chief 'women's adviser' was John DeGruchy, a manufacturing executive with more than 50 years of experience in sports leadership, notably football. In 1931, when DeGruchy became adviser to the newly created Provincial Women's Softball Union, he was 70, and Spalding, the president, just 17. Yet she and her sisters usually held their own in their rulings and negotiations.

If Rosenfeld was the outstanding athlete of the period, the most influential leader proved to be Alexandrine Gibb. She was 'the real pioneer,' Margaret Lord said. The daughter of a woman well known for 'raising eyebrows' by rowing heavy boats across Toronto harbour – a distinctly 'male recreation' – Gibb went to Havergal College, the most athletically advanced of the Ontario private schools at the time. Sports were compulsory, and 'attractive-looking, vigorous and young' British- or American-trained gamesmistresses encouraged students to direct and manage their own teams. Ada Mackenzie was at Havergal about the same time, as was Mary Edgar, who started women's camping in Ontario.[43] After graduation in 1913, Gibb worked as a secretary for a mining broker. The *Star Weekly* described her as 'the kind of girl that a busy man likes to have for a secretary. She is quite capable of bullying a fellow into keeping his appointments.' While Mabel Ray was the driving force behind creation of many women's sports organizations, Gibb gave them ideas and inspiration and quickly became their most articulate spokesperson. She was tough, too, and could always be counted on to support other sportswomen in a fight. It was Gibb, for example, who galvanized the LOBA's resistance to Teddy Oke when the headstrong businessman tried to sign all the best players for his Parkdale squad. She would demonstrate the same resolve throughout her career. In 1934, she was appointed to the Ontario Athletic Commission (OAC) by Liberal Premier Mitchell Hepburn, whom she much admired, and became the only woman ever to hold that office. But when Hepburn tried to dictate to the OAC, she (and fellow Commissioner P.J. Mulqueen) promptly resigned.[44]

Though Ray seems to have been the first to submit articles to the press, Gibb became the most successful at that endeavour. In 1928, she parlayed her experience as a volunteer sports administrator into the position of women's daily sports columnist for the *Toronto Star*, the first post of its kind in Canada, setting the example that many others would follow. Her column was entitled 'No Man's Land of Sports.' Excerpts appeared regularly in newspapers across Canada. Whether in print or behind the scenes, Gibb worked assiduously to advance the chances of female athletes. Irene McInnis remembers her good advice about how to get athletes invitations to American meets. In 1954, ten years after she switched from sports to the features beat, Gibb was instrumental in encouraging Marilyn Bell to take on the American star Florence Chadwick in the Lake Ontario swim.[45]

While the achievement of suffrage throughout the English-speaking world improved the climate for assertive leadership, only a few of the female sports leaders were vocally supportive of women's rights outside sports. In the highly patriarchal world of sports, such views attracted the dangerous epithet 'man-hater.' Margaret Lord used this term, in parentheses, to characterize those who insisted on forming their own clubs, such as her close friend Connie Hennessy, one of the founders of Toronto Ladies, who wanted men removed from all aspects of women's sports. While she admired Hennessy's proud spirit, Lord felt that complete independence was impractical and voicing the desire for it singled women out for ridicule and opposition among the male sports establishment. Happily, circumstances had enabled her to spend most of her sporting career within the supportive atmosphere of the Hamilton Olympic Club, formed in 1926.

Many others have said the same. Men controlled the existing institutions, and they had a wealth of experience and expertise on which sportswomen could draw. As Ann Clark, who rarely deferred to anyone, has said, 'I learned a great deal from the men. The trick was developing an effective working relationship.' Even Gibb, who eventually pursued the non-traditional career of journalism and fiercely defended sportswomen's interests, eschewed causes that could be associated with 'feminism.' Their distance from feminism has been construed as an 'apologetic' to compensate for the emotional conflict involved in directing (as well as playing in) such traditionally masculinizing activity. Ross is perhaps the defining case. 'I would never go to a female doctor, or vote for a female politician – I don't think that's what women should be doing,' she has said, but she spent much of her adult life campaigning for and leading women's sports organizations.[46]

Creating a National Federation

The impetus for the Women's Amateur Athletic Federation (WAAF) in Canada was a response to international developments in track and field. In their buoyant, post-suffrage enthusiasm for new frontiers, women in many countries were competing in record numbers and achieving record times. In 1921, teams from Britain, France, Italy, Norway, and Switzerland took part in an 11-event competition at Monte Carlo. National bodies for women's track and field were established in Britain, Europe, Japan, and the United States. But they still had no chance to compete in the most prestigious form of international competition – the Olympics. A few women had competed in the International Olympic Committee's (IOC) Games, initially in tennis and golf, and then in archery, gymnastics, skating, and swimming, but these events were initiated by Games organizers and sympathetic international federations such as the Fédération internationale de natation amateur (swimming) on an ad hoc basis. They did not enjoy official status. If IOC founder and president Pierre de Coubertin and some of his colleagues had had their way, they would never have been held. The combined opposition of the IOC and the powerful International Amateur Athletic Federation (IAAF), which governed men's track and field, denied women even this provisional place in the Games.

In response, French feminist Alice Milliat decided to organize an Olympic Games for women. A translator by profession, a rower and sports administrator by avocation, Milliat established the Fédération sportive féminine internationale (FSFI) in 1921 at a conference in Paris attended by representatives from Britain, Czechoslovakia, France, Italy, Spain, and the United States. The following year, she and the FSFI organized the Women's Olympic Games, an international track and field meet in Paris. Teams from five countries, including the United States, competed before 20,000 spectators. In a day of dazzling performances, 18 world records were broken. It was too much for the IAAF to ignore. It asked member federations to take over women's activity in the sport.[47]

Prior to this point, Canada's AAU had shown no interest in women's activity, refusing to accept female registrations. Its Olympic committee had never contemplated entering women in the events open to them either. But the IAAF's directive required some action. The AAU had two models to choose from: in Britain, the Amateur Athletic Association (AAA) agreed to respect the jurisdiction of a female-controlled governing body established that year – the Women's Amateur Athletic Association (WAAA) – and to develop a cooperative agreement, while in the United States, the AAU there seized direct control. As Canada had no body for women's track and field, the AAU here followed the American example and claimed jurisdiction. It applied for and obtained Canadian membership in the FSFI.[48]

Despite the new responsibility, the Union moved reluctantly, like a runner who moves to the front of the pack to slow down the pace. In his 1923 report, Norton Crow questioned the 'wisdom and value [of] the growing tendency of women and girls to take part in public track and field.' Though the fledgling Canadian Amateur Basketball Association, which had both male and female members, asked the 'Parliament' to develop a standard policy on women's sport, delegates gave the issue scant attention, sloughing the task off on the incoming president, William Findlay. He took little action. Fifteen-year-old Cecile Eustace Smith of Toronto, a singles figure skater, was included on the Canadian team that competed in the international winter sports festival in Chamonix, France, which subsequently was declared the First Olympic Winter Games. In non-winter sports, the AAU authorized, instead of the full day of track and field events held at the American and British championships, a single national event for Canadian women – a 100-yard championship held in Toronto and sponsored by the CNE. (Rosa Grosse edged Bobbie Rosenfeld.) In his 1924 report, Crow allowed that 'it is no use shutting our eyes to the fact that women's competition, particularly in Track and Field sports, is vastly on the increase and will have to be taken into account.' But no policy was developed. The 1924 'parliament' merely established a committee.[49]

One can only imagine how much longer the AAUers would have dawdled. A.S. Lamb took over the influential position of secretary when Crow retired in 1924. While a supporter of physical activity for women, he opposed highly competitive or physically demanding events. Under his influence, McGill's athletic program 'emphasized skiing and social tennis. We didn't care as much about competition as U of T or Queen's. There was no question but that we would play girls' rules,' Joyce Plumptre

Tyrrell, who played at both Toronto and McGill in the early 1920s, has said. In the McGill School of Physical Education, 'no thought was given to national or international competitive athletics. "Dad" Lamb believed that ladies just didn't compete aggressively.'[50]

Lamb later wrote: 'The nature and characteristics of boys and girls differ very widely ... The tendency for girls to ape the activities of boys is regrettable. In most cases, it is physiologically and psychologically unsound and may be definitely harmful. Nobody would wish to see a return of mid-Victorian fainting frailty and the traditional headaches of that era. There are numerous activities suitable for girls and women without the necessity of using those types of competition which call for such intensive concentration as many which are now being promoted.'[51] The women's committee chair, John DeGruchy, shared these reservations. At the founding meeting of the Ontario Ladies Hockey Association (OLHA), he had 'favored the cutting out of anything which would make the game too strenuous.'[52] Such a restrictive impulse was not likely to initiate additional opportunities.

But in 1925, the AAU received another push from Europe. The WAAA invited it to send ten Canadians, expenses paid, to an international track and field meet at Stamford Bridge in London on 1 August of that year. Findlay and Lamb sat on the invitation for several weeks, then in a panic asked Alexandrine Gibb to conduct selection trials and manage the team. Gibb was already well known as a vocal proponent of women's sport and a 'clever organizer.' It was a rush job – she was appointed 3 July, with the team needing to sail from Montreal no later than 17 July – so there was no opportunity for westerners to make it to the selection trials in Toronto, which fact the nationalist Gibb publicly regretted. But with the help of a quickly assembled committee of sportswomen, she pulled it off. Britain, with eight world record holders, won the three-team competition, but the Canadians 'were by no means disgraced,' placing in virtually every event. Even in the absence of the speedy Grosse and the all-rounder Rosenfeld, who could not make the trip, and the athletes from western Canada, the team finished just behind internationally experienced Czechoslovakia. In the eyes of the *London Sketch*, 'those who did duty for the Dominion appeared to be very fine specimens of athletic woman-hood.' The team captain, Molly Trimmel, was described as 'a sweetly beautiful girl with an air of serious gravity [who] epitomize[d] the steadfast purpose of the strong young nation she and her sisters had been called upon to represent.'[53]

At the AAU's insistence, the team was accompanied by the president's sister-in-law, Mrs Gordon Findlay, a recent graduate of the McGill School of Physical Education, as 'chaperon.' It set a precedent that was followed for another 50 years. 'I always resented being called a "chaperon," ' Margaret Lord, who served in that position on many international teams, said years later. 'It gave the impression that all we did was take the women to teas and socials and see that they got home in one piece. In actual practice, we had little time for that. We organized training and therapy, saw that they got to their competitions, and made many other arrangements. We should have been called "managers" but the times wouldn't allow it.'

The trip inspired Gibb to start a national governing federation. There is some evidence that she had long harboured such an ambition, but if not, the Stamford Bridge experience would have suggested it. Compared to the indifferent treatment that they suffered from the AAU, the Canadian women were 'entertained lavishly' in England and given the assistance of two outstanding coaches, Frederick Webster and Sam Mussabini. Webster was a world authority on the field events, Mussabini the personal coach of Olympic sprint champion Harold Abrahams. Both were strong supporters of women's track and field.[54] They would have reassured the Canadians that there was nothing to fear from vigorous training and competition. Their own accomplishments, the WAAA's competent organization, the stories of other FSFI competitions they heard from competitors, and the full coverage they received in the press must have convinced them that they had everything to gain by creating their own organization.

Almost immediately on her return, Gibb proposed 'a Women's Amateur Athletic Union in affiliation with [the AAU].' At the same time, she announced creation of the Canadian Ladies Athletic Club (CLAC), to provide opportunities in baseball, ice hockey, softball, and track and field for women across Canada. She became the first president. With her on the executive were Mabel Ray and Janet Allen, both of whom had been on the selection committee for the Stamford Bridge team, and Grace Conacher and Tony Conacher (cousins of Lionel), who had competed for it.[55] The name 'Canadian Ladies' was not just Toronto pretension. Though members kept their cards to themselves, the new organization provided the structure for a national governing body in the eventuality that the AAU opposed it.

A few weeks later, at its annual general meeting, Gibb presented the AAU with a fait accompli – a provisional organization for her proposed union, composed primarily of her associates from Canadian Ladies. There could be little doubt about her resolve. The men quickly acquiesced, with more than a touch of admiration. 'Women's athletics should be in the hands of a women's organization and controlled by them,' President Findlay told his surprised fellow delegates. Not wishing to cut themselves off from the amateur centre, Gibb and her sisters responded with gracious praise of the AAU leaders and asked them to serve the new organization as advisers.[56]

The infant union's first step was to organize provincial branches. It was much sounder to build from the bottom up, Gibb believed, so it gave itself a year to stimulate setting up of provincial organizations. In November, she and her colleagues – Janet Allen (who served as provisional president) and Mabel Ray from Canadian Ladies, Marie Parkes from the University of Toronto (provisional secretary, against whom Gibb had played in the Toronto Private School League – Parkes went to Branksome), and Ethel Cartwright from McGill – sent out a draft constitution to known sports groups in other parts of Canada. Branches were soon established in Ontario, Quebec, and the Maritimes.

The founding meeting was held in Montreal on 7 December 1926 at the Mount Royal Hotel. Because they had taken most of the initial decisions themselves, the Torontonians were pressed to cede the first official presidency to a Montrealer. She was Frances Secord, who had graduated from McGill that year. Marion Belding, a Saint John journalist, was elected vice-president, and Parkes and Allen, secretary and treasurer, respectively. But the meeting gave the Torontonians lots to be proud of. It gave their new offspring – christened the Women's Amateur Athletic Federation of Canada (WAAF) – a warm welcome and credited their club, the CLAC, with a world's record for its 4 x 110 yard relay the previous summer.[57] The CLAC fielded successful Toronto teams for many years. When sprinter and 'director of track and field' Myrtle Cook moved to Montreal in 1927, she started a branch there.

The Federation grew rapidly. In each of the next four years, another branch was added from the western provinces. British Columbia was the first, in 1927. Its president was softball executive Victoria Sallis, a sales clerk at Spencer's department store in Vancouver. She was immediately elected national vice-president, though it was several years before the province could afford to send someone in person to national meetings. In 1928, Ethel Cartwright established a branch in Saskatchewan. She had moved to the provincial university in Saskatoon after being arbitrarily fired from McGill by A.S. Lamb during a period of illness, despite years of legendary service on behalf of students.[58] The following year,

B.W. Bellamy and R.J. Foster of the Alberta AAU started an Alberta branch and assigned the task of attending meetings to their wives. Mrs Foster proved a master of parliamentary procedure and was elected WAAF president in 1932. By 1930, only Manitoba remained unorganized, so Gibb, who was then president, and Ontario president Thelma McKelvey stopped off in Winnipeg en route to the annual meeting in Edmonton and persuaded the leading sportswomen there to join. The principal Manitoba organizer was Edith Mackenzie, a 23-year-old stenographer who excelled in basketball, figure skating, golf, and softball.[59]

In 1927, paid membership was 3,190. In the early years of the Depression, it fell to 2,700 (in 1933), but it climbed back to 3300 in 1935, about one-fifth of the AAU registration. Most members came from southern Ontario and English-speaking Montreal. Like the AAU, the WAAF included very few francophones and virtually no members of First Nations or women of colour. Memberships and 'sanction' fees (for the right to hold an officially sanctioned competition) were the sole source of revenue, so funds were always scarce. Nevertheless, the leadership tried to support the branches with as much national activity as possible. Between 1926 and 1939, the annual general meetings and championships were held in nine cities from coast to coast.[60]

The Women's Federation was created when the AAU was at the height of its power. Quite understandably, it modelled itself after the existing union. It directly governed track and field and developed a uniform code of eligibility for all sports. By the mid-1930s, national and provincial bodies in basketball, hockey, and softball recognized its authority and required athletes to have WAAF cards. A few fencing, skiing, and swimming clubs also affiliated.

As an affiliated body of the AAU, the WAAFers had to model their code on the main precepts of the men's, though they won the right to amend criteria to suit their own conditions. The one contentious issue was the status of 'physical directors.' A majority held to the AAU's prohibition, which meant that physical educators and even students in McGill's School of Physical Education, the University of Toronto's diploma program in physical education, and the Margaret Eaton School in Toronto were ineligible to compete. In 1939, Olympic medallist Betty Taylor was told that she was ineligible for the 1940 Games scheduled for Helsinki because she had a job teaching physical education. But the less ideologically inclined pointed out that women in this position could greatly contribute to the development of women's programs by adding their expertise. As a compromise, 'physical directors' were given the right to apply for reinstatement after two years of retirement from professional practice, instead of after five years, as was the case with the AAU.[61]

Debates within Feminism

The Federation kept the fear-mongers and 'moral physiologists' at bay by requiring all athletes to obtain an annual medical certificate of good health. 'It is the desire of the Federation that only physically fit women compete,' Ethel Cartwright told reporters after the inaugural meeting in Montreal. The *Globe*'s sports editor, Fred Wilson, heartily approved.[62] 'We concentrated on the fitness of our members,' Ann Clark has emphasized. 'It ensured that no one who had a heart problem or some other ailment would be seriously hurt through sport. Remember, this was long before medicare. In most cases, it didn't cost anything – girls would simply go to their family doctor, or sometimes one doctor would check a whole team, one by one, the night before the first practice. If girls didn't have their own doctors, we got them one free of charge. But we strictly enforced the rule – no one played without the certificate.'

Clark made the same point over and over again during her terms as BC and national WAAF presidents, and she was as good as her word. In 1935, she even marched onto a basketball court to stop a game involving a team without amateur cards and medical certificates. When she led the Canadian women's team to the 1938 British Empire Games in Sydney, Australia, Clark boasted about this requirement in every interview.[63] There was no corresponding AAU requirement for the men. 'We wouldn't have given [the concern about health] a moment's thought,' Jim Worrall, who competed throughout the 1930s, has remembered.[64]

Even when players said that they could not afford the 25-cent amateur card, the Federation tried to have them medically checked. In 1931, a newly formed 13-team Toronto church league sought to join the WAAF-affiliated Ladies Ontario Basketball Association, so that its best teams could enter the city playoffs, but pleaded poverty when asked to obtain amateur cards. The Ontario WAAFers struck a deal. On the promise that no one would be permitted to play without first passing a medical examination, the league was permitted to register only the two teams that made it through to the playoffs. 'This is a splendid arrangement and gives both the girls and the league the necessary protection regarding the health of the girls,' Alexandrine Gibb told her readers in the *Star*.[65] Other members of the WAAF mention the rule with great pride. 'We all thought it terrific,' Ann Spalding has said. 'Softball officials didn't want to be responsible for anyone who shouldn't have been playing.' The requirement enjoyed widespread support. In 1935, when the WAAF reduced the registration fee to ten cents for women who played only one sport, columnist Phyllis Griffiths expressed the hope that it would encourage more women to get a pre-season checkup.[66]

In making a public issue of participants' health, the Federation followed a well-established tradition among women's organizations. During the struggle for women's education in the previous century, 'vitalist' physiologists threatened women with every sort of illness, even death, if they abandoned their god-given responsibilities for child-bearing and mothering and dared pursue academic study. In response, the first British and American female educators took every precaution to ensure that their pupils' health would not fail. They designed facilities with an eye to comfort, sanitation, and ventilation. They taught health and hygiene, hired doctors and dietitians, encouraged dress reform, and strengthened their students' fitness with a comprehensive program of gymnastics, dance, and sports. Despite the narrowly medicalized view of health that this approach encouraged, it was the best physical education of its time.[67]

Many of these practices were introduced to Canada through the private schools and universities. At the University of Toronto, all first-year students were required to submit to a physical. In addition, any woman who wanted to take part in intramural or intercollegiate sports needed a pre-competition checkup from Dr Edith Gordon, medical director for women. If they wanted to play two or more sports, they had to get her written approval. By comparison male students were also physically examined on entrance to university but did not require a subsequent examination if they took up competition. An ardent advocate of sports for 'the future mothers of Canada,' Gordon was part of the group that Gibb recruited to create the Women's Federation. Whenever doubts were raised about the wisdom of women's athletics, such as after the sudden death of a 17-year-old who had played softball, she assured the public that sports were necessary for 'perfect development along physical and mental lines.' Gordon also refused to act as a judge in beauty contests, arguing that every healthy women is an 'ideal.'[68]

But assuming responsibility for their members' health revealed the ideological divides in the coalition that Gibb and her sisters had pieced together. Then as now, different women held varying views about what constituted women's interests and what was necessary to advance them. While they all agreed that women should control their own physical activity, they fiercely debated the extent to which athletic women should be challenged/protected, what games they should play, or even whether they should be competitive at all. On the issue of health, for example, one group wanted the WAAF to take a much more interventionist approach and mandate weekly medical checkups. Their spokeswoman was Ethel Cartwright. At the founding meeting, Cartwright had called on the WAAF 'to see that women athletes do not try to run before they can walk, to see that they enter the right kind of sports and are not overworked. There has been much adverse criticism of the more violent sports for women.'[69]

Cartwright and her former colleagues at McGill represented the most conservative current of the women's sports movement in the interwar period. Helen Lenskyj has likened them to the 'maternal feminism' of many other women's organizations of the day: they sought better opportunities for women, but in a way that did not contest restrictive patriarchal views on female abilities.[70] Accepting the prevailing medical view that females were not physiologically and tempermentally as strong as males, they argued that sports for women had to be carefully restricted and closely supervised. 'At McGill, moderate physical exercise without jumps or strains was permissible, but vigorous activity was discouraged. Competition was prohibited during menstruation altogether,' Joyce Plumptre Tyrrell, who studied and worked with Cartwright, told me. 'I first learned from "Carty" that being female meant that I was different and somewhat inferior.' Jesse Herriott, Cartwright's successor at McGill, took similar positions at WAAF meetings. The Cartwright-McGill faction was usually outvoted, but only after lengthy debate.[71]

Another thorny issue was 'girls' rules' – the effort by some leaders to create a distinct, and what they hoped would be a more appropriate, experience for sportswomen. In no sport was the path of separate development more controversial than in basketball. At the time of the Federation's founding, women used several 'codes' of basketball – principally, the six-player, 'Spalding rules,' which limited all players to their designated section of the court, and the five-player, men's rules. In the Maritimes and central Canada, most high schools played the 'Spalding rules,' while community teams were split between 'Spalding' and men's rules. With the remarkable success of the Grads, and the relative scarcity of female physical education teachers, most teams in the west played men's rules. One of the first tasks of the federation was the search for agreement on a uniform code.[72] That proved impossible.

Led by McGill, the Quebec delegation insisted that some version of 'girls' rules' be imposed across the country. The distinct women's game was more interesting, with less jarring physical contact, than the men's, they said, and it would give women who played it an advantage in competition for teaching jobs. But they made little headway with delegates from other regions. Though Ethel Cartwright delivered Saskatchewan, they were opposed by the Maritimes, Ontario, Alberta, and British Columbia. In 1928, during the annual elections, the McGill group mounted a slate in an attempt to pack the executive. But Alexandrine Gibb, who had played men's rules herself, out-organized them, defeating the slate and getting herself elected president. She then obtained permission to negotiate articles of alliance with the Canadian Amateur Basketball Association, which conducted the national championship for women under men's rules, and she rubbed it in the next day in her column in the *Star*. 'The six or seven sets of so called "girls' rules" adherents had better get together and decide on one set for themselves before trying to coerce those who have been satisfied with the men's rules for a number of years,' she thundered. (In 1929, they did, agreeing on the 'intercollegiate rules' developed in 1921 by Marie Parkes – similar to the 'Spalding rules,' but allowing each player the range of two-thirds of the court.) But Gibb was no more successful in imposing a single set of rules than her opponents. With neither side prepared to budge, the matter was eventually left to provincial discretion. A national survey in 1941 indicated that the numbers playing the two sets of rules were about even.[73]

The 'girls' rules' movement also sought to reduce the intensity of women's competition. Against the pursuit of records and highly publicized challenges between representative teams, adherents encouraged a more instructional and recreational approach, maximizing participation and development of personal friendship. To this end, they advocated 'play days' in which every student would be involved – rather than inter-scholastic competition, with only a few top players on a single school team – under the slogan, 'A girl for every team; a team for every girl.'[74] The most fervent supporters were middle-class US physical educators, who had considerable influence in Canada. Jesse Herriott of the McGill School of Physical Education was an American who had studied at Columbia. Half of the faculty members of the Margaret Eaton School had had US graduate training. Helen Bryans, director of physical education at the Ontario College of Education in Toronto, took summer courses at Columbia University in New York. According to Helen Gurney, Bryans 'was a very strong advocate of the American philosophy. Her influence was unbelievably powerful – she could influence one's chances for a position all across Ontario.' During the 1930s, Herriott, Bryans, and others persuaded a number of Canadian school boards, including Toronto's, to drop interscholastic competition for girls in favour of 'play days.'

The 'girls' rules' movement was a curious blend of protective and progressive impulses, held together by a desire for female advancement within women's-only institutions. Conservative 'maternal feminists' supported it because they believed that young females were ill prepared for the stress of travel, unfamiliar surroundings, and intense competition. Recognizing that many girls and women took great pleasure in these stresses, they feared that the 'male model' of sports might have a 'masculinizing' influence on participants. Others calculated that if women's sports were significantly different, males would be much less interested in taking them over. Most of the contemporary physical education texts took this approach. Florence Somers adhered to this line in her widely used *Principles of Women's Athletics* (1930). She became director of the Margaret Eaton School in 1933. 'Girls' rules' also resonated with the middle-class tradition of female decorum, leisure, and gentility. None of the factory workers, telephone operators, and secretaries who sweated long hours at work or danced into the night at parties had any compunction about physical intensity.

But other, more assertive readings of 'girls' sports' can be taken. During the 1920s, the 'male model' of sports was changing, too, often in undesirable ways. With legalization of boxing across North America, and the increased popularity of collision sports such as hockey and football, came new legitimation for sports violence and physically combative modes of masculinity. At the same time, school and university sports for boys and young men were becoming fiercely competitive, often to the detriment of athletes' health and education. The female physical educators who led the 'girls' rules' movement were not alone in their criticism of the 'male model.' In 1929, the prestigious Carnegie Foundation for the Advancement of Teaching's special commission on intercollegiate sport in the United States and Canada condemned many of the same high-pressure practices that led women to experiment with 'girls' rules.' Nor were the female physical educators alone in attempting new ways of developing youth through sports. In the state of New York, Frederick Rand Rogers introduced the 'player control' system for all high schools in an effort to increase student athletes' opportunity to make – and learn from – their own decisions. Henceforth, all adult teachers were relegated to the stands. Rogers worked closely with the advocates of 'girls' rules' and 'play days.'[75] In this light, 'girls' rules' represented less an attempt to reduce the challenge of women's sports than a feminist experiment to create something more genuinely educational and developmental in a period of dynamic change.

Initiation of 'play days' was also a stroke for equity. Most schools had little money for women's sport and few qualified teachers. These conditions only worsened during the Depression. Often, a single physical education teacher was responsible for all the female students in a school. It was very difficult for her to organize both an instructional program and highly competitive, interscholastic teams. If she stayed in the school conducting 'play days,' she could give more young women a beneficial athletic experience. To the extent that 'girls' rules' and 'play days' expressed the search for less dehumanizing, more inclusive alternatives, they had a progressive impulse.

The career of Helen Bryans illustrates the difficulty of characterizing 'girls' rules' as simply defensive and protective. Bryans probably achieved greater influence in Canadian physical education during the 1930s than anyone else, male or female. Many of the innovations that she introduced to the women's curriculum at the Ontario College of Education were subsequently adopted for preparation of male teachers, and she virtually dictated hiring of female teachers across the country. Bryans campaigned all her life against the 'evils of [interscholastic] sports,' even when games such as basketball were played under the six-a-side, women's rules. But she never would have accepted the proposition that women were inferior, should be challenged less, or should be steered by the expectation that their lives would be limited to child-rearing and household management. She never stinted in the demands she placed on the teachers she trained. They were all expected to be superbly fit.

Bryans herself was active all her life in physically challenging pursuits and seemed to love 'one-upping' the men. Once, during a guided tour of the University of Toronto's Hart House, from which women were usually barred, the group wandered off while Bryans and a friend were admiring the deserted swimming pool, where men traditionally swam naked. Bryans quickly locked the door, stripped off her clothes, swam two lengths in patriarchy's 'inner sanctum,' climbed out and cheered, to the complete amazement of her friend. She did believe that interscholastic sports made little sense. Though she wanted separate opportunities for girls and women, they were to be nothing less than 'equal.' As Martha Verbrugge has suggested about some of the American advocates of 'girls' rules,' Bryans could more accurately be described as a 'radical feminist' than a 'maternal feminist.'[76]

Today, sports leaders and physical educators have come to realize that no single policy can address the physical activity needs of all girls and women. While some females want to pursue highly competitive sports as ambitiously as their male counterparts – and every effort should be made to ensure that they receive an equitable share of the available resources and honours – those who most value the nurturing of friendship and social networks and the kinaesthetic pleasures of movement are repelled by the fiercely competitive and instrumental expectations of the 'male model'. While some females want to compete with males, other seek different, female-only opportunities. The popularity of dance, aerobics, and many other non-competitive pastimes makes it clear that girls and women are not uninterested in physical activity.[77] This vantage point suggests a nuanced reassessment of 'girls rules.' The leading feminist sports organization today calls itself the Canadian Association for the Advancement of Women *and Sport and Physical Activity* (my emphasis) to signal its belief that the interests of women require, along with improved opportunities, that the very nature of sports be changed.

Ironically, the advocates of 'girls' rules' helped one of the fiercest critics of 'play days' start a career in sports. In 1927, when only McGill, Queen's, and University of Toronto women competed in intercollegiate basketball, McGill vowed to withdraw from the competition unless the other institutions hired a female coach. 'It was felt more likely that a woman would know women's rules, or that a young athlete would approach a female coach during her period,' Tyrrell has explained. The threat prompted Toronto to offer the job to alumna and former player Phyllis Griffiths, who was working as a reporter for the *Toronto Telegram.* The coaching experience encouraged her to try her hand at sports writing, and in 1929 she started a daily column, 'The Girl and the Game,' in the *Telegram.* While a partisan of the women's game of basketball, Griffiths regularly railed against 'play days.' So did columnists Alex Gibb and Bobbie Rosenfeld. The idea of 'play days' never got very far at the WAAF, either. A majority of the national leaders wanted competition, albeit without the obsessions of the male model, and opposed any attempt to dilute it.

International Competition

After their successful expedition to the Stamford Bridge international meet in London in 1925, Gibb and her colleagues were eager to send more teams abroad, but it would be several years till they did so. Even after they had established the Federation, the AAU retained the Canadian membership in the Fédération sportive féminine internationale (FSFI) cutting them off from international developments. It was a heady period for the FSFI. In 1926, it staged its second Women's Olympics in Gothenburg, Sweden. Ten nations entered, including distant Japan. With a spectacular opening march past and ceremony – 3,000 pigeons were released amid a display of pageantry – the full patronage of the Swedish royal family, and several world's records, the Women's Games evoked comparisons with the International Olympic Committee's (IOC's) Stockholm Olympics of 1912. Such was the women's growing prestige that the FSFI's shrewd president, Alice Milliat, was able to use the success of the Games as a bargaining card. She agreed to change the name of her gathering from 'Women's Olympics' – which greatly upset the IOC and the International Amateur Athletic Federation (IAAF) – to 'Women's World Games,' in exchange for at least ten events in the IOC's Games. Milliat kept her part of the bargain, but the IAAF welshed on its, placing only five events on the program for the 1928 Olympics in Amsterdam. A majority within the FSFI reluctantly accepted the watered-down deal, ensuring women's competition in Amsterdam, but they also vowed to continue their own Games.

However, the powerful Women's Amateur Athletic Association (WAAA), which had easily won the team championship at Stockholm in 1926, refused to accept anything less than the ten-event minimum. 'We had 13 events in our championship, including the relays, so it just wasn't enough,' Vera Seale, the reigning 400-metre record holder and a member of the WAAA's executive, has said. 'We circulated all the member clubs and they told us not to go [to the men's Olympics] until there was a full program.' The British women also resented the fact that without any consultation, the IOC and the IAAF had placed a one-handed shot put on the Amsterdam program. At the time and for many years afterwards in most parts of the world, female competitors put the shot with two hands – i.e., first with one and then with the other – with total distance determining the placings. It was felt that such an approach encouraged strength development in both arms and muscular symmetry throughout the body. As a result of these differences, the British women decided to stay away from Amsterdam – the only feminist boycott in Olympic history.[78]

While the Canadian Federation was not party to these discussions, many of its leaders were interested in Olympic competition. At the 1927 annual meeting in Toronto, delegates voted to send a full team to

Amsterdam, with selection trials to be held in Halifax. But participation was not guaranteed, because only the Canadian Olympic Committee (COC) had the right to enter competitors. COC Chair P.J. Mulqueen was encouraging, but he made it clear that the federation could only nominate candidates for the team. He promised them a favourable hearing after Alex Gibb and Marie Parkes were named manager and chaperon. Eventually, six track and field competitors and swimmer Dorothy Prior of Toronto were chosen for the team. Athletically, Amsterdam represented a great triumph for Canadian sportswomen. Saskatoon's Ethel Catherwood (who had moved to Toronto to train) took the gold in the high jump, and the 4 x 100 metre team won with a new world's record. Bobbie Rosenfeld took silver in the 100 metres. She competed in the 800 metres, an event that she had never run before. In the final, she seemed content just to run beside and coax 17-year-old Jean Thompson of Penetang, who was running on an injured leg. Thompson and the effortless Rosenfeld finished fourth and fifth, respectively, behind Lina Radke of Germany's world-record run, earning further points for Canada. The women's team did better than any other contingent. When the 'matchless six' returned to Toronto, they were fêted by 300,000 people lining the streets from Union Station to Sunnyside Stadium.[79]

But throughout the Amsterdam Games, the WAAFers' subordinate status proved frustrating. The trouble began on the track, with a close finish in the 100 metres. The judges, without the advantage of a photograph, were deeply divided. The Canadians were convinced that Rosenfeld had won. When the American Elizabeth Robinson was awarded the race, Gibb, on the advice of Alice Milliat, and with the support of Mulqueen and men's track and field manager Bobby Robinson, started to file a protest. But Lamb, in his position as overall team manager, refused to deliver it, on the grounds that it was 'unsporting' to second-guess the judges. Robinson's victory stood, and the women were incensed. 'We Canadians will never believe other than that [Rosenfeld] had won the first place,' Gibb wrote in her report.

A few days later, Lamb further infuriated them by voting – without any consultation – against further women's participation in the IOC's Olympics. Like many others, including the pope, Lamb found the sight of women straining down the home straight of the 800 metres too much for his patriarchal sensibilities to stomach, and he decided to join with those who wanted an end to the whole experiment. Fortunately, a majority of Lamb's IAAF colleagues outvoted him (though they would not resume the 800-metre race for 32 years). But his action brought home the great vulnerability of the federation's position. He angered it again that fall by appointing Marion Belding – again without consultation – as Canadian representative to the FSFI. Though Belding was the incumbent president, the WAAF executive was upset that this was all done behind its back.

These issues came to a head at the 1928 WAAF meeting in Toronto. The McGill-led Quebec delegation fired the first shot by introducing a motion condemning female participation in Olympic sports, citing its familiar arguments against vigorous competition. It also called for elimination of the 800-metre race from all Canadian track and field meets and moved a vote of confidence in Lamb. Gibb, Parkes, and their supporters replied with all guns blazing. 'Olympic competition stimulates interest in athletics,' Parkes countered. 'International competition makes a definite contribution, not only to athletics, but also to the education of the competitors and to the goodwill existing among the different nations.' Mabel Ray of the Ontario Women's Softball Association told the Montrealers not to worry about the athletes' health. Because most of the Olympic team came from Toronto, she said, they were in superb physical condition. After a long debate, the Gibb forces defeated the Quebec motions and pushed through three of their own: that Lamb be formally asked to explain his actions, that the WAAF pursue FSFI membership, and that it seek articles of alliance with the AAU. Quebec recorded its opposition on every vote. The meeting also left the 800 on the Canadian championship program, enabling interested women to continue to race over the distance.[80]

Belding (who stayed in the chair throughout the bitter meeting), Gibb, and Parkes were elected to negotiate with the AAU. They immediately boarded a train for Port Arthur, where the 'Parliament of Canadian Sport' was about to go into session. When they arrived, they were welcomed as allies, for the knives were being sharpened for Lamb. That fall, he had publicly criticized Mulqueen and Bobby Robinson for their leadership of the Olympic team. They were out to clear their names and remove him from the presidency. Others had had enough of his haughty and humourless style. Lamb continued to patronize the women, reporting that 'I have not favoured granting of an independent status [to WAAF] until we, as a Union were convinced that the administration of their affairs would not fall into the hands of unscrupulous promoters, or those whose chief interest might be self-glorification.' Gibb and her sisters quickly turned his refusal to support the Rosenfeld protest in Amsterdam – and 'the interests and morale of the whole Canadian Team' – into an emotional rallying point. The newspapers called it 'the Battle of Port Arthur,' but it was really a rout. After a dogged defence of his actions, Lamb submitted his resignation, the only interwar president not to seek the traditional second term. The WAAF's motions were approved without other opposition. 'The easiest thing that went through,' Gibb told her readers the next day, 'was the passing of the articles of alliance. [That gave the WAAF] complete control for women's sports nationally and internationally.'[81] Once again Canadian nationalism proved a potent force, this time swamping the combined opposition of paternalism and maternal feminism.

The Port Arthur agreement gave the WAAFers the best of both worlds – a chance to compete in the Women's World Games as well as to enter the traditional men's Games. In 1930, they encouraged the Canadian Basketball Association to send a team to the Women's World Games in Prague, while keeping the track and field team in Canada to compete in 'demonstration' events at the British Empire Games in Hamilton. That experiment brought women a permanent place on the Empire Games program. In 1934, the WAAF entered a team in the Empire Games in London and in the Women's Games, held in the same White City stadium the following week. Canadian women were thus able to participate in the more extensive FSFI program, including 13 events in track and field, among them the 800 metres. There had been only six events and no 800 metres in the Empire Games.

Yet for the most part, the WAAFers concentrated on the opportunities afforded by the AAU. They were not prepared to withdraw from the FSFI. They had great admiration for Alice Milliat and her European colleagues. But with the exception of the McGill contingent, which sought to cut all ties with male organizations, they much preferred the Olympics to the Women's Games. They were happiest with the FSFI when it pressed for a full women's Olympic program.[82] There were several reasons for this. First, the FSFI was primarily a European body, within which the WAAF had very little influence. Second, there was virtually no coverage of FSFI events in the North American press, so from the Canadian perspective the Women's Games were 'merely a sideline alongside the Olympics. The trouble with the FSFI,' Gibb wrote, 'seems to be that the Olympics are getting the call over their world games in popularity with the athletes ... Just ask the girls whether they prefer Olympic games to these women's world games and you will get an unanimous "yes." '[83] In all their publicity the Edmonton Grads claimed Olympic victories for 1924, 1928, 1932, and 1936, suggesting that they had won gold medals in the IOC's

Games. In actual fact, however, these were FSFI championships organized in the same city as the men's Olympics, but with no official connection with the IOC's Games. Third, and most important, it was much easier to raise funds for an Olympic team than for the Women's Games, and in a pinch the WAAFers could fall back on the COC (and subsequently, the British Empire Games Association of Canada).

After several more years of skirmishing, the WAAF won the right to name its own Olympic and Empire Games teams, with fewer events to compete in, but 'half a loaf is better than none.' It proved a wise course. The London Games of 1934 were the last that the FSFI was able to organize. In 1935, Milliat tried to up the ante in her negotiations with the IOC, proposing that it provide a full women's program and full parity for women on the IOC and IAAF. If not, she said, the FSFI should be allowed to run completely separate Women's Olympics in every sport. But the IAAF effectively countered by threatening to seize full control over women's track and field in many countries, the FSFI's strongest suit. 'The FSFI had no recourse; all its cards had been played.' In 1936, in exchange for a nine-event Olympic program, three less than in the Woman's World Games, the FSFI agreed to cancel its Fifth Games, scheduled for 1938.[84] Thus ended a remarkable campaign of advocacy and action.

It would take until 1981 before a woman was appointed to the IOC, and until 1995 before a woman (Canadian Abby Hoffman) was elected to the IAAF.

'Distance and Dollars'

Coordinating the far-flung activities of Canadian sportswomen and asserting women's leadership was 'a fight, I'll tell you. It was really a fight,' Margaret Lord said on several occasions. Then she would pause and smile: 'We just had two problems: distance and dollars.'[85] These familiar Canadian organizational hurdles meant that most communication was by mail and telegraph rather than direct meeting. 'Most of the people I wrote to I couldn't identify by sight,' she said. Spalding told me with considerable pride how she convinced the local telegrapher to send messages for free – until he was fired for it. (She helped him get another job at the Savage Shoe Co. where she worked.) 'You couldn't call the national championships real championships – they were only regionals. It almost defeated the purpose of trying to bring women together. There were about 20 or 30 little knots of activity all over the country, but they rarely got together. [I am still bitter] about some of the selections to the

AAU's Hall of Fame. [One woman] was voted in because she won five national titles in a single day. Well, I was there – she didn't have any competition. There are lots more deserving than her. But the men wouldn't listen.'[86]

During the Depression, these difficulties led to divisive regional conflict. Each branch was allowed three votes at the annual meeting, but few could afford to send more than one delegate unless the session was held in the region. Few of the sportswomen enjoyed independent means. Even those who were employed managed just to scrape by on their meagre salaries. A teacher, Margaret Lord had to take out a bank loan to pay for her ticket to the 1936 Olympics in Berlin, so that she could serve the women's team as 'chaperon.' Family responsibilities also discouraged full attendance. If the provincial leaders could not afford to attend, they had to entrust their votes to others living closer to the meeting. But Ann Clark, the BC secretary after 1929, could always pay her own way. Fully employed (initially as a secretary, ultimately as a personnel manager at the Hudson's Bay store in Vancouver) and living at home with wealthy parents (her father supplied chicken to transcontinental passenger trains and ocean liners), she had no trouble finding time and tickets. Others remember her long winter vacations during the worst years of the 1930s. In 1934, when the meeting was in Toronto, Clark stopped her train journey at Edmonton, Saskatoon, and Winnipeg, collecting three votes each time. When she arrived in Toronto, 'Thirteen Vote Clark' (her position as WAAF secretary entitled her to one vote) took a large suite at the King Edward with Elizabeth Stirling of the Maritimes. The two women were close in age, interests, and outlook. Though they represented the 'extremities' of the country, ideologically they bridged the gap between the defensive 'maternal feminism' of the McGill physical educators and the combative spirit of the Toronto leaders. Between them, they had the meeting locked up. (There were only 26 accredited votes.) Clark and Sterling defeated several attempts to limit use of proxies and elected themselves secretary and president, respectively.[87]

The Ontario and Quebec representatives were livid. Since they had two-thirds of the membership, they felt that they should have more influence. They feared that they had unwittingly created several rotten boroughs: Saskatchewan and Manitoba, with about 50 paid-up members each, had the same voting power as Ontario, with 1,100. 'It wasn't so much that [Stirling and Clark] were poor choices, but that the system of voting was so unjust,' recalled Irene Moore McInnis, who was president of the Ontario branch at the time. She and her colleagues were also concerned that, when so many decisions required correspondence, 'it will take the president and secretary ten days to communicate with each other.' They felt that Clark, by far the stronger personality, would run the organization with little consultation.[88]

Clark was a formidable opponent. She was attractive, bright, and confident, a knowledgeable defender of women's interests, and a gracious listener. But when she had the upper hand, she was rarely willing to compromise. The following year, unable to attend the annual meeting in Halifax because of illness, she delivered 11 votes to Stirling. The Ontario delegates, McInnis and Margaret Lord, became so frustrated with their 'minority' position that they walked out in protest. But the mayor of Halifax and several AAUers, whose session was being held later that week, persuaded them to return. A powerful inducement was their desire to have their athletes' records ratified. So Clark won again. The press called her the 'Czarina,' 'Il Duce,' and 'Hitler' of women's sport – and so she must have seemed to those unaccustomed to strong women in positions of power.[89]

In 1935, with the meeting taking place in Regina, Ontario and Quebec stayed away, with Ontario disdaining even to send proxies. The meeting voted to move to biennial sessions 'for economic reasons,' and Clark was elected to a two-year term as president. Ontario's (mailed-in) proposals for proportional representation and a limit on proxies were handily defeated. Clark told the meeting that they were 'a lot of nonsense. It is very questionable why they want the added voting power. If they need it for the benefit of sport I would say yes, but I question it very much.' 'Ontario and Quebec went to Halifax last year with a chip on their shoulder,' added Stirling. But others were concerned with the growing split. 'We must not act like fools and hog all the important offices,' Ethel Cartwright urged the delegates in a plea for 'harmonious relations.' She ultimately persuaded them to give the two absentee branches positions on the executive.[90]

In the end, it was a proxy vote that ended Clark's six-year reign. Like the AAUers, the cash-strapped WAAF used regional time trials as the basis for selections for the 1938 Empire Games in Australia, but the absence of head-to-head competition between athletes left the Clark-appointed selectors vulnerable to charges of favoritism. When Ontario hurdler (and WAAF branch secretary) Roxy Atkins was left off the team, the Ontario leaders cried foul. When they discovered, after the boat had sailed for Sydney, that Atkins's times were actually faster than those of the hurdler selected, British Columbia's Yvonne Dingley, they were convinced that the fix had been in. Ontario sent three delegates to the 1938 biennial meeting in Winnipeg, including Atkins. Atkins's appearance was an unannounced 'surprise attack.' According to McInnis, 'When we arrived in Winnipeg, the votes and proxies were still stacked against us, the west alone holding twelve votes for Clark. While we were able to swing a few votes, we still needed two more. After much digging, we found two women in the west who had been overlooked and their proxies not requested. We wired them and got their proxies. When Ann found out, she withdrew from the race for president, and Edith [Mackenzie] was elected.'[91] The deciding vote came from the president of the women's section of the Canadian Amateur Basketball Association, who lived in Vancouver, Clark's home town.

Mackenzie quickly moved to patch up east-west relations. Though she had previously opposed proportional representation, she now threw her weight behind it and got the required votes in a mail ballot a few weeks later. A membership of 300 was henceforth entitled to three votes; of 500, to four votes; of 900, to five votes; and of 1,300, to six votes. A branch with less than 300 members got only one vote. Ontario, with 1,400 members, would get six votes, while the smaller branches such as Manitoba and Saskatchewan were reduced to one. The meeting also decided never to resort to regional selection trials again.[92] But the rift had consumed much of the Federation's energy for five years.

The problems of 'distance and dollars' were compounded by a scarcity of leaders. Almost every year, most of the women involved held multiple offices. In 1939, for example, while she was still competing, Roxy Atkins was president of the Ontario Ladies Hockey Association and the Ontario branch of the WAAF. Though the Quebec branch tried to have them declared ineligible for office, all the well-known sportswriters – Lillian 'Jimmie' Coo, Cook, Gibb, Griffiths, and Rosenfeld – were called on to serve in administrative capacities. In many provinces, the same small group soldiered on year after year. Ann Clark served as BC secretary for 27 years. (She was returned to the national executive as vice-president in 1946.) Irene Wall, Margaret Lord, and Ethel Cartwright were active in Quebec, Ontario, and Saskatchewan, respectively, for more than 20 years. When Elizabeth Stirling stepped down from the leadership of the Maritimes branch, after 15 years, she turned the reins over to Aileen Meagher, who had been coached by Stirling's husband. When Meagher could no longer continue, the branch disbanded.[93]

During the bloom of the late 1920s, there were hopes that many more women could be recruited into leadership positions. Seventy women attended the 1929 annual meeting in Montreal. But while the number of athletes participating never dropped significantly during the Depression and climbed to new highs in the late 1930s, the number of officials dwindled. Only eight officials attended the 1938 session in Winnipeg. As Lord observed, very few women had the time or the financial means to take on these responsibilities. Perhaps the lack of exemplars was another factor. Outside the family, there were few spheres in Canadian society in which girls and women saw themselves exercising authority.

The shortage of leaders heightened the federation's reliance on the AAU, and males in general. All of the women I interviewed stressed the double-sidedness of their relationships with the men, the desire for autonomy coexisting with the need for advice and support. 'I couldn't have done it without the men [of the Hamilton Olympic Club],' Lord has said. 'They pushed me into positions of increasing responsibility, saw to it that I attended meetings, and found the funds to send the girls' team to meets across the country.' Despite her resolute public defence of women's leadership, Ann Clark said the same: 'We couldn't have functioned without their expertise and experience. I admired some of the men very much. I learned enormously from them.'

The women's dependence was especially evident in the labour-intensive administration and regulation of competition. The 1930 Ontario championships staged in Toronto by the Canadian Ladies Athletic Club (CLAC) is a case in point. Only 23 of the 50 officials listed in the program were female. The CLAC must have had to pull out its entire membership, for several of the senior organizers also had major responsibilities in the Ontario Women's Softball Association that day. Men performed most of the duties requiring technical knowledge and experience, such as starting, timing, and judging. Eight women served as prize stewards, three as number clerks.[94] Other competitions required much the same male assistance. It was impossible to have a successful event without them.

Pushing the Limits

The WAAF's activities were always tinged with tension, not only between men and women, but among women, as they brought different ideological perspectives, interests, and tactical considerations to bear. Was the project of 'girls' sports run by girls' undermined by financial, technical, and administrative reliance on men? Or conversely, did too much autonomy jeopardize the necessary male support? If a women's club was coached and sponsored by men, who should vote at association meetings? And what about 'male advisers'?

These questions were continually debated. Some organizations accepted male leadership, while others tried to restrict it, giving men voice but not vote, or banning them from meetings altogether. Some men were content to sit back and 'advise,' but others found it frustrating. They either quit, or tried quietly to exert control. Sometimes the women's organizations had to find new male helpers, sometimes to reassert their authority. In 1928, for example, in response to what was perceived to be a 'crisis' of increasing male control, the Ontario WAAF called an emergency meeting to 'present a united front to any serious menace to women's domination and government of their own athletic activities.'[95]

Clearly there were limits to the extent of women's power, but it was not always apparent what they were. The sad story of Mabel Ray illustrates the complexity. Ray first came to public light as a successful equestrian and softball and hockey player, but by the 1920s she was best known as an organizer. A vocal proponent of women-led organizations, she helped found the Canadian Ladies Athletic Club (CLAC), the Ontario Women's Softball Association (OWSA), and the Women's Amateur Athletic Federation (WAAF). She was tireless in her efforts to raise money and promote women's teams. She was one of the very first to persuade the daily newspapers to publish her articles on women in sports. But there was often an edge to her advocacy. She could be sharply critical of male coaches and organizations such as the YMCA, which, she felt, exploited the popularity of female athletes without giving them much in return. In her mid-40s (she was 45 in 1927), she was considerably older than most of her female sporting colleagues, and they often called upon her to take the lead in difficult discussions with the men. When the Toronto Harbour Commission (THC) added lights to Sunnyside Stadium, for example, she fought for additional revenue because 'the lateness of the games will necessitate sending the players home in cars and in some cases teams are not financially able to do so.'[96]

In 1928, when women's softball was enjoying its greatest popularity, Ray obtained the lease on Toronto's Sunnyside Stadium for the Toronto Women's Softball Association (TWSA), of which she was president. She wanted to give every club a chance to benefit from the popularity and revenues of games at Sunnyside, not just those that had played there previously. But in reorganizing the schedule, she angered the organizers, sponsors, and supporters – both male and female – of the National

Ladies Softball League (NLSL), which fielded the city's strongest teams. Previously, NLSL teams had been able to control their own appearances at the park and obtain their share of the revenue directly from the THC. Now they had to go through Ray and take fewer games at the park. They lost no opportunity in attacking her. Ray's decision to 'share the wealth' split the closely knit Toronto women's sporting community. Phyllis Griffiths, Bobbie Rosenfeld, and Hilda Thomas, all associated with the NLSL, made the case against Ray. Alexandrine Gibb supported her.

At the beginning of 1931, Ray was at the height of her power. Despite the onset of the Depression, Sunnyside revenues had remained high the previous season, and she had been able to return $11,993.90 to TWSA member clubs. She was president of the OWSA, the Ontario WAAF, and the WAAF of Canada. But within a year, she was out of sport altogether. Her troubles began when two clubs from the NLSL asked the Ontario Athletic Commission (OAC) to investigate the TWSA's finances, alleging mismanagement. The auditor confirmed that 'while I have seen nothing to suggest any diversion of the Association's funds for the personal uses of any of the members of the Executive Committee, it must be admitted that the funds were not handled in a business like way.' Apparently, Ray did not obtain receipts of the monies she distributed to the clubs. Though this is somewhat surprising, given her occupation as a book-keeper, it is also somewhat understandable in what must have been the hurly-burly of her sports life: she not only ran the TWSA and the OWSA but coached and managed teams, officiated at track meets, and sat on the executives of WAAF – all as a volunteer on top of her day job. The members of the all-male OAC did not see it this way, however, and they recommended that she be expelled from sport for life. They also condemned the THC for 'professionalizing the sport [and] clearly promoting the competitions for their gain.' The main target of censure, though, was William D'Alesandro, president of the Sunnyside League, who could not explain how he spent his team's share of the proceeds. The Ontario AAU immediately endorsed Ray's censure, urging that it be enforced nationally through the articles of alliance.[97]

Neither the national AAU's president, James Morkin, nor the TSWA, OWSA, and Ontario WAAF memberships accepted these recommendations, and Ray kept her offices that year. (Toronto's Tory *Telegram* suggested that Ray survived only through the intervention of prominent Liberals such as COC President P.J. Mulqueen.[98]) But the feud continued at Sunnyside. When the NLSL was unable to persuade the other clubs to impeach her, it withdrew, taking its teams to city parks where they could keep the entire collection. On 9 May, it formed its own rival body, the Provincial Women's Softball Union (PWSU). Attendance at Sunnyside fell drastically, despite the last-minute addition of men's lacrosse, and revenues dropped by more than 50 per cent.

This was where Ray was most vulnerable. When she took over the Sunnyside lease, the THC insisted on a $8,500 guarantee and promissory notes to the value of $2,500 in case the guarantee were not met. In 1931, she obtained five notes of $500 each from local businessmen to cover the guarantee. With the shortfall of $4,893.98, the notes came due. The businessmen balked. Her employer, William Robertson of Robertson's Brothers Chocolates, wrote the commission: 'While I do not believe we are very bad losers, to pay out money for a deficiency of this sort would go against the grain. If we had been on the paper of the Toronto Baseball Club of which we are shareholders, we would have taken our loss without comment but to take a loss on account of these girls squabbling we think is hardly fair.' Though Ray got the THC to forgive the promisory notes, she had to relinquish the lease and withdraw from softball.[99] The PWSU soon took over the entire sport. Though 17-year-old Ann Spalding was elected president, all the other positions were held by men. It would take another 22 years for women to regain complete control of women's softball in Ontario.

Was Ray a victim of her 'dictatorial methods,' of her determination to 'share the wealth' over the 'powerful interests' of the best teams, or of the THC's double standard, for no male leaseholder was ever asked to sign a guarantee? All these factors no doubt played a role in her downfall. But there is also a strong suggestion that she was targeted for her strident feminism. Certainly Ray believed this herself. In a fund-raising minstrel show in the midst of the controversy, she contributed a skit of the Sunnyside investigation in which her own character was harried for interfering with men's work and 'talking too much.'[100] Those I have interviewed speak of her exceptional commitment and organizational abilities and her warm loyalty to friends, but they also term her 'aggressive,' 'forthright,' 'a real battler,' 'woefully misunderstood,' and a 'man-hater.'

Ann Spalding, who was asked to be the first PWSU president, told me that Ray was a lesbian and had to be driven out of sport: 'Everyone said "financial mismanagement" was the reason, but that was the easiest way out. What she was doing – you know, girls with girls and boys with boys, they're trying to make it legal now – would have meant a terrible scandal which would have killed women's sport. The men who formed the new organization said they needed someone from outside of Toronto to give it respectability and I was glad to help.'[101] Spalding, a devout Catholic from a prominent small-town family, was 17. She still speaks about Ray in the white heat of anger. I have some doubts about her memory. No one else raised the issue of sexual orientation in interviews or in the coverage of the day, even in coded language. On the contrary, women freely and openly expressed close feelings and 'crushes' for other women at the time. Susan Cahn, in her careful periodization of popular attitudes to women in sports, found that stigmatization of strong, 'mannish' athletes as lesbians began in earnest only after the Second World War, suggesting that Spalding may have been projecting a subsequent moral panic on the events of 1931.[102] None the less, it is clear that Ray went beyond the bounds of 'femininity' expected of every sportswoman. The PWSU breakaway was actively encouraged by John DeGruchy, the most paternalistic of the AAU's many 'women's advisers.'

Other WAAF leaders, however, sought to enlarge the space for sports-women by temporizing with patriarchal expectations. To a public that expected them to be 'respectable ladies,' they spoke appreciatively of the men, distanced themselves from organized feminism, and dressed conservatively. While frequently ridiculed for their formality, it no doubt contributed to their authority and the legitimacy of women's control. The published photographs of delegates to the annual WAAF and AAU meetings, dressed in dark suits and fur collars (but with bobbed hair), suggest a seriousness and accomplishment far beyond their actual years. In response to all the advocates of caution and protection – male leaders, 'girls' rules' advocates, and public commentators who warned that a woman's physiology and natural destiny put her at great risk – the WAAFers ensured that all athletes had the benefit of a medical examination, and then used the certification of fitness to give girls and women the green light. In short, while they presented themselves as respectful of patriarchal authority, they were not prepared to rein in their ambition for women in sport. On the contrary, they gave them the best opportunities they could and fought to see them 'properly recognized' so that they could inspire others. When it became clear that their nominees had little chance of winning the national sports awards created in the early 1930s – the AAU's Norton Crow Memorial Trophy and the Canadian Press Athlete of the Year – they created their own, named after Velma Springstead, who was selected the best all-round competitor in the Stamford Bridge meet in 1925 but died suddenly of pneumonia the following year. Donated by Alex Gibb, the trophy was first awarded in 1934 to swimmer Phyllis Dewar.

Against the charge that athletic women would lose their 'femininity' – and thus jeopardize the economic and emotional support of men – many of them strove to be 'feminine' with great relish. In the early 1930s, Andy Lytle of the *Vancouver Sun* wrote that female athletes were 'leathery faced Amazons with flat chests and bony limbs and a walk like a knock-kneed penguin.' It quickly became a refrain. In response, Alexandrine Gibb and the other women's columnists stressed the grace, beauty, and matrimonial attractiveness of the best athletes, ridiculing Lytle and his ilk. At the 1933 national track and field championships in Vancouver, Margaret Lord took her entire Hamilton team of young women to meet him, taunting him to 'name one leathery faced, flat-chested Amazon [among the good-looking, well-dressed competitors]. He scurried away in embarrassment.'

The other WAAF leaders did the same in interviews, annual reports, banquet speeches, and letters to the editor. In 1938, Montreal sportswriter Elmer Ferguson told female readers of *Maclean's* that 'the violent sports are no good for your looks, dignity or health. Sorry, but I like a little delicacy.' Though she had no previous writing experience, Ontario WAAF secretary Roxy Atkins immediately demanded that the magazine publish her article-length rejoinder. 'Elmer, you're goofy,' she told him. 'A temporarily strained face doesn't permanently destroy beauty, nor does it reduce a woman's social charm or her ability to bake a pie. You don't understand us girls [and] you don't even know your men. The girls who play the sports you deplore are gilt-edged securities in the marriage market.' At a time when many women were pressured to retire from sport upon marriage, WAAFers encouraged them to continue, even after childbirth, and brought their own children to games and meetings.[103] Perhaps their views constituted an 'apologetic' to deflect reprisals against their invasion of men's culture, but there was a proud, contestative quality to it, too: they tried to forge a new, vigorously active 'woman-hood.'

Accomplishment

After two decades of feminist scholarship, and the cascade of female breakthrough performances in every sport imaginable, there is a tendency to criticize the sports leaders of the interwar period for their failure to challenge directly the dominant, male-privileging sexual division of labour. Most of the women I know who played 'girls' [basketball] rules' remember them as restrictive. By comparison to the now widely televised men's game, the two-zone game seemed to offer them less athletically ambitious and thus less exciting opportunities. 'Girls' rules' also seemed to concede the admirable qualities associated with vigorous physical activity to 'manliness.' Though ever mindful of the contradictions that sportswomen faced – their athletic performances were measured against male standards, while their personal behaviour was held up to a feminine ideal – Helen Lenskyj has stressed the shortcomings of the 'apologetic approaches' of leaders such as Gibb and Atkins. There was enough support for women's athletics that they did not have to concede this ground, she suggests. The consequence was to condemn successive generations of sportswomen to the expectation that they be exceptionally pretty and open the door for homophobic attacks on those who refused to conform.[104]

When I first met such former WAAFers as Margaret Lord when I was a young runner in the late 1950s, I found them conservative, too, and readily empathized with my sister athletes who were frustrated by their protectiveness. But consider the interwar context. After the initial promise of new independence, the underlying expectations of the period became increasingly restrictive. The 'New Woman' was still expected to devote herself to the caring of men and their children. More and more women were encouraged to work for wages outside the home, but as a preparation for a domestic career. 'A few years of business experience ... serve to make [a woman] a more efficient home-maker, a more companionable wife and a better balanced mother,' Mable Crews Ringland told her readers in *Chatelaine*. Many employers insisted that women give up their jobs on marriage. Even university-educated women faced the expectation that their ultimate goal was to be a dependent wife and mother.[105] These pressures intensified during the Depression, as unemployed men argued that they had a prior claim to available jobs.

While the interwar generation established a place in sports for women, they were never allowed to forget the doubts and questions about whether they properly belonged. The female sports leaders, who took their responsibilities for girls and other women very seriously, heard these discouragements louder than anyone else. 'My mother never approved my involvement in sports,' Lord said repeatedly. Male sports leaders and sportswriters and middle-class physical educators in the 'girls' rules' movement continually drew attention to the boundaries and the risks of crossing them. The WAAFers were not social activists. They had been engrossed in sports from adolescence and had time for little else besides work. Most of them were the first in their families and communities to be involved in sports, so they faced all the uncertainties of pioneers. None of them was independently wealthy. A few – Rosa Grosse and Bobbie Rosenfeld, for instance – laboured under the further burden of being non-British immigrants. Yet rather than capitulate to the reigning definitions of 'feminine,' they reworked them to include the right to vigorous physical activity under their own leadership. We should not allow the advances of recent years to dim the light of their accomplishment.

In proportion to numbers, Canadian women have achieved greater success in international competition than their male counterparts.[106] To be sure, many factors contributed to these feats, but the legitimation of intense competition for women was a necessary precondition. That was perhaps the WAAFers' most striking achievement. They not only established a national structure for women's leadership but defended and advanced the idea that women could play as aggressively as they wanted. Given the great reluctance, if not outright opposition, of such conservative AAUers as Findlay and Lamb, there is little reason to believe that Canadian women would have ever had the chance to compete internationally as early as they did without the initiative of Gibb and others. The WAAF also mediated the ideological divide between the 'girls' rules' movement and those who sought unrestricted competition within an accommodation with the traditional male sports organizations, avoiding the deep rupture that split sportswomen in the United States.

US advocates of 'girls' rules' were largely successful in eliminating interscholastic and intercollegiate competition, thus depriving women in those institutions of the training and competition necessary to reach international levels of skill. But the American physical educators completely cut themselves off from the thousands of girls and women who played sports in the community, thereby abandoning them to a structure of male leadership. In Canada, the WAAF, largely because it drew its leaders from both the working and the middle class, was able to encourage Canadian women to aspire to whatever level of competition they wanted, while maintaining women's leadership in both the educational system and the community. It had no presence in French or rural Canada, nor among the First Nations. Yet despite the thinness of its leadership and organization, it was able to preserve and slightly increase urban opportunities during the Depression.

The WAAF leaders missed no chance to improve access. When the big indoor meets in Toronto, Hamilton, and Montreal began to invite American male stars as headliners, they insisted that the top American females be added to the list so that Canadian women could benefit from the extra competition. They fought to obtain as much travel and as many different experiences for their athletes as they could. Judging by the reminiscences of those I have interviewed, these opportunities significantly shaped participants' lives. 'You have to remember that [in the 1930s] it was a big thing if anybody got to Montreal,' Cathy Miller Ray, who grew up in Grimsby, Ontario, has said. 'Sport took me across the country [to the 1933 national championships in Vancouver], and broadened my horizons in many other ways.'[107] Other former athletes exulted in the chance to excel and win public recognition, for which there were few other avenues. They all stressed the importance of meeting other women. More than half a century later, many of them are still in regular contact, even while living far apart. They may remember few of their athletic triumphs, but they speak lovingly of their teammates. Old animosities remain, too. Friends phone each other across the Atlantic, while completely out of touch with former adversaries who live around the corner.

In 1937, the Ontario WAAF began a formal leadership development program, obtaining permission and funds to conduct a two-week residential training program at the Ontario Athletic Commission Camp at Lake Couchiching. According to Margaret Lord, 'There had been a boy's camp for years, but nothing for the girls, and the men wouldn't listen. Then Lionel Conacher became Commissioner and Irene McInnis, Roxy Atkins and I went to see him. He thought it was a great idea and gave us the last two weeks in August. We did it pretty much the same way as the men, dividing the province into ten districts, and taking ten girls from each district, selected from a district competition. We had instruction and competition in a number of sports, and some of the best coaches available, such as Dorothy Walton [who became the world's champion] in badminton and Alex Wilson [an Olympic medallist] in track and field. In the evening, we had skits and games. It was just terrific.'

Conacher had reason to be sympathetic. His cousins Grace and Tony Conacher were successful athletes who had benefited from the WAAF initiatives, and his wife, Dorothy Kennedy, was a graduate of Margaret Eaton School. If he was not otherwise convinced of the value of sports for women, they would have made the arguments. Conacher undertook to have the province pay all expenses. The camp brought many of those selected from the north and northwest together with the WAAF leadership for the first time. Participants were expected to pass along what they had learned to their clubs and teammates on their return. The camp generated favourable publicity and extended the network of athletic women. Other WAAF branches sought to emulate it in their own provinces. It might well have enabled them to replenish the ranks of leadership if it had survived the Second World War.[108]

Some historians have argued that women's participation in sport declined during the 1930s, in response to the Depression-induced return to conservative values, the effect of the 'girls' rules' ban on competition in some jurisdictions, and the increasing preoccupation of the mass media with commercial sport, which was primarily male.[109] Each of these factors did discourage involvement, particularly at the leadership level. But the effect was not as great as has been stated. Participation was reduced in some sports and some regions, such as softball in northern Ontario and the Maritimes generally. Press and radio coverage declined as well, often becoming ghettoized in the 'women's sport' columns. But in ice hockey, softball, and track and field, in the cities of Ontario and the west, participation and spectatorship were on the rise. In 1939, a record 1,528 athletes took out WAAF cards in Ontario, and both Alberta and Manitoba reported registrations of close to 400, giving the Federation a total membership greater than that of the team-sport–depleted AAU.[110]

After the outbreak of war, the WAAF continued to operate for several years, and activities continued to grow. But eventually mobilization brought almost everything but fund-raising to a halt. In order to stave off cancellation of the Couchiching Camp, the Ontario WAAF gave participants training as Red Cross leaders, but in 1943 the camp, too, was stopped. In 1942, Edith Mackenzie went to Washington, DC, to work for the British Purchasing Commission, leaving the organization without a president. Some women's sports continued under industrial auspices – Gladys Gigg Ross played for Vickers Aircraft – but many community teams folded. Both the Edmonton Grads and the Preston Rivulettes lost their facilities. Columnists such as Alex Gibb and Phyllis Griffiths were assigned to other beats, depriving sportswomen of a regular source of news and legitimation.

After the war, a few leaders tried to regroup, but the current ran harder than ever against them. 'The immediate legacy of the Second World War was an indisputable reaction against war's upheaval, including the unsettling extent to which women had crossed former sex/gender boundaries ... For more than a decade, feminism was once again sacrificed to feminity.'[111] In 1953, a majority of WAAF provincial representatives decided to amalgamate with the AAU. 'We had given it a good try, but we had no money, and few new leaders,' Margaret Lord explained. Ann Clark and Irene Wall bitterly opposed the decision. Wall refused to surrender the records and eventually burned them.

The collapse of the WAAF was disastrous for the interests of girls and women in sports. It eliminated an accepted advocate and a national network and helped marginalize, if not obliterate, sportswomen in newspapers, radio, and television. During the 1960s and 1970s, when the federal Fitness and Amateur Sport Program and its provincial counterparts were transforming the amateur structures into a state-directed system of high performance, women lacked an identifiable leadership to represent their interests and a forum to discuss issues and strategy. Very few women at all participated in the major decisions, and those who did were actively discouraged from speaking from a 'women's point of view.'

When second-wave feminism began to make its voices heard in sports, in demands for better, more numerous opportunities, young athletes such as Petra Burka, Abby Hoffman, and Marion Lay had to start the task of women's organizing all over again, from outside the athletic establishment, as if WAAF's control of women's sports and the networks they created had never existed. Nor did they have the relatively clear field that their predecessors in the 1920s enjoyed, because males were firmly in control, even though most opportunities continued to be segregated by gender. Girls and women gradually won new opportunities to participate, but with second-wave feminism's rejection of 'separate spheres,' those women who aspired to positions of leadership lost ground. Many of the once-separate women's programs that had long existed in schools and universities were brought under male leadership, and men got most of the jobs created by the expansion in female participation. Today, despite the recent acceptance of gender equity by many sports organizations, women remain woefully underrepresented in positions of leadership.[112]

'Women's sports run by women' is so utopian an ideal that it cannot be imagined. As a result, girls and women struggle to develop identities of healthy womanhood in a cultural practice largely controlled by males and steeped in discourses of masculinity. In the absence of the sort of vigorous feminist debate about alternatives that the WAAF facilitated, there is little to challenge the naturalization of the male model. That so many women succeed does not discount the enormous contradictions they experience.

These concerns deeply trouble Irene McInnis, now in her 80s. She was one of those who opposed the decision to wind down the WAAF, and she believes more than ever that it was a mistake. I first interviewed her in the summer of 1989, during the hearings of the Commission of Inquiry into the Use of Performance Enhancing Drugs and Other Banned Practices (the Dubin Inquiry), appointed to investigate Ben Johnson's disqualification from the 1988 Olympics in Seoul. It was not only the male track stars, weightlifters, and footballers who admitted to training on drugs, but several prominent female athletes, including perennial sprint champion Angella Taylor Issajenko. 'If women were still running it, there never would be a steroid problem,' McInnis insisted. 'The men got too lax about safeguarding track and field. They completely lost sight of what sports should be about.'

4

Workers' Sport, Workers' Culture

Ever since the mid-1870s, when rower Ned Hanlan brought back the first of his many international prizes, Toronto's Union Station had been the site of athletic farewells and celebrations, as friends and relatives, fellow athletes, admirers, hangers-on, and sportswriters flocked to wish their heroes good luck, bask in their glory, and catch first-hand accounts of great triumphs. But the athletic procession that began at the station on Saturday, 24 November 1934, was somewhat out of the ordinary. Instead of fans and dignitaries flocking to greet triumphant athletes, more than one hundred uniformed athletes joined thousands of other followers to cheer a 'victorious' revolutionary. He was the leader of the Communist Party of Canada (CPC), Tim Buck, who had been discharged that day from Kingston Penitentiary. Buck had served less than three years of a five-year sentence for 'belonging to an unlawful organization.' He had been convicted under the notorious section 98 of the Criminal Code, which the 'red-scared' Borden government had passed in 1919 in the aftermath of the Winnipeg General Strike. The law was modelled on New York legislation of the same year. Buck's unannounced release, and that earlier in the year of six of his comrades sentenced to identical terms in the same Toronto show trial, came despite the threat by Prime Minister R.B. Bennett that 'these men will serve every last five minutes of their sentences.' They were in large part the result of the aggressive public campaign waged by the CPC's 'front' organization, the Canadian Labour Defence League (CLDL), led by A.E. Smith. While officials at all three levels of government had hoped that jailing the communist leaders would seriously damage, if not destroy, their organization, the strength of public support for Buck's release and his enthusiastic welcome at Union Station showed otherwise.[1]

The athletes who marched in Buck's honour were members of the Workers' Sports Association (WSA) of Toronto, an affiliate of the Workers' Sports Association of Canada (WSAC). In the weeks that followed, they accompanied Buck to several large and small rallies in and around the city. At the Alhambra Hall on Spadina Avenue, they warmed up the audience by performing daring human pyramids, jumps and spins, and a series of fast-moving, choreographed exercises. Dressed in white gymnasts' tights, red belts, and white singlets with star-shaped red crests that read 'WSA,' they were fit, graceful, and strong. At Maple Leaf Gardens, they carried Buck on their shoulders into the arena and up to the speaking platform. When he addressed the 17,000-strong crowd, among baskets of red roses and carnations and below 30-foot high photographs of Lenin and Stalin, they guarded the podium and kept all but designated officials from approaching.

To sympathetic onlookers such as Winnipeg's communist leader, Andrew Bileski, the WSA symbolized the courage and vitality of an organization that had survived five years of state repression. But to those such as Alexandrine Gibb who feared the red menace, or who strenuously objected to the 'politicization of sport,' it seemed less an athletic group than a para-military unit that might support the CPC in street battles in the manner of the *croix de fer*, the Red Brigades, and the Stormtroopers of Europe.[2]

Neither characterization is very close to the mark, but the workers' sports movement – of which the WSAC was a major part – played a noteworthy counterpoint to the dominant themes in Canadian sport during the interwar years. At a time when more working people were joining middle-class and corporate associations to play sports and even greater numbers of them were being drawn into the capitalist leisure market as consumers of spectacles and other sports-related commodities, the workers' sports movement offered the possibility of class-centred and -controlled athletic activity. The publications that championed its growth, particularly the sports pages of CPC newspapers the *Worker*, the *Young Worker*, and the *Clarion*, presented a critique of dominant institutions and practices and an alternative vision of what might be. The clubs associated with it provided a range of new opportunities. Unlike other sports-persons, their members went into the streets to campaign publicly for their causes – usually against Coubertin's Olympic Games and for increased state spending on sport and recreation. In these and other ways, the movement sought to redirect the energies of working-class sportspersons along socialist lines. Despite their fascination with parties of the left, Canadian historians have barely noticed the Workers' Sports Association, but its activities throw the key developments of the period into sharp relief.

Beginnings

When working people – most often boys and men – engaged in sporting activity in the late nineteenth and early twentieth centuries, they usually did so within the ambit of class-centred institutions such as the tavern, mutual benefit or friendly societies, and trade unions. Baseball was a particular favourite. Playing with mates from the same workshop or factory could 'illuminate class inequalities and generate fierce opposition to the fundamental wrongs of the social order.' Many unions, from the respectable crafts of the American Federation of Labor (AFL) to the revolutionary International Workers of the World (IWW), held team games, track and field, boxing, and wrestling as part of their summer and Labour Day picnics. The fraternal ties encouraged by these activities were no doubt strengthened when working people had to improvise diamonds and equipment and defy laws that forbade use of public parks on Sundays in order to engage in them. Many working people resented and resisted the middle-class proselytizing of the YMCA, and the police, church, and company sports associations which extended opportunities to them under the banner of 'rational recreation.' Trade unions and socialist clubs were in the forefront of campaigns against sabbatarian restrictions and for public parks. In the 1890s in Vancouver, for example, it was the labour leadership that led the eventually successful campaign to end private ownership of the beaches of English Bay and turn them into a public park.[3]

But in the struggle for political and cultural allegiances, other sporting experiences had the effect of weakening workers' consciousness of class. In nineteenth-century Montreal, workers rarely formed their own clubs and leagues but joined those already created by industrialists, professionals, and white-collar clerks. Even when the best players were mechanics and labourers, as in the case of the famous Shamrocks Lacrosse Club, the dominant team in Canada for almost two decades, 'the subscription list read like a Who's Who of Irish Montrealers [including Mayor James McShane] ... and the leadership and organizational expertise [were] provided by the middle class and those workers with clerical training.' Most working-class athletes in Montreal were 'upwardly mobile [men] who accepted the basic Victorian ethic – true muscular Christianity.'[4] As many workers' picnics were sponsored by charitable institutions and employers as by unions. Commercial entertainments may have drawn upon working-class sentiments, and tavern owners and impresarios may have been sympathetic to the interests of the working class, as was the case with Montreal's legendary 'Joe Beef,' but their satires and narratives 'accepted class divisions and the distribution of wealth as part of the natural order of things.'[5] The spread of these amusements helped undermine non-market, associational forms of cultural expression.

But among working-class leaders, the harsh conditions of working life in late nineteenth-century Canada and the gradual formation of collective institutions inspired the dream of a distinct, proud, workers' culture, with control over its own activities, including sports. Such a culture would enable workers and their families to conduct their social lives as much as possible within their own institutions. It would not only affirm the nobility of labour but openly contest the injustices of the dominant order, providing 'an alternative hegemony in transition.' The best-known source of these ambitions, the Holy and Noble Order of the Knights of Labor, faded from view almost as quickly as it had appeared in the 1880s. For the most part, workers' culture was '*alternative* but not *oppositional*.'[6] But the dream of a self-conscious workers' culture lived on. It was kept alive by the attempt by professional baseball players in the United States to form unions and even to mount their own league – the short-lived Players' League of 1890[7] – and reflected in the fears of the radical press that workers were being coopted by capitalist sports. In 1909, for example, *Cotton's Weekly* warned its readers that 'if a wage slave can be got to turn his attention to Jim Jeffries or Jack Johnson, he will not be thinking how much Lord Strathcona or Colonel Carson or Sir Frederick Borden is taking out of his pay envelope.'[8]

The One Big Union (OBU) showed that even the dominant forms of sports could sometimes be used for workers' benefit. On 8 December 1921, at the suggestion of a member of the Winnipeg Labour Council, the OBU began to conduct a weekly soccer lottery, based on the scores of the British leagues, to boost the circulation of its newspaper, the *Bulletin*. In the summer, the contest drew on Major League Baseball scores. Entries had to be printed on coupons from the *Bulletin*. The contest brought in an extraordinary revenue. In its first six months of operation, the *Bulletin* paid out more than $500,000 in prizes, and $63,479 in a single week. The enraged provincial government tried repeatedly to have the lottery closed down, but the OBU simply rejigged the rules to stay within the law. After the Manitoba Court of Appeal declared wagering on the outcome of games illegal in 1922, for example, the contest was altered to require entrants to predict whether the mean temperatures of 15 Canadian cities would be higher or lower than those of the previous year. After another challenge, the OBU was forced to turn it into a 'Great Subscription Campaign' – for 25 cents, you could get a month's subscription and one draw – but the contest brought heavy sales for many years.[9]

The editors initially hoped that the contest would draw sports fans to their other pages. 'To Football Fans,' one such appeal read: 'Comrades! Many of you have only become acquainted with the One Big Union Bulletin through our competition. We hope, however, that many have read some of the articles appearing in the paper. They are written for you; the majority of you are members of the working class; perhaps you are out of employment; or are only partially employed. We have a message for you. Contrast [it] with the articles appearing daily in your newspaper. You will obtain a far better idea of world events from the Bulletin than from any other paper published in Canada.'[10]

Though the OBU made no effort to give these readers a radical analysis of sport, the lottery supported the OBU Athletic and Social Club in Winnipeg and a program of activities that included baseball, boxing, cricket, curling, football, hockey, quoits, road running, rowing, swimming, tennis, water polo, and wrestling. My father-in-law, Ben Berck, only son of an immigrant bus conductor, learned to box and play tennis there during the 1920s. 'It was very well organized. I don't think I could have afforded to go anywhere else,' he has remembered. OBU boxers and wrestlers were regularly featured in Amateur Athletic Union (AAU) competitions.[11]

The European Precedent

The dream was also kept alive by the example of a strong, autonomous, and class-conscious workers' culture in Europe. In sports alone, European clubs and associations boasted a total membership of four million adults and children. In several respects the workers' sports movement was significantly more successful than the rival amateur organizations, such as the Coubertin-led International Olympic Committee (IOC). Canadian workers were familiar with its activities through the labour press and the recollections of immigrants.

Germany was always at the centre. The first association was formed in Leipzig in 1850 by left-wing gymnasts who had managed to escape the repression that followed the collapse of the liberal revolution of 1848 and the Frankfurt Assembly. Others were started in the 1860s as breakaways from the conservative German Gymnastics Association. In 1893, these bodies met to form the Workers' Gymnastics Association. At the outbreak of the First World War, German combined membership was 180,000.[12] Other European workers and socialists formed sports groups as well. In France, the first clubs were a cover for socialist political activity, outlawed during the 1880s. In England, Robert Blatchford and the Christian socialists formed the Clarion Cycling and Rambling Clubs in 1894 to distribute the *Clarion* newspaper and other propaganda more effectively. Many members soon became ambitious weekend adventurers. National federations were formed in Switzerland in 1874, in Austria in 1892, in Belgium in 1904, in Finland in 1905, and among the Czechs in the Austro-Hungarian Empire in 1910. By the First World War, opportunities in bowling, boxing, chess, cycling, fencing, mountain climbing, soccer, swimming, tennis, track and field, weightlifting, and wrestling were provided by workers' organizations in Europe.[13]

'The battle for socialism demanded an affirmation of life and this affirmation is sport,' proclaimed German socialist Carl Shreck, a member of the Reichstag. 'Through sport, an enthusiasm will be awakened for the great task which we socialists have placed before ourselves, namely to make man free and to create a classless society.'[14] The European workers' sports organizations sought to invigorate their members in ways that encouraged class solidarity and dramatized the growing strength of the movement to the population as a whole. They made their own rules, raised their own funds, conducted their own events, and settled their own disputes, having nothing to do with the amateur, church, school, or voluntary bodies that the middle and upper classes created at the same time. They started summer camps for children and purchased insurance against members' accidents and injuries. Many associations drew on the populist, ceremonial traditions of physical-activity movements such as the German Turners and Czech Sokols. They loved to parade on holidays, at workers' rallies, and at their own festivals and competitions behind elaborate flags and banners. At least once a year, they staged a gigantic gymnastic carnival in which thousands of uniformed participants performed complicated routines in unison in a stadium or city square, before moving on for banquets and dancing. As sports became more popular, there was a gradual shift from non-competitive to competitive activities – the German federation added 'sport' to its title in 1919 – but the ceremonial and social characteristics remained.

Class issues were never far from the forefront. Most associations restricted membership to workers, socialists, and their families and stressed the importance of creating and supporting the institutions of the class *for itself*. The extent to which they engaged in overt political activity varied widely, but most of them gave their support to trade union struggles and agitated for better public sports and recreation facilities. The German federation contributed significantly to the physical education reforms and the ambitious construction of facilities undertaken by the Weimar Republic after the First World War. The Fédération sportive et gymnastique travailliste (FSGT) in France agitated against subsidization of commercial sport and religious instruction in the schools and for improved physical education, a shorter work week, subsidized health care, and birth control. In 1936, it participated in the massive sit-in strikes which enabled the Popular Front government of socialist Léon Blum to break a legislative log jam and enact its program, which included statutory paid holidays complete with state-subsidized travel and accommodation in French resorts. During the strikes, the FSGT organized games and social activities in occupied plants. The British Workers' Sports Federation (BWSF) led the 'mass trespass' of Kinderscout, the Manchester-area (and Baden Powell–owned) peak kept out of bounds to hikers and picnickers by armed gamekeepers and police. It opened up many parts of rural Britain to recreation where generations of polite lobbying had failed.[15]

Many European associations were able to publicize their events and campaigns and shape the interpretation of all forms of sport through their own newspapers and magazines. In Germany alone, there were 65 such periodicals in 1930. In addition to news, gossip, announcements, and advice, popular columnists provided ready-made judgments of events, praising heroes and castigating villains in a popular catechism of 'socialist sport.' During the interwar years in France, for example, worker sports enthusiasts could choose between René Thuillier, in *L'Humanité*, and Pierre Marie, in *Le Populaire* – the former usually flaying sports entrepreneurs for exploiting athletes, the latter criticizing them for stealing players from workers' teams and for causing the moral decline of athletes. The two writers' loyalty to class-centred sports was never in doubt. Marie even refused to attend the entrepreneurs' press conferences: 'For years, I have consistently refused these self-serving invitations. The coulin sauce câpres and the tournedos champignons hold little attraction for me. I prefer my simple fare, and above all, the freedom to write what I think ... Why do they hold these banquets? To announce future events? Surely a typed note would suffice. The real reason is to get into the good graces of sports reporters who otherwise might be difficult, to flatter them and feed them at a well-laden table. This, plus some envelopes judiciously distributed at the end of the month, established the "atmosphere" necessary to promote a given match, which otherwise would be quite unimportant.'[16]

Workers sports columnists continually warned readers against the evils of capitalist sport and stressed the need for publicly funded recreation. Even party leaders gave their authority to these campaigns. Writing in the BWSF's *Worker Sportsman*, British Communist Party leader Harry Pollitt argued:

Hundreds of thousands of pounds can be found for all forms of capitalist sports, where only hired professionals participate; where sport is corrupted; where bribery is rampant; and where the whole aim of sport is prostituted for the sake of making a profit both for the speculators and a few hired sports-men. But nothing can be done to provide the wherewithal to give the young workers the chance of developing all forms of sport facilities. ... If cheaper fares can be provided for people to travel to watch other people play football (like they do for the Cup Final) why cannot similar cheap fares be arranged for those workers and their supporters who want to play themselves, the providing of good dressing rooms, of good refreshment rooms, of cheaper facilities for buying the sports requisites and clothes?[17]

Early in the twentieth century, several national associations became interested in establishing an international body. Through the auspices of the Socialist International (SI), a founding congress was held in Ghent in 1913, attended by delegates from Belgium, England, France, and Germany, with fraternal greetings from Austria. They elected a four-person bureau to carry out the necessary tasks, but a second congress scheduled for Frankfurt a year later had to be postponed because of war. The organization was firmly established in Lucerne in 1920. Though formally named the International Workers' Association for Sport and Physical Culture, and then the Socialist Workers' Sports International (SWSI) (after 1926), it was known best as the Lucerne Sports International (LSI). At its formation, it had almost one million members in six countries. Its chief aims were to assist national organizations, to create international sport activity for their members, and to re-create the unity that had been shattered by the war.[18]

The SWSI's crowning achievement was the Workers' Olympics. Throughout the interwar years, international exchanges took place on a regular basis. The major festivals were designated 'Olympics.' Though Pierre de Coubertin was horrified when Alice Milliat called her international women's games 'Olympics,' he seems not to have minded in the SWSI's case.[19] The first Workers' Olympics, hosted by the Czechoslovakian Workers' Gymnastics Association, took place in Prague, 26–29 June 1921. Worker-athletes from 13 countries, including the United States and the Union of Soviet Socialist Republics, competed in sports, performed together in mass gymnastic displays, and attended choral recitals, political plays, and pageants staged by the organizers. The festival ended with the entire stadium singing revolutionary songs. The SWSI held Workers' Olympics in Schreiberhau (winter events) and Frankfurt am Main (summer events), both in Germany, in 1925; in Mürzzuschlag (winter) and Vienna (summer), both in Austria, in 1931; and in Johannisbad, Czechoslovakia (winter), and Antwerp (summer) in 1937. The Czech socialists hosted another well-attended Olympics in Prague in 1934.

The Vienna Games of 19–26 July 1931 were perhaps the most successful athletic festival ever held; 76,245 athletes from 23 countries competed in 220 events in 15 sports (including 'military sport' and motorcycling). There was a children's program, a fitness biathlon (run and swim) for tourists and citizens, artistic displays, dramatic performances, fireworks, and mass exercises. On opening day, an estimated 250,000 people watched 100,000 men and women parade to the new stadium, constructed by the socialist Viennese government. Some 65,000 watched the soccer finals and 12,000 the cycling finals. The Workers' Olympics differed from the Coubertin version in several important respects. Whereas the IOC's games encouraged competition along national lines, the SWSI stressed international solidarity. After the First World War, the IOC allowed the Belgian and French governments to bar athletes from the 'aggressor nations' of Germany and Austria from the 1920 Antwerp and 1924 Paris Games. In response, the SWSI held its 1925 Olympics in Germany under the slogan 'No more war.' The centrepiece of the opening ceremonies was a mass artistic and gymnastic display symbolizing working-class solidarity. Athletes marched and competed as part of national teams but, instead of national flags and anthems, carried identical red flags and sang revolutionary hymns such as 'The Internationale.' Whereas the IOC set a stiff performance standard for entry, the SWSI invited both the record-holder and the novice and set no limit on the size of teams. In Vienna, 36,600 worker-athletes were entered by the host Austrian federation,

29,054 by the Germans. The SWSI actively encouraged female participation. Some 25,000 women competed in Vienna. A year later at the IOC's Games in Los Angeles, only 107 females took part. The inclusive character of the Workers' Olympics extended to children and those beyond their athletic prime. At the 1934 Prague Olympics, an entire day of the program was devoted to children's activities and there were special displays by participants over 35.[20]

Despite these successes, the movement could rarely boast of unity. For much of the interwar period, the SWSI faced a far more troublesome rival than the IOC within the ranks of workers' sport. The events of the war and its aftermath had split the international left into warring socialist and communist parties, trade unions, and cultural organizations, and these divisions were reproduced in sport. As early as 1919, the Berlin club Fichte broke with the national body over its demand that clubs be neutral in disputes between working-class parties. Fichte wanted to restrict executive committee membership to Communists and Independent Socialists. In 1923 in France, the majority voted to affiliate with the communists, causing the socialists to walk out and form their own organization. For much of the period, there were also two bodies in Britain, the communist British Workers' Sports Federation (BWSF) and the unaligned British Workers' Sports Association (BWSA). Pro-communist bodies were affiliated to the International Union of Red Sport and Gymnastics Associations, later renamed the International Union of Workers and Peasants Sports Associations and best known as the Red Sport International (RSI). It was formed by the Communist International (CI) at its third congress in 1921 as an explicit alternative to the SWSI.[21]

The struggle between the two internationals was bitter and long-lasting and extended well below the leaderships. The SWSI was a decentralized federation of relatively autonomous associations whose leadership was primarily concerned with the conditions and opportunities for working class athletes in sport, while the Moscow-dominated RSI was intended as an instrument of the class struggle; 'it was not interested in developing a better sports' system for workers in a capitalist world.'[22] Initially, the RSI sought to win adherents by infiltrating SWSI clubs, condemning their leaders, and pushing its own line, without formally affiliating as an organization. When the SWSI, understandably, did not invite the RSI clubs (95 per cent of which were in the Soviet Union) to the Frankfurt Olympics, the RSI tried to stage counter-demonstrations. Soon afterwards, the SWSI broke off relations completely and the RSI began its own multi-event international festivals, which it called Spartakiads. The term was first applied to an athletic festival set up by Czech communists in 1921.[23] RSI manoeuvres were conducted within the lurches of Comintern policies, which were continually being redrafted in response to the internal political struggles and foreign policy concerns of the Soviet Union. It was not until the Comintern entered the 'common front' phase in late 1934 – after Hitler had destroyed workers' sports in Germany – and a number of national associations began to push for unity that the two internationals tried to patch up their differences. But while they jointly sponsored the ill-fated 'Peoples' Olympics' of Barcelona in 1936 and Soviet athletes competed in the SWSI's Antwerp Games of 1937, they were never able to agree on a basis for fusion.

Transplanting the Movement to Canada

The idea of an explicitly class-conscious, Canadian workers' sports movement came from Europe and the Communist International. In 1924, Tom Hill, the Canadian delegate to the Fourth Congress of the Young Communist International (YCI), took the RSI campaign against the SWSI to Canada, advising his comrades in the Young Communist League (YCL) that 'our duty is to work within the workers' sports organizations, mobilizing them against exploitation, militarism and fascism, and for revolutionary understanding.'[24] Sports would help them mount a 'total culture' of opposition to the harsh capitalism in which they lived and show the way to a new society. Since workers' sports organizations on the European model did not exist in Canada, they had to be created. Soon thereafter, the YCL's newspaper, the *Young Worker*, instructed every branch to form a Workers' Sports Association (WSA) so that comrades and sympathizers could have opportunities for 'exercising the body and all the mental benefits accruing from sport.' Baseball would probably be the most popular, but WSAs should also schedule boxing, hiking, running, and swimming. 'These sports must be turned from commercial antagonistic games into "Red Sports," ' readers were admonished. 'They are recruiting agencies because they are beneficial to YC membership and develop a feeling of comradeship and vitality.' The League sought to build the WSAs into one of the most powerful of the Communist Party of Canada's (CPC's) 'mass organizations' designed to win sympathetic and uncommitted non-party members to the cause. Though any number of non-communists could be signed up as WSA members, the organization would in fact be controlled by a 'faction' of YCLers that was acting under party discipline.[25]

The YCL was quick to take up the challenge. In 1925, soccer teams were started in Montreal, Toronto, and Winnipeg (which had the Hammer and Sickle Club). Oshawa, Renfrew, and Kirkland Lake, in Ontario and Lethbridge, Sylvan Lake (the 'Red Hope Club'), and Drumheller in Alberta reported field days, team games, boxing clubs, swimming parties, picnics, 'tramps', and 'rambles.' By 1926, WSAs were established in 17 centres. Toronto's operated a seven-team softball league, with two teams of cigar makers, one of jewellers, one from the Earlscourt Labour Party, and three WSA teams. Montreal's fielded senior and junior soccer and basketball leagues and attracted a large following. 'You didn't have to be a communist to go to Fletcher's Field on a Saturday afternoon and cheer for the WSA,' recalls Dave Kashtan, who grew up in Montreal and eventually became national secretary of the Workers' Sports Association of Canada (WSAC). During the 1930s, the Toronto and Montreal WSA soccer teams played each other on an annual basis, and these games attracted crowds as large as 5,000. (Montreal usually won.) Games were followed by speeches, songs, a collection, and an invitation to the WSA dance in the evening.[26] They complemented other cultural activities of the communist movement, such as the children's camps, choral societies, literary societies, and theatre groups such as the Progressive Arts Club.[27]

The WSAs encouraged a range of activity, but the staples of most clubs were the mass drills, acrobatics, and stunts of gymnastics that could be practised and performed in most community halls Though the YCI was wary of the too-close association of sports and other cultural groups (lest enlarged cultural organizations weaken political and trade union activity), gymnastic routines could be set to music and combined with choral and theatrical performances in movement 'concerts' of great appeal. Particularly popular were the statuesque 'tableaux,' in which semi-naked, bronzed (glycerine and bronze powder) adolescents enacted famous historical moments and sculptures before audiences of their parents, relatives, and friends. Gymnastics had the organizational advantage of continuity, as the *Young Worker* once ruefully admitted after one WSA concentrated all its energies on a softball league and then dissolved with the end of the season.[28]

In Toronto, the Jewish WSA held competitions in the Olympic events, but elsewhere gymnastics were pursued for mass exercise and display. Usually an entire group would participate in sequences of carefully coordinated field or floor exercises, while smaller groups and individuals would perfect statue posing and apparatus, tumbling, and acrobatic stunts – hand and head balancing; teeter, trapeze, and trampoline twists and spins; and sometimes juggling. Clubs also sought to develop comedy routines for their regular 'concerts.' The most frequently performed routine was the multi-person pyramid, which the YCL encouraged because it was believed to depict the importance of working-class solidarity during the class struggle. But the pyramid also brought out the intergenerational tensions that sports touched off in immigrant households where these activities were unfamiliar. Ben Burston remembers that as the youngest member of one club, it was his task to climb to the top of a ten-man pyramid. Once during a concert, just as he was about to scramble up to his perch, his mother screamed out from the audience, 'Benele, don't do it!'[29]

During the 1930s, the Winnipeg WSA developed gymnastics to such a level that many of its members subsequently made careers for themselves as circus and night-club performers. The driving forces were Walter Kaczor and his younger brother, Fred. They came from a left-wing family, they had been members of the YCL, and their older brother Mike had been a circus acrobat. Walter had successfully competed in gymnastics for the YMCA but became disillusioned by its 'failure to do anything for anybody who wasn't a star.' He wanted to create a more accessible club. In 1931, with $100 in savings from his job at the CPR, 'he bought and cleaned all the remaining equipment from a defunct Y on Selkirk Avenue and set up shop in a room we rented above a store.' According to his brother Fred, 'In no time at all, we had so many members that we had to get our own hall. We found an old ballroom on Dufferin Street, with a beautiful hardwood floor, a stage and a balcony, and a kitchen in the basement. It cost $60 a month in the winter, $40 in the summer so we paid the rent by holding dances every Sunday, charging 10 cents admission, five cents for checking. We usually made enough to hire a live band. At first, some gangs and then the cops gave us trouble, but we got 20 of our most muscular gymnasts to put on a show at intermission and then serve as bouncers and that seemed to intimidate them.'[30] Club membership was 25 cents a month – free for the unemployed and their children – and it gave admission to all activities and a subscription to the mimeographed newsletter, 'The Universal Sportlite.' As the membership grew – by the late 1930s, it averaged 500 – the Kaczors developed their own leadership training program and recruited sympathizers with professional skills to help with administration.

During its most successful period, the club offered twice-weekly classes in bodybuilding, boxing, skiing, snowshoeing, swimming, table tennis, weight training, and wrestling; it conducted summer camps for children; and it fielded teams in basketball, volleyball, and softball ('never hockey – it was already well organized'). It was best known, however, for gymnastics. Almost every week, its top squad travelled to small towns in Manitoba, northwestern Ontario, and North Dakota to stage displays. 'These were farming communities,' Fred Kazor recalled; 'they always wanted to feed us, and most of our kids were always hungry. Sometimes they ate so much they had trouble performing.' Twice a year, the club staged a choral and gymnastics festival in the 1,000-seat Winnipeg Auditorium. In 1940, Russ Saunders, one of the club's featured performers, moved to Los Angeles, where he became a stalwart of Muscle Beach, an influential centre of American physical fitness, and a Hollywood stuntman (for stars such as Errol Flynn and Gene Kelly) and model (for artists such as Salvador Dali).[31]

From the outset, the YCL sought to create a national organization. In 1927, the first attempt to link up the various WSAs failed when no club outside Toronto was able to send a representative to the founding convention. But a second attempt a year later was successful, and the WSAC was established. Twenty clubs joined directly, and the 20-club Finnish Workers' Sports Association of Canada (FWSAC), the Ukrainian Labour Farmer Temple Association (ULFTA), whose member organizations often provided the WSAs with facilities, and the Canadian Party of Labour became affiliates.[32] The national committee began to organize leadership training and regional and national events. In 1929, the WSAC joined the RSI. In 1932, the Finnish clubs agreed to dissolve the FWSFC and join directly, enabling the WSAC to claim a total membership of 4,000 in 50 clubs from New Waterford, Nova Scotia, to Ladysmith, British Columbia. In 1933, membership was 5,000.[33] Though turnover was high, the organization had a presence in many communities – no mean accomplishment.

The Finnish Canadians

In Michael Ondaatje's novel about the construction of public works in Toronto, *In the Skin of a Lion*, the protagonist remembers a night when he had been drawn out into the cold by

lightning bugs within the trees by the river. But this was winter! He moved forward. ...

The ice shone with light. It seemed for a moment that he had stumbled on a coven, or one of those strange druidic rituals. ... But even to the boy of eleven, deep in the woods after midnight, this was obviously benign. Something joyous. A gift. There were about ten men skating, part of a game. One chased the others and as soon as someone was touched he became the chaser. Each man held in one hand a sheaf of cattails and the tops of these were on fire. This is what lit the ice and had blinked through the trees.

They raced, swerved, fell and rolled on the ice to avoid each other but never let go of the rushes. When they collided sparks fell onto the ice and onto their dark clothes. ...

Patrick was transfixed. ... It was not just the pleasure of skating. They could have done that during the day. This was against the night. The hard ice was so certain, they could leap into the air and crash down and it would hold them. Their lanterns replaced with new rushes which let them go further past boundaries, speed! romance!

To the boy growing into his twelfth year, having lived all his life on that farm where day was work and night was rest, nothing would be the same.

Years later, while working and living alongside immigrants, Patrick realized that the magical, midnight skaters of his childhood had been Finns.[34]

Though a work of fiction, Ondaatje's sketch of the athletic exuberance of the Finnish-Canadian worker-sportspersons is based on interviews and archival photos. He could well have been describing their real-life passion for the out of doors, their endless energy, and their ability to transform almost any setting into an arena of athletic drama. The haunting imagery of the bewitching hour is appropriate, too, because as working men (and women) they had little time during 'normal' hours for leisure pursuits and often ran, skied, swam, and competed late into the night. Like many other immigrants, the Finns pursued these activities outside the middle-class, staunchly pro-British mainstream of Canadian sports.

The Finnish Canadians were the best organized and most athletically gifted of the worker sports participants in Canada. Their love of vigorous physical activity seemed to be a national characteristic. In the late nineteenth century, despite, or perhaps because of, their inclusion in the Russian Empire where sports were virtually unknown, many Finns were quick to adopt them. From the very beginnings of international competition, they strived to enter distinct Finnish teams and they excelled. With renowned champions such as Hannes Kohlmainen, who won the 5,000 and 10,000 metres at the 1912 Olympics in Stockholm and the marathon at the 1920 Olympics in Antwerp, and Paavo Nurmi, who won eight

Olympic medals during the 1920s, Finns like to boast that they 'ran their way onto the map of the world!' Finnish athletes also competed with great success in the Workers' Olympics. The enthusiasm for sport seems to have been shared by men and women of all classes and political perspectives. Finnish women have always been much more actively involved in organized sport than their sisters in English-speaking countries, perhaps because of the early successes of suffrage and other feminist campaigns there. Women gained the vote in Finland in 1906, and 14 women won seats in parliament the following year, the first in the western world to do so.[35]

Finnish immigration to Canada began in the late 1880s. Some Finns sought to escape tsarist conscription and repression, others to obtain the farm land promised by the dominion government and railway recruiters or simply for adventure. By the First World War, 17 per cent of all Finnish emigrants were living in Canada. After the Civil War in Finland, the flow resumed. While most were described as 'farmers' on their immigration cards – even political refugees such as Finland's first prime minister, Social Democrat Oskari Tokoi – very few ever settled on homesteads. The land they were given was often unsuitable for agriculture, or they lacked the capital and the commitment to make a go of it and ended up as wage labourers in the mines and lumber camps of the resource hinterlands of northern Ontario and British Columbia or as tradespersons in the cities. They quickly developed a reputation for labour radicalism. Many of them had been socialists or active in the cooperative movement in Finland, so it was hardly surprising that they formed similar organizations to combat difficult economic conditions, racial prejudice, exploitative employers, and a repressive state in Canada.

Finnish forestry workers played a leading role in organizing the Lumber Workers Industrial Union of Canada and the Finnish Socialist Organization of Canada, later renamed the Finnish Organization of Canada (FOC). They also made common cause with Canadian socialists, being active in the Socialist Party of Canada, the Social Democratic Party of Canada, and the CPC. Though such activity led to their removal from Ottawa's 'preferred immigrants' list in 1919, they continued to arrive in large numbers throughout the 1920s, many to escape the persecution of left-wingers that followed the Civil War.[36]

Wherever they settled in numbers, Finns created a rich social and cultural life for themselves, usually in their community halls, or *haali*. They ran educational meetings and camps for their children, published and discussed their own newspapers, novels, and political literature, wrote and performed their own plays, and listened and danced to their own choral groups and orchestras. They also formed sports clubs. By 1910, there were clubs in Toronto, Cobalt, Copper Cliff, Garson Mine, Port Arthur and Sellwood, with such heroic names as Endeavour (Yritys), Frolicking Brothers and Sisters (Kisa Veljet – Kisa Siskot), Energy (Tarmo), and Hard Blow (Isku).

While they restricted their own membership to working-class Finns, they were quite prepared to compete against all comers. In 1920, one Toronto Yritys wrestler, Enok Lopponen, represented Canada in the IOC's Olympics in Antwerp. In northern Ontario and British Columbia, they arranged meets and games with athletes from nearby Native reserves. Toronto Yritys contributed money to the founding of the Workers' Sports League (TUL) in Finland in 1919 and to the sending of the Finnish team to the 1921 Workers' Olympics in Prague. Both events were discussed at length in the Finnish-Canadian press. With the YCL's growing interest in a sports movement, the Finnish-Canadian clubs sought to create their own federation. In 1924, the clubs in the Sudbury area formed the Central Ontario Gymnastics and Sports Federation. A year later, northern and northwestern Ontario joined, and the new association was renamed the Finnish Workers' Sports Association of Canada (FWSAC). Its objectives were 'to raise the physical, intellectual, and cultural level of workers by promoting an interest in physical activity; and to further the country's militant labour movement.'[37] The FWSAC was closely associated with, but never formally affiliated to, the FOC. The first secretary was Hannes Sula, a former Finnish champion in the 100 metres, who had been a fierce Red partisan during the Civil War. He was also the editor of *Vapaus*, the FOC's daily newspaper.

In the long days of summer, Finnish Canadians pursued track and field and gymnastics. In winter, they skied and the men wrestled in the 'classical,' or Greco-Roman style, which they liked because of its spectacular, over-the-head throws. Even if they had only a small clearing or a corduroy road, they tried to race, throw the javelin, and perform mass drill. In many communities, they blasted rock and cleared trees and stumps to level out athletic fields and running tracks (usually 300 or 400 metres and always metric) and constructed haali, which could serve as gymnasiums. They built most of their own equipment, including track and field implements, wrestling mats, gymnastic apparatus, and skis. The Finnish Canadians competed in track and field with the spirit of *sisu*, or indomitable courage. In 1933, at the peak of membership, they held all of the WSAC's senior men's records.

Most WSAC competitions were held at Finnish grounds, such as Toronto Yritys' Camp Tarmola (in the Don Valley until 1927, and then near Woodbridge). While Finnish Canadians rarely competed in gymnastics, each year a central committee determined a set of routines to be practised by individual clubs. These would then be performed en masse at the annual summer festival, the *liittojuhla*. In winter, skiing was a way of life. 'You skiied to the outhouse, you skiied to work and the grocery,' several participants told me. They raced, too – for sweaters and socks, 'not that useless bourgeois stuff, cups and medals.' In the mining districts, many practised at night with the aid of their miners' lamps. Girls and women were encouraged to participate in everything but wrestling.

Most practice sessions, competitions, and festivals ended with the sauna. Max Ilomaki was a U.S.-born stonecutter who travelled throughout the United States and Canada in search of work during the Depression. 'You'd be sitting on a freight train and see a curl of smoke coming out of the woods and you knew it was a sauna. So you'd get off the train and join them. If you did it after a competition, you'd dive into a snowbank and then go back in. It invigorated you.'

The Finns were always prepared to travel long distances to engage in these events, even if it meant hopping freight cars ('the slide-door pullman') or bundling up in open trucks. Several Toronto participants told me about travelling to Sudbury in winter in an open truck to compete in wrestling. In the collection of Montreal's Jousi ('Cross-bow') Athletic Club, a photo shows 22 men and women from Toronto Yritys who had ridden there in a small truck for a track meet. While there are mattresses laid out on the truck bed, there is almost no room for sitting. One other annual trek is noteworthy. During the 1930s, when many people were unemployed, with lots of time on their hands, the clubs around Beaver Lake (near Sudbury) and South Porcupine (near Timmins) would each stage a ski race. One week, the men from Beaver Lake would ski to South Porcupine, a distance of some 240 kilometres, stopping at lumber camps along the way, race, and then return. Two weeks later, the South Porcupine men would do the same in the opposite direction. By comparison, the longest ski race in Canada today, the Canadian Ski Marathon from Lachine to Ottawa, is a mere 160 kilometres.

The Ukrainian Canadians

Radical Ukrainian immigrants and their children made up the second most numerous ethnic group within the workers' sports movement.

Ukrainian immigration to Canada began in the 1890s, increased dramatically in the decade prior to the First World War, and quickened again when peace came. Between 1925, when the dominion government gave the railways the right to recruit agricultural and domestic workers from central and eastern Europe, and 1930, when it effectively shut down Canada's borders, the annual intake grew from 2,245 to 16,000. These numbers probably understate the arrivals, because, given the statelessness of the Ukrainian people, many were classified as 'Russian' or 'Polish' by Canadian officials. Most immigrants had been peasants in the over-populated western Ukraine and went straight to the prairies, where they struggled with the soil, the railways, the bugs, and the banks to eke out a living on their homesteads.

Despite constant Anglo-Saxon chauvinism, they were politically conservative. They would agitate against the Soviet Union and contribute to the movement for an independent Ukraine. But a few ended up in cities and the industrial projects in the resource hinterlands and worked as unskilled or semi-skilled labourers. These became the radicals who joined or formed trade unions, participated in socialist political struggles, and created cultural organizations to provide a social base for this activity. The first of these, the Taras Shevchenko Society, was formed in Winnipeg in 1904, with a membership of 400. The establishment of the Soviet Union inspired many more, and by 1924, there were enough to establish a national federation, the Ukrainian Labour Farmer Temple Association (ULFTA).[38]

But unlike the Finns, the Ukrainians did not have a strong sports tradition of their own. While they could use their community halls and summer camp grounds for gymnastics and other forms of athletics, they rarely did so. 'Most Ukrainian immigrant parents viewed sports if not as an unnecessary luxury at least as a wasteful activity ... Economic stability and security were foremost on their minds.'[39] When the YCL began to organize sports groups under the WSA banner, a number of young Ukrainian-Canadians signed up directly, even when they were members of the ULFTA. In fact, Dave Kashtan, national secretary of the WSAC from 1930 to 1932, has argued that many of the Ukrainian-Canadian members would never have taken up sport but for the WSAs.[40] While the Ukrainian-Canadian members rarely entered track and field and other sports, they became outstanding gymnasts. Many of them became very successful leaders and instructors.

There were also Czech, Hungarian, and Jewish clubs, though the WSA leadership sought to discourage ethnic identification, and Canadian- and

British-born members. Most athletes were involved in trade union or left-wing activities or came from working-class families.

Against 'Bosses' Sports'

While the YCL leadership was no doubt pleased with the extent of activity, it always sought to steer it into a more explicitly political practice and discourse. The identities that it wanted to foster were socialist and internationalist. The YCL's approach was heavily influenced by its reading of Marxist-Leninist theory and its directives from the YCI. During the 1920s and early 1930s, its primary concern was advancing the possibilities for revolutionary change, a task well beyond the day-to-day activities of most sports programs. Except for the years 1925–6, when it pursued a policy of uncritical alliances with other left groups, the CI and the communist parties and youth movements that affiliated with it adopted a stance of uncompromising militance against all opponents, bourgeois and non-communist left alike. This was especially the case after 1927, when the CI leadership came to believe that the world was entering a period of capitalist crises. If the gradualist, parliamentary tendencies of the social democrats and other reformers (labelled 'social fascists') were defeated and clear communist alternatives established, they felt, the resulting uprisings would lead to the overthrow of capitalism. During this period the CPC took few positions independent of the CI. Ian Angus argues that it sought to be neutral in the Trotsky-Stalin debates, Norman Penner that it advocated an independent Canadian strategy, but on both questions it soon fell into line and expelled those who did not.[41]

In keeping with the Marxist-Leninist ambition to link theory and practice, the YCL sought a fuller understanding of the role of sport in capitalist society. These explorations, published in a series of articles during the mid-1920s, prefigure, albeit in vulgar, materialist form, the social history of sports published in the 1970s and 1980s. Sports developed in step with the very conditions of industrial capitalism and urban concentration that gave birth to the proletariat, the YCL hypothesized. This occurred first in Britain and the United States, with their 'gigantic industry' and 'large towns.' 'Peasants have no interest in sports.' From this starting point, the YCL argued that workers and their families took part in sport because they had a 'natural' desire to pursue health and recreation and 'to develop their bodies for efficient service in the class struggle. It is only weaklings and morons who decry sport.' Workers' desires were intensified by the 'unwholesome atmosphere of the workshop' and 'the overcrowed tenement houses of the proletarian quarter.'

It was clear that all workers need space, fresh air, and exercise, the YCL told its cadres. 'In spite of the systematic misuse of sport in the various sports clubs,' the young worker engaged in sports to escape from the factory and the misery of life in the slums. 'Two things must be remembered,' YCL speakers and editorials thundered in conclusion: 'Sports result from the physical need of the young worker. Sports movements, which for a great part are made up of proletarians, grew with the development of industry. These two facts are significant enough to induce all YCLers to pay greater attention to sport.'[42]

This syllogism became the basis for YCL strategy. Because it naturalized working-class participation in this way, the YCL concentrated its efforts on those workers already participating in sports and on turning them from 'bosses'' or 'bourgeois' sports to 'revolutionary sports.' The leadership accordingly gave considerably less attention to extension of opportunity to those who had none. Though the YCL was quick to point out the many disadvantages workers faced in other spheres – lack of adequate education and vocational training, exhausting working conditions, low wages, lack of unemployment insurance, the high cost of medical and dental care, and the law prohibiting abortion[43] – it rarely did so in sport. 'Of course we knew about the difficulties the working-class faced in getting adequate recreation. They were obvious,' Dave Kashtan, WSAC national secretary during the early 1930s, responded when I asked him about this. 'What wasn't obvious to everybody was the bourgeois control of sport and its effect upon the working class. Company sports teams were invariably used against union organizing. That's why we opposed them.' Whatever the reason, the YCL gave first priority to 'getting contact with the bourgeois-minded youth' (through sports) and winning them over to socialism. This approach was fully supported by the YCI.[44]

The YCL sought to break bourgeois ideological hegemony in sports by demonstrating their class character through education and propaganda. 'Sports are [not] neutral,' the Young Worker stressed: 'The bosses today use sports as a means of drawing the workers away from the class struggle, they use it as a means of drawing the workers into the cadets, preparing them for future wars, ... to combat the radicalism of the workers, for increasing productivity by building up stronger bodies, and so on.'[45] Many of its articles were devoted to such ideological deconstruction. When Toronto teenager George Young went from rags to riches after winning the $25,000 first prize in the Catalina swim marathon, the Young Worker demurred at the widespread celebrations: 'The young proletarian's splendid performance has been prostituted to serve the needs of capitalism. The immediate financial gains the moving picture magnates, theatre owners, and other exploiters of his feat derive, are the least part of what his battle with the waves yields capitalism. The whole capitalist class profits by a system that keeps workers excitedly interested in trivial matters remote from their true concerns ... The brain-numbing narcotic of the sporting page is perhaps more deadly to the average worker than the more active poison of the editorial page.'[46]

When Canadian newspapers published an admiring photograph of George V patronizing a soccer match at Wembley Stadium in London, the *Young Worker* instructed readers: 'It is important to note what an interest the ruling class takes in sport. It is not only because they are "unemployed" and have nothing else to do but grin and shake hands. There is another reason. The sports life of capitalist countries, although it recruits so large a proportion of the workers, is under the control of the capitalist class. The training is aimed to make labour-haters and strike breakers of the workers ... Their energy and attention are directed away from their everyday struggles and toward boss-controlled sports, where they forget the class struggle.'[47] These arguments were repeated by YCL leaders at WSA field days and exhibitions.

The YCL especially sought to discredit the organizations that it regarded as competitors – the YMCA and YMHA, Boy Scouts, cadet training programs in high schools, industrial recreation programs, the AAU, and Coubertin's Olympics. In particular, it wanted to discredit the developmental promise of 'rational recreation' – what it called 'sports for sports' sake' – by drawing attention to the contradictions between their seemingly benevolent provision of sports and the anti-labour hostility of their other activities. The YMCA was repeatedly 'exposed' for its 'despicable role in suppressing workers in India, China, Korea, etc.' and for strike-breaking and masking the fundamental antagonisms of class relations in North America: 'One of the cleverest schemes devised by the great railway companies for doping their workers is the Railway Y [which makes] the workers "contented" with their slavery and thankful to the boss for exploiting them. [Recently] Ontario CNR Superintendent R.H. Fish declared "the spirit of cooperation was making itself felt in increased efficiency and earnings." And yet the roads had refused to grant a miserable two cents an hour raise to those of their slaves who were receiving less than 40 cents an hour, although an arbitration board had recommended it.'[48] The Boy Scouts, frequently described as 'future

White Guards,' were picketed for their militaristic exercises and their loyalty to British imperialism.[49]

These attacks were stepped up after the Comintern's Sixth Congress in 1928, which proclaimed the doctrine of 'socialism in one country,' the effect of which was to subordinate the communist movement throughout the world to the needs of the Soviet Union. The congress predicted that capitalist collapse would ignite further wars between the imperialist powers and possibly an attack against the Soviet Union. It called for a new revolutionary upsurge and asked the sports clubs to play their part. In response, the Jewish WSA in Toronto staged a demonstration against the 'bourgeois' AAU gymnastics championships at the Canadian National Exhibition (CNE), while other branches held their annual summer events under Counter-Olympic banners. Coubertin's Games were assailed as 'demonstrations of international counter-revolution where the athletes who participate become the advertising agents of the capitalist countries.'[50] The first British Empire Games in Hamilton in 1930 became another target. The *Young Worker* warned that while 'the bosses are cutting the wages of the working class, young and old, they spend millions of dollars for such propaganda as the Empire Sports Games. In this way, they intend to blind the working class to their conditions, and [draw them] into the war preparations of the bosses, against the Soviet Union and the struggle between England and America.'[51]

The WSA sent its own best athletes, invariably the Finnish Canadians, to the RSI's Spartakiads. In 1931, decathlete Eric Kempainen of Port Arthur travelled to Berlin to compete, only to find that the Social Democratic municipal government had refused permission for the Spartakiad to take place in the German capital, necessitating its transfer to Moscow. He continued on to the Soviet Union and competed there. In 1932, WSA athletes competed in the Counter-Olympics in Chicago. In 1934 the WSAC sent its national secretary, Jim Turner, and Sulo Huhtala to the International Conference and Track Meet against War and Fascism in Paris.[52]

In what was known as the tactic of 'united from below,' WSA members were encouraged to join the 'bosses' sports organizations' – the Ys, the AAU clubs, and the industrial teams and leagues – to turn working-class members against their leaders. After the CPC began its own trade union–organizing drive (through the Workers' Unity League, or WUL, formed in 1929), the YCL sought to assist this campaign by creating factory sports leagues. According to Dave Kashtan, writing in the *Party Organizer*. 'There are thousands of young and adult workers who belong to factory teams in some of the most important industries where the Party has as yet no contacts whatsoever. These teams are utilized by the employers as a weapon of keeping down the militancy of the workers. The development of factory workers' sports would assist the Party greatly ... It must also be a weapon in the struggle against the bourgeois sports organizations through raising the issue of workers' sports vs. bosses' sports. Very serious emphasis must also be laid on the organization of sports clubs alongside the Revolutionary Trade Unions ... and the building up of the Workers' Defence Corps.' The WUL actively supported the campaign.[53]

The alternative to 'bosses' sport,' the YCL believed, was a militantly partisan movement that would play a leading role in union organizing, strikes, and other mass struggles. All recreational activity, it argued, ought to be explicitly linked to the needs of class struggle. Games, picnics, and children's camps were to be organized around collective tasks and the legends and aspirations of communism. The polemic against 'sport for sport's sake' constantly reminded members that these activities had an ultimate, external purpose. 'Recreations are serious work, even if the work is done in an atmosphere of laughter and frolic,' N. Gollam explained in the *Worker*. 'Social activities tie those who belong to the League in that closer comradeship that comes from common understanding. They keep the youth in contact with the work that is being done for the union of all the militant youth into one organization for the great task that lies before the workers of the world.'[54] It was 'rational recreation' for revolutionaries.

Needless to say, the best example of socialist sport was provided by the Soviet Union. In the years immediately following the revolution, groups hotly debated the proper role of organized physical activity in the new society. Two of these – the proletkul'tists and the hygienists – stood squarely against development of competitive sport. Following the teachings of Alexander Bogdanov, the proletkul'tists rejected sport on ideological grounds, claiming that physical activity should embody and celebrate a workers' culture that would be distinct from the sports of the capitalist countries of western Europe. They developed, taught, and performed a theatrical gymnastics that drew on and extended the motions of various factory skills. The hygienists believed that sporting contests (particularly boxing and soccer) simply added to the physiological damage that workers and peasants had undergone during centuries of exploitation. They advocated an elaborate system of rehabilitative exercises. Yet both groups had to contend with the growing popularity of sport within Komsomol (the Communist Youth organization), the police, and the military, who found it useful in training, and among ideologues, who thought the struggle for records in sport as attractive as the Stakhanovist pursuit of new quotas in industry. The debate was eventually resolved in the early 1930s in favour of a comprehensive program of physical and health education (which came to be known as 'physical culture') and high-performance sport. Stalin favoured the scientific management of sport.[55]

The *Worker* and the *Young Worker* tended to side with the critics of sports. Their campaign against 'sport for sport's sake' was clearly proletkul´tist in character, if not in origin. Several Canadian columnists echoed hygienist concerns as well. In an early feature on 'Sport in Russia,' William Moriarty extolled the campaign to construct gymnasiums in factories and child care centres, stressing that the 'keynote is not to fool and delude the workers, but to develop their bodies and their minds as benefits a nation that is free from capitalist influence. [This] one day will be the envy of the world. Not a nation where one or two specialists or record breakers stand out, but a nation of consistent health and active life.'[56] Readers were told that Soviet athletes 'vied with each other in raising production' and trained for defence of the revolution. In 1930, for example, a relay of cross-country skiers assisted the Red Army in its offensive against 'Chinese bandits' along the Manchurian border, by delivering messages about the fighting. The *Young Worker* reported: 'This was no mere "endurance test" as we see in capitalist sports. This was no crazed effort to break a "record." The Soviet sportsmen have given the lie to the empty slogan of "sport for sport's sake"! In all their campaigns, they have taken their full share as the physically most perfect specimens of the Russian working class in the construction of socialism. The working sportsmen of Canada must take their full share also in the struggles of the Canadian working class.'[57] This was the example that YCL leaders had in mind when they invited WSA athletes to perform at rallies and demonstrations.

How successful was the YCL in creating a politically conscious, militant sports movement in the Soviet mould? Some WSAs undertook political activity along the lines advocated by the YCL. In 1931, a Calgary baseball club won over the membership of a team from the 'Ukrainian fascist organization.' The Vancouver branch took advantage of the drawing power of its baseball league to solicit signatures and contributions in support of the national CPC leaders facing trial in Toronto. In 1932, during a wrestling tournament, it persuaded YMCA members to join it on a march in support of the unemployed. The Elspeth club from Sylvan Lake, Alberta, recruited nine members from 'boss sport clubs' to its new hockey rink. Several clubs staged 'Tom Mooney Runs' in solidarity with their American comrades' campaign for release of the well-known socialist leader from San Quentin Penitentiary in California. A fierce opponent of U.S. involvement in the First World War, Mooney had been sentenced to life imprisonment in 1916 on trumped-up murder charges. In Montreal, Toronto, and Winnipeg, WSA athletes tried to keep the police, 'the fascists,' and anti-union thugs at bay.

Yet the WSAs had little impact on factories, even less on 'bourgeois sports organizations.' The WSAs are 'completely isolated from the general sports activities of the working class youth,' National Secretary Dave Kashtan wrote in a pre-convention article in 1931. 'Due to the lack of working class education, [many clubs] bear the character of ordinary sports clubs while carrying the name of the WSA. We cannot hope to build up a revolutionary sports organization with the absence of bodies to direct and lead the work. The issue of workers' sports vs. bosses' sports has not been brought out clearly to expose the bourgeois sports organizations. The activity must be broadened out and must be of a far wider and collective character than up to now.'[58]

This was a frequently voiced lament. When an outstanding WSA soccer player from Montreal sought to transfer to a 'bourgeois' team because it promised to massage his legs, it brought howls of outrage from the leadership: 'That such a state of affairs should exist in a revolutionary organization is beyond comprehension. The ideological orientation of the workers in the mass organizations to the necessity of revolutionary struggle and an understanding of the role the party plays, can only come about as a result of the systematic enlightenment in the ranks of the mass organizations. There must be no "Sport for Sport's Sake!" The WSA must serve the general movement by raising the class consciousness of its members, by bringing them into active participation in the general class front against capitalism.'[59]

Not surprisingly, these criticisms did not sit well with members of local WSAs. One of the great attractions of the WSAs was that they brought together people of similar backgrounds for shared moments of recreation and culture and to have some fun. Most of the members were sympathetic to the concept of a working-class sports movement and to left-wing causes generally, but they wanted to get on with it and do some sports.

The daunting task of infiltrating other organizations for the purpose of propaganda and recruitment was an additional stress they did not need. Their greatest challenges were organizational and financial, not political. If there was no sympathetic 'mass organization,' WSAs had to scramble to find facilities and equipment. In Drumheller, Alberta, the WSA went inactive the entire winter of 1927–8 when local businessmen refused to rent it enough space. Clubs lost members because they moved to find work or sought the better equipment and coaching provided by the Y. Other needs were knowledgeable leaders, rulebooks, uniforms, and funds for travel. In these circumstances, club secretaries wrote that they needed practical help, not words. 'We must maintain a proper balance between propaganda and serious athletics,' the Alberta secretary advised. 'A successful team should give us all the propaganda we care for.' On the few occasions it chose to acknowledge these criticisms, the national WSAC committee responded by urging more YCLers to become involved, but to no avail.[60]

The best clubs were reluctant to drop what they were doing for the unlikely projects the YCL wanted – trying to win members away from the YMCA, or leafletting plant gates in an attempt to establish factory leagues. They resented any suggestion that they were letting down the side. 'I guess I was primarily interested in what they called "sport for sport's sake,"' Emmanuel Orlick, once director of the London WSA and a national training school for WSA leaders, has recalled: 'I shared some of their criticisms of the Y – I was upset that it wouldn't lower its membership fees for the unemployed, for example – so I helped them form the London WSA (actually we called it the London Unemployed League). But I had no intention of publicly discrediting the Y or running a campaign against it – I was working there at the time and I got a room at the Y for the League to use. I was always prepared to defend the WSA in public, but I wanted a career in physical education, and it didn't look like the WSA had anything like that in mind. They wanted me to do everything myself.'[61]

Orlick would remain a thorn in the side of the 'bourgeois sports organizations' for the rest of his life,[62] but he 'eventually lost interest in the WSA and left.' The Kaczors never quit – in fact, in 1935, Fred travelled to Toronto to become national organizer – but they have said much the same. As their reputation grew through the 1930s, they continued to be critical of the sports establishment, and they lobbied for improved public programs, but they abhorred the idea that the athletes they coached were regarded as a defence corps by the party. They welcomed invitations to perform and parade because these activities gave them something to train for, not because they advanced the class struggle. 'Most athletes – even the political ones – came to the gym because they wanted to work out,' Walter Kaczor said. 'They didn't want to discuss the political questions there.'

Of course, the YCL had other worries and responsibilities, especially when the Depression greatly exacerbated the economic and social difficulties of working people. 'I was once walking down St. Lawrence Avenue [in Montreal] posting notices for the Spartakiad campaign,' Dave Kashtan remembers: 'I came across 200 French-Canadian ladies who had just walked off the job because the foreman had fired somebody. So I spoke to them briefly and led them back to our office. They needed someone to negotiate for them, find strike support, places for people to live because they didn't have any money, and so on. It was two weeks before I even looked at the Spartakiad posters again.'[63] In addition to sports and union organizing, Kashtan and the few other full-time leaders were also responsible for writing for party journals, establishing youth centres, and conducting political education. Most of them had very little previous experience in sport. Several, including Kashtan and his brother Bill, were arrested for their activities. 'My first arrest came when I was leafletting against "bosses' sports" outside the Vickers plant in Montreal, the second time for addressing a meeting of the unemployed. It got me a year in Bordeaux jail for "sedition," ' Dave Kashtan recounted. His imprisonment came shortly after he had started to work on a WSA magazine, the *Sports Parade*. It set back publication three years.

Several WSAs were victims of the same repression. Clubs in Lachine, Oshawa, and Toronto reported that the police forced them to cancel events or burst in to break them up as they started. In Vancouver, the police seized schedules, membership lists, and equipment in a raid on the WSA.[64] There was also the time-consuming struggle to maintain 'life and love' during the Depression. 'During the first two years of our marriage, we were evicted 14 times,' Dave Kashtan remembers. Frightening police attacks, the movement's economic difficulties, and the not inconsiderable personal pressures they created help explain why the YCL leaders had little time and patience for the more mundane tasks of developing the WSA as a sports movement.

The YCL's failure to address WSAs' sports-related needs eventually cost it the strongest section, the Finnish-Canadian clubs. After the WSAC was founded, the YCL began to press the Finnish-Canadian members to give up their separate identity. This demand took two forms, both stemming from Comintern directives. First, in keeping with the 'bolshevization' of the CPC, which ordered dissolution of the language sections and their replacement by units organized around the workplace, the WSAC sought to 'liquidate' the FWSAC in the interests of building a 'unified' national organization. Second, Finnish Canadians were also urged to take up 'mass Canadian games' and throw their considerable organizational skills into recruiting English-speaking workers. 'We do not wish to be too critical of the Finnish Workers' Sports, which form the vanguard of our movement,' the *Young Worker* wrote during this campaign, 'but there is a strong need for augmenting these individual sports with popular group sports such as hockey, basketball, football and baseball, which will more readily interest the broad strata of workers in mines, factories, and farms.'[65] In 1932, the FWSAC accepted this edict and agreed to dissolve on condition that it be allowed to keep its own sports. The Finnish clubs became direct members of the district associations. Yet the experience proved so disappointing that five years later they re-established their own national organization, the Finnish-Canadian Amateur Sports Federation, and ended all formal ties with the WSAC.

Other scholars have stressed the ethnic divisions in the working class. Within the communist movement, divisions were so strong that they ultimately defeated the 'bolshevization' campaign.[66] Ethnic loyalties also helped produce the Finns' walkout and the ultimate breakup of the WSAC. The Finns deeply resented the 'Canadianizing' campaign and loss of the distinct identity that their own organization gave them. They also felt that they got little in return for all their efforts on behalf of the WSAC. While they put out the welcome mat for athletes from other communities, they were impatient with the other groups' relative lack of competitiveness and came to feel that it would be easier just to go their own way. There was another factor, too. Many of the Finnish-Canadian sportspersons felt uneasy with the political line of the WSA. This discomfort must have been difficult for English-Canadian leaders such as Kashtan to perceive, for the Finnish sports leaders shared the CPC's revolutionary goals and openly campaigned for them. During the Comintern's militant period the FWSAC maintained a hard line, restricting membership to trade unionists and those associated with the FOC. Some clubs even opposed competition with anybody else. One participant recounted a family that had been 'run out of Beaver Lake because the father had travelled through Amsterdam to watch the bourgeois Olympics [of 1928] on his way back from Finland.'[67] A number of the Finnish-Canadian members volunteered for Soviet Karelia and the Spanish civil war.

Yet the Finnish-Canadian sportspersons were not prepared to reduce every aspect of participation to an instance of class struggle. Many of them liked to run or ski or wrestle better than anything else. They were also heavily influenced by the social democratic traditions of the SWSI. The few communists who remained in Finland after the civil war did not form their own sports organization but stayed as a faction within TUL and competed in the Workers' Olympics. They continually pushed for fusion of the two internationals. The Finns in Canada avidly read the extensive TUL sports press and occasionally brought in TUL instructors and athletes to conduct clinics and stage exhibitions. They, too, believed in a measure of 'sport for sport's sake.'

The split was precipitated by the WSAC's perennial lack of organization. Though the Finnish athlete Jim Turner (Terho Tuori) took over from Kashtan, the Finns became convinced that 'the WSAC was going nowhere. It couldn't in reality fulfill the organization's goals. Meetings were never called, debts grew, and the level of activity declined. The district executives seemed neither interested nor capable of organizing any ongoing events. Only the Finnish clubs were paying dues. There were 40 Finnish clubs with 2,000 members, men were idle because of the depression, and we had nothing to do.' Most participants held Turner, who died in the USSR in 1974, responsible for the organizational shambles. 'He was a beautiful speaker, he could translate from Finnish to English faster than you and I ordinarily speak, but he could never finish a task. We were always discovering letters he'd never mailed out,' William Heikilla has recalled.[68]

In 1935, at the urging of Toronto Yritys, the Finns pushed for a more active national executive and created a technical committee, composed entirely of their own members, to coordinate their own events. But the frustrations continued. A year later, the technical committee complained that 'the [national] executive has for a long time been totally incapable of directing affairs and it has apparently gone to sleep.' After another year of unfulfilled promises, the Finnish-Canadian members decided to re-establish their own association. They would continue to associate with the other clubs, and invite them to their events, but they had given up on the national movement.[69]

The Turn to the Popular Front

In 1934, after the prohibition and repression of communist and socialist parties, trade unions, sports clubs, and cultural organizations had begun in Germany and fascism had started spreading in France, the Comintern changed course and ordered new anti-fascist defensive alliances 'without difference of party or religion.' These 'popular front' alliances were prompted in large part by western European communist party members who saw the need for a broad progressive mobilization against fascism. They were confirmed by the Seventh Congress of the CI in 1935. In sport, the RSI softened its polemic against the SWSI and sought a joint campaign against the 1936 Olympics in Germany. In France and Norway, warring communist and socialist workers' federations were reunited in anticipation of the signal from the top. In Canada, the WSAC quickly buried the hatchet in its relations with the YMCA and the AAU.

The 'united front' promised new gains. The WSAC announced that it would send a team of 40 Canadian athletes and coaches for competitions and to see sports schools, health clinics, factory fitness programs, and Young Pioneer summer camps in the Soviet Union. The tour would serve as an advertisement for new members and even 'arouse the interest of bourgeois sportswriters.' The trip to Russia did in fact intrigue athletes and reporters. Initially, a number of national champions agreed to go, including 1932 Olympic high-jump bronze medallist Eva Dawes and 1934 Empire Games winners Eric Coy and Thelma Norris. Em Orlick, who had just been appointed assistant director of physical education at the University of Western Ontario, agreed to serve as delegation head. But the AAU changed its mind at the last minute and forbade the athletes to go. When Dawes went ahead, she was suspended. The resulting controversy generated more publicity in the daily press than the WSA had ever received.

In the end, nine athletes, organizers, and public health officials travelled to the Soviet Union for a four-week stay. They competed in two track meets, attended numerous other competitions and cultural events, and toured historic sites, factories, hospitals, parks, and schools, in the first significant sporting exchange between Canada and the new socialist state. The *Toronto Star* took advantage of the occasion to send Alexandrine Gibb for a series of features on the Soviet Union. Both Gibb and Orlick, who wrote articles and gave a series of speeches after the delegation's return, reported at length on the Soviet system of 'mass sport.' While Gibb was critical, Orlick was greatly impressed by the Soviets' scientific approach to health and physical activity and their 'pride, the fire, the spirit of cooperation or lack of selfishness' in the face of extreme hardship. 'It lifts you from a dull sordid world of personal gain, selfish grasping principles, hunger, unemployment, hate, greed, jealousy, everything contemptible, yes it lifts you to a higher, cleaner, brighter life.' Orlick's detailed observations indicate that the institutional supports for high-performance sport – the vaunted Soviet model of sports development, which transformed competition in the 'bourgeois Olympics' following the Second World War – were already well in place by 1935.[70]

The workers' sports movement gained even more publicity and supporters during its year-long campaign against the 1936 Olympics in Nazi Germany. Hitler had no delusions that 'sports and politics do not mix.' Soon after he seized power in 1933, he ordered all Jewish, communist, and socialist sports clubs to be shut down and all others to accept Nazi direction and 'Aryan cleansing' or face the same fate. It was not only the vast workers' sports movement and the Jewish sports clubs that were repressed in this way, but the Catholic Youth Organizations and many Protestant clubs. At the same time, Hitler made elaborate plans to turn the 1936 Olympics, which had been awarded to Berlin and Garmisch-Partenkirchen (Winter Olympics) under the Weimar Republic, into a showcase for Nazi propaganda. In response to an American protest, the IOC obtained a promise from Hitler that persecution of Jewish athletes would end and declared that the Games would go ahead as planned. But Nazi atrocities increased in every sphere of German society, and protests mounted around the world. In the United States, a broad campaign of opposition fell just $2\frac{1}{2}$ votes short of taking the Amateur Athletic Union out of the Games. The pro-Berlin forces were led by Avery Brundage. When those opposed to the Nazi Olympics either resigned or were turfed out, Brundage became AAU president and a member of the IOC.[71]

Canadian opposition to participation in the 1936 Olympics was led by the WSAC. True sportsmanship requires peace and respect for human rights, neither of which existed in Nazi Germany, spokespersons such as Pat Forkin argued. He sought to have the Games transferred to a site outside Germany. The campaign won the support of the Canadian Trades and Labour Congress, Toronto Mayor James Simpson, the Ontario CCF, and prominent church and university leaders but made little headway among the AAU and the WAAF. Like most Canadians and the dominion government of W.L. Mackenzie King, the amateur organizations chose to ignore destruction of the Jews and the other victims of fascism. Except for Bobbie Rosenfeld and *Vancouver Sun* sports editor Hal Straight, the major sports writers weighed in against the boycott. Alexandrine Gibb suggested that the Olympics were none of the communists' business. Ted Reeve suggested that 'any good athlete who lets the threats of a little trouble in

Berlin keep him away ... doesn't rate as a champion, no matter how fast he can run or how high he can jump.'

When the AAU and the WAAF decided to go ahead, the WSA picketed fund-raising activities. In Sudbury, its protests prevented Alex Hurd, an Inco miner and speedskater who had been named to the Winter Olympic team on the condition that he raise his own boat fare, from making the trip. Inco had agreed to help if the miners followed suit, but they refused, on the slogan 'No money for Hitler,' so Hurd stayed home. Several prominent Jewish athletes stayed away from the AAU's Olympic Trials. In July, the WSAC sent five non-WSA athletes, including Eva Dawes and popular Toronto boxers Sam Luftspring and Norman 'Baby' Yack, to the counter-Olympic 'People's Games' in Barcelona. But the People's Olympics never took place, as Hitler's ally Francisco Franco began his uprising against the republic on the morning of the opening ceremonies. The struggle to defend the Spanish Republic would unite the left for another generation.[72]

The turn to the 'popular front' stimulated a round of new activity. A number of clubs began to offer swimming instruction to their members, using public pools and lakeside beaches. The Montreal club added boxing and table tennis to its program and began to challenge for the supremacy of city leagues in soccer and basketball. The Vancouver branch created the Progressive Hikers' Association for students and unemployed youth uninterested in competitive sports. In Toronto, local union leaders long hostile to the CPC started their own leagues in bowling, ice hockey, and softball, in conjunction with the existing workers' clubs. 'Playing and competing against each other in games and on gym floors would develop a strong bond of friendship between every trade union member and this would aid us greatly in our organization of the unorganized trades,' explained Joe Robson, secretary of the Allied Printing Trades (of Toronto), in clear echo of the earlier WUL line.

In 1937, the Trades and Labour Congress passed a resolution favouring workers' leagues. One stimulus was the support given union sports programs by the AFL and the CIO in the United States, but the WSA's Fred Kaczor and his wife, Florence, played a significant role. When funds were available, Fred was spared from his job in the CPC printing plant so that he could work as a full-time organizer and instructor, and Florence started programs for girls and women. The Kaczors helped found four new clubs in Toronto and one in Cobourg. Other new clubs and events were reported in Le Pas and Vancouver. There was still opportunity for political action. Clubs regularly passed the hat for striking workers, Finnish volunteers in Soviet Karelia, or Canadians fighting in Spain, such as Alberta boxer and WSA organizer Bill Medvenko, who became director of physical fitness for the Mackenzie-Papineau Battalion. WSAers Leige Claire of Toronto and Charles Martin and Scott McGrindle of Vancouver lost their lives in Spain.

Without the obligation to discredit 'bosses' sports,' the movement turned its full attention to the challenge of obtaining adequate workers' leisure, health, and sports. Many clubs began to campaign for better public recreation. In the winter of 1937, the WSA persuaded the Toronto Labour Council and the Toronto and District Football League to join it and five clubs – the Clarion Football Club (the 'Redshirts'), the Cosmopolitan Athletic Club, the Deltas, the Spadina Avenue Labour Sports Club, and Yritys – in a delegation to city hall to ask for improvements in parks and recreation. Party leaders seeking elected office often spearheaded these efforts. In Toronto's ward 5, aldermanic and board of education candidates Stewart Smith and John Weir promised better amenities in Trinity-Bellwoods Park in their 1936 and 1937 campaigns, and when Weir was elected he persistently lobbied for greater funding.[73]

But in the attempt to prove popular, the WSAC lost some of its distinctive character. At the 1935 annual meeting, the rule prohibiting competition against bourgeois clubs was dropped and the name of the national organization was changed to the less contestative Canadian Amateur Sports Federation (CASF), with most local associations becoming 'Universal' and 'Cosmopolitan' Athletic Clubs. In 1937, the CASF reluctantly accepted the AAU's ban against Canadian participation in the Workers' Olympics and decided not to send a team to Antwerp.[74] A number of clubs abandoned left-wing causes altogether. The Winnipeg UAC described itself as a 'non-political independent sports club. [Our] purpose is to provide physical training and recreation to all young people irrespective of their nationality or beliefs.' Among the new members was Duff Roblin, who would become a Conservative premier of the province. The club stayed away from any political demonstration. In 1939, it turned down an invitation to participate in the annual May Day celebrations 'due to the varied opinions towards May Day. It holds no grievances towards anyone who does or does not participate ... but the club as a whole will not take part.'[75]

The Toronto-based *Clarion* (the renamed *Worker*) began to cover commercial and intercollegiate sports and to handicap the horses. Sports editor W.E. 'Stuffy' Richards defended the turn on the grounds that 'horse racing and sports are of interest to the masses.' Replying to readers who complained that commercial sports 'are a racket,' he pointed out that 'everything is a racket under the capitalist system. But are we going to get anywhere by taking narrow-minded opinions to the daily enjoyment that the masses get under the rotten conditions that exist at the present time?'[76] Leaders such as Fred Kaczor agreed with him. Richards's eye for swift thoroughbreds – once he predicted seven winners on a nine-race card – proved more beneficial to circulation than years of Leninist bombast.

The *Clarion* nevertheless maintained its regular coverage of workers' and Soviet sports and never lost its feisty character. It added a gossipy women's column and began to campaign for the unionization and labour rights of athletes. It decried corrupt judging and the lack of safety in boxing and horse racing, the 'slave wages' of journeymen NHL and Major League Baseball players, and the arbitrary firings of coaches and managers who disobeyed their 'owners.' Following the lead of New York's *Daily Worker*, the first non-Black newspaper to campaign for the integration of Major League Baseball, it extolled the feats of such Negro League stars as Satchel Paige and Josh Gibson and argued for their ability and right to play in any 'big league.' (Neither has been given much credit for it, but the Black and communist press 'played a major role in mobilizing left and liberal opinion to fight for the integration of Major League Baseball.')[77] For the Olympic sports, it called for abolition of amateurism and replacement of the AAU by a national board elected by athletes and coaches. 'It is time the athlete ran his own affairs. There are too many careerists supposedly governing sport and too few real athletes intelligently cooperating with each other.'[78]

The *Clarion*'s most persistent campaign was for better fitness and recreation opportunities for Canadians. It called for repeal of sabbatarian legislation, vast expansion of public facilities, and wholesale distribution of protective equipment to cut down on the number of injuries in sports. Whenever a cash-strapped municipal government considered implementing user charges for recreation, as the city of Toronto did in 1938, or a softball or soccer league increased its entry fees, sports editor Bert Whyte (who took over from Richards) mobilized readers against such moves. At the same time, the paper gave full publicity to the innovative British Columbia Pro-Rec Program, which provided new facilities and physical fitness activities to thousands, especially women and the unemployed, and the efforts of Em Orlick's National Physical Fitness League and others to bring about national fitness legislation. In 1938, the *Clarion* began to publish a daily, full-sized afternoon edition, and its sports pages were among the liveliest in the country.

Yet the CPC's leaders seemed to lose interest in directing workers' sports. Perhaps they felt lingering resentment because the movement had been completely captured by 'sports for sport's sake,' but most probably they recognized the real limitations to their own energies and resources and the ethnic divisions in the membership. On 2 August 1937, when the Finnish Canadians officially withdrew from the CASF, the national executive decided to dissolve what remained, except for an advisory commission. Individual clubs continued to prosper, but without any pretense of belonging to a national organization.[79]

Most of the activity conducted by the various sports clubs came to a halt in 1940, when the dominion cabinet ordered the RCMP to seize the facilities of the Communist Party of Canada's (CPC) 'mass organizations.' Only a few Finnish-Canadian clubs not officially tied to the Finnish Organization of Canada escaped the crackdown. When Germany invaded the Soviet Union and the CPC endorsed the Canadian war effort, a number of former Universal Athletic Club (UAC) instructors enlisted and became physical fitness instructors. After the war, the Ukrainian Labour Farmer Temple Association revived a number of gymnastic groups and they, along with a few Finnish Canadian Amateur Sports Federation clubs, flourished for several decades, providing many cherished programs for members and their friends. But the UACs were never resumed. Workers' sports organizations still operate in Austria, Finland, and France, and there is still a workers' sports international – the Comité sportif international du travail (CSIT), based in Brussels – but the Canadian movement died with the Canadian Amateur Sports Federation. Despite the interest of several CCF clubs during the 1930s, the social democratic parties in Canada have rarely thought about sports. The defection of the Soviet Union to the 'bourgeois Olympics' hastened the demise of the international communist sports movement. With the mounting success of Soviet athletes – by 1939 they claimed 44 world records – Soviet leaders became much more interested in beating the capitalists at their own games. The Red Sport Internation (RSI) was dissolved sometime in the late 1930s, and in 1952 the USSR and its satellites in central and eastern Europe entered the IOC's Olympics. Many of those who continued to champion workers' sports were executed or imprisoned in Stalinist purges.[80] Until the collapse of the Soviet system, the CPC regularly boasted about the remarkable achievements of Soviet-bloc athletes.

As a political movement, workers' sports failed to take root in Canada. Its smartly uniformed athletes may have discouraged Canadian fascists from attacking communist rallies in Montreal, Toronto, and Winnipeg, but they did not completely protect CPC leaders from the police. Though the WSAs supported a number of political campaigns initiated by the RSI and the YCL, they never became the path of recruitment into the party they were hoped to become. Some workers who joined through the Workers' Unity League knew of the WSAs' existence. So did the AAU and WAAF athletes and officials who were forced to respond to their campaign against the 1936 Olympic Games. But for the most part, as the *Young Worker* frequently lamented, 'the WSA was too isolated from the masses of the working youth.' It was clearly an opposition, but never one that achieved a major presence, let alone an 'alternative hegemony.'

The reasons for this failure include scarcity of skilled leadership, ethnic divisions within the membership, and police repression, all exacerbated by the hardships and struggles of the Depression. The YCL's militant sectarianism during the WSAs' formative years blinded it to the enormity of the challenge many workers and their families faced just obtaining good recreation and led it into insensitive polemics against 'sport for sport's sake.' Neither the leaders nor the locals managed to achieve a 'balance between propaganda and athletics.' At the same time, the WSA was buffeted by the same rising tide of commercial sport that washed over the AAU. Despite its go-for-the-jugular militancy, the WSA's approach was increasingly framed by the same expectations as the competitions popularized by the sports cartels and the mass media. The WSA was no more successful than the amateurs in holding back penetration of the popular commercial teams and spectacles into their members' experience.

But the WSA was not without accomplishment. The culture that it provided may not have been oppositional, but it warmly welcomed and affirmed workers and their interests. Member clubs provided much-needed recreational opportunities for a sizeable number of people who did not enjoy access to, could not afford, and were not very welcome in the middle-class, pro-British organizations that dominated amateur sports during the period. It was not just radical immigrants who faced such difficulties. 'Ethnicity, language, religion and other barriers defined [all] Ukrainians as outsiders, causing many young people to shy away from mainstream Canadian clubs ... Those who did venture into the non-Ukrainian world were often disappointed [by] discrimination, indoctrination and exclusion.'[81] There were also familial pressures. 'Many immigrant parents and most immigrant religious and ethnocultural leaders [saw sports] as a threat to group solidarity, a process of deprivation which meant the loss of ethnoculture, parental control, esteem between generations, and sometimes salvation itself.'[82] For working-class immigrants, and left-wing immigrants in particular, the WSA provided a supportive atmosphere for mediation of the newly discovered interest in sports. Participants fondly remember personal challenge, social interaction, travel, and adventure.

In the case of gymnastics and cross-country skiing, the WSAs often provided the only opportunities to be found anywhere. During the interwar years, Canadian gymnastics were on the decline. Outside the YMCA and a few schools, the sport was largely forgotten – the AAU discouraged it because it was 'ethnic.' Cross-country skiing had yet to develop any organizational base apart from the Scandinavian immigrants and college students who held races on a local basis.[83] In both sports, as the Finnish Canadians and the Kaczors discovered, those interested had to provide opportunities for themselves if they wanted them at all. By helping out, the WSAs provided another familiar reference for immigrants who loved to pursue sports. In addition, the WSAs encouraged, perhaps even influenced, a small number of future leaders in Canadian sport and physical education. Em Orlick and Fred Kazor played key roles in the revival of Canadian gymnastics after the Second World War. George Nick used the skills he learned at the Winnipeg UAC to develop the first provincially initiated recreation program in Manitoba.[84]

Though their influence is harder to measure, the WSA and the communist press provided the first systematic critique of capitalist sports to be heard in Canada. Others shared their concern about the alienating nature of professional, and highly competitive sports. But the WSA was the first to draw attention to the ideological aspects of the Olympic, professional and industrial sports and the legitimizing implications of sports coverage in the mainstream press. It was one of the few organizations during the period to apply the logic of industrial relations to sports and campaign for unionization of professional and Olympic athletes. The questions that the WSA posed are now critically explored as part of the growing sociology of sports. To be sure, the WSA shut down its critical faculties when it considered physical activity in the Soviet Union or its own propaganda. But organizers such as Dave Kashtan and Em Orlick, and sportswriters such as 'Stuffy' Richards and Bert Whyte, encouraged both enjoyment of sports and physical activity and critical scepticism about many dominant practices. It is a stance we could well emulate today.

5

Brand-Name Hockey

On 22 November 1917, in the midst of a dominion election and bitter debates about conscription, five sports entrepreneurs met in Montreal's Windsor Hotel to launch a new venture. Ostensibly, it was the annual meeting of the eight-year-old National Hockey Association (NHA), but in the absence of Toronto owner Ed Livingstone they created a new organization, the National Hockey League (NHL), to exclude him. They wanted to increase their profits from hockey. 'Livingstone was always arguing,' Tommy Gorman, representing the Ottawa club, told Elmer Ferguson of the *Montreal Herald.* 'Now we can get on with the business of making money.'[1]

The men who formed the new league – Gorman, George Kendall (sometimes known as Kennedy) of the Montreal Canadiens, Sam Lichtenheim of the Montreal Wanderers, and NHA Secretary Frank Calder, who became the NHL's president – were mavericks in the sports world of wartime Canada. At a time when most sports bodies had cancelled operations for the duration of the war, the NHA spared no effort to stay in business. In 1916, in the interests of enhancing reinforcements to the depleted Canadian forces in France, the Ottawa club asked permission to withdraw from that year's competition but retain the franchise. The NHA refused, transferring the franchise to Edgar Dey, manager of the local arena. It also recruited a team from the 228th Battalion Team and then took out insurance on the contingency that the players would be called up before the season was over. Several players were no more patriotic, enlisting only to play hockey with military teams.[2]

Moreover, as their candid boasting suggested, the promoters of the new league were unabashed sports capitalists. They sought to forge identities that could be turned into consumer loyalties. If in order to profit, they needed to alter the rules, transform the labour relations of the game, or move their operations to other communities, even another country, they were prepared to do it. In short, while the amateur leaders were preoccupied by the use value of men's sports, the NHL sought to enhance the exchange value of one of them – ice hockey.

Initially, it was an uphill battle. It took another week for the NHL to obtain a team in hockey-mad Toronto without Livingstone, several years to get rid of him altogether. The new Toronto franchise was given to the owners of the Toronto Arena Co. Three weeks into the inaugural schedule, 1917–18, the Montreal Arena was destroyed by fire, and Lichtenheim disbanded the Montreal Wanderers, a celebrated team with four Stanley Cups to its credit. For the first few years, the NHL had to struggle along with just three teams. In 1918, Livingstone sought to get another franchise by threatening legal action against the 'conspirators' who had formed the NHL. Unsuccessful, he then sought to revive the NHA, forcing the other clubs to attend a meeting just to vote it out of existence. In 1920, Livingstone tried to form a rival league; his attempt came to naught, but it caused the NHL considerable embarrassment.

The public reception was no more certain. The NHL was just one of many fledgling commercial leagues. Elmer Ferguson was the only reporter to attend its founding meeting. When the results filtered out many accounts were derisive. 'Same Old Story: NHA Uncertain,' mocked the headline in a brief, one-paragraph story in the Toronto *Globe*. Newspapers were accustomed to giving amateur games the major play. The notion lingered in many circles that professional sports were somewhat shady. Anyone who would take money to win might also take it to lose. Though the amateur game could be just as rough, many held professionalism and 'shamateurism' accountable for the violent and loutish hockey behavior that brought down the censure of editorial page, pulpit, and bench. Even those who admired the ability of professional athletes might not want to have anything to do with them. In 1920, University of Toronto star Bill Box turned down an NHL contract because his parents objected to his playing with the pros.[3]

But eventually the promoters realized much of their ambition. In just two decades, the NHL became the best-known sports organization in Canada, with its players household names and the term 'professional' synonymous with 'excellence.' Revenues increased many times over. In 1917–18, the Ottawa club, playing in the second largest rink in the league, the 7,000-capacity Dey Rink, took in a total revenue of $18,500 and made a profit of $1,000. Two decades later, the Montreal Canadiens earned the lowest revenue in the league, yet averaged $185,683. If prices for franchises can be taken as a measure of profitability, they too increased significantly. In 1921, George Kendall's widow sold the club to Joseph Cattarinich, Leo Dandurand, and Louis Letourneau for $11,000. In 1935, the Canadian Arena Co., which owned the Montreal Forum, where the team then played its games, purchased it for $165,000.[4]

During the 1930s, except for horseracing, the NHL enjoyed greater revenues in Canada than any other form of commercial sport.[5] Only the long-established International (Baseball) League came close, but its Montreal and Toronto franchises limped through the Depression. The Royals lost money for seven consecutive years. The baseball Maple Leafs could never match their NHL rivals at the box office. In 1932, the baseball Leafs drew a paltry 49,963 paying fans, fewer than the women's softball teams at Sunnyside Park. In 1934, with the introduction of night games and a winning season, the baseball Leafs increased total attendance to 211,670, in their best Depression season. By comparison, during the 1930s the NHL and the hockey Leafs attracted a regular-season high of 282,211 (1937–8), a low of 204,377 (1932–3), plus an average of 55,462 for playoffs. In addition, thousands of spectators paid their way to other attractions in the club's Depression-built facility, Maple Leaf Gardens. Total paid attendance for all events averaged 887,399 per year. While the baseball club lost its stadium for back taxes in 1931, the parent corporation of the hockey club, Maple Leaf Gardens Limited (MLG), operated in the black from its very first game. During its first ten years, it averaged annual revenues of $363,186, and net annual profits of $84,724. The value of MLG common shares increased from $1 in 1931 to $8 in 1939.[6]

The success story of the NHL is well known, in broad outline if not in specifics. But there is a tendency to take it for granted, as one of the eternal verities of Canadian life. Popular historians of the game, such as Dick Beddoes, Stan Fischler, Trent Frayne, Neil Isaacs, and Brian McFarlane, assume an unchanging superiority and dominance of the NHL even when they try to convey the differing conditions of earlier periods. In his insightful, unpublished doctoral thesis, Frank Cosentino documents the growth and legitimation of 'professional' sport in Canada, but he too suggests that it was an inevitable consequence of industrialization and rapid urbanization.[7]

It is important to assert a note of contingency here. The social transformations that accompanied development of industrial capitalism certainly provided favourable conditions for sale of sport spectacles. In many ways, they were augmented by the First World War. Recruitment and expanding wartime production accelerated urbanization. The call to self-denial and sacrifice and the horrors of the trenches contributed to a desire for peacetime 'frivolity' and entertainment. The emphasis on military manliness reinforced the fetish of the body and the fascination with sport that had begun a century before.[8]

But commercial sport did not take off as if its success were guaranteed. Growth was slow and uncertain. Sports entrepreneurs collected only a fraction of the revenue garnered by other popular entertainments of the day, such as motion pictures. During the 1930s, for example, reported motion-picture theatre revenue in Canada averaged $29.2 million per year, compared to $750,000 for professional hockey.[9] More NHL franchises failed than succeeded. Between 1917 and 1940, eight teams went under: Hamilton Tigers, Montreal Maroons, Montreal Wanderers, Ottawa Senators, Philadelphia Quakers, Pittsburgh Pirates, Quebec Bulldogs, and St Louis Eagles. The Canadiens almost failed as well. 'Things got so bad during the Depression that there was even talk of transferring the franchise to (horror of horrors) Cleveland.'[10]

In 1933, the Detroit Falcons went bankrupt, but they were purchased by James Norris, who owned the Olympia Arena. He subsidized the team for years from the huge profits he made from his vast holdings in grain, railways, and real estate. The Boston franchise would also have collapsed if Norris had not helped owner Charles Adams pay his mortgages.[11] In 1936–7, the NHL acquired the New York Americans and tried running the franchise itself for several years, only to abandon the effort and disband the team in the fall of 1942. Outside the NHL, entire leagues failed. Despite a growing population base and several Stanley Cup teams, the Western Canada Hockey League was disbanded in 1926. An attempt was made to revive it in 1932–3, but it failed after one season. The professional lacrosse league that thrived in British Columbia prior to and immediately after the war folded in 1924. The professional football league that Lionel Conacher started in Toronto in 1934 lasted only one season.[12]

It is not readily apparent that the NHLers were cleverer than their competitors. Were they simply favoured by circumstances? How did the strict amateurs' triumph of 1909 and the uneven development of the Canadian economy structure their choices? What were the consequences of the promoters' triumph for Canadian sports as a whole? These matters need to be reinserted into the story.

The Origins of Commercial Sport in Canada

As we saw in chapter 1, the same dynamic that enabled 'reconstruction' of game contests – development of a rapidly urbanizing industrial capitalist economy – enhanced possibilities for production and sale of sport-related goods, services, and spectacles. The interrelated transformations of work, urban space, and culture all helped create a market for commercial leisure, which entrepreneurs eagerly sought to expand and fill. In sports, they constructed rental facilities, manufactured equipment, established instructional programs, published inspirational and technical information, and staged highly publicized contests. The aggressive advertisement of these new commercial opportunities furthered the popularity and accessibility of sports, thereby adding to the potential market.

Most early commercial sports contests were one-time events, pitting two competitors against each other or involving very small fields. These had the advantage of requiring only small capital outlays and rarely needed specialized facilities. This was the entrepreneurial stage of commercial sport: a single promoter staged a single contest involving a small number of athletes. If events were well publicized and did not become too predictable, they could attract a segment of the limited market available. As late as 1912, as the professional careers of Tom Longboat, Fred Meadows, and Alf Shrubb readily demonstrate, a single, matched race – two runners chasing each other around a small track for distances up to a marathon – could draw sellout crowds in many Canadian and American arenas.[13]

Development of profitable entertainments from the team games codified in the latter half of the nineteenth century proved more difficult, requiring the cooperation of two or more clubs or associations, larger and more specialized facilities, and ultimately abandonment of the 'challenge' system in favour of a league schedule. Because more athletes were involved, even if they were amateur and only their travelling expenses had to be covered, the potential revenue had to be greater to cover the costs. The impetus for commercialization of team games came from several directions. By the 1870s, land costs, taxes, and the expense of uniforms, equipment, and travel led amateur baseball and lacrosse teams to pass the hat for donations. Initially there were debates about the propriety of doing so, but admission was soon charged without question.[14] In the case of hockey, the first ticket sales were made by the rink owners who rented the ice to amateur teams. When they discovered the great popularity of the new sport, they began booking games between successful teams, offering a percentage of the gate to the teams as inducement. The early rinks were built primarily for pleasure skating, so fans were often jammed into the narrow corridor between the walls and the boards.

Commodification of games was inextricably caught up with the representational character of teams and the appeal of 'winning.' Athletes and strongmen had long been regarded as 'champions' or 'defenders' of individuals and collectivities in European societies, in both deadly combat and symbolic game-contests. Despite their emphasis on social interchange and the possibilities for character-building afforded by sports, early amateur leaders clothed their own activities in this tradition, claiming representational status for not only teams but events and entire games. In 1867, the lacrosse game that George Beers promoted was played only within the Montreal region, yet he awarded a 'national championship' to the best team and demanded that Parliament declare his creation 'Canada's national sport.' His astute public relations led to a long-standing myth that he was successful, but there is 'no evidence in the parliamentary debates or Acts to support the contention that [lacrosse] was proclaimed Canada's national game' in the nineteenth century.[15] (Not until 1994 did Parliament recognize lacrosse as 'Canada's national summer sport' and hockey as 'Canada's national winter game.') Local boosters, politicians, sportswriters, and bookmakers were also eager to confer representational status on athletes and press them to excel, as the careers of any of the successful individuals or teams of the late nineteenth century attest. Of course, Hanlan was the most important example, but every community had its favourite champion.[16] These associations were reinforced by the desire of elites to create popular images that would transcend and therefore blur class differences and that of new arrivals to find common points of identity with their new neighbours.

Professionalism began as an outgrowth of stake gambling. It grew when facility owners sought to obtain exclusive use of popular players and players sought a share of the gate in return. Because many of the best athletes excelled in both hockey and lacrosse, they carried their demands from sport to sport. The ready association of athletes with local booster-ism proved a powerful stimulus. If a town's reputation was on the line, then 'its team' had to have the best players. That eventually meant freeing players from their other jobs to enable them to practise, encouraging them to develop specialized skills, and 'importing' and 'adopting' better players from outside the community. It also meant that one or more persons sought control of the team, creating a regime of rules and sanctions similiar to that employed in other areas of wage labour. Professionalism thus reinforced a division of labour between managers and players, both on and off the field. Financial compensation and inducements were especially necessary when teams from different towns and cities began to bid for athletes and managers. Growth of these practices added to the stakes riding on a contest and the desire to market it.[17]

Two Spectator-Sport Traditions

Because of the bitterness of the amateur-professional debates, both protagonists and scholars have made the remuneration of players the analytical demarcation line in their accounts of the early development of Canadian sports. Given the deep divide that these differences created, such categorization is entirely justified. But in considering the economic organization of teams and leagues, I believe that a further distinction is necessary, between 'not-for-profit' or 'community' teams and leagues, on the one hand, and 'full market' or 'capitalist,' on the other hand.

As much as the practices of commercialism (selling sport spectacles) and professionalism (paying athletes to perform and managers to organize) fed on each other in the proliferating fin-de-siècle sport marketplace, they did not always go hand in hand. Nor did they necessarily lead sports producers to direct all their energies to the market. Many clubs that sold their games remained rooted in communities and such institutions as universities. They used whatever surpluses they earned to improve facilities and opportunities. If revenue fell short of expenses, they balanced the books with members' contributions, reduced the program, and sometimes folded, but they would not transfer their operations elsewhere. The Montreal Victorias, winners of four Stanley Cups in the 1890s, put together competitive hockey teams on this basis until 1939.[18]

Many teams that imported 'outsiders,' paid players, and began to treat them as employees strongly identified with the cities and towns where they operated. Formed to enhance local prestige or to provide a diversion for an isolated and potentially militant workforce, they were not preoccupied with direct profit. While they had accepted the necessity of paying players, they did not completely eschew the public-spiritedness imbedded in the ideology of amateurism. When merchants in Kenora, Ontario, made it possible for the local team to 'import' eastern stars to bolster its Stanley Cup challenges in 1905 and 1907, they knew full well that they would not recoup their investment, but they did it anyway as a gesture of community boosterism and to enhance their own prestige within Kenora. Kenora's rivals in the 1905 challenge, the Ottawa Silver Seven, were organized along the same lines, as was the Edmonton team that challenged for the Stanley Cup in 1908.[19]

Whether the players were paid openly or 'under the table,' whether they drew sizeable salaries or 'shared the wealth' after the season's books were closed, whether they were 'owned' by private businesses or run on a membership basis, these teams were essentially 'not for profit.' Though managers would promote ticket sales as much as possible, and sponsoring merchants were keen to bask in any reflected glory, the teams main purpose was to provide gifted athletes with opportunities to play, local residents with exciting entertainment and a winning team. I do not wish to romanticize links between these teams and an organic 'community' – the role of teams differed widely from place to place and was profoundly shaped by the prevailing class, gender and ethnic relations – but it is clear that organizers felt a strong loyalty to a particular people and place. They always kept one foot solidly in the cities and towns where they lived and worked. This tradition would become the backbone of the Canadian Amateur Hockey Association and the Canadian Rugby Union (subsequently the Canadian Football League).

The community-focused, not-for-profit approach was similar to that taken in Britain. In cricket, county clubs were operated by volunteer community boards of directors, many of them led by former players. They hired professionals and marketed their games, but they did not personally profit. In soccer, while many clubs were incorporated as businesses, and treated their players no better than other corporations of the day, they gave little attention to profit. In 1894, the ruling Football Association limited dividends to 10 per cent of net profits and barred directors from profiting at all. Many shareholders simply framed their dividend cheques as a sign of prestige. In both sports, teams stayed where they began, regardless of performance on the field or at the box office. The 88 teams in the Football Association have remained the same for almost a century. A similar approach shaped the development of professional soccer in Europe and Australian Rules Football in Melbourne.[20]

But team sport production solely for profit – 'full market' or 'capitalist' sport – had taken place in the United States since the 1870s. Commentators might rue the unbridled self-interest and the absence of 'local patriotism' of managers and investors who moved teams to other cities when revenues fell or greater profits beckoned, but the entrepreneurs themselves made no bones about the practice. As much as they appropriated the symbols of community to develop a loyal following for their contests – one of the first by-laws of the National (Baseball) League required member teams to name themselves after the cities where they were located – they made decisions according to the balance sheet, not love of sport or community pride. The entrepreneurs developed the concept of operating leagues as cartels, with an eye to maximizing joint profits as a means of optimizing individual franchise profits. Teams were created, dropped, and moved to strengthen the overall interests of the league, regardless of local interests. They developed internal rules to govern the entry and movement of players. This was commercial team sport on a corporate scale.[21] Canadians encountered these practices when they competed against American baseball teams and sought franchises in U.S.-based leagues. They increasingly read about them in the mushrooming sporting press.

The history of fully capitalistic sports production in Canada has been studied only as a backdrop to the growth of professionalism. Little is known about the economic operations of the pre-1914 professional hockey leagues – the short-lived International Professional League and the Timiskaming League (sometimes called the New Ontario League), which operated in northern Michigan and northern Ontario, respectively; the Maritime Pro League; the Ontario Pro League (sometimes referred to as the 'Trolley League' because the players travelled in radial streetcars to and from games in Toronto, Berlin [Kitchener], Brantford, and Guelph); and the Manitoba, Northwestern, and Boundary leagues in western Canada. Foster Hewitt suggested that the owners of many of these teams, especially in the rapidly expanding mining areas, hoped to profit from wagers rather than from revenues.[22]

In the Montreal-based leagues out of which the NHL was formed, teams assembled and organized on an amateur-club basis took on an entrepreneurial form only gradually, as they were taken over by a small group of individuals, usually a player-manager and one or more significant backers, and turned into a business. At first, such teams continued to play against all comers. In the Eastern Canadian Amateur Hockey Association (ECAHA), which operated in 1907–8 in Quebec, Montreal, and Ottawa, the liberal policies of the Amateur Athletic Federation enabled completely amateur or 'mixed' teams from the Montreal Amateur Athletic Association (MAAA) and the Victorias to compete against fully professional 'community' teams such as Ottawa and entrepreneurial teams such as the Shamrocks and Wanderers.[23]

But the amateur wars and the fierceness of unregulated competition for players made the combination of 'community' and entrepreneurial teams extremely volatile. In 1908, the Victorias and the MAAA left the ECAHA so that they could stay amateur. The rest of the league became the Eastern Canadian Hockey Association (ECHA). The following year, because of a disagreement with Wanderers' owner James Strachan over where the team's games would be played and how revenue would be shared, the majority of the organizers reconstituted the league as the Canadian Hockey Association (CHA), without the Wanderers. In retaliation, Strachan combined with M.J. O'Brien of the Timiskaming League (Cobalt, Haileybury, and Renfrew) to form the National Hockey Association (NHA). In the process, they formed a new club, the Canadiens, to be represented on the ice entirely by French-Canadian players.

A short but spectacular bidding war ensued in December 1909. Star players were offered up to three times what they had previously earned to switch allegiances. O'Brien paid 'Cyclone' Taylor $5,250 to play the 12-game season for his Renfrew 'Creamery Kings,' and Lester and Frank Patrick $3,000 and $2,000, respectively. By comparison, Ty Cobb, the American (Baseball) League batting champion, earned $6,500 for 154 games that year. In Montreal, where there were five teams, the two leagues also waged an intense battle for fans. Backed by the mining profits of O'Brien and Noah Timmins, the NHA appeared to have the upper hand. Within a month Ottawa and the Shamrocks jumped to the rival league and the CHA folded. The NHA executive quickly moved to reduce costs to their former levels by cutting salaries, easily checkmating Art Ross's plan to form a players' union by threatening to banish any player who refused to go along.[24]

The NHA combined both entrepreneurial and 'community' elements, but with considerable tension. O'Brien's primary goal, for example, was not profits but the Stanley Cup. He most wanted to 'rub Ottawa's nose in it' for denying him a franchise in the CHA.[25] (Though his high-priced help beat Ottawa, the Creamery Kings never did win the Stanley Cup. He lost $11,000 on the 1909–10 season.) The Ottawa franchise was held by a voluntary membership organization, the Ottawa Hockey Association, until forcibly transferred to a profit-seeking private corporation in 1917.[26] Team managers continued their rivalries off the ice and so made few efforts to act in concert to strengthen the league as a whole. In 1913, for example, when Ottawa sought to sell scoring star Skene Ronan to the Pacific Coast League, Lichtenheim of the Wanderers objected that other teams should be allowed to bid for Ronan so that he would not be lost to the league. The practice that Lichtenheim recommended would subsequently become known as 'placing a player on waivers' – i.e., giving other teams in a league, usually in reverse order of standing, the first right of purchase at a stipulated price. But in 1913, Ottawa insisted on selling Ronan to the rival league and NHA President Emmett Quinn upheld them. Teams regularly raided each other's rosters and disobeyed the rulings of the elected president.[27]

The first hockey organization to enter the market with both feet was the Pacific Coast League (PCL), established by the Patrick family in Victoria, Vancouver, and New Westminister in 1912. The Patricks epitomized the early entrepreneurs of hockey. Like many of the others who would finance teams, Joe Patrick made a small fortune in the pre-war frenzy for natural resources – in his case, BC lumber. His sons Lester and Frank were outstanding athletes. Both played at McGill. Lester later starred with the Wanderers, playing for their Stanley Cup-winning teams of 1906 and 1907. He headed west to work in the family business but returned in 1910 to captain the heavily bankrolled Renfrew Creamery Kings. Frank, younger by three years, refereed in the ECHA while only 20 and still at McGill. After a year as 'walking boss' in his father's lumber camp, he joined Lester on the Creamery Kings. Both men were full of ideas about how to 'improve' the sport and its saleability. Their father's successful sale of the Patrick Lumber Co. in 1911 gave them the financial backing to try them out.[28]

The PCL was frequently referred to as 'syndicate hockey' (after the attempt a few years earlier by New York Giants owner Andrew Freedman to turn the National [Baseball] League into a single corporation, or 'syndicate,' to be called the National Baseball Trust).[29] The Patricks ran all the teams under unified management; there were no franchises. They constructed their own arenas in Vancouver and Victoria, with artificial ice, the first in Canada, to guarantee the schedule in the uncertain west coast climate. Frank Patrick was playing manager of the Vancouver team, and league president. Lester was playing manager for Victoria. Games were officiated by players from the team that was not playing that night. Players were lured away from other leagues and evenly distributed around the PCL. Sixteen of the 23 original players came from the NHA. In 1913, the PCL offered contracts to all but two of the players on the

TABLE 5.1
Agents producing and selling sport spectacles, c. 1914

- Not-for-profit sports clubs, amateur. Example: Queen's University football
- Not-for-profit sports clubs, professional. Example: Kenora Thistles, Stanley Cup winners, 1907
- Facility owners staging both amateur or professional events or renting the facility for a percentage of the gross. Example: P.J. Doran, owner of Montreal's Jubilee Rink
- Transportation companies staging amateur and professional events to sell combined rail-ferry-spectacle. Example: Toronto Street Railway
- Event entrepreneurs, staging single amateur and professional events and challenge games, usually in rented facilities. Example: Pat Powers, promoter of the World's Professional Marathon Championship, 1908–9
- Team entrepreneurs managing single teams in loosely federated leagues, usually in rented facilities. Example: W.P. Lunny of the Montreal Shamrocks
- Cartels with internal arrangements for player regulation and revenue sharing among franchises in the interests of joint profits. Example: the International (Baseball) League
- 'Syndicate hockey,' in which a single ownership operated an entire league as an integrated enterprise. Example: the Patricks, operating the Pacific Coast League

Stanley Cup–winning Quebec Bulldogs. In 1915, the PCL took virtually the entire Toronto team to stock its new Seattle team; though the two leagues eventually signed a non-raiding pact, it was frequently broken. When the PCL's teams did not attract the crowds it wanted, the syndicate moved them elsewhere. In 1914–15, the New Westminister Royals became the Portland Rosebuds. In 1916–17, the Victoria Aristocrats became the Spokane Canaries. (They would later return as the Victoria Cougars and win the Stanley Cup.) For several years, the Patricks also operated a club in Seattle. The PCL quickly challenged NHA teams for Stanley Cup honours. Its raids on other leagues accelerated the process of player mobility throughout the sport.

It should be clear from the foregoing that the organization of sports for public sale in pre–First World War Canada was far more complex than the familiar labels 'amateurism,' 'professionalism,' and 'commercialism' suggest. As Table 5.1 indicates, both amateur and professional events were 'commercialized' – i.e., produced as commodities for sale to spectators. Even when players were paid and subject to wage discipline, teams were not always conducted on a full market basis. Many of the 'backers' who put up the cash to buy outstanding players were motivated by a sense of community service or loyalty rather than by profit. Different beliefs and practices frequently intertwined. In multi-sport clubs such as the MAAA, amateurism and professionalism briefly coexisted, as various sports presented different eligibility requirements and revenue opportunities.[30] Facility owners and transportation companies joined hands and sought working arrangements with amateur and professional clubs alike.

If we imagine ourselves surveying the situation in 1914, we would see that it was not clear that the pattern of fully capitalist professional sport that is so familiar today would come to dominate in Canada. Nevertheless, events and circumstances combined to increase the pressures and incentives for hockey managers to commercialize their activities. Ironically, the Amateur Athletic Union's (AAU's) victory in 1909 contributed to these forces. After the decision had been made to outlaw pro-am 'mingling' and make 'once a pro, always a pro' the reigning doctrine, no athlete would agree to risk his chance to play organized sports for the rest of his life unless the rewards were significant. Strict amateurism thus increased the wage bill for professional teams. The AAU's refusal to contemplate the sort of compromise that governed British soccer also cut the promoters off from the facilities, expertise, and goodwill of many strong clubs. Both circumstances forced the pros to intensify the search for revenue. For the National Hockey Association, the Patricks' annual player raids added to the upward pressure on salaries. Nevertheless, the growing crowds for sports, amusements, and spectacles of all kinds in the buoyant urban leisure markets gave the promoters hope that there were paying customers to be won, if only they could find the right formula.

Capital and Capacity

Like the Patricks, the NHLers continually sought ways of making hockey more profitable. Initially, growth was slow. After the Montreal Wanderers' sudden demise in 1917, there were only three teams for the first two seasons – the Montreal Canadiens, Ottawa Senators, and Toronto Arenas (renamed the St Pats in 1919–20). In 1919–20, they recruited the Quebec Bulldogs, but the last-place anglophile team drew very few spectators and the franchise was transferred to Hamilton the following season. For the next four years, the league remained unchanged, languishing in the shadow of amateur hockey. Prospects were so uncertain, and there was so little mutual trust, that in 1923 the four clubs signed a legal agreement pledging that they would stick together come what may.[31]

Physical plant constituted one barrier to growth. Most arenas were cramped, cold, fire traps. Except for Toronto's Arena Gardens, opened in 1912, they were built out of wood and dangerously vulnerable to fire. Several did burn down, fortunately at times when they were empty. After the Montreal Arena was destroyed by fire in 1918, the Canadiens moved to the Jubilee Rink. It burned down in 1920. Many non-NHL teams lost their facilities to fire, too. Calgary's Sherman Rink burned down in 1915, the Patricks' Victoria's Arena in 1929, their Vancouver Arena in 1936. Because managers relied on the weather to freeze the ice, arenas were kept unheated and could be almost as cold and uncomfortable as the out-of-doors. Seats were narrow and hard and many spectators had to stand. In Ottawa's Laurier Arena, for example, 2,500 of the 7,000 'places' for spectators were for 'standees.' It was not an environment to encourage any but the devoted fan.

Natural ice kept the season short and unpredictable and often diluted the quality of play. After a sudden thaw, games had to be cancelled or tranferred to other cities. Except in arctic weather, the ice could only be scraped between periods – not flooded. (Flooding between periods did not become mandatory in the NHL until 1940.) As a result, the ice was often deteriorating as the game was drawing to its climax. In late-winter playoffs, sections of the ice would often become unplayable. Attendants sprinkled the most dangerous spots with sawdust to warn off players, but these areas were difficult to avoid, often ruining the contest for both fans and players. In the second game of the 1920 Stanley Cup finals between Seattle and Ottawa in Ottawa, for example, 'both teams suffered with the poor ice conditions, there being large pools of water that made combination play difficult.' The third game was 'contested on a slushy surface that was atrocious. Time and again players would rush with the puck to be relieved of it by slush rather than an opponent.' Both managers then agreed to transfer the remaining games to Toronto, where artificial ice was available at the Arena Gardens.[32]

Capacity was another problem. Ticket sales were the largest source of revenue. If arenas were filled to capacity, revenue could be be increased only by raising prices. Up until 1923–4, the largest was Toronto's Arena Gardens, with 8,500 seats. In the early 1920s, games in Montreal, Ottawa, and Toronto regularly sold out, suggesting that additional seats could be readily sold. Differences in franchises' revenues also affected the quality of play. If one team had significantly more to spend, it could eventually buy up the best players, creating an imbalance in play that would result in predictable games and lopsided scores.

Other issues included control of dates and times and share of gate and concessions revenues. If the franchise did not own an arena itself, it had to share the calendar with other teams, even leagues. In Toronto, the most popular time for hockey was Saturday night. But when a Conn Smythe–led group bought the St Pats in 1926 (and renamed them the Maple Leafs), it was able to get only two alternate Saturdays a month from the Arena Gardens. The other nights 'are reserved for use by teams playing amateur hockey.' The Gardens also limited the Leafs to one hour of practice per day and took 50 free complimentary tickets plus two private boxes for each game, 30–35 per cent of the gate, and the right to sell refreshments.[33]

Early in the 1920s, team owners began to upgrade their facilities. The first to do so was the Ottawa group, made up of Frank Ahearn, Edgar Dey, and Thomas Gorman. Dey was a co-owner of the existing arena, Ahearn a veteran sports promoter, and Gorman a former athlete and sportswriter who had managed the Ottawa club since 1915. In 1923, Dey built the Ottawa Auditorium, with an ice-making plant and a seating capacity of 10,000, and sold it and his interest in the team to Gorman and Ahearn. The new facility enabled the Ottawa club to practise for several weeks before the season opened and host an exhibition series against one of the western clubs. It seemed to justify the investors' confidence. The Senators set attendance records throughout the season, and bookings were full, with amateur games and figure skating.[34]

In 1924, a new group headed by James Strachan and Senator Donat Raymond built the Montreal Forum, a 9,500-seat arena with artificial ice. Many in the anglophone business elite invested, including Montague Allan, Edward Beatty, J.W. McConnell, William Southam, and the Molsons. They had been promised a new franchise, which they would call the Maroons, and there is good reason to believe that they had an eye on the Canadiens' business as well. Though the existing team had a contract with the Mount Royal Arena, Mount Royal had notoriously poor ice and fewer seats (8,000). When no ice was available for Canadiens' home opener on 29 November 1924, the Habs played in the Forum. In 1925–6, the Canadiens broke their contract with Mount Royal and moved all their games into the larger Forum. The move cost them $83,000 in court, but they more than made up for the loss in additional revenue.[35]

The new artificial ice surfaces permitted the league to extend the schedule to 30 games without threatening the popular Stanley Cup series. Up until 1926, the finals annually rotated between east and west. When it was held in one of the Pacific Coast League (PCL) arenas, timing was not a problem, because they were all equipped with mechanical refrigeration. But if held in an NHL city where ice was uncertain, the schedule and the preliminary rounds of the playoffs had to be completed by mid-March. In 1924, when the finals were scheduled for the east, the deciding game of the three-game western playoffs between the Calgary Tigers of the Western Canadian Hockey League (WCHL) and the PCL Vancouver Maroons of the PCL was played in Winnipeg, to reduce the time required for transcontinental travel. Even then, the final game between Calgary and Canadiens had to be transferred to Ottawa's new artificial ice. The benefits of the artificial ice at the Forum were demonstrated again in 1926 when it permitted the Stanley Cup final to begin on 30 March, two weeks later than ever before in the east.

The most significant increase in the league's capacity came with expansion to the United States. In 1924–5, the promoters created two new franchises, the Maroons and the Boston Bruins. Each team played in a large, new arena. In 1925–6, they added two more, the New York Americans and the Pittsburgh Pirates. In 1926–7, the NHL entered two other U.S. cities with the Chicago Black Hawks and the Detroit Cougars and transferred the Hamilton Tigers to New York, where they became the Rangers. In just three years, they had expanded the league to ten teams, four in Canada and six in the United States (see Table 5.2). The Bruins played in the 12,000-seat Boston Garden, the Americans and Rangers in the new 17,000-seat Madison Square Garden, and the Pirates in the 10,000-seat Duquesne Gardens. Though the Detroit and Chicago franchises began operations in smaller facilities – the Cougars played their first season in Windsor's 6,500-seat Kennedy Arena – their owners were committed to building new facilities. The 14,000-seat Detroit Olympia opened in 1928, and the 16,500-seat Chicago Stadium in 1929. Total seating capacity for the league thus grew from 27,000 (an average of 6,800 for four franchises) in 1917 to 112,000 (11,200 for ten franchises) in 1929. With expansion of the schedule – to 44 games in 1926, 48 in 1931 – the NHL increased its potential regular season revenue (number of seats multiplied by number of games) tenfold.

The new arenas provided the spectator with a much more comfortable viewing experience, making spectator sports appealing to affluent new audiences, women, and children. Madison Square Garden, for example, was designed to be 'a beauty of faultless technical proportion,' to be as pleasing in itself as the sporting events that it would facilitate. It boasted the latest in technological advances, including 'manufactured weather,'

TABLE 5.2
National Hockey League franchises, 1917–43

Year	Franchise				
1917–18	Montreal Canadiens	Montreal Wanderers *Folded*	Ottawa Senators	Toronto Arenas	
1918–19				↓	
1919–20				St Pats	Quebec Bulldogs
					↓
1920–1					Hamilton Tigers
1921–2					
1922–3					
1923–4					
1924–5					
1925–6					New York Americans
1926–7					
1927–8				Maple Leafs	
1929–30					
1930–1					
1931–2			*Inactive*		
1932–3					
1933–4			↓		
1934–5			St Louis Eagles		
1935–6			*Folded*		
1936–7					*Purchased by league*
1937–8					
1938–9					
1939–40					
1940–1					
1941–2					Brooklyn Americans
1942–3	↓			↓	*Folded*

NOTE: To its 6 teams of 1942–3 the league added 6 in 1967, 9 in the 1970s (including 4 from the short-lived World Hockey Association), and 5 in the 1990s, for a current total of 26.

TABLE 5.2   (*Concluded*)
National Hockey League franchises, 1917–43

Year	Franchise					
1917–18						
1918–19						
1919–20						
1920–1						
1921–2						
1922–3						
1923–4						
1924–5	Montreal Maroons	Boston Bruins				
1925–6			Pittsburgh Pirates			
1926–7				Chicago Black Hawks	Detroit Cougars	New York Rangers
1927–8						
1929–30			↓		Falcons	
1930–1			Philadelphia Quakers ↓			
1931–2			*Inactive*			
1932–3						
1933–4			↓		Red Wings	
1934–5			*Folded*			
1935–6						
1936–7						
1937–8	↓					
1938–9	*Inactive*					
1939–40						
1940–1						
1941–2						
1942–3		↓		↓	↓	↓

which would ensure that, regardless of temperature or humidity, 'everyday would be a good day' inside the Garden. The best seats were plushly padded. As Conn Smythe, the future managing partner of the Toronto Maple Leafs, admiringly noted, it would encourage 'people [to] go in evening clothes, ... everything new and clean, a place that people can be proud to take their wives or girl friends to.'[36] Several of the new arenas became tourist attractions in their own right.

American promoters had long been interested in hockey. Amateur leagues flourished in several northern cities. Well before the war, Canadian college and professional teams played exhibitions there. In 1908, for instance, Cyclone Taylor and the Ottawa Senators defeated the Stanley Cup–champion Wanderers in two exhibitions in New York's St Nicholas Arena. The sport was so popular that a post-season New York series became an annual event. In 1911, another series was staged in Boston, prompting press gossip that a new American league would be created with Canadian stars.[37] But it was a Montreal promoter, Thomas Duggan, who launched the NHL's American expansion. Duggan had been one of the unsuccessful bidders for the Canadiens in 1921. He was connected with the group that created the Montreal Maroons and built the Forum. Several of them, such as James Strachan, had been with the Wanderers during their pre-1914 American exhibitions, and they may well have nursed for some time the idea of expansion into the United States. In 1924, Duggan offered to sell two new NHL franchises in the United States. His proposal promised a greatly expanded market for NHL hockey. Commercial sports were undergoing a tremendous boom in the war-expanded industrial and commercial centres of the U.S. northeast. A new generation of heroes – pitcher-slugger Babe Ruth, boxer Jack Dempsey, running back Red Grange, and golfer Bobby Jones – mythologized by sportswriters skilled in hyperbole such as Grantland Rice, attracted greater crowds than ever before. The decade would be known as 'the Golden Age of American sport.' Hockey promoters were eager to cash in.

The prospects for hockey were greatly enhanced by a boom in boxing and wrestling shows, which stimulated construction of arenas and an interest in other physically aggressive, 'manly' contests. Prior to the war, prize-fighting was prohibited in many states, but mobilization gave it new respectability. Military instructors considered boxing the basis for bayonet drill, and wrestling, for hand-to-hand trench combat, and boxing and wrestling cards were a regular feature of troops' entertainment. After the war, boxing was quickly legalized, and promoters began to stage as many events as they could. It quickly overtook wrestling as combative entertainment. Boxing's popularity was the main reason that promoter Tex Rickard rebuilt Madison Square Garden in 1925. Rickard and his competitors in other cities, such as Canadian-born James Norris of Chicago, needed additional attractions to fill out the week's calendar, and they turned to hockey, exploiting the insight in the old joke, 'I went to a boxing match and a hockey game broke out.'[38]

In fact, it could be argued that the American franchises in the NHL survived the Depression only because of hockey's cultural and organizational links to boxing. By 1935, James Norris owned or controlled the Detroit Olympia and the Red Wings, New York's Madison Square Garden (where the Rangers and Americans played), and the Chicago Stadium (where the Black Hawks played), and he stood behind the mortgages on the Boston Garden (where the Bruins played). His primary interest was controlling the lucrative boxing business and becoming the 'virtual Dictator of U.S. Indoor Events.' With a little help from organized crime, Norris, his partner Arthur Wirtz, and his son Jimmy created a boxing monopoly that lasted until it was was broken up by the courts in 1957. Apart from the Red Wings, he took little interest in hockey.[39]

At a special meeting on 31 August 1924, the NHL's Board of Governors unanimously voted to accept Duggan's offer to create two American franchises. It did so not without trepidation. Expansion would bring needed capital and capacity into the league, but directors also knew that significantly richer teams would put their own clubs in jeopardy. The previous year, the fear that Duggan would 'link up with the powerful Townsend interests in Pittsburg[h] to launch a [rival] American group' had led them to bind themselves together for a five-year period. Admitting Duggan to the NHL only changed the nature of the threat. Successful franchises in the more populous U.S. cities might undermine their own ability to keep the best players, eventually forcing them to move to the United States themselves or sell out to American owners. Tommy Gorman was so conscious of the risks that he carefully recorded the decision and his copy of the duly signed undertaking in his personal papers, under the notation, 'for the hockey archives.' The promoters knew that the smaller-city Canadian franchises would be in jeopardy in an expanded NHL. They had to stay united, but how could they trust each other? Just to be sure, they each signed another special agreement promising to keep their teams in the league for the next ten years.[40]

Six weeks later, they transferred the first Duggan franchise to millionaire grocer Charles Adams, whose team, the Bruins, would play in the Boston Garden. On 11 April 1925, they granted Duggan a second franchise for New York's Madison Square Garden. Duggan briefly stayed with the new team, called the Americans, but its official representative was J.S. Hammond, managing director of the Garden, who fronted for Rickard and bootlegger William Dwyer. Despite his recent pledge to stay with the Senators for ten years, Gorman cashed in his chips. Two days after selling his interest in the Ottawa club to Frank Ahearn for $50,000, he became the Americans' manager.[41]

The next to bolt was Percy Thompson, principal owner of the Hamilton Tigers, who had also signed the ten-year moratorium. At the conclusion of the 1924–5 season, players on the first-place Tigers announced that they would not skate in the playoffs unless they were each paid a $200 bonus. Under the rules that year, the second and third teams played off for the right to meet the first-place club in the league finals. Led by Captain Wilfrid 'Shorty' Green, the Tigers claimed that they had signed contracts for a 24-game season, not the 30 games they had just completed. Thompson refused their demand, countering that the NHL and Stanley Cup playoffs were part of the 'scheduled playing time' each player had contracted for. After a meeting of the players, Thompson, and league president Calder failed to reach a settlement, Calder suspended all the players and declared the Canadiens, winners of the semi-final, league champions.[42]

Speculation mounted that Thompson would sell the team. Even Ed Livingstone jumped into the fray, threatening to sign the suspended players for a new league. In September, a group of 'concerned Hamilton sportsmen' announced that it would seek the franchise to keep professional hockey in the city. But in what has become an all-too-familiar pattern in commercial sports, Thompson denied that the team was for sale.[43] *Hamilton Spectator* sports editor Walter McMullen was not convinced. With remarkable prescience he described the political economy that has left most Canadian commercial sports franchises vulnerable to this day:

The manner in which the National Hockey League is expanding means that it will be only a matter of time until the largest cities will have the best teams, for with the greatest populations to draw from and great seating capacity of their arenas, they will be in a good position to pay top prices for players and will make better salary offers to the budding young stars. New York, with its six millions of population and an arena which will seat over 20,000 people, will have to have a winning team to keep the seats filled, while Boston, Montreal, Toronto, and Pittsburg, if the latter city is admitted, are all much larger than Hamilton and Ottawa ... The expansion may be a good thing for the league, but it is only a matter of time until the smaller cities will have to look to other sources for their entertainment in professional sport.[44]

Eight days later, with only Ahearn from Ottawa objecting, the other owners allowed Thompson to sell the players to the Americans for $75,000 (a tidy capital gain of 1,500 per cent on his original $5,000 purchase) and resign from the league. At the same meeting, the league granted a franchise to a Pittsburgh group, headed up by Ed and Harry Townsend. For several years, the NHL would list the Hamilton franchise as 'inactive,' but no effort was ever made to revive it.[45] For the Hamilton fans, many of whom had strongly identified with the Tigers, it was a bitter betrayal. Thompson had often equated the Tigers with the fortunes of the entire city, but rather than settle with the workers who were about to bring home the championship he made his fortune privately and left the city without a team.

What led Gorman and Thompson to sell out so quickly? It was not that either of them was eager to get out of hockey. Gorman stayed in the NHL another two decades, working for the Americans, Black Hawks, Maroons, and Canadiens, helping to bring Stanley Cups to all but the New York club. Thompson continued to manage the Hamilton rink for many years. It was not only promoters located in smaller cities who contemplated selling out at this time, either. The owners of the Toronto St Pats – J.P. Bickell, Paul Ciceri, N.L. Nathanson, and Charlie Querrie – almost sold their franchise to a Philadelphia partnership. Selling to the Americans was nothing new to Nathanson. His 1920 sale of his string of theatres to the U.S. chain Paramount Pictures enabled it to form a Canadian subsidiary, Famous Players, of which Nathanson became first president. Did these promoters just want to make a quick buck? Was the power of American capital simply too great? Or did they lose their nerve, and, like many other Canadian capitalists before and since, prefer working in the branch plant? It was certainly a period of American take-overs. Between 1913 and 1926, American investment increased from 21.5 per cent to 53 per cent of total foreign investment in Canada. By the 1930s, much of automobile production (82 per cent), electronics (68 per cent), rubber (64 per cent), machinery (42 per cent), and chemicals (41 per cent) was American owned.[46]

Why didn't the NHLers act to protect their interests before the sale to

Duggan, by strengthening their player allocation system, or increasing revenue sharing between teams? They were familiar with these mechanisms and frequently discussed them. My guess is that Gorman and Thompson, as owners who played an active role in team management, were so deeply imbued with the ethos of competition that they were unable to contemplate any significant joint undertaking.

In 1926, liquidation of the Western Hockey League (WHL) facilitated the NHL's creation of the Rangers, Chicago, and Detroit franchises. The WHL had begun as the Western Canada Hockey League (WCHL) in 1921 when the professional teams in the Saskatchewan and Alberta senior amateur leagues 'had come out of the closet.' Teams operated in Calgary, Edmonton, Regina, and Saskatoon. From the beginning, the league champion challenged representatives from the NHL and the PCL for the Stanley Cup. In 1922, the last-place Saskatoon Sheiks gained national publicity when they traded the then-unknown Auriel Joliat to the Canadiens for headliner Edouard 'Newsy' Lalonde and doubled his salary. The Canadiens traded Lalonde without first asking 'waivers,' infuriating their NHL partners. In 1924, the WCHL added the remnants of the PCL. Despite the boom in commercial sport in the eastern United States, the Patricks were unable to make a success of it west of the Rockies. When the Seattle arena they rented was demolished for a construction garage, they wound up the PCL and took their Vancouver and Victoria teams into the WCHL. In 1925, they bought the Regina franchise and moved it to Portland, and the WCHL became the WHL.[47]

While competitive on the ice, western teams were in constant financial and organizational difficulty. In the middle of the 1921–22 season, Saskatoon owner Bob Pindar transferred the team to Moose Jaw in hopes of drawing more fans. He brought it back the next season and added 'Newsy' Lalonde but then sold it. Pindar said that he sold the team because whenever it lost people would stop shopping at his drug store. The Regina and Calgary teams also changed hands several times. The one owner who kept his team, Edmonton's Ken McKenzie, regularly lost money.[48]

After the 1926 season, the WHL announced that it would no longer operate. In response, the NHL created three additional franchises. The promoters had promised another group of New Yorkers a franchise for $15,000 (which became the Rangers), and they got $50,000 from each of the Chicago and Detroit groups in the booming market. Claiming to hold the rights for the majority of the WHL players, the Patricks invited them-

TABLE 5.3

Markets pursued by the Western (Canada) Hockey League (WCHL/WHL) and the Pacific Coast League (PCL), 1921–6

City	Population*	Rink capacity	Artificial ice?
Calgary	83,761	5,000	No
Edmonton	79,197	7,000	No
Moose Jaw	21,299	2,500	No
Portland	278,000 (1924)	5,000	No
Regina	53,209	5,600	No
Saskatoon	43,291	6,000	No
Seattle	315,312 (1920)	7,000	Yes
Spokane	109,000 (1926)	5,000	No
Vancouver	246,593	11,500	Yes
Victoria	39,082	4,000	Yes

*Except where noted, population figures are from the 1931 census.
NOTE: From 1921 to 1925, the Western Canada Hockey League (WCHL) operated in Calgary, Edmonton, Regina, Saskatoon, and briefly in Moose Jaw, and the Pacific Coast League (PCL) in Vancouver, Victoria, and briefly in Portland, Seattle, and Spokane. In 1925, the PCL folded, and the Vancouver and Victoria teams moved into the WCHL. In 1926, the Regina franchise was transferred to Portland and the league became the WHL.

selves to the NHL's next meeting and sold it the WHL players for $300,000. They had no legal title to the players they sold, who could have bargained for themselves as free agents. But Saskatoon had already sold six of its players to the Maroons for $60,000, and the Patricks convinced everybody that they controlled the rest. Lester Patrick subsequently became the Rangers' manager and Frank an NHL official.[49]

In just three years, the NHL had expanded its market enormously. In the 'original three,' the largest city the league played in was Montreal, with a population of 618,566 (1921 census). In the expanded NHL, the Boston, Chicago, Detroit, New York, and Pittsburgh franchises drew upon municipal populations of 787,000, 3,048,000, 1,290,000, 5,924,000, and 637,000, respectively (1926 estimate).[50] But in the process, some of the original entrepreneurs had been replaced by much wealthier capitalists from outside hockey and outside Canada, a change that radically altered the balance of power in the league. To build the Forum and Madison Square Garden cost $1 million and $5 million, respectively. Such investments could not have been made from the profits of hockey alone.

If the WHL had survived, the expanded NHL would have provided it with much stiffer competition in the bidding for players. As Table 5.3 indicates, the western league drew on significantly smaller populations and played in smaller, pre-1914 arenas. Only the BC clubs enjoyed artificial ice. Their reported average attendance was but 3,000–5,000 a game. Financial records confirm this figure. In 1923–4, the Regina Caps earned a total revenue of $65,000, or $4,312 a game. League records for the 1924–5 and 1925–6 playoffs show an average gross revenue of $4,013 per game. In 1926–7, the Prairie Hockey League, with teams in Calgary, Edmonton, Saskatoon, and Regina, was scraped together to continue professional hockey. Its most successful team at the box office, the Saskatoon Sheiks, drew 19,275 adults and 2,335 children in 16 regular-season home games and 6,000 for two playoffs, for an estimated revenue of $44,000, or $2,500 a game.[51] By comparison, in 1927–28, the first year of Maple Leaf operations at Arena Gardens, the Toronto team grossed $123,468, or $5,703 per game. In their first year of operations at Maple Leaf Gardens in 1931–2, the Leafs grossed $355,930 from ticket sales, or $14,830 per game.[52] Under these conditions, the western teams would have found it increasingly difficult to attract and keep the best players.

Nor were the westerners in a position to match the capital investments in arenas and players that their eastern competitors had obtained through the U.S. franchises. New capital had always been hard to find on the prairies, and it was especially so during the 1920s, when fluctuations in the international price of wheat and the U.S. tariff on cattle and beef kept savings low and investors uncertain. It was not only hockey entrepreneurs who felt forced to sell out to central Canadian and foreign capitalists. In 1920, Calgary Petroleum, which had made the first significant oil strike in Alberta, faced bankruptcy because it could not attract sufficient capital to continue. It was then taken over by Imperial Oil. In 1928, Dominion Securities bought out the Burns meat-packing interests.

Despite these disadvantages, it is surprising that the WCHL/WHL collapsed without a fight. It was a decade of bitter regional antagonism, during which sports teams were highly regarded as champions of the west. In the years that followed, western football clubs were never daunted by the disparity in the resources they had available.[53] In its agreement with the NHL, the WHL had first call on all players from the western provinces – certainly a political rallying cry, if not legally binding. There was obvious interest in professional hockey, as the creation of the Prairie Hockey League demonstrated. With the best players gone to Montreal, New York, Chicago, and Detroit, the west lost its chance to challenge for the Stanley Cup. In Hamilton, the Tigers' sale had unleashed a nationalist outcry. 'Our national game has been prostituted, our sports fans cheated,' commentators such as Walter McMullen lamented.[54] But in the west, there was no public protest against the Patricks' opportunistic sale. D'Alton Coleman, vice-president of the Canadian Pacific Railway (and father of sportswriter James Coleman) wrote the Patricks offering to subsidize the WCHL to keep it going. But his letter arrived too late.[55] The NHL was able to sweep up the best of western Canadian hockey by default.

The capital requirements necessitated by the NHL's rapid expansion also forced out another of the NHL's original owners, Charles Querrie of the Toronto St Pats. Frank Selke, who subsequently worked for both the Leafs and the Canadiens, says that Querrie 'was astute enough to cope with any situation, [but] did not have the funds with which to buck the well-heeled gentlemen from Montreal and the United States who were franchise-holders.' Querrie and his partners put the St Pats on the market in 1926, eventually selling them to an investors' group put together by Conn Smythe. Like Gorman and the Patricks, Querrie was reduced to a salaried position – in his case, managing the Arena Gardens.[56] Big capital had taken over.

Winning New Audiences

Placing new franchises in larger cities did not by itself guarantee bigger audiences. Consumers had to be sufficiently interested in the game and the competing teams to buy tickets. Selling hockey was not overly difficult in Canadian cities, where males and some females played it as children and avidly followed the fortunes of their favourites, but the NHL had to compete with the best amateurs for their customers. In the United States, where the game was 'foreign' to most regions and cities, it had to be carefully explained and popularized. In both countries, the NHL pursued a number of strategies to increase the attractiveness of their 'product.' The foremost of these was speeding up the game.

Cultural historians have often speculated on the declining popularity of lacrosse relative to hockey in the first two decades of the twentieth century. Did lacrosse suffer from its historic association with the Aboriginal peoples, at a time when the urgency of belief in the white civilizing mission was at its height? More prosaic explanations focus on the competition that lacrosse matches received from baseball and other forms of summer recreation, such as camping and cottaging, and on the superior organizational and entrepreneurial abilities of the hockey promoters.[57] In this latter category, we must include the hockey executives' successful renovations of the rules. As Foster Hewitt observed in 1934, during a period of steady innovation, 'rule changing by amateur leaders was inspired by necessity, but with the coming of professional executives, alterations were animated more by the desire to make hockey speedier, more spectacular and crowd-pleasing.'[58]

The first to experiment in a systematic way were the Patricks. As players, they were frustrated by frequent slowdowns and stoppages in play, and they openly talked about ways to keep the game moving. When they played for the Renfrew Creamery Kings, they loudly criticized Cyclone Taylor for his habit of shooting the puck into the crowd to relieve pressure, even though he was a valued teammate and they all had to play the entire game without substitution. If they ever ran their own league, they vowed, they would penalize any attempt to interupt play. 'Our followers are entitled to action,' Lester Patrick said, 'not for a few brief moments, but for three full twenty-minute periods.' When they did create their own league, they put this and other ideas into practice. Along with the two-minute penalty for delaying the game, they instituted numbering of players, player substitution, the penalty shot, and awarding of assists (which not only gave fans another statistic to argue about, but spread 'stardom' around the team), and they were the first to allow and encourage the goaltender to fall down to block a shot.[59]

In 1913, the Patricks broke the confinements of the off-side rule that had governed the game and players' strategic thinking up to that time. The original, Montreal rules were adapted from soccer, rugby, and grass hockey. They required a player to 'always be on his own side of the puck' and prohibited passing to any teammate who was closer to the opponent's goal – i.e. a forward pass. There were no divisions (blue or red lines) on the ice. The puck carrier had to lead the attack, placing a premium on stickhandling. After a game in which there were 15 whistles for offside in the first five minutes, the Patricks decided to allow a measure of forward passing to encourage players to 'freewheel' and simultaneously cut down on stoppages. They devised the 'blue lines' – which divided the ice surface into three equal sections – to regulate the new method of attack. Forward passes could be made in the centre or the neutral zone created by the blue lines. Because a good pass travelled much faster than a player could skate, the new rule opened up the game significantly. It proved a great hit with both players and fans, though eastern professionals did not adopt it until the NHL was formed in 1917.

When the NHL promoters took the game to the United States, they encouraged even greater use of the forward pass. To be sure, the necessity of carrying the puck from the blueline into the goal had stimulated the great duels of the sport's folklore, as stickhandlers such as Taylor, Newsy Lalonde, Joe Malone, and Howie Morenz strove to slip between impassable defencemen as Harry Cameron, Sprague Cleghorn, Art Duncan, and Eddie Shore. But where hockey was less well known, at a time of ever-increasing emphasis on speed and mobility in everyday life, many felt that a faster, higher-scoring game was necessary to attract and retain customers. The men who controlled other sports had 'modernized' their rules with great success. Stodgy baseball introduced the 'rabbitball' and outlawed the 'spitter' to give the offence more power, and attendance seemed to grow with the cascade of homeruns. After years of shying away from it, the men who governed football adopted the unrestricted forward pass and found themselves basking in a new popularity. Should hockey do the same?

In 1927, the NHL authorized the forward pass within the defending team's zone, as long as it carried the puck across the blue line. This permitted a team to pass the puck up to its own blueline, carry it across, and then pass it forward to the other team's blue line. The change sped up the game considerably. But the original Montreal offside rule remained in effect from the opponent's blue line to the goal, and teams simply responded by fortifying their defences. In the 1928–9 season, there were 120 shutouts in the league – a record. Canadiens' goaltender George Hainsworth, who had been purchased from the Saskatoon Sheiks of the WCHL, blanked the opposition in 22 of 44 games. His goals-against average was 0.98, another record.

In response to this goal drought, the league experimented some more. Goalkeepers were prohibited from holding the puck. Infringement meant a faceoff ten feet from the goal, with no defending player other than the goaltender allowed between the faceoff and the goal. So that forwards could not stay back, they were required to leave the defensive zone with the puck. Infringement drew a two-minute penalty. The most drastic change was in the passing rule. The league simply abolished offside. Though players could not pass across any blue line, they no longer had to be alongside or behind when the puck crossed it. It meant that a player could park in front of the goal at any time of the game and wait for a teammate to cross the blue line and pass.

The changes had their intended effect, and more. Such players as Cooney Weiland and Nels Stewart took full advantage of the new rule and rarely left the other team's goal crease. Scoring more than doubled, from an average of three goals per game in 1928–9 to seven during the first quarter of the 1929–30 schedule. This was too much for the promoters. They called an emergency meeting to reintroduce offside at each blue line. Increased scoring continued, but not at the same frantic rate. By the end of the season, goaltenders had still compiled 26 shutouts. But the net result was a much more dynamic game.

Still the NHL did not stop experimenting. At the close of the 1931–2 season, the Bruins and the Americans, both out of the playoffs, were asked to try another version of the unlimited forward pass. In that game, only one line – a centre red line – was used. As long as players were onside when the puck crossed it, unlimited passing was permitted. Press critics gave the high-scoring game – the Americans won 8–6 – mixed reviews. Columnist Victor Jones complained that it took away body-checking, 'one of the things that has sold hockey to the crowd.' In 1933–4, the same two teams tried a modification of the no-offside rule that the league had briefly tried in 1929–30. Teams could pass without restriction, but once the defending team took the puck out of its zone, all players on the attacking team had to leave the zone; players could not permanently park on the goal crease. In 1934–5, the NHL asked two farm clubs to try still a different rule: players could pass from anywhere in the defending zone to the other team's blue line without restriction. In the end, none of these further amendments was adopted. The league did not make another change in the passing rule until it introduced the red line in 1943–4.[60]

Another 'product improvement' was the playoff system. In other leagues, designating the first-place team at the end of the regular schedule as champion was the accepted practice. The NHL did that, too, awarding the O'Brien Trophy to the first-place team in the regular season, calling it league champion. But then the hockey promoters created a second season to establish another 'champion.' The idea was probably inspired by the post-season exhibition series held in New York and Boston before the war. It was first tried by the NHA in 1914 to bolster attendance. The first and second teams at the end of the season played off for the right to represent the NHA against the PCL in the Stanley Cup. In 1917, the NHL divided the schedule in half and required the winners of each half to play off. The following year, the Patricks created a PCL playoff 'to provide a second chance for teams that for whatever reason have fallen too far behind to make a race of it.'

In 1921–2, the NHL abandoned the split schedule but playoff revenues were too large to lose, so it continued the post-season series, making it between the first and second teams. In 1924–5, the league expanded to six teams, all of them enjoying artificial ice. It enlarged the playoffs to a two-game, total goals semi-final between the second and third teams and a best-of-three final against the league leader. It was this addition, along with the extension of the schedule, that prompted the Hamilton Tigers' strike.

With the collapse of the WHL in 1926–7, the NHL claimed sole possession of the Stanley Cup. With its expansion to ten teams, it could mount a major event. 'Canadian' and 'American' divisions were created. Teams in the 'Canadian' division, comprising Ottawa, Toronto, Maroons, Canadiens, and the New York Americans, played six games a year against each other and four games against each of the five 'American' division teams. Each division held three-team playoffs, and these were followed by an inter-divisional Stanley Cup final. Some series stretched out so long, the refereeing was so erratic, and the results were so bizarre that critics charged that the games were fixed.[61] But the playoffs became an important source of revenue. Even though six of ten teams qualified, the promoters claimed that 'making the playoffs' was the measure of a 'successful' season. For teams that did so, it helped enormously with advertising and greatly increased the number of regular season games that could be billed as 'crucial' to a team's fortunes. It could also boost overall attendance. In 1932–3, when the Maple Leafs had six post-season games at home, the playoff crowds boosted attendance by 82,723, or 40 per cent. While average attendance per game was 8,515 during the regular season, it was 13,787 for the playoffs.[62]

Of course, as the NHL billed itself as the 'best hockey in the world,' it had to deliver a steady supply of outstanding players – a task that it could not always fulfill. In the early years, the PCL and the WCHL regularly raided the NHL (and each other's teams) and vied for the best amateurs. The promoters also had to contend with the tendency of some of their own partners to sell and trade good players out of the league. It took the persistence of NHL president Frank Calder, a former *Montreal Herald* sports editor, to bring the player market under control. In 1922, after several attempts, he got all clubs to agree upon a waiver rule. He also obtained territorial and non-raiding agreements with the rival leagues. After the collapse of the WHL, Calder moved quickly to relegate the remaining professional leagues to 'minor league' status. These included the Prairie League, the Canadian Professional League (Hamilton, Kitchener, London, Niagara Falls, Stratford), the Canadian-American League (New Haven, Philadelphia, Providence, Quebec, and Springfield), the American Hockey Association (Duluth, Kansas City, Minneapolis, St Paul, and Winnipeg).

In a 'memorandum of agreement' that Calder dictated to all minor-league presidents and franchise holders and forced them to sign, NHL clubs obtained the right to take one player from each minor-league club every other year for the stipulated price of $5,000. They also gained the right to buy other players without their having to pass through waivers in their own league. The agreement required all clubs to use the standard NHL player's contract and designated Calder as the arbiter, without appeal, of all disputes over players' contracts. Apparently, no one tried to call his bluff. In return, Calder promised that the NHL would respect the other leagues' markets – i.e., not to establish franchises where they were operating – though it broke this agreement whenever that suited its purposes. In 1934–5, for example, it let Ottawa operate its team out of St Louis, as the Eagles, without seeking permission from or paying compensation to the St Louis club in the Canadian-American League.[63]

But Calder was much less successful in establishing a competitive balance around the League, another now familiar requirement of successful sports entertainment.[64] In the interwar years, sports cartels sought to maximize competitiveness through various player allocation schemes and revenue sharing. Though such manoeuvres have prompted player strikes and lockouts in all the major leagues in recent years, the early NHL enjoyed a free hand over players by virtue of the 'reserve clause' and a punitive system of player relations. First employed in American baseball as a means of controlling players and keeping salaries down, the reserve clause bound a player to the team he had signed with (or to which his contract had been sold or traded) after expiration of the contract – i.e., in perpetuity. When respected by other teams, the reserve clause enabled clubs to dictate players' salaries and working conditions. The reserve clause was brought to Canada by the NHA and continued by the NHL.[65]

Though the reserve clause gave the NHL the means to redistribute players at will, owners and managers were too antagonistic with each other to use it for that purpose. Directors talked about the need for competitive balance, but few were prepared to weaken their own teams. In 1920–1, when it was felt that clubs should donate some players to the Hamilton team, which had won only two games the previous season, the champion Ottawa Senators refused. Toronto contributed four players but recalled one of them, Cecil Dye, when he scored two goals in his first game. He went on to win the scoring title. The same disparity was evident when Boston and the Maroons entered the league in 1924–5. The 'original three' refused to share, forcing their new partners to raid the WCHL and PCL and scurry around for minor league and amateur players. Not surprisingly, the newcomers quickly sank to the cellar. The Bruins managed only six wins in the 30-game season, the Maroons nine. The Maroons were also disadvantaged by the right of first refusal that the Canadiens enjoyed vis-à-vis all French-speaking players. That provision would limit the Maroons' appeal to Montreal's anglophones.[66]

The animosities between teams also torpedoed development of gate sharing and salary caps. To a considerable extent, as the history of the Winnipeg Jets and the former Quebec Nordiques readily attests, a club's ability to put together an outstanding team is a function of relative revenue. Then as now, teams in smaller cities sought to increase their relative revenue through gate sharing, so that they would benefit from playing in larger arenas and in cities where tickets were more expensive. In the early years of professional hockey, teams had shared the net receipts equally, but in the NHL the visiting team received only 3½ per cent. After expansion, Ottawa repeatedly proposed that the visiting team's share be raised to 15 per cent, but to no avail.

As an accompanying strategy, poorer franchise holders tried to establish limits on expenditures to prevent richer clubs from simply buying the championship.[67] In 1925, the directors agreed that no franchise should be allowed to have more than 12 active and two inactive players under contract. They also agreed to an annual total salary cap of $35,000 (with expansion clubs being able to spend $45,000 a year for two years).[68] But such agreement did not last, and in 1927, at the instigation of the Rangers, the cap was removed. The cap was reinstituted in 1932, but too high (at $70,000) and too late to help Ottawa and Pittsburgh, which by then had begun to sell their best players to the richer teams in a desperate effort to keep afloat. Both teams sat out several seasons, paying off debts by renting their remaining players to the league, and they tried to operate in other cities (in Pittsburgh's case, in Philadelphia; in Ottawa's, in St Louis). In 1934 and 1935, as the Depression continued to cut into revenues, the cap was lowered to $65,000 and then $62,500, respectively. But the disparity between what the teams received in revenue and what they would have had to pay out to become competitive was too great, and by 1935 both franchises had folded.

The Montreal Canadiens almost disappeared too. Losing money steadily, they tried selling off their best players to stay afloat. The charismatic superstar Howie Morenz was sold to Chicago in 1934. But that only weakened the team even further. By 1937, the Habs had sunk to seventh place in the eight-team league, playing to half-empty houses. The Montreal Arena Co. which by then owned the Forum, the Canadiens, and the Maroons, was so badly in debt that 'there was serious talk of turning [the Forum] into a streetcar barn to serve the west end of the city.' But the Maroons were winning regularly, taking the Stanley Cup in 1935 and placing first in the regular season in 1936, and enjoyed a loyal following, so owner Senator Donat Raymond decided to keep one of the two teams alive. He chose the Canadiens, because of the overwhelming majority of French–speakers in the city. The NHL allowed him to 'suspend' the Maroons without losing the franchise. The players were sold or rented to the league, which distributed them in a draft. The Canadiens got star and future coach Hector 'Toe' Blake. In 1940, Raymond requested and obtained a further suspension for the Maroons. But they never played again.[69]

Despite much puerile bickering – the Leaf's Conn Smythe, the Bruins' Art Ross, and the Red Wings' Jack Adams fought incessantly with each other in public and in private – Calder did manage to get the owners and managers to cooperate in other ways. Eventually they honoured each other's contracts and reserve lists and complied with the waiver rule. They allowed Calder to negotiate on their behalf with hotels and railways, new franchise applicants, and other leagues and to resolve disputes between clubs. Slowly they came to agree that the league, not individual franchises, should be the effective unit of operation – the mark of a cartel. With expansion, they gave each franchise holder a monopoly in the markets in which they were located and a veto over any new franchise in its area. They also required those who entered existing markets to pay the original club 'recompense.' Of the $15,000 that the Maroons paid for their franchise, for example, $10,000 was paid to Canadiens for sharing the Montreal market. The Ottawa and Hamilton representatives on the NHL's board of directors, Tom Gorman and Percy Thompson, respectively, voted against 'recompensing' Canadiens, requiring Calder to cast the deciding vote.[70]

Forging New Loyalties

After the demise of the WHL in 1926, the NHL pursued a strategy of what we would call 'product differentiation' to consolidate its position in the sports entertainment market. To distinguish itself from its remaining professional competition, it refused all challenges for the Stanley Cup, claimed as the 'world championship' after the cup's trustees allowed the PCL's Portland Rosebuds to challenge the NHA's Canadiens in 1916. In 1928, another group of sports entrepreneurs created the American Hockey League in direct competition with the NHL. The AHL was led by Tom Shaughnessy, who had been fired as manager of the Chicago Black Hawks, and quietly financed by James Norris, who had been refused a second Chicago franchise for his Chicago Stadium. (The original franchise owner, Fred McLaughlin, had used his veto to stop him. Norris was not able to gain control of the Black Hawks until later in the decade.) Shaughnessy persuaded several NHL stars to jump to AHL teams, signed a number of American amateurs, and made them headliners.

In Chicago, where the Shaughnessy-managed Shamrocks played in the stadium, the AHL outdrew the NHL by several thousand fans a game. In 1931, the AHL challenged the NHL for the Stanley Cup. The NHL refused. It would rather forfeit the cup, President Calder said, than play against an 'outlaw' league. Calder's decision was upheld by the cup's trustees – the men appointed by Lord Stanley to determine the conditions for cup challenges and to settle all disputes.[71] Unable to benefit from the prestige and gate receipts that a Stanley Cup series would provide in the lean markets of the depression, the AHL subsequently disbanded.

In Canada, the NHL still faced stiff competition from the junior and senior teams of the Canadian Amateur Hockey Association (CAHA). In the cities where the NHL operated, franchises had to vie with amateurs for both arena dates and fans. Comparisons are difficult to make, because eligibility rules prohibited the best amateur teams from playing professionals, but a number of observers remembered them as every bit as good. Ted Reeve, who covered sports for Toronto newspapers for more than 50 years, always said that 'the Granites [who won the Allan Cup in 1922 and 1923 and the Olympic championship in 1924] could beat the St Pats [who won the Stanley Cup in 1922] on their lunch hour.' According to Frank Selke, 'up until [Smythe took over the Leafs], all NHL players reported to their clubs a day or two before opening game. The boys had one or two practices. Then they depended upon their games more than anything else to put the team in condition. Generally, the season opened in the third week of November. Christmas came around before the boys were in shape to give the customers a run for their money, which may explain why enlightened fans in Toronto and many other Canadian cities still preferred the senior amateur brand of competition.' This was Foster Hewitt's recollection, too.[72]

Outside the NHL cities, CAHA teams enjoyed even greater popularity. 'The NHL was like the Cincinnati Redlegs – they were a thousand miles away,' Stan Spicer, who lived in Winnipeg at the time, remembered. Winning teams such as the Port Arthur Bearcats, who won the Allan Cup in 1925, 1926, 1929, and 1939, were popular across the country. 'I'm much better known for my games with the Bearcats, even in Montreal and Toronto, though I played ten years in the NHL and won the Stanley Cup,' said Edgar Laprade.[73] The local and national celebrity of the top CAHA teams made it much more difficult for the NHL to sign the top amateurs. By the late 1920s, many CAHA clubs were finding their top players well-paying jobs in the community, and some were even paying them under the table. Players who signed with the NHL had to leave family and community and they risked never playing hockey again if they did not make the cut. NHL rosters were small – 15 players and a goalie in the 1930s – and men, once signed, could not return to the CAHA.

But gradually, the NHL was able to win Canadian fans away from these other teams and leagues, so that they identified more strongly with the Leafs, Canadiens, or even one of the American teams, rather than their local club. Promoters benefited from the redefinition of professionalism that occurred in all sports. By the mid-1930s the dominant meanings no longer dwelt on ethical motives and 'avarice' but focused on ability and implied 'excellence.' The NHL also gained from the more open new rules and a bevy of skilled and exciting players, such as 'Babe' Siebert, Nels Stewart, and Cy Wentworth of the Maroons, Morenz and Aurel Joliat of the Canadiens, and Syl Apps, Charlie Conacher, and 'Happy' Day of the Leafs.

The promoters left nothing to chance, actively contributing to reconstruction of vocabularies and reshaping of fans' identities. They paid a few star players unprecedented amounts and energetically publicized their signings. In 1930, the Maple Leafs bought Frank 'King' Clancy from Ottawa in a cash-and-trade deal worth 'about $50,000, the most paid for a hockey player to that time. Around the league, people wanted to buy tickets to see what kind of a hockey player was worth $50,000.'[74] The NHLers assiduously courted the men who wrote about sports for the newspapers. In New York, Tom Gorman supplied reporters with 'the most flamboyant Hollywood-type stories' about the players while Lester Patrick gave newsmen formal seminars on strategy and tactics. In Toronto, the Leafs management did much the same, offering reporters pre-written features, statistical information, privileged access to stars, and 'scoops' if they filed stories on a daily basis. Many reporters got part-time jobs to supplement their income. During the 1920s, Mike Rodden and Lou Marsh, sports editors of the *Globe* and the *Toronto Star* respectively, worked as NHL referees. Other hockey reporters 'wrote' regularly for the clubs' programs. The Leafs created such deep dependence that *Toronto Telegram* columnist Ted Reeve later quipped, 'The Leafs haven't changed the way they practice for 40 years, but we cover every practice just the same.'[75]

To get exposure for the NHL at the expense of the amateur leagues, the Toronto Maple Leafs 'invented' the training camp. According to Frank Selke, assistant manager at the time, 'the physical rewards of early season training were great, but of greater importance was the fact that our team practically eliminated Senior and Junior amateur hockey gossip from the sports pages. Everybody suddenly became Leaf conscious. Other teams, quick to realize the advantages of this pre-season publicity, soon followed suit.'[76]

In some cases, the entrepreneurs bribed reporters outright. W.E. 'Stuffy' Richards, the *Clarion*'s sports editor during the 1930s, recounted: 'I had a press pass to the Gardens and used to go quite a bit. One day I was ordered to come down to Smythe's office. There were three well known hockey writers there. "Look at this," Smythe told me and he held up the latest *Clarion*. "Did you write this?" 'Yes," I said, somewhat afraid of what he was going to do. Smythe turned to the other men. "If he can do this in the Communist Party newspaper, why can't you in yours? I don't pay him a cent, and you're getting $4,000."'[77]

If reporters repeatedly failed to write what the promoters wanted, they were dropped from the payroll and cut off from their sources of information. Bruce McFarlane documented the same practices in Montreal in his pathbreaking account of sportswriting during the 1950s. Reporters made as much as half of their income in handouts from the promoters whose entertainments they covered. At out-of-town games they lined up with the players for meal money. Despite all the cant about the 'objectivity of a free press,' most publishers went along, grateful that someone else was paying their employees.[78] The *Toronto Star*'s Joseph Atkinson seemed troubled by the practice, but he was not prepared to lose revenue over it. His solution was to get Smythe to use the $20,000 he was annually paying *Star* reporters to purchase advertising in the paper, on the promise that Atkinson would increase reporters' salaries. Apparently, Smythe followed through, but it took certification of the Toronto Newspaper Guild in 1948 after Atkinson's death to make a significant difference to reporters' salaries.[79]

Two of the most important steps in the development of the NHL's hegemony in Canada were taken in 1931 – construction of Maple Leaf Gardens and creation of an NHL radio network. In 1926, during the NHL's rush to find US markets and buyers, it was rumoured that the Toronto St Pats were to be sold to a Philadelphia syndicate. Smythe, who had successfully managed hockey teams in the Canadian armed forces and at the University of Toronto and briefly coached the New York Rangers, used nationalist arguments to convince the most powerful shareholder – mining magnate J.P. Bickell – to postpone the sale. He then persuaded Bickell to keep his money in the team and found enough other investors to enable the group to buy it. To broaden its appeal, he renamed it the Maple Leafs and changed its colours from green and white to the blue and white of his alma mater. It is widely believed that Smythe bought the team outright, but, like many of the other Canadian hockey entrepreneurs of the time, he did not have the resources himself to match the massive capitalization of the new American teams. His main role was putting the new ownership together, on the promise of running the team. Initially, he owned but a small percentage of shares.[80]

With a good eye for talent and a shrewd managerial sense, Smythe gradually improved the team, taking it from last in 1926–7 to second in 1930–1. But he felt that the 8,500-seat Arena Gardens cost it the extra revenue necessary to produce a winner. 'I had the players but we were still playing in the Mutual Street Arena [sic],' he wrote in his autobiography. 'About half the time we were packing in 9,000 counting standees, but still weren't grossing enough to pay our players what they could have been getting with the richer teams in the U.S.' Though their contract enabled the Leafs to ask for construction of an additional 800 to 2,000 seats, in 1929 the team had these provisions deleted. Smythe wanted a brand new arena, 'a temple dedicated to The Game.'[81]

Smythe persuaded Eaton's department store, which owned the site he wanted, to '[sell] us the property for considerably less than its actual value.' Despite the depression, he found additional capital. When the the Montreal-based Sun Life Assurance Co. agreed to invest $500,000, others were persuaded to join in. The resulting board included representatives from the major banks, trust and insurance companies, mining and oil companies, and retailers. Smythe and Bickell also made a public offering of stock in the new company, Maple Leaf Gardens Inc., which they created to run the new arena and team. The propectus advised: 'Not only is the new building essential if big league hockey is to remain in Toronto, but it will fill a long-felt want in our civic life generally. For years, the need of such an amphitheatre for mass meetings, conventions, display shows, etc., has been apparent. In Maple Leaf Gardens we hope to create a centre that will not only cater to sports of one kind or another, but will prove to be a real asset in many other ways to our beloved city ... Montreal, Boston, Detroit and Chicago have all built new arenas in recent years. Toronto dare not lag behind.'

The prospectus tried to attract every interest imaginable. It combined careful architect's drawings with the raucous cartoons of the sports page. It played on the financial expertise of new directors such as Sir John Aird, president of the Canadian Bank of Commerce, Leighton McCarthy, president of Canada Life Assurance, and J.Y. Murdock, president of Noranda Mines, and on the heroics of such stars as 'Happy' Day and 'King' Clancy. It appealed to community hockey traditions and the competitive spirit, claiming that 'Conn Smythe and his associates on the Maple Leaf Directorate started hockey on the Public School teams of the city, and by sheer persistence and honest dealing have gradually elevated themselves to the position they now hold at the top of the heap.' (Actually, Smythe attended a public school, Jarvis Collegiate, for only a single year. He learned his hockey at St Alban's and Upper Canada College, both private schools.) Extra revenue was promised from the shops that would be located on the street fronts on Carlton, Church, and Wood streets. Female investors were encouraged 'to take up small holdings in the company.' The prospectus even held out the promise of a Stanley Cup, suggesting that 'the enthusiasm that radiates from a crowd in a new sports building rouses the players to superhuman heights.'

Bickell, Smythe, and their partners helped themselves to ample stock in the new corporation, turning their original $160,000 investment into majority control of a new $2-million corporation. Just to make sure, Frank Selke, a card-carrying union electrician, got the men in the building trades to take some of their salaries in stock and then bought them back at a discount.[82] But the Bay Street investments, the shares offering, and the new arena garnered Smythe and his partners even more value in new legitimacy and public standing.

When the Gardens opened, on 12 November 1931, the largest crowd ever to attend an indoor event in Toronto – 13,342 – was in attendance. Selke's proud reminiscence was not far off the mark: 'When Maple Leaf Gardens opened its doors to the general public, the overall cleanliness and swank of the new building ushered in a new era for long suffering hockey patrons. It was only natural that women, who previously hated to dress for the stodgy old arenas of yesteryear, were glad to wear their best to see the Maple Leafs in their new arena. And just as surely as the apparel of the lady fans stepped up in quality, that of the young men followed suit. Hockey crowds now had real class. At times, special parties of young men and women attended the games in formal attire. They looked as glamorous and appeared to belong just as truly as the occupants of any box at the opera.'[83]

The Gardens was an instant financial success. In the first season, the team grossed $154,000 more than the previous year at Arena Gardens, more than enough to compensate for the $30,000 it had to pay for breaking the contract. Not all the promised shops at street level were opened, but the directors' hopes were quickly realized in other respects. The Gardens did become a prime facility for major events, from public school gymnastic displays to political rallies and ballet, a familiar scene of front-page stories. The Leafs did win the Stanley Cup for the first time later that season, topping off professional hockey's rise to respectability in Toronto.

One of the features of Maple Leaf Gardens was a radio broadcast booth, or 'gondola' as it came to be known, designed for play-by-play announcer Foster Hewitt. Radio stations had been sending out sports information and live accounts of events almost from the beginning of regular broadcasting in the early 1920s. In 1924, the Canadian National Railways broadcast an account of the final Stanley Cup game between the Canadiens and the Ottawa Senators on its recently opened Ottawa station, CNRO. By the late 1920s, live reports of men's baseball, basketball, boxing, football, horseracing, lacrosse, motorboat and motorcycle racing, rowing, swimming, tennis, and track and field and women's basketball, hockey, and softball were being carried. Hewitt, working for the *Toronto Star*'s CFCA, was one of the first to 'call' a large number of live sports events, but he did not specialize in sports to begin with. Throughout the 1920s, he also described and broadcast concerts, conventions, and church services.[84]

When Smythe took over the Maple Leafs in 1927, he wanted Hewitt to broadcast the games on a regular basis. Though he first had to overcome the fears of Maple Leafs directors that the new medium would cut into paid attendance, he got CFCA to carry games, with Hewitt as the commentator. When the Gardens was being planned, Smythe hired Hewitt as 'director of radio,' to produce and broadcast all Gardens events and sell the advertising. During the initial season, the games were carried on three Toronto stations and were sponsored by General Motors (GM), in an arrangement initiated by advertising executive Jack MacLaren. GM paid $500 a game for the rights. The same year, the Canadiens' games were broadcast in French, the Maroon's in English in Montreal and parts of Quebec. By 1933, Hewitt's Saturday-night broadcasts from Maple Leaf Gardens were carried on a 20-station, coast-to-coast network. In 1936, Imperial Oil became the broadcast sponsor, initiating the custom of the 'three star' post-game awards to advertise its gasoline of that name.[85]

Radio quickly enabled the NHL teams, especially the Toronto Maple Leafs, to broaden their following far beyond the cities in which they played. The new medium had a revolutionary impact on the consciousness of Canadians, transforming living habits and discourse overnight. The mysterious 'ether' brought top-flight entertainers, orchestras, and theatre companies that hitherto most Canadians had barely read about, let alone heard, right into people's homes with an immediacy and intimacy that seemed completely unmediated. Radio turned the focus of leisure inward towards the home, and the set itself became the meeting place in many households.

The broadcasts helped sell not only the early stations, but the technology. Despite the hardships of the Depression, sales of receivers increased each year, from 112,272 in 1933 to 348,507 in 1939.[86] Advertisers quickly discovered that radio gave them an unprecedented audience and legitimacy. In 1931, a cosmetic company sponsored a program called 'An Evening in Paris.' So many women asked by name for the non-existent perfume that the firm created an 'Evening in Paris' product and promptly outsold all competitors. Sports broadcasts had a similar effect on men. In 1939, the Gillette razor blade company promoted special 'World Series' shaving sets during its sponsored broadcasts of the Major League playoffs and sold its entire production of 2.5 million sets in just four games.[87] The same occurred with Maple Leaf broadcasts. In 1931, a brief Hewitt advertisement for mail-order Maple Leaf programs led to immediate sale of 3,000. Another Hewitt ad for a special booklet about the proposed new arena led to sale of an extra 60,000 copies.

Far beyond southern Ontario, Canadians listened to the Maple Leaf network in growing numbers. Many adopted the Leafs as their team. In 1934, an estimated 72 per cent of the roughly one million radio sets in Canada tuned into Hewitt's broadcasts of the Stanley Cup semi-finals. Hewitt and the Leafs became national celebrities. The Leafs enjoyed their CBC monopoly in English-speaking Canada for more than four decades. This fact explains why, even where there are now other NHL franchises, they remain a popular team.

The Power of Capital

Where the National Hockey Association had stumbled, the corporation that the NHL promoters created transformed the landscape of Canadian hockey after the First World War. By recruiting outside capital, building attractive new arenas, selling franchises to powerful U.S. interests, and speeding up the game, the NHL greatly expanded its market and gained the revenue to buy up virtually any player it wanted. By 1932, with the collapse of the American Hockey League, it controlled all of professional hockey. Though it limped through the Depression in every city but New York and Toronto, it had access to the deep pockets that enabled it to survive.

The NHL's triumph was facilitated by and reflected three interrelated changes in Canadian society: further spread of the 'universal market,' accelerating penetration of American industry and culture into Canada, and increasing concentration of corporate capital generally. The first of these processes – commodity production of objects of everyday life – is also called 'Fordism,' because the success of Henry Ford in assembly-line automobile production both opened up the possibility and necessitated creation of mass markets for manufactured goods.[88] During the 1920s, investment was increasingly directed toward production and sale of consumer goods – automobiles, household furniture and appliances, stylish clothing, toiletries, and cosmetics. The extent of consumer culture has always been exaggerated, because real wages rarely increased to permit many outside the middle class to participate. In 1929, the average Canadian wage of $1,200 per year was $230 less than the dominion Department of Labour's estimate of the 'minimum standard of health and decency.'[89] But a growing population expanded the potential market.

Increasing urban densities, along with the accelerating pace of everyday life, added to the attractiveness of 'ready made' goods and entertainments. Popular entertainments such as movies, radio shows, comic books, and commercial sports advertised the new consumer products directly and indirectly through sponsorships and plot lines while they sold themselves. The mass media played a pivotal role in this process, proclaiming the advantages of the new products and anointing the stars of the new entertainments, while selling readers and listeners to advertisers. Motivational messages equated consumption with endless happiness, from fulfilment of romantic fantasy to enhanced gender identity and social status: consumption itself was offered as a form of cultural expression and identity.

The NHL rose with the tide of consumer culture. While the mass media enlarged the general audience for commercial entertainment, and consumer advertising encouraged men and women to purchase new identities, able publicists such as Tom Gorman, Lester Patrick, Frank Selke, and Conn Smythe fashioned similar narratives in hockey. In addition to presenting the excitement and drama of the contest, they offered men vicarious participation in the rituals of heroic masculinity and membership in a broad and powerful 'community.'

The growth of the NHL was furthered by another trend – the growing interpenetration of Canadian and American economies. Following the First World War, U.S. expansion greatly increased demand for Canadian raw materials, particularly minerals (for cars, radios, and electrical goods), pulp and paper (for newspapers and magazines), and hydro-electric power. Between 1922 and 1930, the value of Canadian base-metal production increased by more than four times, from $20.9 million to $85.1 million. Annual production of Canadian newsprint more than doubled, from 1,081,000 tons to 2,498,000 tons. Almost 85 per cent of output went to the United States.

U.S. investment in Canada doubled during the 1920s. Under the stimulus of staple exports and foreign investment, the consumer industries grew as well, led by U.S. branch plants, such as Ford, General Foods, and Procter and Gamble, their products made popular by Hollywood movies and American magazines and radio programs. In 1929, Canadians purchased two million cinema tickets per week, most for films made by American studios. They bought 50 million U.S. magazines. In terms of sales, the *Saturday Evening Post* was 'Canada's leading magazine.' Canadian manufacturers, retailers, and media entrepreneurs contributed, too. *Maclean's*, Saturday supplements such as the *Star Weekly*, and a host of other publications, as well as a growing number of private radio stations, prospered from the advertising.[90]

While these changes were transforming the way people in Canada worked and thought about themselves, 'the greatest merger movement in Canadian history' was taking place, primarily to reduce competition among domestic firms. Much of it was orchestrated by the banks and brokerage houses such as Wood Gundy. By 1927, the Bank of Commerce, the Bank of Montreal, and the Royal Bank controlled 70 per cent of banking resources and, in alliance with a number of life insurance and trust companies, enjoyed hitherto-unmatched economic clout and productive power. After creation of the Canada Power and Paper Co. in 1928 by the Gundy group, five companies controlled 90 per cent of

Canada's pulp and paper production.[91] Penetration by American industries, products, and cultural icons legitimized the NHL's new continental alignment, while American expansion gave it the capacity to dominate the rest of Canadian hockey. Monopoly profits in gold (the Bickells were the largest Leaf shareholders) and banking financed construction of Maple Leaf Gardens, while two American-based multi-nationals, General Motors and Imperial Oil, sponsored the spectacular transcendency of Hockey Night in Canada.'

After the NHL achieved its professional monopoly, the only effective competition that remained was the Canadian Amateur Hockey Association (CAHA). Community-based senior hockey thrived during the Depression. Diversions were few, so the stands were often full. The promise of a steady job was enough to keep lots of good players in the amateur leagues. The NHL was not for everyone. For all but the stars, salaries were low and opportunities uncertain, and anyone who signed a pro contract could never be reinstated if he was cut from a team. After the acceptance of professionalism in 1936, some CAHA players made as much money as the pros. But the NHL had the bankroll to bring the amateur clubs into line. Because the purpose of the CAHA was to foster playing opportunity, available sponsorships and gate receipts tended to be shared among a number of teams, rather than captured by a single franchise. In the mid-1930s, for example, there were eight senior amateur clubs from Toronto in the Ontario Hockey League, while the Leafs held a monopoly in professional hockey. None of the amateur teams could engage in a signing war for very long. The sudden signing of one or two top players could cripple a club and demoralize its supporters.

In 1936, to minimize the potential damage, the CAHA agreed to respect the NHL's reserve lists and have all players learn NHL rules, in exchange for a promise that NHL clubs not sign junior-age players. The CAHA also wanted the NHL to limit itself to one player per amateur club per season and to refrain from approaching any player during the amateurs' training camp period, but the promoters refused. After the Second World War, with most senior teams reeling from the disruptions caused by mobilization, the NHL forced the CAHA into complete surrender. For the next 25 years, the NHL turned the vast network of CAHA teams and leagues into a tightly controlled feeder system. 'The money barons of the NHL have relegated Canada to the role of a gigantic hockey slave farm,' CAHA Secretary-Manager Gordon Juckes said bitterly during the 1960s. 'We have become the Gold Coast of hockey.'[92]

NHL teams have brought untold pleasure to millions of Canadians. Apart from politics, NHL hockey has no equal as pan-Canadian theatre. The trials and achievements of the favourite players, the impassioned dramas of the annual Stanley Cup playoffs, and the richly textured symbolisms of the great rivalries provide many of us with an endless source of cultural narratives to ponder and share. For many, episodes from the histories of favourite teams contextualize the passages in our lives and link fathers and sons, teachers and students, long-standing residents and newcomers. The NHL's appeal is in part the game itself, the 'Canadian specific,' as poet Al Purdy once said. The promoters and their partners in 'Hockey Night in Canada' did much to make it attractive. That millions of Canadians so enthusiastically and consistently embrace NHL hockey is the measure of their accomplishment.

But the success of the NHL changed Canadian sport in other, unsettling ways. In the first place, it accentuated the metropolitan tendencies in Canadian economic and cultural development. By 1939, using the surpluses that the Bickells and their associates had drawn from the resource hinterlands, the NHL octopus drew talented athletes from every part of Canada to teams in six financial and manufacturing centres – Toronto, Montreal, New York, Boston, Detroit, and Chicago. Consumer purchases from every part of Canada contributed to the broadcasting fees that advertisers such as General Motors and Imperial Oil paid to the Leafs and the Canadiens. In the absence of revenue sharing, the NHL's policy of giving franchises municipal monopolies meant that only those in the largest, richest markets could survive. One of the best teams in the early NHL, the Ottawa Senators, winners of four Stanley Cups, succumbed to these economics during the lean 1930s. It became accepted wisdom that no other Canadian city could ever have a top team. Ironically, the whole complex process of packaging the best of a coast-to-coast cultural production for sale in central Canada and the United States was celebrated over the public radio network formed to promote Canadian unity and culture.

Though 'Hockey Night in Canada' encouraged a liberal, bi-national Canadianism, it simultaneously legitimized, even celebrated, those economic forces and discourses that undermined the ability of Canadians to sustain the communities and institutions they needed for their own lives. The subtext to the aura of accomplishment that the promoters and the mass media gave to the exodus of so many gifted players to the metropolitan centres of central Canada and the United States was that the cities and towns they had left had no right to them, nor to the rich, athletic dramas that they produced. It was hardly the 'export' of the best of Canadian culture, as it was often approvingly styled, when it left many of the communities that nurtured hockey without any top-flight hockey to enjoy for themselves. 'Cultural asset stripping' would be a more appropriate label.

The legacy of the NHL's 'original six,' as the teams that survived the league's first 25 years came to be called, was a Canadianism of contradiction and alienation. While the players' explosive artistry on the ice held out the promise of national strength, creativity, and grace, that potential was largely unrealized, subordinated to the dictates of continental capital. My generation grew up dreaming of emulating heroes who were forced to leave home at an early age in order to practise their craft, hardly circumstances that encouraged us to develop a strong commitment to our own society. I have long believed that the NHL's example served to accelerate the uncritical Americanization of so much of Canadian sport and retard development of opportunities for athletes who choose to stay in Canada. In their best moments, hockey players became Canadian Prometheuses, imprisoned by the gods of capital and guarded by vultures for the temerity of exciting our national ambition and pride. But in their worst moments, they became our tragedies, like Felix Batterinski in Roy McGregor's poignant novel *The Last Season*, or friendly buffoons, like Pierre St Pierre in Tomson Highway's play *Dry Lips Oughta Move to Kapuskasing*.

Moreover, the issues of subordination and impotence were very real to the thousands of boys and men who played the game. On the one hand, the NHL promised a meritocracy based on ability. Until the 1970s, it was the only pan-Canadian sporting organization that provided significant opportunity to French-Canadian athletes, though research indicates that only the exceptionally gifted could count on making it into the league.[93] The NHL also sought out and encouraged promising youngsters living outside the major cities. But on the other hand, it subjugated them all to a harsh and despotic system of labour relations. 'Professionalism' gave players nothing of the self-regulation, economic power, and security of other 'professionals' – lawyers and dentists, for instance. Smythe, Jack Adams, Art Ross, and other managers demanded military-style discipline, and the reserve clause gave them the means to enforce it.

Any attempt by players to exercise their rights was brutally suppressed. In the 1950s, even all-star players such as Ted Lindsay, Bert Olmstead, and Jim Thompson were traded to losing teams or demoted when they tried to form an association to question the league's unilateral management of their pension fund. Expecting players to devote themselves entirely to their teams, managers actively discouraged their attempts to acquire formal education and other forms of post-hockey qualifications – 'the nonsense of going to college,' as University of Toronto grad Smythe often put it – and eventually created a system of teenage apprenticeship that made it virtually impossible. Players were penalized or ridiculed for developing relationships outside of hockey and starting families. Smythe kept Bill Ezinicki in the minors for several years because he had got married without permission. To be sure, players enjoyed the satisfaction of working at something that they loved and much excitement, celebrity, and camaraderie. But while the NHL was not entirely responsible for the image of brutalized and brutalizing masculinity that is all too readily associated with hockey, it actively cultivated it.[94]

There are a number of 'what ifs' for historians. Was it inevitable that the NHL would stick to the 'full market' model of sport development, with the subjection of athletes into waged labourers, move into the United States, and take most of Canadian hockey with it? Or that so many from other parts of English-speaking Canada would come to identify uncritically with the team from hated Toronto (and, less frequently, Montreal)?

Certainly the American example exerted a powerful influence. In baseball, the capitalist model had been accepted well before the turn of the century. At the same time, Canadians had become much less interested in the British sports of soccer and cricket, where commercialization was modified by the motives of philanthropy and social control, so that most professional teams were kept in the communities where they were formed and run on a not-for-profit basis. Canadians had long been accustomed to playing against teams in the United States and welcoming American athletes in Canada. After The First World War, the cross-border traffic increased, as Canadians went south to work for American professional and college teams, and American athletes and coaches were 'imported' to work in Canada, even in rugby, where rules were significantly different. For example, in 1931, the Montreal Winged Wheelers won the Grey Cup behind the passing of Warren Stevens, an 'import' from Syracuse University. Stevens later became the football and basketball coach and first paid athletic director at the University of Toronto.

Canadian mass media coverage increasingly focused on American events and stars, since the Associated Press provided most of the news on the early wire services, including Canadian Press, established in 1907. With radio, many Canadians could hear U.S. sports news and events directly. While some Canadian stations tried to reconstruct the play-by-play of popular American events such as baseball's World Series, employing telegraph reports to do so, most Canadians preferred the live broadcasts emanating from the United States. In fact, the selling point of most radio advertisements was that sports fans could receive American signals directly. A study of the best-known athletes of the interwar period, as measured by headline frequency in the *Globe* and the *Winnipeg Free Press*, found that eight of ten in 1924–5 and seven of ten in 1935–6 were American. Babe Ruth scored highly in both decades. Of the other 19 athletes identified, only boxer Jim McLarnin was Canadian. It should also be said that in other enterprises, and in other areas of cultural production, Canadians were quite accustomed – and usually encouraged – to seek careers and capital in the United States.[95]

According to Frank Selke, decisive step in the NHL's rise to power was made in the winter of 1926–7, when Conn Smythe persuaded J.P. Bickell to keep the St Pats in Toronto and allow him to run it as the Maple Leafs. If Smythe's considerable energy and imagination had not been channelled into the NHL, it might never have succeeded in the way it did. There is good reason to believe him. The Maple Leafs were the NHL's flagship team throughout the depression, and the league might well have collapsed without them. If Toronto had continued as a CAHA stronghold, a Canadian Hockey League might well have developed along the lines of the Canadian Football League.[96] Alan Metcalfe suggests an even earlier turning point. He has argued that with the victory of the 'strict amateur' faction of Canadian sport in 1909, and rejection of a form of amateur-professional coexistence similar to that adopted in British soccer and cricket, Canadian hockey was irreparably split. As a result, the professionals could never call on sufficient resources to mount a major league entirely in Canada and were therefore drawn to the larger markets of the United States.[97]

Metcalfe's speculation leads us back to the amateur side. During the 1920s when the crucial decisions about the NHL were being taken, the amateur leaders had no fear about the national character of Canadian hockey because they were still very much in control and enjoying unprecedented success. They might have worried about the consequences of the NHL's flight to the United States, but they certainly did not think that their cities were losing 'representative' teams. Even during the 1930s, they must have felt confident. While the NHL lost four franchises, and many professional leagues folded altogether, most CAHA teams enjoyed record attendance. After the liberalization of eligibility in 1936, teams got stronger than ever. I think that this explains why there was so little outcry about the Americanization of the NHL. When the CAHA woke up to the changes a decade later, it was too late.

NHL franchises now operate in Ottawa, Calgary, Edmonton, and Vancouver – cities where fans could only read and hear about the NHL in the 1930s. Between 1979 and 1995, there were also NHL teams in Quebec and Winnipeg. These franchises were created in much different circumstances, including the brief boom in western resource-driven economies, willingness of provincial and municipal states to invest in the necessary facilities, and failure of the NHL to find comparable US markets. In cities such as Calgary, they were obtained by elites who sought a professional team as an expression of community pride. Today many of these franchises are in jeopardy. Despite record revenues, they find themselves unable to compete in the bidding for players from their rivals in larger cities. As a result, several owners have threatened to move their teams to the United States unless they are bailed out with huge tax subsidies. Vibrant cities once wooed as 'proud communities' when season tickets were in the offing are now demeaned as 'small markets.' The owners' only strategy to balance revenue around the league was to try to take it from the players in the form of a salary cap and/or a payroll tax – an approach that led to the lengthy 1994–5 lockout. Though the players were forced into major concessions in the 1995 agreement with the NHL that ended the lockout, they managed to defeat both the salary cap (except for rookies) and the payroll tax, thus renewing the Canadian owners' interest in franchise flight. Shortly after the 1995 season, the owners of the Quebec Nordiques chose to sell the team to the Comsat Entertainment Group in Denver rather than stay in Quebec with 'only' $21 million in public subsidy. The sale netted them a profit of $85 million.[98] In 1996, the Winnipeg Jets were sold to Phoenix businessmen despite an unprecedented outpouring of public support for keeping the team in the Manitoba capital and the willingness of three levels of government to contribute to a $200-million new arena.[99]

In each of these cases, the public policy options are extremely difficult. It can well be argued, as did Thin Ice, the Winnipeg group that opposed public subsidies to the Jets, that preserving top-flight hockey for Canadian cities should have much lower priority than sustaining public education and social services. But the sale and disappearance of popular teams like the Nordiques and the Jets disrupt and confuse many strong loyalties.

Except for the question of public subsidy, the issues are identical to those 70 years ago, when the NHL first expanded to the United States. If they are left to the NHL and the market to decide, the same sorry outcome is likely to result.

6

Capturing the State

In 1936, the dominion government contributed $10,000 towards the costs of sending Canadian athletes to the Olympic Games in Germany, and the minister of pensions and national health, Charles 'Chubby' Power attended a swirl of parties and events in Berlin on Canada's behalf. The donation evoked the bitter condemnation of the religious, university, labour, and veterans' leaders and organizations that opposed the Nazi Olympics and 'the despicable glorification of fascism in sport.' Prime Minister Mackenzie King tried to wash his hands of the whole affair, telling the House of Commons: 'I think it is very doubtful that anyone participating in the Olympic Games is a representative of the government of this country,' but this response satisfied no one. It not only infuriated those who supported the Workers' Sports Association–led boycott of the Games but provoked almost as much fury among the amateur leaders whose cherished national team was the recipient of the grant. For the latter, the money was not enough. It covered less than 30 per cent of the Canadian Olympic Committee's pared-down expenses, forcing officials and most athletes to pay their own way and those who could not find or raise the necessary funds to stay home. Olympic head P.J. Mulqueen, a prominent Toronto Liberal, put it as tactfully as he could: 'Canada as a nation cannot afford not to take these Games seriously and must make it possible for her athletes to worthily represent her. I trust that our national leaders will ponder deeply over this situation, and take measures to make it possible.'[1]

Not every governmental intervention in sports in Canada has touched off such impassioned politics, but no matter how public-spirited the rhetoric, none has been impartial to competing interests. In the nineteenth century, dominion, provincial, and local governments encouraged rifle-shooting and team sports, while prohibiting prize-fighting. They closely regulated the use of leisure in the general interests of male hegemony, middle-class morality, and capitalist production.[2] These attempts to shape the practice and meaning of sports were extended during the early years of the twentieth century, amid rapid economic expansion, political and ideological conflict, and public debates about use and display of the body.

In 1906, at the instigation of a coalition of Protestant churches and organized labour, the Laurier government passed the Lord's Day Act to impose uniform requirements across Canada, with the approval of the provinces. Except in Quebec, where the wide-open 'continental Sunday' continued to be accepted, the sabbatarian forces were successful in closing most public facilities, including parks, playgrounds, and swimming pools, and in eliminating commercial entertainments, on Sunday. In 1912, for example, they persuaded Toronto city council to close the popular toboggan runs in Riverdale and High parks on Sunday, despite the labour council's appeal for the 'inherent right of the people to spend Sundays as they please.' With Saturday employment common, the Lord's Day Act meant that most working people had few opportunities to use their own parks for active recreation. Public spectator events were also prohibited in most places. Of course, in the private clubs, sports continued to 'go on full blast.'[3]

The dominion government initiated several other long-lasting projects. In 1907, in the midst of the amateur wars, Governor General Lord Grey initiated establishment of the Canadian Olympic Committee (COC) through his secretary, John Hanbury-Williams, and henceforth Ottawa made a regular grant to the COC. In 1909, the minister of militia, Frederick Borden, strengthened the emphasis on military drill in the physical education curricula of most provinces through the trust fund put up by his arch-imperialist friend Lord Strathcona.

Middle-class concerns about health, urban civility, and the moral order pressed provincial and municipal governments to take greater responsibility for provision of facilities and programs. The campaign for inner-city supervised playgrounds, led by the National Council of Women (NCW), social workers such as J.J. Kelso, Ontario's superintendent of neglected and dependent children, and small businessman such as Thomas Boyd of Winnipeg, was motivated by the same spirit that inspired the 'rational recreation' favoured by the Amateur Athletic Union of Canada (AAU). 'The basic principle is PREVENTION,' Mabel Peters, the NCW's convenor of vacation schools and supervised playgrounds, told the 1913 annual convention. Our work in playgrounds 'seeks to eventually dispense with the curfew, the juvenile court, the jail and the reform school for the young of our land.' Though women's groups initially staffed the new playgrounds themselves, they eventually succeeded in getting cities and towns to take them over.[4]

People located within the state also contributed to these developments. In 1909, for example, Ontario education officials introduced regulations requiring high schools seeking the benefits of 'collegiate status' to build gymnasiums. The resulting additions did much to stimulate girls' and women's sport. Of course, with improved opportunity came closer scrutiny. In the schools, public health legislation allowed authorities and professionals further scrutiny of children's bodies through the powers of inoculation, quarantine, and medical and dental examination.[5]

The Amateurs' Holy Grail: A National Ministry of Sports

Of the four groups examined in this study, none tried harder to woo the state to intervene on its behalf than the Amateur Athletic Union. Throughout the period, the AAU's national leadership tried repeatedly to get the dominion government to create a national ministry of sports. Unlike many conservatives today, the middle-class patriarchs of the AAU harboured no ideological compunctions about seeking state assistance, even if that meant active intervention and a measure of state regulation over their own activities. Like many others in the voluntary sector of Canadian society (and among big business, too), they understood the Canadian social economy to be inextricably mixed, with governments advancing upper- and middle-class interests in a myriad of direct and indirect ways. Eminently practical, they hoped to advance their own social and cultural ambitions through the resources and legislative leverage of the state.[6]

It was the centrality of sports to the training and motivation of the Canadian Expeditionary Forces that first inspired the AAUers to push for a full-fledged ministry. During the summer of 1918, Norton Crow, W.A. Hewitt, Bruce MacDonald, Francis Nelson, and the other members of the Union's 'Reconstruction Committee' became convinced that the strength and self-confidence that sports had inculcated among the troops could be developed in the nation as a whole and sustain Canadians through the difficult transition to peacetime and the urgent tasks of social regeneration. The national promotion of sports would also serve as a fitting memorial to the thousands of young men killed and maimed by the guns in France. But without a proper program, they feared, the fitness of the troops would atrophy, and little would be done for the general population. In October, an AAU delegation to Ottawa received a 'favourable reception' from the health minister, Newton Rowell, who assured it that 'it was not necessary to argue the importance of sport in the life of the nation.'

Encouraged, Crow and his colleagues drew up elaborate plans for the dominion and provincial governments and their own associations. First, the department of soldiers' re-establishment would facilitate the rehabilitation and resettlement of soldiers by providing them with 'properly organized recreation' after their return. As a second step, Ottawa should 'nationalize playground and kindred work' with an ambitious program of facility construction. Town planning experts would create designs to a national standard and coordinate their construction with redevelopment of existing areas and the development of new ones. A national ministry of sports would then provide programs in these facilities and give ready access to the amateur sports bodies and clubs. Third, the plan called for the provincial governments to improve and extend physical education in the schools and to foster sports and recreation in rural areas. In both cases, the AAU would provide the necessary policy and technical advice.

The British North America Act, 1867, made no mention of sports, but the AAUers correctly assumed that both levels of government would assume jurisdiction. The reconstruction committee also recommended that both levels provide annual grants to the AAU, so that it could expand its own programs. The monies would be used to increase AAU representation at important meetings, standardize and improve championships, and extend technical assistance to coaches and clubs. The committee proposed that details of the plan should be fleshed out by a national sports planning conference in Ottawa to which delegates from all sports governing bodies, provincial ministries of education and municipal recreation departments would be invited. It asked the Canadian Pacific Railway (CPR) to provide members with free or subsidized rail passes, so that a large number could attend.[7]

But neither the Union government in Ottawa nor the CPR was prepared to meet the AAUers' demands. The government was exhausted by the war and preoccupied with the labour agitation that led to the Winnipeg general strike, the country-wide influenza epidemic, the delicate political task of refinancing the new transcontinental railways, and its own political future. Those Liberals who had joined with Prime Minister Borden in support of conscription were openly preparing for their departure. Agriculture Minister Thomas Crerar was the first to leave, in April 1919, to lead farmers' protests against central Canadian business domination. Sports were a distant concern. In the case of the demobilized soldiers, 'reconstruction' was limited to resettlement and re-employment schemes.

Even if he had been contemplating a sports program, Newton Rowell would have been discouraged by the response that he received in the House of Commons in April 1919 when he introduced the bill to create his new department of health. He used many of the arguments that the AAUers had presented him about the sorry state of the nation's health. Fifty per cent of the adult population of military age had had to be rejected as physically unfit, showing 'the room there is in caring for the health and well-being of the people of this country,' he told the House. But members of the opposition were uneaasy about the new initiative. Some claimed that health was properly a matter of provincial jurisdiction. Others decried the government's ambition to assume responsibility for social welfare. Thomas Tweedie of Calgary 'thought this social welfare business could be carried to an extreme. Social welfare leaguers were already attacking the use of tobacco. He feared that this clause gave the Government power to regulate the habits of the people.' The 'venom' against the bill was so great that Rowell was forced to dilute the bill's preamble to get it through second reading.[8] Shortly afterwards, Finance Minister Thomas White wrote Norton Crow that 'government support [for the AAU's plan] would not be possible.'

Undaunted, the amateur sports leaders kept up the pressure upon dominion politicians throughout the period, with personal letters and delegations, formal resolutions from the 'Canadian Parliament of Sport,' and planted appeals in the press. During the Depresssion, the AAU's plummeting revenues dashed its hopes of improving opportunities for Canadians living and training in Canada. The curtailment of their own development plans made the record medal haul from the Los Angeles Olympics in 1932 bittersweet: most of the Canadian medals were won by US-trained athletes. Henry Roxborough, increasingly the voice of amateurism through his regular features in *Maclean's*, berated Ottawa for its 'miserly' support of the Canadian Olympic Committee. The 'failure to [create] a better system of development and discovery can be attributed to the failure of the federal government, which failed to supply adequate funds. Why place the financial responsibility on Government? Surely the reasons are obvious.' The international goodwill and 'national advertising' would repay the costs many times over, he argued.[9]

On those few occasions when the national government was prompted to think about sports, it preferred to do so in connection with cadets. The defence department sponsored the after-school training of approximately 100,000 public, separate and secondary schoolboys each year and gave a smaller number of them a week-long advance course in summer camps across the country. The cadets received instruction in first aid, signalling, scouting, marching drill, and rifle shooting and took part in physical fitness activities, including sports. The annual estimates could always be counted upon to produce a lengthy debate in the Commons. When Liberal finance ministers tried to pare down the appropriation, they found themselves under attack from both the left and the right. Staunch imperialists such as Toronto Tory Thomas Church condemned them for cutting 'the backbone of the militia' and discouraging patriotism, while pacifists such as the Ginger Group's J.S. Woodsworth and Agnes Macphail urged elimination of the program altogether.

But both defenders and abolitionists agreed on the need for public expenditures on sports. Church complained that 'if the work of these camps is stopped, the rising generation who come from places where the conditions are not good for physical development will suffer and have no recreation.' Woodsworth 'sympathize[d] with any movement in the direction of giving an impetus to athletics.'[10] But neither Liberal nor Tory governments were prepared to take advantage of this middle ground in support of sports. In 1924, the International Labour Conference of the League of Nations recommended that member governments develop sports facilities to enhance workers' hygiene and spare time, but Canada's justice minister, Ernest Lapointe, counselled against dominion action on the grounds that this was a provincial responsibility.[11]

Another attempt at establishing a national sports program was made in 1937 by Liberal MP Hugh Plaxton, who introduced a resolution in the House of Commons calling for a ministry of sports. Plaxton had starred for the University of Toronto team that won the 1927 Allan Cup and the 1928 Olympics and briefly played for the Montreal Maroons before practising law. In 1935, the 31-year-old celebrity was elected in Toronto's Trinity riding on the promise of health insurance, 'a fair and living wage for everyman,' and a better deal for youth. The previous year, in separate interventions, Conservative Thomas Church and health minister 'Chubby' Power stimulated considerable press comment over their proposals that Ottawa assume responsibility for sport and recreation. Plaxton incorporated these ideas and the salient points of the public discussion into his resolution. The program he proposed would oversee administration of amateur sport, particularly selection of Canadian Olympic teams, and initiate a 'national scheme of physical training' in conjunction with the provinces.[12]

Plaxton stressed the national prestige that could be won or lost through international sport. Ironically, because the AAU had long advocated a dominion sports department, his greatest concern was the failure of amateur leaders to avoid an embarrassing defeat in the 1936 Olympics hockey tournament. Initially, the Allan Cup–winning Halifax Wolverines had been slated to go, but the Canadian Amateur Hockey Association (CAHA) had suddenly declared them ineligible and had nominated the runners-up, the Port Arthur Bearcats, in their place. In Garmisch-Partenkirchen, the Bearcats lost what they believed was a preliminary game 2–1 to a British team led by two Canadian-trained players. They fully expected that the gold medal would be decided in the final. The two teams proved to be the top qualifiers, but Olympic officials said that a final game was unnecessary because Britain had already beaten Canada. They awarded the championship to Britain, stonewalling the Canadian Olympic Committee's protest. (The British manager who outsmarted Canadian officials in the committee room was A.F. 'Bunny' Ahearn. He subsequently became president of the international ice hockey federation and frustrated Canadian efforts again and again.) The whole episode called the competence of amateur officials into question, Plaxton told the House. 'The time is long past when any athlete or group of athletes who presume to represent Canada should be permitted to do so without proper supervision and control by someone responsible to this government.' Plaxton also advanced the AAUers' familiar arguments about the importance of sports to national health. The major governments in Europe had taken responsibility for sports and fitness, in part to prepare for war, he said. Canada should do the same.

The ensuing debate brought home the length to which the amateurs still had to go to demonstrate that public responsibility for sports was in the national interest. The Conservatives enthusiastically endorsed the idea of dominion contributions, especially if they would assist municipalities in construction of playgrounds and other facilities. 'I know of no better influence for good in the community than clean, well regulated amateur sport,' Frank Lennard of Wentworth told the Commons. But they did not believe that taxpayers would support a full-blown ministry. Tommy Douglas of Weyburn, Saskatchewan, who spoke for the newly formed Cooperative Commonwealth Federation (CCF), urged another course altogether. He would support dominion encouragement of 'national cultural development, national drama, national music festivals, and some type of national recreation,' but not of sports, at least not as a health measure. Though he recognized the contribution that sports made to 'healthy bodies,' Douglas felt that full access to medical and hospital care had much higher priority.

These cautions no doubt enabled the government to climb down from any suggested undertaking. 'Chubby' Power directed Plaxton to withdraw his resolution, killing the dream of a national ministry of sports one more time.

The Ontario Athletic Commission

But the amateur leaders did achieve a breakthrough in Ontario, the province in which they were strongest. In 1919, they persuaded the Conservative government of William Howland Hearst to fund construction of community centres and athletic fields. Under the Community Halls Act, municipalities that established recreation committees were eligible for 25 per cent of the costs of building new facilities. The grants contributed to a slow but steady expansion of public sports facilities in the years that followed.[13] In 1920, the AAUers took advantage of a favourable convergence of circumstances – the efforts of returning soldiers to get boxing legalized and the 'social purity' campaigns of the newly elected United Farmers of Ontario – to engineer a modest provincial version of their reconstruction plan.

Enforcement of the 1881 ban on 'prize-fighting' had always been uneven. Police forces were reluctant to prosecute, and magistrates and juries to convict. Their concern for order conflicted with their admiration for the manly and democratic virtues of physical self-defence. Many of them shared Senator William Almon's reservations about the ban, believing that 'settling disputes [by fisticuffs] was better than to resort to the stilletto of the Spaniard and Italian, or the revolver and bowie knife of our cousins across the border.'[14] In acquitting the defendants in a bout staged by the Hamilton Bowling and Athletic Club in 1911, Presiding Judge Snider declared: 'I am as much opposed to prize fighting and brutality and intentional injury in boxing, football, hockey or lacrosse, as any person can be. At the same time, I feel confident that it will be a long time before Parliament will think it wise to so hedge in young men and boys by legislation that all sports that are rough and strenuous or even dangerous must be given up. Virility in young men would soon be lessened and self-reliant manliness a thing of the past.'[15]

The common law was contradictory. Middle-class amateur boxing was not included in the prohibition. As court decisions accumulated, exhibitions of professional sparring came to be allowed as well, as long as the encounter was not intended to inflict injury and no winner was declared. The distinction between sparring and fighting to the finish was almost impossible to determine, as one superintendent informed Ontario premier James Whitney, making the police even more reluctant to intervene.[16]

By the 1910s, sports organizations such as the Montreal Canadiens Hockey Club and promoters such as Toronto's Tom Flanagan were staging professional contests before audiences that included 'some of the best people in the city and some of the worst.'[17] The threat of arrest and conviction remained, nevertheless. After a bout in Calgary in 1913 billed as the 'White Heavyweight Championship of the World,' Arthur Pelkey was charged with manslaughter when Luther McCarty died from his punch. Chief Justice Harvey of the Alberta Supreme Court advised the all-male jury that an illegal contest had taken place. It none the less returned a verdict of 'not guilty.' A Montreal bout was declared illegal in 1918.[18] The possibility of fines and imprisonment and the rule against the declaration of winners hindered the promotion of boxing as a popular and profitable entertainment.

Developments during the Great War challenged public authorities to liberalize the law. Along with wrestling, boxing was encouraged as training for the infantry – sparring was considered excellent preparation for the bayonet plunge of trench warfare – and as entertainment behind the lines. Matches were staged between the best from each unit, and winners were freely declared. While no one was paid, admissions were collected and wagers taken, often producing considerable income for canteens. When the soldiers returned home, many stayed in touch with each other in the cities and towns where they were demobilized and sought to continue the fraternal social life that they had enjoyed overseas, organized around boxing. The sport provided them with a reassuring, masculinist narrative of continuity in the face of a 'new world order' transformed by war-accelerated urbanization and industrialization, temperance restrictions, and women's suffrage. But to enjoy boxing with impunity, they had to change the law. In Ontario especially, they vigorously pressed their elected officials to do so. They argued that professional boxing had won acceptance in many of the adjoining U.S. states which had also once outlawed it.[19]

In this campaign, the veterans worked closely with the amateur leadership. The AAUers had enthusiastically supported the close association of sports with the war effort. Many had actively campaigned for militarization of physical activity in schools. Now they were confident that boxing could contribute to postwar social discipline. 'No boy physically fit should be allowed to leave school without having learned to contend with others. It is to be regretted that boxing cannot be taught in every school in the land,' Bruce MacDonald told the Ontario Educational Association. Headmaster of the private St Andrew's boys' school in Aurora, Ontario, MacDonald was elected national AAU president in 1920. Francis Nelson, another widely respected AAU leader, argued in the *Star* that the encouragement of boxing, in the context of an overall program of state support for sports, would enable Ontario to keep apace with governments in Europe. In France, he pointed out, the state and the army conducted sports 'to combat the evils of drink, debachery and laziness.' In Britain, 'a moral foundation is being established by the encouragement of boxing among the Boy Scouts ... The finals were held at Holborn Stadium and the spectators included the younger generation of the royal family.'[20]

Both vets and the AAUers found unlikely allies in Ontario's farmer-labour government, headed by E.C. Drury, which had been elected, to the surprise of everyone, including its own members, in 1919. During its single term in office, the Drury government introduced a number of progressive social measures, including the first mothers' allowances and a minimum wage for women, and increased workers' compensation. But the farmers in power drew the most press and public comment from their espousal of moral reform. Convinced that 'rural depopulation and the beguiling attractions of city life were dangerously eroding the superior values of the agrarian way,' they were determined to do something to elevate standards of personal conduct throughout the province.[21] This meant a vigorous effort by Attorney General William Raney to strengthen and enforce the Ontario Temperance Act, which prohibited sale of alcoholic beverages except under medical supervision. Raney also campaigned forcefully against racetracks and gambling. Both were protected by dominion legislation, but he could tax them, and he did – slapping an onerous daily levy of $5,000 (for half-mile tracks) and $10,000 (for one mile) and 5 per cent of the pari-mutuel gross upon all racecourses in the province. The AAUers must have quickly warmed to him. Both shared the same strict, 'improving' spirit.

These various interests and ambitions were brought together by Dugall

Carmichael, a 35-year-old, Scots Presbyterian farmer and decorated veteran from Meaford, who was minister without portfolio in the Drury cabinet, and AAU Secretary Norton Crow. Early in 1920, Carmichael won public and legislative approval for creation of an Ontario Athletic Commission (OAC) to regulate boxing and 'assist, promote and encourage amateur sport and recreation in schools, community centres and through associations of amateur sportsmen.' It seems probable that Crow, who was seconded from his position in the provincial treasury to serve as Carmichael's secretary throughout the process, drafted the actual legislation.

The Ontario Athletic Commission Act of 1920 provided a politically palatable formula – regulation – for the legalization of boxing, overcoming the ambiguities and inconsistencies in dominion and common law. Ottawa sanctioned Ontario's approach in an amendment to the Criminal Code in 1933, paving the way for similar regulatory agencies in other provinces.[22] In relaxing the restrictions against boxing – a popular and perhaps inevitable step, given the legitimation that the war brought to all forms of combat – the Drury government simultaneously brought it under tight control. The profits promised by a visible industry gave veterans' clubs and promoters an incentive to obtain a licence, while legalization encouraged pro-boxing police superintendents and constables to enforce the new law. At the same time, the regime that the OAC established reined in the most barbarous features of the clandestine game, encouraging a more 'scientific' code of physical manliness.

From the outset, the regulations required all clubs and promoters to obtain a medical examination for each boxer each time he fought. Instead of the underground 'fight to the finish,' bouts were restricted to ten rounds of three minutes each. In 1921, the commission imposed the strict British amateur rules on professional contests, explaining that 'it goes on record as favouring the boxer as opposed to the fighter.' It did, however, enforce discrimination against Blacks, banning the ageing Jack Johnson in 1924 and prohibiting 'mixed bouts,' even when the Black boxer was a returned soldier.[23]

The commission was expected to be self-supporting, financing development of amateur sport from the taxes and licence fees that it was empowered to collect from professional boxing and wrestling. Though these powers and resources fell significantly short of Crow's dreams, they none the less strengthened the AAUers' authority and legitimacy and gave them new access to the corridors of government. While American legislation provided the precedent for the commission structure, no other

North American jurisdiction provided direct financial support to amateur sport or gave amateur leaders direct say in how the monies would be spent. All five initial commissioners were prominent AAUers. Francis Nelson became chair of the boxing board, and Olympic President Pat Mulqueen headed up the athletic board. As vacancies occurred or governments changed, new commissioners were appointed, but whatever the party in power, at least some of them came from the AAU. In 1923, the act was amended to give the Ontario branch of the AAU the right to ask the commission to conduct a study into 'any matter which [it] considers should be investigated in the interest of amateur sport in the province.'[24] No other athletic organization was mentioned in the legislation.

In keeping with the AAU's mission of 'making men,' the OAC's initial focus was on broadening opportunity for schoolboys across the province. In its very first intervention, it conducted a seminar for student teachers at the Toronto Normal School. It assisted teachers in the field with free distribution of relevant rules and educational materials. In 1922, it made an agreement with A.G. Spalding to prepare and distribute 10,000 copies of a booklet containing the rules of indoor and outdoor baseball, basketball, handball, hockey, lacrosse, rugby, soccer, tennis, and volleyball, thought to be the most popular games played in Ontario schools. By the late 1920s, it operated a lending library of technical literature from its office in Toronto.

To ensure that teachers and athletes were familiar with the most up-to-date techniques and training methods, the OAC sent prominent coaches around the province to conduct clinics in public, private, and industrial schools and in community clubs. The famed Walter Knox of Orillia, who once held the world's All-Around Championship (an earlier, multiple-event, track and field competition) and coached the Canadian team at the 1912 and 1920 Olympics, was one such itinerant coach. In 1922, Knox spent 105 days (at $10 a day, plus expenses) offering clinics for the commission. Each involved a two-hour demonstration, 'showing by example,' followed by a practice period. He took a 'motion picture machine' with him and usually screened one of the commission's three instructional films. As much as possible, he taught in a central location, so that teachers and athletes from several schools could attend, coordinated by the local school board. In 1923, Knox spent all but 11 of the 97 days he worked for the OAC outside of Toronto. He taught in every region of the province except Ottawa, where Nick Bawlf, who coached at Cornell, visited the schools. In 1928, the commission sponsored more than 200 clinics in 73 Ontario cities and towns. It also initiated learn-to-swim programs. Between 1924 and 1928, 20,000 children took part. 'The point' of all this, J.P. Fitzgerald wrote in his annual report for 1922, 'is that play is necessary and natural. The view of the Commission is that properly directed, it will get infinitely better results, in health and pleasure, apart altogether from the making of champions.'

But like the AAU leadership, the OAC gradually shifted its focus to the making of champions. To stimulate competition, the commission provided medals and other prizes. Outside the major cities, it took the initiative in organizing schools into district associations, creating the structure that became the Ontario Federation of School Athletic Associations in 1948. It started a provincial schoolboys' track and field championship and subsidized travel and accommodation for qualified athletes – provided that they achieved passing grades in school. In 1928, more than 5,000 boys took part in the district meets, and 214 participated in the Ontario finals in Toronto. Out-of-town competitors were given an extra day's expenses so that they could take advantage of the 'education' offered by the Canadian National Exhibition (CNE). Promising senior athletes received coaching assistance as well. The commission claimed that 90 per cent of the Ontario athletes who won places on the Olympic team received instruction from its coaches.[25]

Gradually, the OAC began to address another of the amateur leaders' goals – assistance to governing bodies and sports clubs. It provided office space and secretarial services to the Ontario AAU and meeting rooms for other provincial sports governing bodies. It subsidized the travel of Ontario athletes to national championships, Olympic Trials, and special competitions. For example, before he turned professional (and won the $25,000 first prize in the 1927 Catalina Marathon) swimmer George Young was able to race in Ottawa, Montreal, and New York with the commission's assistance. The commission helped pay for construction of special facilities, such as the indoor track at the CNE Coliseum. In the late 1920s, it undertook 'a long desired work for the restoration of Canada's National sport, Lacrosse,' starting several leagues and stocking them with coaches. It had a hand in the origins of the British Empire Games, subsidizing Commissioner M.M. Robinson's travels to Europe to win support for the plan. When the first Games were held in 1930, it held the schoolboy championships in Hamilton at the same time, so that participating athletes and coaches could benefit from watching top-flight competition.[26]

Given these growing programs, the AAUers on the OAC sought to obtain revenues from other professional sports. A minute of 1925 set the tone: 'Hockey has contributed neither time, attention, encouragement or money toward the development of the very players whose early training and development make [the pros' large dividends] possible. The same facts apply more or less to professional baseball and football. Nothing has been contributed by these sports to the development of the amateur.'

That indictment became a refrain as professional sports grew rapidly in the booming urban economy of Toronto. In 1927, the OAC persuaded the Conservative provincial government of Howard Ferguson to give it the power to collect a 2 per cent tax on the gross box-office receipts of all professional events. The existing 5 per cent tax on boxing and wrestling was lowered to conform with the new levy, though promoters, fighters, managers, and referees were still liable for fees and fines that were not collected from the other sports. (In many years, these additional charges brought in more revenue than the gate tax.[27]) In the legislature, the health and labour minister, Dr Forbes Godfrey, promised that the additional revenues would enable the OAC to campaign more effectively for 'healthy citizenship,' which in turn depended on 'healthy boyhood.' 'We want boys raised in this country who are not afraid to fight. This "sob-sistering" and "too-much-military-training" talk [referring to the anti-cadet speeches of Agnes Macphail] is all nonsense.' Godfrey then singled out Ferguson as a 'first class fighting boy in the Village of Kemptville. He licked every kid in the place and twice tried teachers twice his size.' It is impossible to gauge the effect of such bluster on the legislature, but the bill sailed through without opposition. 'No fault will be found with the proposal,' *Globe* sports editor Frederick Wilson told his readers.[28] Though Conn Smythe and other professional managers resented the tax, they did not yet have the political clout to stop it.

The new levy more than doubled the commission's budget. Twelve sports, including boxing and wrestling, contributed to the revenue, though hockey (51 per cent), wrestling (20 per cent), boxing (11 per cent) and baseball (11 per cent) produced 93 per cent of it. The range of sports provided some stability during the depths of the Depression, when the bottom fell out of boxing and the Toronto Maple Leaf Baseball franchise went bankrupt. Nevertheless, revenues in 1936–7 were only 69 per cent of those of 1928–9, the last year before the Great Crash. The commission estimated that 90 per cent of its revenues came from events in Toronto. As Table 6.1 indicates, the proceeds provide a telling measure of the uneven development of commercial sports in that city.

TABLE 6.1
Ontario Athletic Commission revenues from gate tax (dollars), 1927–40

	1927–8	1928–9	1929–30	1930–1	1932–3	1933–4	1935–6*	1936–7	1937–8	1938–9	1939–40	Summary
Baseball	3,642.77	2,544.01	1,846.89	1,430.53†	‡	2,592.44	1,858.72	1,486.56	2,322.71	1,885.25	2,622.45	22,292.33
Boxing	4,364.20	4,747.57	2,394.53	1,900.32	539.63	221.76	469.74	702.98	4,258.43	2,212.54	1,030.63	22,842.33
Hockey	8,609.63	10,985.33	11,421.26	11,218.63	11,449.13	8,825.36	8,526.47	8,544.17	8,726.40	8,480.60	9,333.12	106,120.10
Soccer	275.07			258.22	85.16							618.45
Swimming§	1,100.00	1,167.84	678.30	576.00	323.44	238.00	183.00	150.00	115.20			4,531.78
Wrestling		1,617.33	3,340.96	4,201.04	5,346.99	6,659.59	4,569.79	3,295.62	4,569.79	5,395.74	2,017.87	41,014.72
Lacrosse				556.37								556.37
Cycling					493.02	1,252.37	739.95	332.89	137.27			2,955.50
Rowing						100.00				60.00		160.00
Tennis							65.58	35.09	93.32	92.10	23.76	309.85
Ice skating										3,185.37	1,444.47	4,629.84
Roller skating											113.75	113.75
Totals	17,991.67	21,062.08	19,681.94	20,141.11	18,237.37	19,889.52	16,413.25	14,547.31	20,223.12	21,311.60	16,586.05	206,085.02

NOTES: The tax was 2 per cent. In boxing and wrestling, the OAC also levied fees and fines and took a percentage of the purses awarded, but this revenue is not shown here. No report was filed for 1931–2.
* In 1935, the commission changed its fiscal year from 1 November–31 October to 1 April–31 March. The revenue for the five months 1 November 1934 to 31 March 1935 has not been included.
† Does not include $936 in uncollected tax
‡ Tax of $1206, paid in $600 instalments in each of 1933–4 and 1934–5
§ Sometimes levied on gates, sometimes on purses.

The gate tax enabled the OAC to provide direct financial assistance to sports governing bodies and clubs. In 1938–9, 40 provincial or regional associations and clubs received annual grants totalling $6,000 – about 20 per cent of the commission's budget (Table 6.2). The new monies also enabled the commission to realize a long-standing dream of the amateur leaders – a provincial training centre. In 1929, playing fields, a 440-yard cinder track, a swimming dock, and accommodation for 66 athletes plus staff were constructed on 17 acres of farmland along Lake Couchiching, near Orillia. As soon as it was ready, the Ontario Athletic Camp began to hold two three-week summer training sessions each year for high-school athletes from around the province. A select few from every district were sent on scholarship, while others could enrol at $10 a week. Pride of place was given to track and field and swimming. Hockey and wrestling, whose professional activities gave the commission the bulk of its revenue, were not offered at all. The camp was also made available to the Department of Education for the upgrading of physical education teachers and to the amateur sports governing bodies for their own training camps. Here women first significantly benefited from the OAC's work. In 1934, the Department of Education began to hold an annual week-long workshop for female physical education teachers from all parts of Ontario. In 1937, after several refusals, the leaders of the Women's Amateur Athletic Association of Ontario persuaded Commissioner Lionel Conacher to let them use the camp for their own leadership development program and then to subsidize participation of young women from across the province.[29]

British Columbia Pro-Rec and Its Impact

Canada's organized amateur sports movement had very little to do with the other major governmental initiative of the period – the Recreational and Physical Education Branch of the Adult Education Division of the British Columbia Department of Education, or 'Pro-Rec,' as it became widely known – established in 1934. While the AAUers increasingly concentrated on developing top athletes, BC Pro-Rec was started to meet the recreational and fitness needs of the thousands of unemployed and destitute young men who rode the rods to the warm-winter cities of Vancouver and Victoria during the depths of the Depression. The instigators were Ian Eisenhardt, Vancouver's superintendent of playgrounds, and George Weir, education minister in the 'Little New Deal' Liberal government of Duff Pattullo. Though cash-strapped Vancouver

TABLE 6.2
Ontario Athletic Commission, grants to sports bodies, 1938–9

Organization	Amount ($)
Argonaut Rowing Club	200
Athletic Board, St Patrick's College	200
Brockville Rowing Club	200
Canadian Canoe Association, Northern Division	150
Cataraqui Aquatic Club	100
Catholic Youth Organization	300
Don Rowing Club	200
Leander Rowing Club	200
Mercury Athletic Club	50
91st Highlanders' Athletic Association	250
Ontario Amateur Basketball Association	150
Ontario Amateur Lacrosse Association	500
Ontario Amateur Softball Association	300
Ontario Bantam and Midget Hockey Association	150
Ontario Baseball Association	400
Ontario Church Basketball Association	150
Ontario Education Association, Men's Physical Committee	150
Ontario Juvenile Hockey Association	150
Ontario Rugby Football Union	100
Ontario Rural Hockey Association	150
Ontario Section, Canadian Amateur Swimming Association	250
Ottawa Rowing Club	200
Premier Athletic Club	50
Provincial Women's Softball Union	200
Toronto Amateur Baseball Association	100
Toronto Amateur Hockey Association	113
Toronto Hockey League	150
Toronto Rugby Union	75
Western Ontario Secondary Schools Association	100
Women's Amateur Athletic Federation	700
Total	5,988

was forced to eliminate most of its formal recreation programs, Eisen-hardt struggled to provide some organized activity for the swelling numbers of 'hobos' who congregated in the city's parks and playgrounds looking for something to do.

A recent emigrant from Denmark, where gymnastics and sports were conducted by volunteers as part of the Danish folk school movement, Eisenhardt began a system of volunteer-led games and classes. But there were always far more who wanted to take part than leaders and facilities available, so he approached Weir for assistance. Weir needed no convincing. A former professor of education at the University of British Columbia, he was already a strong believer in the benefits of physical activity. 'An A1 intelligence cannot function adequately in a C3 physique,' he had written in 1925 in support of recommendations for a comprehensive program of physical education in a commissioned report on BC schools. Weir was also a proponent of provincial health insurance. Agreeing that the 'demoralizing influences of enforced idleness' could only retard the government's 'Work and Wages' job creation initiatives, he got Eisenhardt to sketch out a province-wide program and pushed it through cabinet in less than a month, hiring Eisenhardt to be the director.[30]

From the outset, Weir and Eisenhardt went far beyond the initial impulse of sports and fitness for unemployed young men. They set up Pro-Rec centres wherever there was interest, whether application came from a municipality no longer able to provide activities itself, a service club, or an unorganized group. The programs were free to anyone who wanted to participate. By 1939, 155 centres had been established, not only in Vancouver, Victoria, and the lower mainland, but in the northern parts of Vancouver Island and throughout the interior of the province. Initially, Pro-Rec set up and equipped each centre, but demand became so great that soon it required the local group to provide the facility. Schools, community halls, even commercial cinemas and theatres during their 'dark' times were used. The first leaders and instructors came from existing institutions, such as Ys, municipal playgrounds, and schools, but growing demand forced the branch to recruit and train many with no previous experience. The enthusiasm brought by these 'converts' provided an added boost.

During winter, centres usually operated twice a week, conducting two-to-three-hour sessions of dancing, gymnastics, keep-fit routines, and sports. The men's program featured apparatus gymnastics, basketball, boxing, handball, volleyball, weightlifting, and wrestling, while the women's program offered a wide variety of dance, gymnastics, and sports. Skiing instruction and outings were arranged on a co-gender basis where there was snow. An extensive summer program, which included swimming lessons, was offered as well. For those who could not attend a centre, a weekly radio program took listeners through a program of exercises set to music – today's aerobics participants would feel right at home – and gave them health and nutrition tips. In addition, Pro-Rec sponsored sports teams, youth hostelling, mass displays, film screenings, drama groups, provincial championships in a number of sports, activities for the blind and deaf, and social dances.

The programs were so popular that enrolment jumped from 2,768 in 1934 to 43,869 in 1937. A majority of registered participants – 24,077 – were women, making Pro-Rec the most 'female-friendly' public recreation program in Canadian history. Instead of the emphasis upon military drill and competition found in programs elsewhere, Pro-Rec's slogan was 'Health, Beauty, Diet and Sports.' Women found the comprehensive mix of fitness, sports, outdoor activities, and social events highly attractive. The department's monthly newletter, the *Gymnast*, stressed involvement of women at all levels of leadership and participation and was remarkably free of the infantilizing treatment of women that characterized most other publications of the time. By 1939, Pro-Rec's annual budget was $79,441, almost three times that of the Ontario Athletic Commission.[31]

The success of Pro-Rec encouraged a broad sprectrum of interests in Canada to press for a dominion initiative. The Calgary Leisure Time League, the Canadian Council on Child Welfare, the Canadian National Parks Association, the Canadian Physical Education Association, the Workers' Sports Association, the YM and YWCAs, and others began citing the BC example in their calls for a national recreation program. In its widely discussed *Social Planning for Canada*, the League for Social Reconstruction proposed vastly improved public recreation as part of an ambitious program of social welfare measures that included national unemployment and health insurance. The Canadian Youth Congress demanded better recreation as a basic right of citizenship: 'We know the values of games and sports in the maintenance of body, alertness of mind and discipline and cooperation in social relations. We want public facilites and trained leaders and workers, as are now provided for more formal education, for wholesome recreation for all people, rural and urban.' Municipalities and employers put forth a mixture of humanitarian, developmental, and social-control arguments to the same end, convinced that recreation could help alleviate Depression misery, halt the rapid decline in the skills, health, and morale of the idle labour force, and restore public stability and morality.[32]

The continuing economic and social devastation caused by the Depression, and the soul-searching and agitation that it provoked across the country, were by far the most important factors underlying these appeals. The growing pressures for dominion recreation policies must be understood in the context of the shifting interplay of corporate, political, state, labour, and popular interests as they struggled to address capitalism's failure to provide for a large part of the population. In 1935, half a million Canadians, including about 20 per cent of those aged from 16 to 30, remained out of work, and despite modest recovery many industries continued to operate well below capacity. Many local and provincial governments were driven close to bankruptcy in the effort to help them with emergency relief payments.

It was clear that the Bennett government's principal attempt to address the crisis – the notorious work camps for unemployed young men – was not the solution. Harsh conditions there were detested by their inmates, provoking them to ever more angry protests such as the ill-fated 'On-to-Ottawa' trek of 1935, prompting church and business leaders to criticize the camps, too. Opposition leader W.L. Mackenzie King promised to abolish them, one of the few concrete undertakings he made in the 1935 election campaign. The example of so many European governments enacting national fitness programs also increased pressure for a national recreation scheme.

It was not only the totalitarian states such as fascist Italy and Germany and the Soviet Union that appeared to mobilize the energies and public-spiritedness of youth through national fitness programs, but democratic countries such as Britain and Czechloslovakia. In 1937, the British government created a national physical training and recreation council to develop facilities and train leaders. Deploring the low levels of fitness in 'in most countries in large sectors of the population,' the Health Section of the League of Nations called on member governments, including Canada's, to embark upon a national fitness and nutrition program.[33]

In Canada, a focal point for these representations was the National Employment Commission appointed by the new Liberal government in 1936. The commission's Youth Committee quickly recognized the dilemma: 'The slackening of the economic machinery has produced a large volume of leisure which was not marginal but total, and which bore with particular severity upon youth. Young people finding their usual or expected avenues of opportunity closed, found themselves face to face with their own and society's deficiencies in the matter of leisure. Work is undoubtedly a necessity for all, but the real end to be achieved for a satisfactory balance between work and "play" is not mere loafing or mere off-side amusement, but activity of a truly recreational character which tends to sustain morale in times of idleness and to maintain employability at the highest possible level at all times.' The National Employment Commission subsequently recommended a $20-million package of reforms, including a national employment service, a voluntary work program similar to U.S. President Franklin Roosevelt's Civilian Conservation Corps, and creation of training centres for young men to 'assure their physical and mental fitness and raise their level of employability.'

King had other ideas – he wanted the commission to recommend cutting relief costs to 'lessen the burden of taxation' – so he rejected most of its proposals. Health Minister Power rejected the idea of a national physical fitness program on the grounds that 'medical authorities were not agreed' that beneficial results would follow.[34] But the cabinet was ultimately persuaded by Labour Minister Norman Rogers to aquiesce in a $1-million stopgap of farm placements and youth training to occupy the men turned loose from the camps that the government had closed. It was enacted as a shared-cost dominion-provincial program by the Unemployment and Agricultural Assistance Act of 1937 and was continued in the Dominion-Provincial Youth Training Program of 1939.

These meagre measures did little for youth employment. Barely a quarter of participants obtained jobs after their training. But the program did provide a new stimulus to public recreation because 'physical training projects designed to maintain the health and morale of the young unemployed' were eligible for support. Brtish Columbia immediately took advantage of the funds to strengthen its leadership training program – a six-week course that included a medical examination, nutrition counselling, and instruction in first aid. New Brunswick, Manitoba, Saskatchewan and Alberta soon developed versions of Pro-Rec for their own citizens – in the case of Alberta, with direct BC assistance. In 1939–40, 20,105 participants were subsidized by dominion funds in these provinces. The promise of Pro-Rec and the structure of the Dominion-Provincial Youth Training Program provided the basis for the wartime National Physical Fitness Act (NPFA) of 1943. Pro-Rec's Ian Eisenhardt was appointed director of the program that the NPFA created.[35]

The prominent role of Pro-Rec in the developments of the late 1930s illustrates the extent to which the AAU's preoccupation with amateurism and its turn to high performance sport had isolated it from the movement for public recreation. A generation earlier, the AAU had been vocal in its advocacy of opportunities for all, but by the early 1930s it had grown silent on social issues. It was the YM/YWCAs, the Workers' Sports Associations, and broadly focused agencies such as Pro-Rec that organized sports and recreation for the victims of the Depression, and only rarely the amateur clubs. Not surprisingly, while the AAUers and Hugh Plaxton got nowhere in their campaign for a ministry of sports, those advocating more inclusive programs of recreation and fitness found themselves in the company of many other groups galvanized by the Depression into struggling for a Canadian welfare state.

The only AAU leader to play a role in the lobbying for a national fitness program was A.S. Lamb, who by the late 1930s had been marginalized within the Union. Pushed by Em Orlick, who moved to McGill in 1938, Lamb helped that same year to create the National Physical Fitness League, which publicized the costs and benefits of improved fitness in a number of imaginative special events, radio broadcasts, and publicity campaigns that prefigured today's familiar campaigns of ParticipAction. Nor were any of the AAUers prominent in the National Physical Fitness (NPF) council created by the dominion legislation of 1943.

But those who wanted to advance national development through sports had found a charismatic new champion. Eisenhardt and the new NPF council were committed to realizing the popular aspirations for a better life that grew out of the Depression and the 'war against the dictators.' They were convinced that the national fitness program would soon complement a national health insurance plan and that there would be universal access to many other long-denied developmental opportunities. Health Minister Ian McKenzie seemed to promise as much in his presentation in 1942 to the Special Committee on Social Security, to which he first proposed the NPFA. Though the government provided a modest budget of only $250,000, nine-tenths of which was to go to the provinces, the new NPF councillors did not rein in their ambition. They defined the 'fitness' they felt it was their mandate to foster as 'the best state of health ... necessary for a life of service to one's family and country. [It] is spiritual, moral, mental and physical, and that total fitness must originate in the home, the church, the school and the community.' They would encourage 'all activities relating to the development of the people through sports, athletics and other similar pursuits.' While one of the many NPF committees was concerned with the Olympics, the primary emphasis was on mass participation. This developmental spirit quickly spread across the country. In Ontario, the newly formed Community Programmes Branch, which had eclipsed the Ontario Athletic Commission, set out to 'teach and promote democratic living' through recreation.[36]

Yet realization of these goals was not to be. Just as it dashed the hopes of those expecting creation of a significant welfare state as the reward for Canadians' wartime sacrifices, the King government disappointed the aspirations for a broad national fitness program. Though flush from the taxes generated by the frenzied production and full employment brought about by mobilization, the government quietly pulled back from its 'Green Book' promises for postwar reconstruction. It failed to increase the NPF program budget, amend the legislation, or assist with any of the other improvements recommended by the NPF council, despite pledges to do so. In frustration, Eisenhardt left for the United Nations in 1946. The remaining members of council refused to acquiesce in the government's about-face. They continued to agitate for a comprehensive national program, publicly critical of their 'political masters,' while spending their limited funds on innovative pilot projects and public education. In 1947, Health Minister Paul Martin told them: 'I do not see the hope of giving another cent just now. People are demanding the curtailing of government expenditures.' In response, the council sought legal advice on how it could enlarge the executive powers that it had been given under the act so that it could conduct programs independently of Treasury Board and cabinet. The protracted feuding was too much for the Liberals. Encouraged by the business-sponsored Citizens Research Institute, which recommended that 'the [fitness] Act be revoked and the whole scheme abandoned,' they did exactly that. In 1954, when the existing obligations expired, the NPFA was repealed, much to the chagrin of eight provinces and North west Territories, which had started and extended programs on the basis of federal support.[37]

The NHL and the CBC

But if Ottawa was reluctant to fund national physical fitness and opposed to financial support of amateur sport, one influential arm of the federal state – the Canadian Radio Broadcasting Corporation and its successor, the Canadian Broadcasting Corporation – gave corporate sport a gigantic boost. During their formative years in the 1930s, the CRBC and the CBC legitimized and then extended the radio network initially put together by Conn Smythe and Jack MacLaren in English-speaking Canada, and by the Montreal Canadiens in Quebec, thereby consolidating the NHL is monopoly and privileging it with 'prime time' access to Canadian homes. These broadcasts featured only the NHL variant of Canadian hockey, and for most listeners they emanated from only one rink. Though soon called 'Hockey Night in Canada,' it was really 'A Night of NHL Hockey from Maple Leaf Gardens in Toronto.'

The promoters benefited most from the slow reaction time of the

Canadian government to the revolutionary implications of radio. By 1927, both the British and American governments had realized that the new technology required a careful, comprehensive policy framework. The former created the state-supported, advertising-free British Broadcasting Corporation, while the latter decided on a private system financed by advertising, with minimal state regulation. But when Smythe and MacLaren first began to plan Leaf broadcasts, the parameters of Canadian policy were still being hotly debated. The few regulations that did exist were being drafted on an ad hoc basis by the electrical engineers who headed up the radio branch of the dominion government's department of marine.

In 1929, the Royal Commission on Radio Broadcasting chaired by banker John Aird recommended a national network of publicly owned stations financed by a public subsidy, receiver licences, and 'indirect' (i.e., institutional) advertising, but private broadcasters fought fiercely for the right to stay in business. The King government promised legislation but took no action before calling the 1930 election. While the victorious Conservatives under R.B. Bennett waited for a Supreme Court reference on the constitutionality of dominion jurisdiction, lobbyists for and against publicly owned radio besieged them with delegations and telegrams.[38]

It was not until 1932, after the Supreme Court and the Judicial Committee of the Privy Council upheld the dominion power, that the Bennett government finally determined the system Canadians would have. It was to be a mix of public and private. The Canadian Radio Broadcasting Corporation would operate a network of publicly owned or leased stations. Private broadcasting would be allowed to continue alongside the public system, but under the regulation of the CRBC. By the time the new corporation released its first regulations on 1 April 1933, MacLaren's Saturday-night Maple Leaf Gardens broadcasts were being carried on a 20-station, coast-to-coast network. The CRBC made no effort to change them. It was the only program regularly broadcast across Canada at the time. In 1936, after the Conservatives had been defeated, the King government strengthened public broadcasting by creating a new corporation, the CBC. But the CBC did the same with hockey, simply taking over the broadcasts as they were.[39]

It is easy to understand why the fledgling CBC decided to continue the 'Hockey Night in Canada' broadcasts. By the early 1930s, it was the North American norm for commercial programs to be produced by the advertising agencies representing the sponsors. The public system that emerged from the long Canadian debate was still highly dependent upon commercial advertising. Though the Aird Commission recommended against it, the private radio stations, the advertisers, and, strangely, the most vocal proponent of a public system, Graham Spry's Canadian Radio League, all called for a measure of advertising. One telling argument was the plea by Canadian manufacturers that if advertising were banned from the Canadian airwaves, they would be at a disadvantage vis-à-vis their American competitors, whose catchy messages were regularly being heard over American stations reaching Canada. The Bennett government acted on this advice and set up the CRBC in the expectation that it could be financed primarily through advertising.

Although the Liberals, when they regained power, gave the CBC more revenue – licence fees collected from sales of receivers – the CBC too had to seek advertising to survive. At the same time, the new corporation was under tremendous pressure from private broadcasters and influential cabinet ministers such as C.D. Howe to 'slow down public ownership.' In this environment, the network that Maclaren had created was probably too powerful to dismantle. The NHL show was already popular with audiences. It was similar to popular sports broadcasts that Canadians heard from the United States. It promised the CBC an instant following and a ready income. Moreover, the board of Maple Leaf Gardens comprised some of the most powerful capitalists in Canada, including representatives of large manufacturers such as General Electric and retailers such as Eaton's. Their advertisements and goodwill could be useful to the new corporation. Toronto was the industry's largest and most competitive English-language market, so the hockey broadcasts would provide a financial anchor to its flagship station. It would not be the last time that the CBC equated Toronto interests with those of the rest of the country.[40]

But it has always puzzled me that the decision to carry on with the MacLaren hockey network was never contested. It has always seemed an abrogation of public trust and a colossal failure of imagination. The public networks were under constant scrutiny to safeguard their 'objectivity' from political, religious, or commercial interference. In fact, it was a series of 'scurrilous and libellous' Conservative election campaign broadcasts on the CRBC in 1935 that convinced the Liberals to create the CBC. In a subsequent regulation for all broadcasters, the CBC declared that 'the air must not fall under the control of any individuals or groups influential by reason of their wealth or special position.'[41] Yet the CBC turned over the prestigious Saturday-night time slot to an advertising agency, MacLaren's, for commentary by the paid publicist of the principal corporation involved, Foster Hewitt of Maple Leaf Gardens.

No tapes of Hewitt's early broadcasts have been kept. At the national sound and film archives in Ottawa, I was told that those purporting to be broadcasts of pre-war games were actually 'recreated' in the 1970s. But Hewitt's written accounts repeatedly praise the Leafs and the NHL. On the major hockey issues of his postwar career – roughness of play, the NHL's subjugation of the Canadian Amateur Hockey Association (CAHA), the relationship between sport and education – he ably parroted the NHL's line. It was like turning over the news department to the campaign director of one of the political parties, the music department to RCA records, or farm broadcasts to the Winnipeg Grain Exchange. One narrow, vested interest was given virtually unrestricted opportunity to define the hockey culture for us all.

The CRBC and CBC were also under public and parliamentary expectation to further the development of Canadian culture. All commentators in the radio debates, even the private station's lobby, the Canadian Association of Broadcasters, accepted the Aird Commission's recommendation that radio be developed in the public interest. R.B. Bennett thought that the CRBC would be 'the agency by which national consciousness [will] be fostered and sustained and national unity still further strengthened.'[42] During the mid- to late 1930s, when the decisions about hockey broadcasts were taken, there were *excellent* hockey teams and sports broadcasters in other regions where CBC stations were located.

With the liberalization of eligibility in 1936, the community-based, not-for-profit CAHA was stronger than ever. In 1940, Ralph Allen, former sports editor of the *Winnipeg Tribune*, observed that 'the CAHA is now, in effect, running a vast professional league, a league that is strongly entrenched, not only in the big cities, but in a score of relatively new fields like the colliery country of Cape Breton, the manufacturing empire at Oshawa, the rich mining belt around Sudbury and Kirkland Lake and farther west at Geraldton and Flin Flon, Saskatchewan wheat towns like Yorkton and Weyburn, bustling coal and oil strongholds in Alberta like Lethbridge, Drumheller, Olds and Turner Valley, and in British Columbia, fruit or smelter centres like Nelson, Kimberley and Trail.'[43] In many of these cities and towns, games were broadcast locally, often to large audiences.

It was to the Gardens' and MacLaren's advantage to develop a large audience for the Leafs and their sponsors, but it would have provided a much more accurate sense of the reality of 'hockey night' in Canada if the CBC had featured different teams, regions, and broadcasting styles each week. Such an approach would have affirmed the efforts and sporting traditions of all Canadians. Instead of offering the metropolitan monoculture of 'Hockey Night in Canada,' it would have strengthened the vibrant, participatory use of the public airwaves being tried with such programs as 'Citizen's Forum,' 'Farm Forum,' and 'Labour Forum' and helped build reciprocal links among people of different regions. Yet none of these other games was ever covered on the broadcasts that MacLaren controlled, and only a few Allan Cup finals were ever broadcast on the CBC. The symbolic landscape of hockey presented by the public network failed abysmally to portray the actually lived one.

The capture of the CBC gave the NHL and its Toronto franchise complete victory in its campaign for 'product differentiation.' Smythe and MacLaren ably exploited the powerful new medium to convince English Canadians that Maple Leaf games were the best there were and to assemble listeners for MacLaren's principal advertiser, Imperial Oil (after 1935). Some active hockey enthusiasts stayed proudly loyal to the teams to which they first gave their hearts. My father lived almost his entire adult life in Montreal, Ottawa, and Toronto, but he first became a sports fan in Vancouver, where he grew up, and as difficult as it was to get scores in the eastern papers he was always closest to the fortunes of the teams from western Canada. Other men of that generation have said the same. But just as the magic of radio could sell a non-existent perfume, it could turn millions of Canadians into Leaf fans. 'Hockey Night in Canada' transformed the allegiances of many die-hard fans, marshalling them, along with youngsters forging their first hockey identities and adult listeners with little or no previous interest in sports, as devoted adherents of the blue and white.

In 1934, a few weeks after the Stanley Cup playoffs, the Leafs and the Detroit Red Wings travelled to western Canada for a series of exhibition games. The Wings had easily beaten the Leafs in the semi-finals, before losing the cup to the Chicago Black Hawks. The playoff games had been broadcast by Hewitt to record audiences. According to Charlie Conacher, one of the Leafs' leading scorers during the western tour, the huge crowds that showed up at every station kept asking, 'Where's Foster?' Frank Selke has published a similar memory: 'In Winnipeg, as elsewhere, the games attracted sellout crowds ... From the first morning, when our train stopped at Jackfish, north of Lake Superior, the Maple Leafs were mobbed by the fans Foster Hewitt's voice had won for them. Detroit, which was a better team than ours on the season, was practically ignored.

I remember a young boy asking Eddie Goodfellow, Detroit's fine player, for his autograph. When he read the name, he said, "Who's that guy?" and dropped the paper in the slush at his feet ... That sort of thing was repeated in various degrees in every city where we detrained.'[44] With such trophy anecdotes, it was no wonder that the Toronto executives made no effort to change the format.

From its inception, 'Hockey Night in Canada' was one of the most successful programs in Canadian history. Millions tuned into it avidly at some point of their lives, and during the spring Stanley Cup playoffs it brought many other social activities to a halt. During the bleak days of the Depression and the Second World War, it gave many people their strongest sense of pan-Canadian identity. It was not only the immediacy and intimacy of radio that ensured its broad appeal, but the sense of sharing that it created. 'It helped the anonymous individual feel more like a person and the mass more like a community.' One commander told a civilian audience during the war that 'more than anything else, the men in England want hockey broadcasts, then cigarettes, and then your parcels.' After 1952, when 'Hockey Night in Canada' went to television, the innovative genius of the production crews made the athletic artistry and drama of top-flight sport visually accessible to millions. Like Hewitt, many of the play-by-play men and commentators who followed in his footsteps have been as popular as the players themselves.[45]

But in other ways, the CBC's partnership with the NHL – what sociologists would later call the 'state monopoly capitalist sports-media complex' – distorted the development of Canadian sport and Canadian culture. In the first place, it contributed to the steady marginalization or 'symbolic annihilation' of women's sports from the mainstream media.[46] Despite the pioneering efforts of Alexandrine Gibb, Phyllis Griffiths, and others to see that female athletic performances were fully reported, women's coverage fell off considerably during the late 1930s, and it has remained a rarity to this day. While 'Hockey Night in Canada' was not solely responsible for this sorry omission, its powerful example seemed to sanction the practice with public authority.

It was not that there were no strong counter-examples from which to choose. Just as there were outstanding non-NHL men's hockey teams drawing crowds and radio listeners during the 1930s, there were superb women's teams, not only in hockey, but in basketball and softball. Before he became publicity director for Conn Smythe, Foster Hewitt broadcast women's games, as did many of his colleagues. Ralph Allen told his

Winnipeg readers that 'as a sporting spectacle, the Edmonton Grads belong right up there at the top.'[47] The Grads' home games on CJCA were followed attentively throughout rural Alberta. But few of their thrilling games or long streaks (of 147 and 78 games) or the games of the top hockey teams in hockey such as 'Bobbie' Rosenfeld's Pats or the Preston Rivulettes were broadcast by the public network.

Here, too, advertising undoubtedly was a factor. It was during the 1930s that advertising and radio executives gradually discovered the remarkable ability of sports broadcasts to assemble affluent male consumers for their sponsors' appeals. The most dramatic demonstration of this relationship occurred during the 1939 World Series. As an experiment, the sponsors packaged a special 'World Series razor' and advertised it during the broadcasts. In just four games, they sold 2.5 million sets.[48] That relationship became the driving logic of the industry. Despite the large numbers of men who paid to watch women's games, it was felt that only men's sports would attract a male audience. While girls and women listened to the Hewitt broadcasts, they did not have the spending power or perceived household influence to attract the interest of sponsors such as General Motors and Imperial Oil. As a result, the fundamental production function of the sports-media complex was designed for an all-male universe. It helped keep women's sports off the air.

The subtext of what was presented on 'Hockey Night in Canada' was disturbing as well. The show always seemed to suggest that the thrilling heroics justified the talent stripping of the regions, the harsh exploitation of the players, and the 'Big Bobby Clobber' masculinity encouraged by Smythe and other managers. The history of Canadian hockey is replete with examples of athletes who have articulated a more intelligent approach to training and competition; coaches and managers who helped young men and women integrate their hockey with education, career, and a social life; teachers, parents and community leaders who tried to stamp out the senseless violence; and journalists who spoke out for athletes' rights. Most players managed to develop post-hockey careers and live full lives despite the repressive conditions they faced in the NHL. But few of these voices and counter-arguments were ever allowed on the public network, and the few that raised them were never invited back. As every hockey fan should know, the CBC sanctions the NHL's censorship.

During the interwar period, the Canadian state was called on to extend its influence over sports development in a variety of ways. While on the whole, policies were formulated and implemented within the politics of capitalist development, male hegemony, and social control, given the diversity of state agencies and the pressures to which they responded there were contrasts and contradictions. Men's boxing, both as middle-class character training and as a commercial spectacle with working-class professionals, was legalized, but it was done only under the close scrutiny of provincial and local regulatory agencies. While all levels of government expanded parks, playgrounds, and facilities for sports and recreation, in most parts of Canada the sabbatarian laws were just as strictly enforced in 1939 as they were in 1919, severely restricting working people's use of the new opportunities created.

In ministries of education, the Strathcona Trust was gradually replaced in the curricula by more developmental forms of gymnastics. There was much greater effort to offer challenging instruction for girls and an ambitious program of after-school sports for both genders. But what was actually taught depended on the principal and the teachers available, and those who had no interest in or commitment to these new approaches or the subject of physical education as a whole could cancel them as a form of classroom 'discipline.' In Ontario and the western provinces, new provincial programs enhanced opportunity, in the former primarily for the most promising young male athletes, in the latter for citizens of all ages and abilities. These programs prefigured the postwar growth of programs within the expansion of the welfare state.

In this competition for the resources and power of the state, it was the Toronto capitalists' radio show that won the biggest prize. With legitimation of the public network, the Smythe-MacLaren-Hewitt team transformed discourse and ideology. Throughout the 1920s and 1930s, government leaders at all levels patronized and endorsed the efforts of amateur leaders to strengthen the sense of 'Canadianism' by forging cross-country institutions and the full apparatus of Canadian championships, records, and national teams. With the successes of the Edmonton Grads, the 'magnificient six' at the 1928 Olympics, and many others, Canadian female athletes were slowly being brought into these affirmations and endorsements. But by the end of the period, the loudest, most influential public voice on the subject of sports came from the CBC. 'Hockey Night in Maple Leaf Gardens' confounded the Canadianism of independence and self-sufficiency championed by the AAU and obliterated the assertive womanhood encouraged by the WAAF, in the interests of continental and metropolitan capitalism.

7

Conclusion: The Triumph of Capitalist Sport

It has become commonplace to attribute a broad identity of purpose and meaning to sports. Participants and commentators alike refer to a 'community of sport' within which intentions and values are essentially the same. But few observers would have made that assumption during the interwar period. Each of the organizations examined in this study was rocked by internal conflict, often over basic principles, and they often locked horns with each other. The hegemony that the amateurs enjoyed in the early 1920s was never complete. The NHL challenged them for the top athletes, fans, sponsors, and the largess and leverage of the state. During the Depression, the NHL hired away male amateur stars, not only in hockey, but in football and track and field, boosting its own legitimacy and audiences in the process. In 1936, right after the Berlin Olympics, the Toronto Maple Leafs signed Syl Apps, the popular pole vaulter of the Canadian team. Apps's abstemious habits, charitable works, and articulate common sense greatly improved the image of the professional hockey player and helped discredit the amateurs' conservative ideology. It was not only the NHL that raided the ranks of the Amateur Athletic Union of Canada (AAU). The Workers' Sports Association of Canada (WSAC) scored its greatest publicity coup in the mainstream press when it sent a team of AAU and Women's Amateur Athletic Federation (WAAF) champions to the Peoples' Olympics of 1936. While the WAAF worked closely with the AAU, there was always tension about the extent of women's activity and who should control it.

The national organizations energetically competed for the attention and 'slant' of the mass media, cultivating reporters, publishers, and broadcasters, supplying them with prepared copy, photos, and illustrations, treating them with gifts and free lunches, and sometimes bribing them outright. They were greatly aided in this endeavour by the uncritical boosterism that reigned in most sports departments and from which publishers profited. In many cases, there was little boundary between the 'reporters' and the organizations they covered. W.A. Hewitt ran amateur hockey and edited the *Toronto Star* sports page at the same time. Henry Roxborough covered amateur sports for *Maclean's* and other magazines while a member of the AAU's publicity committee. Neither Alexandrine Gibb (*Toronto Star*) nor Myrtle Cook (*Montreal Star*) stopped writing about the WAAF when they served on its executive. Toronto sports editors Mike Rodden and Lou Marsh moonlighted as NHL referees and then wrote about the games they worked in. Foster Hewitt was publicity director for the Toronto Maple Leafs. Because it was shut out of the capitalist media, the WSA saw to it that its members could obtain a socialist viewpoint on sports in the communist press.

In other ways, the divergent projects described in this book led their participants down separate paths. Most athletes spent their entire sporting careers within the same organization, oblivious to what was happening elsewhere, whether they embraced the larger project it sought to advance or not. Outside hockey, the amateur leaders rarely communicated with the professionals and tried to ignore the WSAs altogether. The AAU and NHL were equally distant and unpalatable to the WSA member in Montreal's Fletcher's Field, the Finnish settlements in northern Ontario resource towns, and the North End of Winnipeg. Gender was another divide. Despite the striking growth of women's sport, male and female athletes spent little time together, even while members of the same club. 'We rarely saw them,' marathoner Johnny Miles has remembered about his female teammates on the Hamilton Olympic Club. 'Except at Olympics, they trained at their own times and ran in their own meets.'[1]

But by the outbreak of the Second World War, the NHL had begun to impose a new unity of practice and discourse on the most popular sectors of Canadian sports. The commercial hockey league was the big winner of the period, supplanting the AAU as the dominant body in Canadian sports. These processes were by no means complete by 1939, but they were well under way. By the 1950s, hockey promoters enjoyed the power to 'structure sport in preferred ways, define the range of "legitimate" practices and meanings, and establish selective traditions.'[2] More Canadians played and watched hockey than any other sport organized on a national basis. Through their 1936 agreement with the Canadian Amateur Hockey Association (CAHA), the NHLers extended their playing rules to virtually all levels of participation.

In 1947, the NHL extended this control by turning amateur hockey into a vast feeder system, thereby accelerating the process by which the framework for participation was transformed from voluntary recreation into wage labour, and the basis of recruitment from community loyalty to a continental labour market. At the same time, the NHLers aggressively, and often shrewdly, advanced the 'product development' and marketing of the spectacle. The 'sponsorship system' that they imposed on the CAHA, in the context of the first wave of the postwar 'baby boom' and full employment, sharply reduced the opportunity for all but the most talented boys to play hockey after 15, the age by which full promise was thought to be evident, thereby swelling the numbers of those who would identify with hockey as consumers.[3]

In short, the 1920s and 1930s witnessed the triumph of capitalist cultural production over the more avocational or associational forms of cultural activity pursued by the middle and working classes. Purchased identity replaced the loyalties of roots and self-realization. The public-spirited attempt to develop a pan-Canadian system of sport with organic links to communities across the country was subordinated to the profits of metropolitan and continental interests. The success of the capitalist model was facilitated by and reflected the rapid spread of the 'universal market', the escalating power of corporate capital generally, and the American takeover of much of Canadian industrial production and popular culture.

The NHL was able to legitimate these practices, turning them into everyday 'common sense,' by developing close working relationships with the press and a partnership with the Canadian Broadcasting Corporation (CBC). Hockey Night in Canada became so popular that millions of Canadians began to devote their Saturday evenings to NHL broadcasts, and so powerful that it could regularly pre-empt the nightly national news. The NHL used its monopoly over the game's most prestigious trophy, the Stanley Cup, to create one of the most enduring of Canadian traditions, so that people dropped everything – election stumping, final exams, religious observances – to watch the playoffs. By the late 1930s, 'professional' and 'the National League' had become synonymous with 'the best in sport.' Today, the popular history of Canadian hockey is virtually the history of the NHL.[4]

The NHL-CBC collaboration drastically narrowed the possibilities and meanings of sports for women as well. 'Hockey Night in Canada' broadcast men's hockey exclusively, stressing that it was a 'man's game' and extolling a physically violent code of masculinity. The program contributed significantly to the 'symbolic annihilation' of women from public policy and everyday discourse about sports, setting back many of the important gains of the interwar period.

While these changes were swept along by the growth of commercial culture, which flooded over and submerged all other forms of associational culture throughout the capitalist world, the particular forms they took were not inevitable. If the major players had chosen other options, especially in 1909, when the majority of Canadian sports leaders refused to contemplate any manner of professionalism; or in 1924, when the NHL expanded into the United States; or in 1932, when the Canadian Radio Broadcasting Corporation took over the Maple Leaf Gardens hockey network and expanded it into 'Hockey Night in Canada,' the trajectory of Canadian sports might have been different.

In several major respects, the amateur leaders themselves contributed to the growth of the corporate model. While they sought to check what they believed to be the harmful effects of professionalism, they were never foes of capitalism. Long before the NHL was created, the AAUers accepted and then actively pursued the sale of games and major events. They also championed the idea that successful athletes and teams were 'representative' symbols of community and desirable values. Both practices elevated athletic skill and winning. The AAUers' growing preoccupation with the Olympics increased the appetite for highly skilled performances, thereby contributing to the market that the NHLers so successfully exploited and the supply of outstanding athletes on which they relied. Their stern moralism left the field wide open for the NHL to link sports with the pleasures of an entertaining spectacle, the lights and comforts of new arenas, and the rush and status of a hot ticket.

The NHL's rising star cannot be separated from the growing fascination of Canadians with ice hockey. The period between the World Wars was an era of increasing audiences for many sports, but none aroused the passions quite like hockey. Research into the complex social, psychological, and situational determinations by which different people are drawn to different sports is still in its infancy.[5] But we know that hockey was fast and fluid, providing relentless, unpredictable drama, and the NHLers' rules made it more so. Unlike lacrosse, which had been adapted from the First Nations' game, or baseball, which the Americans claimed, or rugby football, still evolving from a British game, hockey was Canadian in its modern origins and in its essential character. It stemmed from the elements of winter everyone suffered through and offered challenge, excitement, and the opportunity for human contact at a time when first instincts might be to stay put at home.

While hockey was played and followed by women as well as men, its soaring popularity was also closely bound up with the ways in which the most able publicists and players wove reassurances of masculine prowess, solidarity, and dominance into the legends, controversies, and rituals of the game. The terrifying bombardments of war, the uncaring power of the huge new corporations, the bewildering challenge of feminism, the staggering breadlines of the Depression, and the other uncertainties of modernity all served to nullify the possibilities of self-realizing manhood promised by bourgeois ideology. But the breathtaking feats of the great players, recounted in the familiar codes of male accomplishment, male bonding, and male pride, provided a brief, joyous respite.

Certainly no other sport inspired as extensive an investment nor as far-flung an organizational network. Organizers in every sport preached the ethic of openness to all, but none actually drew players and fans from such a wide cross-section of the population as did hockey, offering spectators the chance to cheer for players from across the Canadian 'mosaic' and creating moments of cultural communion in what was otherwise bewildering diversity. As many men and women played baseball, and the World Series rivalled the Stanley Cup in popularity, but the summer game was experienced as an extension of American culture. It was never successfully organized on a national basis in Canada.

In 1919, Canadian sport was divided between amateur and professional, east and west, male and female, 'bourgeois' and workers' organizations. The realignments of the interwar years emphasized a single line of demarcation – between a well-publicized commercial, continentalist, and exclusively male sector on the one hand, and an increasingly marginalized, not-for-profit, nationally organized sector, in which at least some attempt to provide opportunities for women was made, on the other. There were thousands more participating in the latter, but fewer and fewer of their activities were mentioned in the big city media.

To be sure, some of the earlier differences remained. Amateurism still made it extremely difficult for the working class to train and compete at the highest levels of performance. Though women had won the right to compete at every level, including the Olympics, their sports were still ideologically distinct from the men's, and both women and men continued to fight over the nature and position of the boundaries. During the 1930s, the CAHA and the regional football associations affiliated with the Canadian Rugby Union developed a 'third way' – community-based, not-for-profit professionalism. But the deepest fault line fell between the commercial and the Olympic sectors. The two realms were separated not only by different labour processes, but by corporate-community, continental-national, and male-female divides as well.

Canadian sports thus reinforced the 'conundrum of culture' – the simultaneous penetration of continental mass culture and the conscious celebration of Canadian achievement.[6] NHL hockey both played on the metaphors of Canadian nationalism and undermined the very idea of a distinct Canadian society by contending that even the 'national game' had to be sold primarily in the United States. Canadians have always been accustomed to such cultural ambiguity, as they wrestle with the opposi-tions of history (Native/colonial, French/English, federal/provincial), geography and climate (east-west, empty northern tundra/dense southern urbanization, frigid Newfoundland/balmy British Columbia), and identity (bilingual/multicultural). Canadian literature abounds in irony and many-sidedness as well.[7]

But sports posed the cultural riddle more explicitly than any other cultural form by casting the athlete as community surrogate. By the interwar period, athletes and teams enjoyed wide representational status, symbolizing cities, provinces, nations, regions, and, at the highest levels of ability, the pan-Canadian state. Even the American players who toiled for the Montreal and Toronto franchises in the International (Baseball) League and the western Canadian football teams had to conform to this expectation, accepting symbolic 'adoption' in team press releases and publicity.

In this dialectic, the representational status of athletes and teams (along with other ambitions, fissures, and changes) has kept the terrain of Canadian sports stirring with conflict. While the overall pattern established between the wars remains much the same, and capitalist sport has prospered beyond its promoters' wildest dreams, their hegemony has never gone unchallenged.

In the decades following the Second World War, in several cities, the 'third way' of not-for-profit professionalism, pioneered by Syd Halter and others in western Canadian football, provided a source of regional and national sporting pride that rivalled the NHL. The success of this approach led to formation of the Canadian Football League (CFL) in 1958, with teams in Vancouver, Calgary, Edmonton, Regina, Winnipeg, Hamilton, Toronto, Ottawa, and Montreal. Though the CFL's creation came at the expense of teams in smaller centres such as Brantford, Kitchener, and Sarnia, it fostered athletic rivalries that affirmed the geography and political economy of Canada rather than the continentalist lure of the

United States. It fashioned an exciting, distinct, Canadian style of play and kept franchises viable and jobs for Canadian athletes through creative revenue-sharing and player quotas. For many fans, the CFL's annual Grey Cup championship was the highlight of the sporting calendar.[8]

In 1961, amid Cold War rivalries and the rapid growth of the federal state, public health campaigners, social welfare advocates, and admirers of the Ontario Athletic Commission and BC Pro-Rec persuaded Conservative Prime Minister John Diefenbaker to pass the Fitness and Amateur Sport Act. The resulting federal programs, expanded by the Trudeau government during the 1970s in the interests of pan-Canadian unity and cloned in most provinces/territories, have helped thousands of athletes reach international standards of performance. With adoring Olympic and Commonwealth Games coverage from CBC and CTV television, they provide Canadians with another alternative source of cultural heroes. The heart-felt outpouring of telegrams and faxes during events such as the Lillehammer Olympics suggests that such 'made-in-Canada' champions as Susan Auch, Myriam Bedard, Jean-Luc Brossard, Kurt Browning, Corey Hirsh, Ed Podivinski, and Elvis Stoyko, are more genuine and accessible exemplars than the pampered stars of the continental 'big leagues.' Fitness and Amateur Sport programs were never allowed to challenge the NHL's authority. But they revived and helped realize the amateurs' dream for a nationalist sports movement, at least for the urban middle class.

The new state programs also provided a significant measure of support for girls' and women's sports, though their activity and achievement are still largely ignored by the mass media. New advocacy groups – the Canadian Association for the Advancement of Women and Sport and Physical Activity, for example – which have had to push hard for every gain, employ the universalist language of rational recreation (along with the gender-equity demands of second-wave feminism) in their campaigns. Some of them have begun to explore 'female-friendly' alternatives to the 'male model' of contemporary sports which echo the ambitions and approaches of the 'girls' rules' movement of the 1920s and 1930s.

In the 1990s, in the wake of the long, agonizing debate about sport and public policy that followed the Dubin Inquiry into Ben Johnson's disqualification for use of anabolic steroids in Seoul in 1988, the developmental ideal has been revived and updated within the 'high-performance Olympic sector. The National Association of Professional Coaches Association and the Canadian Athletes' Association, among others, seek to implement an 'athlete-centred' model of training and competition. The idea is to enhance the athletes' health, education, and social capacities, as well as their sporting skills, and to provide them with an environment free from sexual harassment and discrimination. In addition, a host of educational institutions, non-governmental bodies such as ParticipAction, new games such as intercrosse, and new ventures like the Special Olympics, the Gay Games, and the North American Indigenous Games keep the spirit of rational recreation alive in other ways, in an effort to inoculate their constituents against the ills and anxieties of postmodern life that recalls the concerns of their predecessors a century ago. Innovative outreach programs, such as Toronto's summer softball for the homeless, Ottawa's 'On the Move' activities for girls and women, and Halifax's 'midnight' basketball league, extend the benefits of physical activity to those long ignored by the mainstream.

One of Fitness and Amateur Sport's achievements was creation of Hockey Canada, which helped convince the Canadian NHL teams to contribute to the national hockey team created by Father David Bauer in the early 1960s. The Canadiens provided the greatest support, perhaps because their principal owner, David Molson, resented 'the increasing American influence, the new breed of hockey player and his demands,' and general manager Frank Selke 'fear[ed] that once [NHL president] Clarence Campbell is gone the Americans will take over and Canada will be the poor relation.'[9] Beginning with the storybook, last-minute win over the Soviet team in 1972, the Teams Canada created by Hockey Canada did much to rejuvenate hockey as the pan-Canadian game.

Other aspirations briefly weakened the continental dynamic as well. In the 1970s, elites in Quebec, Winnipeg, Calgary, Edmonton, and Vancouver, aided by the brief boom in resource-based economies, the willingness of all levels of the state to invest in the necessary facilities, and the failure of the NHL to find comparable markets in the United States, obtained NHL franchises. A new Ottawa franchise was achieved in 1992. Moreover, in the NHL and the other cartels, player unions arguing that 'we are the game' overcame the employers' unilateral bargaining power and now share significantly in the monopoly superprofits enjoyed by the industry. In minor hockey, an anti-NHL core of parents, assisted by the CAHA and many provincial governments, has sought to shift the emphasis back to participation for all, skill development, and winning without violence.

Regrettably, some of these counter-hegemonic initiatives have begun to fade. The CFL has become a commercial, continental league just like the NHL, and years of disastrous decisions have cost it much of its audience and legitimacy. Fitness and Amateur Sport and other state programs have been savaged in the neo-conservative onslaught. The vocabulary of 'athlete centredness' has yet to percolate down to the level of day-to-day training and competition. In the scramble to keep programs alive in the face of disappearing resources, amateur sports leaders are ever more preoccupied with the podium and the legitimation, grants and sponsorships that medals are hoped to bring. These pressures intensify the proletarianization and commodification of athletes, further blurring the boundaries between the Olympic and corporate modes of cultural production. They also diminish the possiblities of overcoming the historic inequality of access to sporting opportunity.

By the late 1980s, Hockey Canada experienced the fate of not-for-profit professional CAHA hockey a generation earlier and became an NHL feeder team. The federal government and the CAHA wisely put it to rest. The NHL has gone the way that David Molson and Frank Selke feared. With NHL power resting in New York, it is the American Fox Broadcasting Co. that alters the playoff schedule to suit its needs. Commissioner Gary Bettman shows little sympathy for the interests of Canadian cities and fans. The Quebec and Winnipeg franchises now operate under new names in Denver and Phoenix, and the Ottawa, Calgary, and Edmonton franchises are at risk, in large part because of the same sort of disparity in revenue that led to collapse of the Hamilton and Ottawa franchises, and the Western Hockey League, in the 1920s. Fortunately, recent campaigns to keep teams in town – in 1995 in Winnipeg, fans and boosters pledged $40 million in an unsuccessful effort to save the Jets – indicate that at least this time franchise flight will not occur without a fight.

As they vie for scarce resources and political support, the new progressive initiatives must confront the consumer loyalties, conventional wisdom, economic power, and political clout forged by the sports corporations in the 1930s, and which they have strengthened and extended exponentially in the years since. Other continentalist cartels such as Major League Baseball and the National Basketball League have expanded to Montreal, Toronto, and Vancouver with the help of provincial and municipal financial support, while global pressures threaten the entire material and ideological basis of cultural expression in Canada. In this context, the effort to create alternatives to the commercial sport culture will continue to be an uphill fight.[10]

But such alternatives do exist. They have a long, rich, and proud history.

Notes

Introduction

1 Canada, *Sport Participation in Canada* (Ottawa 1994), 9
2 Michael Novak, *The Joy of Sports* (New York 1976), 126; Bruce Kidd, 'Toronto's SkyDome: "The World's Greatest Entertainment Centre," ' in John Bale and Olof Moen, eds., *The Stadium and the City* (Keele 1995), 175–96
3 *Statutes of Canada* (SC) 1881, ch. 30. Sabbatarian legislation also prohibited or discouraged many forms of sport. See especially Chris Armstrong and Viv Nelles, *The Revenge of the Methodist Bicycle Company* (Toronto 1977); Gene Homel, 'Toronto's Sunday Tobogganing Controversy of 1912,' *Urban History Review*, 10 no. 2 (1981), 25–43; and Barbara Schrodt, 'Sabbatarianism and Sport in Canadian Society,' *Journal of Sport History*, 4 no. 1 (1977), 22–33.
4 Eric Broom and Rick Baka, *Canadian Governments and Sport* (Calgary 1979); Donald Macintosh, Tom Bedecki, and C.E.S. Franks, *Sport and Politics in Canada: Federal Government Involvement since 1961* (Kingston 1987); and Bruce Kidd, 'The Philosophy of Excellence: Olympic Performance, Class Power and the Canadian State,' in Pasquale Galasso, ed., *Philosophy of Sport and Physical Activity* (Toronto 1988), 11–31
5 *Globe*, 2 Aug. 1924; see also Brian M. Petrie, 'Sport and Politics,' in Don Ball and John Loy, eds., *Sport and the Social Order* (Reading, Mass., 1975), 185–237, and Richard Lipsky, *How We Play the Game* (Boston 1981).
6 Pierre Bordieux, *Distinction: A Social Critique of the Judgement of Taste* (Cambridge 1984); Richard Gruneau, *Sports, Class and Social Development* (Amherst, Mass., 1983); Suzanne Laberge and David Sankoff, 'Physical Activities, Body *Habitus*, and Lifestyles,' in Jean Harvey and Hart Cantelon, eds., *Not Just a Game: Essays in Canadian Sport Sociology* (Ottawa 1988),

267–86; and Michael Messner and Don Sabo, *Sport, Men and the Gender Order* (Champaign, Ill., 1990)

7 Canada, *Report of the Commission of Inquiry into the Use of Drugs and Other Banned Practices Intended to Increase Athletic Performance* (Ottawa 1990), and Peter Donnelly, 'Problems Associated with Youth Involvement in High Performance Sport,' in B. Cahill and A. Pearl, eds., *Intensive Participation in Children's Sports* (Champaign, Ill., 1991), 95–126

8 Tanis Talbot, 'Hockey as a Symbol of Patriarchy: Welcome Home,' *Femspeak* (University of Alberta Women's Law Forum), Jan. 1993, 11–12; cf. Stuart McLean, *Welcome Home* (Toronto 1992), and Ken Dryden and Roy MacGregor, *Home Game* (Toronto 1989).

9 Barthes, 'Of Sport and Men,' post-production script, National Film Board, 8 Sept. 1961; John MacAloon, 'Audiences without Athletes, Sacrifices without Victims,' Stanford Humanities Centre, 17 April 1986; and John Hoberman, 'The Sportive-Dynamic Body as a Symbol of Productivity,' in Tobin Siebers, ed., *Heterotopia: Postmodern Utopia and the Body Politic* (Ann Arbor, Mich., 1994), 199–228

10 Cited by S.F. Wise and Douglas Fisher, *Canada's Sporting Heroes* (Toronto 1974), 88

11 E.g., Jean R. Duperault, 'L'Affaire Richard: A Situational Analysis of the Montreal Hockey Riot of 1955,' *Canadian Journal of Sport History*, 12 no. 1 (1981), 66–83; and Rick Salutin, *Les Canadiens* (Vancouver 1977)

12 E.g., Ontario, *Report of the Investigation and Inquiry into Violence in Amateur Hockey* (Toronto 1974); Quebec, Haut Commissariat à la jeunesse, aux loisirs et aux sports, *Final Report of the Study Committee on Violence in Hockey in Quebec* (Quebec 15 Nov. 1977); Michael D. Smith, *Violence and Sport* (Toronto 1983); and Richard Gruneau and David Whitson, *Hockey Night in Canada* (Toronto 1993), 175–96

13 S.F. Wise, 'Sport and Class Values in Old Ontario and Quebec,' in W.H. Heick and Roger Graham, eds., *His Own Man: Essays in Honour of Arthur Reginald Marsden Lower* (Montreal 1974), 94

14 My list would include Frank Cosentino, *Canadian Football: The Grey Cup Years* (Toronto 1969); Colin D. Howell, *Northern Sandlots: A Social History of Maritime Baseball* (Toronto 1995); Donald Morrow, Mary Keyes, Wayne Simpson, Frank Cosentino, and Ron Lappage, *A Concise History of Sport in Canada* (Toronto 1989); Alan Metcalfe, *Canada Learns to Play* (Toronto 1987); and Gerald Redmond, *The Sporting Scots of Nineteenth Century Canada* (Rutherford, NJ, 1982).

15 E.g., W.A. Hewitt, *Down the Stretch* (Toronto 1958); Henry Roxborough, *Great Days in Canadian Sport* (Toronto 1957), *Stanley Cup Story* (Toronto

1964), and *One Hundred Not Out: The Story of Nineteenth Century Canadian Sport* (Toronto 1966); Scott Young, *War on Ice: Canada in International Hockey* (Toronto 1976) and *Hello Canada: The Life and Times of Foster Hewitt* (Toronto 1988); Eric Whitehead, *Cyclone Taylor: A Hockey Legend* (Toronto 1977) and *The Patricks: Hockey's Royal Family* (Toronto 1980); Brian McFarlane, *Fifty Years of Hockey: A History of the National Hockey League* (Toronto 1967); William Houston, *Inside Maple Leaf Gardens: The Rise and Fall of the Toronto Maple Leafs* (Toronto 1989) and *Maple Leaf Blues: Harold Ballard and the Life and Times of the Maple Leafs* (Toronto 1990); and David Cruise and Alison Griffiths, *Net Worth: Exploding the Myths of Pro Hockey* (Toronto 1991)

16 E.g., Wise and Fisher, *Canada's Sporting Heroes*, 28

17 Personal communication. See also Rick Gruneau, 'Modernization or Hegemony: Two Views on Sport and Social Development,' in Jean Harvey and Hart Cantelon, eds., *Not Just a Game: Essays in Canadian Sport Sociology* (Ottawa 1988), 9–32.

18 Canada, *House of Commons Debates*, 27 April 1994, 3594–608

19 E.g., Nancy Howell and Maxwell Howell, *Sports and Games in Canadian Life* (Toronto 1969); Maxwell Howell and Reet Howell, eds., *History of Sport in Canada* (Champaign, Ill., 1981); Cosentino, *Canadian Football*; Don Morrow, *A Sporting Evolution* (Montreal 1982); Redmond, *The Sporting Scots of Nineteenth Century Canada*

20 Alan Metcalfe, 'Organized Sport and Social Stratification in Montreal, 1840–1901,' in Richard Gruneau and John Albinson eds., *Canadian Sport: Sociological Perspectives* (Don Mills, Ont., 1976), 77–101; Ann Hall and Dorothy Richardson, *Fair Ball* (Ottawa 1983); Richard Gruneau, *Sports, Class and Social Development* (Amherst, Mass., 1983); and Helen Lenskyj, *Out of Bounds: Women, Sport and Sexuality* (Toronto 1986)

21 E.g., Cantelon and Harvey, *Not Just a Game*; Gruneau and Albinson, *Canadian Sport: Sociological Perspectives*; Gruneau and Whitson, *Hockey Night in Canada*; Ann Hall, Trevor Slack, Garry Smith, and David Whitson, *Sport in Canadian Society* (Toronto 1991): and Donald Macintosh and David Whitson, *The Game Planners* (Montreal 1991). For a full discussion of the development of sport studies in Canada, see Bruce Kidd, 'Improvers, Feminists, Capitalists and Socialists: Shaping Canadian Sport in the 1920s and 1930s,' PhD thesis, York University, 1990, 11–40.

22 William Humber, *Diamonds of the North: A Concise History of Baseball in Canada* (Toronto 1995); and John Herd Thompson and Allen Seager, *Canada, 1922–1939: Decades of Discord* (Toronto 1985), 187

Chapter One: The State of Play

1 M.I. Finlay and H.W. Pleket, *The Olympic Games: The First Thousand Years* (London 1976); David Young, *The Myth of Greek Amateur Athletics* (Chicago 1985); R.G. Sipes, 'War, Sports and Aggression,' *American Anthropologist*, 75 (1973), 64–86; and Richard D. Mandell, 'The Invention of the Modern Sports Record,' *Stadion*, 2 no. 1 (1976), 250–64

2 Norbert Elias, 'The Genesis of Sport as a Sociological Problem,' and Nobert Elias and Eric Dunning, 'Folk Football in Medieval and Early Modern Britain,' both in Eric Dunning, ed., *The Sociology of Sport* (Toronto 1972), 85–132

3 Gerald Glassford, *Application of a Theory of Games to the Transitional Eskimo Culture* (New York 1976); Victoria Paraschak, 'The Heterotransplantation of Organized Sport: A North-West Territories Case Study,' in B. Kidd, ed., *Proceedings of the Fifth Canadian Symposium on the History of Sport and Physical Education* (Toronto 1982), 424–30; and Janet C. Harris and Roberta J. Park, *Play, Games and Sports in Cultural Context* (Champaign, Ill., 1983)

4 For a fascinating account of one version of folk football still played in its pre-sport form, see John Robertson, *Uppies and Doonies* (Aberdeen, Scotland, 1967).

5 Elias, 'The Genesis of Sport as a Sociological Problem,' 92 (he admits that the term 'sounds rather unattractive'); and John Hargreaves, *Sport, Power, and Culture* (Cambridge 1986), 38–56

6 Kevin Sheard and Eric Dunning, 'The Rugby Football Club as a Male Preserve,' *International Review of Sociology of Sport* 3–4 (1973), 11–23

7 Mel Adelman, *A Sporting Time: New York City and the Rise of Athletics, 1820–1970* (Chicago 1986); Hugh Cunningham, *Leisure in the Industrial Revolution* (London 1980); Eric Dunning and Kevin Sheard, *Barbarians, Gentlemen, and Players* (Oxford 1979); Sheila Fletcher, *Women First: The Female Tradition in English Physical Education, 1880–1980* (London 1984); Allen Guttmann, *Games and Empires: Modern Sports and Cultural Imperialism* (New York 1994); Robert Malcolmson, *Popular Recreations in English Society* (Cambridge 1973); J.A. Mangam, *The Games Ethic and Imperialism* (Harmondsworth 1986); Kathleen McCrone, *Sport and the Physical Emancipation of English Women, 1870–1914* (London 1988); and Benjamin Rader, *American Sports: From the Age of Folk Games to the Age of Spectators* (Englewood Cliffs, NJ, 1983)

8 George Eisen, 'Games and Sporting Diversions of the North American Indian,' *Canadian Journal of the History of Sport and Physical Education (CJHSPE)*, 9 no. 1 (1978), 58–95

9 Alan Metcalfe, 'Form and Function of Physical Activity in New France,'
   CJHSPE, 1 no. 1 (1970), 45–64; Robert Day, 'The British Garrison at
   Halifax: Its Contribution to the Development of Sport in the Community,'
   in Barbara Schrodt, ed., *Proceedings of the Fourth Canadian Symposium on the
   History of Sport and Physical Education* (Vancouver 1979); Ann Hall,
   'Women's Sport in Canada prior to 1914,' paper presented to First
   Canadian Symposium on the History of Sport and Physical Education,
   Edmonton, 14 May 1970; Edwin Guillet, *Early Life in Upper Canada*
   (Toronto 1933); and Donald Guay, 'Problèmes de l'intégration du sport
   dans la société canadienne, 1830–1865 : le cas des courses de chevaux,'
   CJHSPE, 4 no. 2 (1973), 70–92
10 William Humber, 'Baseball and Town Life in 19th Century Ontario, 1864–
   1869,'in Kidd, ed., *Proceeding of the Fifth*, 189–92; Donald Morrow, Mary
   Keyes, Wayne Simpson, Frank Cosentino, and Ron Lappage, *A Concise
   History of Sport in Canada* (Toronto 1989), 48–52; and Morris Mott, 'The
   Winnipeg Vics, 1890–1903: The Meaning of Hockey at the Turn of the
   Century,' in Kidd, ed., *Proceedings of the Fifth*, 1–10
11 Alan Metcalfe, 'Organized Sport and Social Stratification in Montreal,
   1840–1901,' in Richard Gruneau and John Albinson, *Canadian Sport: Sociological Perspectives* (Don Mills 1976), 77–101; and Richard Gruneau and
   David Whitson, *Hockey Night in Canada* (Toronto 1993), 39
12 Don Morrow, *A Sporting Evolution: The Montreal Amateur Athletic Association,
   1881–1981* (Montreal 1981)
13 See also Alan Metcalfe, William Humber, and Lynne Marks, 'Organized
   Sport,' in Donald Kerr and Derek Holdsworth eds., *Historical Atlas of
   Canada*, vol. 3 (Toronto 1990), 35
14 Ian Jobling, 'Urbanization and Sport in Canada, 1867–1900,' in Gruneau
   and Albinson, *Canadian Sport: Sociological Perspectives*, 64–76; and Trevor
   Williams, 'Cheap Rates, Special Trains, and Canadian Sport in the 1850s,'
   Canadian Journal of the History of Sport (CJHS), 12, no. 2 (1981), 84–93
15 Alan Metcalfe, *Canada Learns to Play* (Toronto 1987), 189–90
16 Peter Levine, *A.G. Spalding and the Rise of Baseball* ((New York 1985);
   Metcalfe, *Canada Learns to Play*, 68; Steve Hardy, 'Entrepreneurs,
   Organizers and the Marketplace,' *Journal of Sport History (JSH)*, 13 no. 1
   (1986), 18: and National Archives of Canada, (NA), 28, 150 I, Amateur
   Athletic Union of Canada (NA), 1909 Minutes, 12
17 Tim Hutton kindly made this calculation from the Canadian censuses.
18 Mott, 'One Solution to the Urban Crisis: Manly Sports and Winnipeggers,
   1900–1914,' *Urban History Review*, 12 no. 2 (1983), 57–70; L.M. McKee,
   ' "Nature's Medicine": The Physical Education and Outdoor Recreation

Programs in Toronto Volunteer Youth Groups,' in Kidd, ed., *Proceedings of the Fifth*, 128–39; Varda Burstyn, *The Rites of Men* (Toronto forthcoming); and Steven Reiss, *City Games: The Evolution of American Urban Society and the Rise of Sports* (Chicago 1989), 171–202

19 Province of Canada, *Statutes of Canada*, 1845, Ch. 45, 263–4

20 K.B. Wamsley, 'Cultural Signification and National Ideologies: Rifle-Shooting in Late Nineteenth-Century Canada,' *Social History*, 20 no. 1 (1995), 63–72

21 Canada, *House of Commons Debates*, 1881, 11 Feb. 1881, 935–40. The bill originated in the Senate.

22 Gerald Redmond, 'Imperial Viceregal Patronage: The Governors-General of Canada and Sport in the Dominion, 1867–1909,' *International Journal of The History of Sport*, 6 no. 2 (1989), 193–217

23 Metcalfe, 'Working Class Physical Recreation in Montreal,' *Working Papers in the Sociological Study of Sport and Income*, 1 no. 2 (1978), 27–34

24 Frank Cosentino and Max Howell, *History of Physical Education in Canada* (Toronto 1971)

25 S.F. Wise and Doug Fisher, *Canada's Sporting Heroes* (Toronto 1974), 305

26 E.g., *Toronto Daily Star*, 25 July 1908

27 E.g., Adelman, *A Sporting Time*; Michael Oriard, *Reading Football: How the Popular Press Created an American Spectacle* (Chapel Hill, NC, 1993); and Charles Fountain, *Sportswriter: The Life and Times of Grantland Rice* (New York 1993)

28 Barbara Schrodt, 'Changes in the Governance of Canadian Sport,' *CJHS*, 14 no. 1 (1983), 15; Nationl Archives of Canada (NA), MG 28, I 151, AAU, 1911 Minutes, 26

29 AAU, 1894 Minutes, 3–4

30 AAU, 1911 Minutes, 45–50

31 Wise and Fisher, *Canada's Sporting Heroes*, 13

32 Don Morrow, 'The Great Canadian Lacrosse Tours of 1876 and 1883,' in Kidd, ed., *Proceedings of the Fifth*, 11–22; J.E. Collins, *Canada under the Administration of Lord Lorne* (Toronto 1884), Appendix Y, 502–63.

33 'Champions of Europe,' *Globe*, 5 March 1910

34 Metcalfe, *Canada Learns to Play*, 97–8; and Humber, 'Cheering for the Home Team,' 196

35 Roy Rosenweig, 'Middle–Class Parks and Working-Class Play,' *Radical History Review*, 21 (1979), 43

36 Bruce Kidd, *Tom Longboat* (Toronto 1980), 3; Metcalfe, *Canada Learns to*

Play, 64 and 196–7; and Gerald Redmond, 'Some Aspects of Organized Sport and Leisure in Nineteenth Century Canada,' in Morris Mott, ed., *Sports in Canada: Historical Readings* (Toronto 1989), 96

37 Mary Fallis Jones, *The Confederation Generation* (Toronto 1978), 70–9; Working Lives Collective, *Working Lives* (Vancouver 1985), 131–41; and Bryan Palmer, *A Culture in Conflict* (Montreal 1979), 52–9

38 Robert Harney, 'Homo Ludens and Ethnicity,' *Polyphony,* 7 no. 1 (1985), 1–12; and Paul Voisey, *Vulcan: The Making of a Prairie Town* (Toronto 1988), 163–5

39 AAU, 1914 Minutes, 9

40 Sheard and Dunning, 'The Rugby Football Club as a Male Preserve'; Morris Mott, 'The British Protestant Pioneers and the Establishment of the Manly Sports in Manitoba, 1870–1886,' *Journal of Sport History,* 7 no. 3 (1980), 25–36; Bruce Hailey, *The Healthy Body in Victorian Culture* (Cambridge 1978); Norman Vance, *The Sinews of the Spirit* (Cambridge 1985); Elliott Gorn, *The Manly Art: Bare-Knuckle Prize Fighting in America* (Ithaca, NY, 1986); Joseph Kett, *Rites of Passage* (New York 1977); David MacLeod, *Building Character in the American Boy* (Madison, Wis., 1983); David Howell and Peter Lindsay, 'Social Gospel and the Young Boy Problem, 1896–1925,' *CJHS,* 17 no. 1 (1986), 75–87

41 *R. v. Wildfong and Lang* (1911), 17 CCC 251 (Ont. CC)

42 Helen Lenskyj, ' "Moral physiology" in Physical Education for Girls in Ontario, 1900–1930,' in Kidd, ed., *Proceedings of the Fifth,* 139–49; and Paul Atkinson, 'Fitness, Feminism, and Schooling,' in Sara Delamont and Lorna Duffin, eds., *The Nineteenth Century Woman: Her Physical and Cultural World* (London 1978), 92–133

43 Ann Hall, 'Women's Sport in Canada prior to 1914'

44 Elizabeth Mitchell, 'The Rise of Athleticism among Girls and Women,' *Report of the Third Annual Meeting and Conference of the National Council of Women* (Montreal 1896); and Marion Pitters, 'Women's Participation in Sporting Activity as an Indicator of a Feminist Movement in Canada between 1900 and 1914,' in Reet Howell, ed., *Her Story in Sport* (West Point, NY, 1982), 141–53

45 Lois Banner, *American Beauty* (Chicago 1983); James Whorton, *Crusaders for Fitness* (Princeton, NY, 1982); and Michael Smith, 'Graceful Athleticism or Robust Womenhood: The Sporting Culture of Women in Victorian Nova Scotia,' *Journal of Canadian Studies,* 23 no. 2 (1988), 120–37

46 *Constitution and Bylaws of the Montreal Pedestrian Club* (Montreal 1873), 8

47 Peter Bailey, *Leisure and Class in Victorian England: Rational Recreation and the Contest for Control, 1830–1885* (Toronto 1978); and Mott, 'One Solution to the Urban Crisis'
48 Gruneau, *Sports, Class and Social Development*, 108–10; John Holt, "Amateurism' and Its Interpretation: The Social Origins of British Sport,' *Innovation in Social Science Research*, 5 no. 4 (1992), 29; and Alan Ingham and Rob Beamish, 'The Industrialization of the United States and the Bourgeoisification of American Sports,' in Eric Dunning, Joe Maguire, and Robert Pearton, eds., *The Sports Process: A Comparative and Developmental Approach* (Champaign, Ill., 1993), 169–206
49 Harry Braverman, *Labor and Monopoly Capital* (New York 1974), 278–9
50 Nancy Bouchier, ' "The 24th of May Is the Queen's Birthday": Civic Holidays and the Rise of Amateurism in Nineteenth-Century Canadian Towns,' *IJHS*, 10 no. 2 (1993), 159–92
51 *Hamilton Spectator*, 1 July 1867
52 John Cumming, *Runners and Walkers* (Chicago 1981), 101–28, and David Blaikie, 'Bennett's 1891 Record,' *Ultramarathon Canada*, 6 no. 1 (1994), 2
53 H.J.P. Good, 'When Hanlan Won the World's Championship,' *Globe*, 6 Dec. 1878
54 Andrea Brown, 'Edward Hanlan: The World Sculling Champion Visits Australia,' *CJHSPE*, 11 no. 2 (1980), 1–44
55 Canada, *House of Commons Debates*, 11 Feb. 1881, 935–40; and Henry Roxborough, *One Hundred – Not Out (Toronto 1967)*, 207
56 Bill Humber, *Cheering for the Home Team* (Erin Mills, Ont., 1983), 45–9
57 Frank Cosentino, 'A History of the Concept of Professionalism in Canada,' PhD. thesis, University of Alberta, 1972, 154, 197; and Morris Mott, 'The Problems of Professionalism: The Manitoba Amateur Athletic Association and the Fight against Pro Hockey,' in Elise Corbet and Anthony Rasporich, eds., *Winter Sports in the West* (Calgary 1990), 132–42
58 R.S. Lappage, 'The Kenora Thistles' Stanley Cup Trail,' *CJSH*, 19 no. 2 (1988), 86–92
59 Foster Hewitt, *Hockey Night in Canada* (Toronto 1961), 55–7; see also Scott Young, *One Hundred Years of Dropping the Puck: A History of the OHA* (Toronto 1989), 72–4
60 Bruce Kidd, 'In Defence of Tom Longboat,' *CJHS*, 15 no. 1 (1983), 49–51
61 AAU, 1909 Minutes, 4–5; Fred Tees Papers, Canada's Sports Hall of Fame; Don Morrow, 'A Case Study in Amateur Conflict: the Athletic War in Canada 1906–8,' *British Journal of Sport History*, 3 no. 2 (1986), 173–90; and Metcalfe, *Canada Learns to Play*, 113–4

62 Morrow, 'A Case Study in Amateur Conflict,' 190; and Metcalfe, *Canada Learns to Play*, 132

63 S.F. Wise, 'The Annexation Movement and Its Effects on Canadian Opinion,' in S.F. Wise and R.C. Brown, eds., *Canada Views the United States* (Toronto 1967), 94

64 Paul Rutherford, *A Victorian Authority: The Daily Press in Late Nineteenth-Century Canada* (Toronto 1982), 170–6

65 J. Lee Thompson and John H. Thompson, 'Ralph Connor and the Canadian Identity,' *Queen's Quarterly*, 79 no. 2 (1972), 161; and David Brown, 'Images of Sports in Canadian Fiction: The Contribution of Ralph Connor,' in Kidd, ed., *Proceedings of the Fifth*, 23–32

66 Though strict amateurism was always a minority current within the United States, 'a fanatical zeal for "simonpure" athletic amateurism' characterized the early leadership of the American AAU; see John Lucas, 'The Hegemonic Rule of the Amateur Amateur Athletic Union, 1888–1914: James Edward Sullivan as Prime Mover,' *IJHS*, 11 no. 3 (1994), 355–71

67 Betty Lee, *Love and Whisky: The Story of the Dominion Drama Festival* (Toronto 1973), 66–8

68 Metcalfe, *Canada Learns to Play*, 220

69 AAU, 1914 Minutes, and Hall, 'Women's Sport in Canada prior to 1914,' 18–9

70 T.A. Reed, *The Blue and White* (Toronto 1944), 43–5; and David Bourbon, 'Sport and Patriotic Expression during WW1,' in Kidd, ed., *Proceedings of the Fifth*, 391–401

71 J.L. Granatstein and J.M. Hitsman, *Broken Promises* (Toronto 1977), 22–4

72 AAU, 1908, 1911, and 1913 Minutes

73 Carl Berger, *The Sense of Power* (Toronto 1972)

74 AAU, 1913, 1909, and 1911 Minutes

75 John MacKenzie, ed., *Imperialism and Popular Culture* (Manchester 1986)

76 Berger, *The Sense of Power*, 251–7; Des Morton, 'The Cadet Movement in the Moment of Canadian Militarism, 1909–1914,' *Journal of Canadian Studies*, 13 no. 2 (1978), 56–68; and David Brown, 'Militarism and Canadian Private School Education: Ideal and Practice, 1861–1918,' *CJHS*, 17 no. 1 (1986), 46–59

77 Don Morrow, 'The Strathcona Trust in Ontario,' *CJHSPE*, 8 no. 1 (1977), 73

78 NA, photo collection, C97800, n.d.

79 Bourbon, 'Sport and Patriotic Expression,' 393–6

80 Cosentino, *Canadian Football*, 42; Murray Ross, *The YMCA in Canada* (Toronto 1951), 280–1; C.W. Bishop, *The Canadian YMCA in the Great War* (Toronto 1924); and AAU, 1919 Minutes, 13–4 and 24

81 Conn Smythe with Scott Young, *If You Can't Beat 'Em in the Alley* (Toronto 1981), 34–8

82 Jean McGill, *The Joy of Effort* (Bewdley, Ont., 1986), 96–9. McKenzie describes his programs in his *Exercise in Education and Medicine* (Philadelphia 1909) and *Reclaiming the Maimed* (New York 1918).

83 Ross, *The YMCA in Canada*, 280; David Barthwick, 'Max Schmeling on the Canvas: Boxing as an Icon of Weimar Culture,' *New German Critique*, 51 (1991), 134

84 Coleman, *The Trail of the Stanley Cup*, vol. 1 (Montreal 1966), 312–13; Ross, *The YMCA in Canada*, 291–4; and Aristotle, *Politics* (London 1967), 7.14.8

85 Bourdon, 'Sport and Patriotic Expression,' 399

Chapter Two: 'The Making of Men'

1 National Archives of Canada (NA), MG 28, I 150, AAU, 1919 Minutes, 12

2 Richard Allen, *The Social Passion: Religion and Social Reform in Canada, 1914–1928* (Toronto 1973), 74; and Marlene Shore, *The Science of Social Redemption: McGill, the Chicago School, and the Origins of Social Research in Canada* (Toronto 1987), 25–31

3 Richard Gruneau and David Whitson, *Hockey Night in Canada* (Toronto 1993), 46–8; and Paul Boyer, *Urban Masses and Moral Order in America, 1820–1920* (Cambridge, Mass., 1978), Robert MacDonald, *Sons of the Empire: The Frontier and the Boy Scout Movement* (Toronto 1993), and Mariana Valverde, *The Age of Light, Soap and Water* (Toronto 1991)

4 Henry Roxborough, 'What Is Sport Worth to Canada?' *Maclean's*, 1 Dec. 1926, 13

5 AAU, 1920 Minutes

6 AAU, 1924 Minutes

7 E.g., Michel Foucault, *Discipline and Punish: The Birth of the Prison* (New York 1979) and *The History of Sexuality: Volume 1: An Introduction* (New York 1980); Bryan Turner, *Regulating Bodies: Essays in Medical Sociology* (New York 1992), and Susan Bordo, *Unbearable Weight: Feminism, Western Culture and the Body* (Berkeley, Calif., 1993)

8 *Toronto Star*, 1 Jan. 1923

9 D.B. Caswell, 'A History of the Development of the Secondary School Physical and Health Education Programme and the Teacher Education that Accompanied Their Growth during the Period 1900–1965 in Ontario,' North York Board of Education, 1965; and Don Morrow, 'The Strathcona Trust in Ontario, 1919–1939,' *Canadian Journal of the History of Sport and Physical Education* (*CJHSPE*), 8 no. 1 (1978), 72–90

10 Employers' Association form letter, signed by Merrick, 19 Oct. 1904; and James Naylor, *The New Democracy: Challenging the Social Order in Industrial Ontario, 1914–1925* (Toronto 1991), 52–9

11 Roxborough, 'What Is Sport Worth to Canada?' 13

12 AAU, 1928 Minutes, 70–1; and John R. Schleppi, '"It Pays": John H. Patterson and Industrial Recreation at the National Cash Register Company,' *Journal of Sport History (JSH)*, 6 no. 3 (1979), 20–9, and Elizabeth Fones-Wolf, 'Industrial Recreation, the Second World War, and the Revival of Welfare Capitalism,' *Business History Review*, 60 (1986), 232–57

13 Metropolitan Toronto Police Athletic Association, *Centennial Book* (Toronto 1983), Elmer L. Johnson, *A History of YMCA Physical Education* (Chicago 1979), Murray Ross, *The YMCA in Canada* (Toronto 1951), and Richard Moriarty, 'The Organizational History of the Canadian Intercollegiate Athletic Union Central, 1906–1955,' PhD thesis, Ohio State University, 1971

14 Robert Korsgaard, 'A History of the Amateur Athletic Union of the United States,' EdD paper, Teachers' College, Columbia University, 1952

15 AAU, 1909 Minutes, 4–11 and 65–79

16 AAU, 1920 Minutes, 7–8

17 John Thompson and Allen Seager, *Canada, 1922–1939* (Toronto 1988), 158; and Mary Vipond, 'National Consciousness in English-Speaking Canada in the 1920s: Seven Studies,' PhD thesis, University of Toronto, 1974, 218–23 and 542

18 AAU 1927 Minutes, 1 and 68

19 Cf Metcalfe, 'The Anatomy of Power in Amateur Sport in Ontario, 1918–1936,' *CJHS*, 22 No. 2 (1991), 64

20 M.J. Shea, 'Down the Sport Trail,' *Manitoba Free Press*, 30 Sept. 1924

21 AAU, 1919 Handbook

22 Henry Roxborough, 'Cash or Character,' *MacLean's*, 15 April 1928, 82–3

23 Leslie Roberts, 'Does Sport Pay a Dividend?' *Canadian Magazine*, Aug. 1931, 46

24 Roxborough, 'Money Talks,' *Maclean's*, 15 March 1930, 17, and 'Is Worship of Mammon Killing Amateur Sport?' *Maclean's*, 15 Feb. 1928

25 AAU, 1925 Minutes, 24

26 'Amateur vs. Professional,' *Ottawa Journal*, 7 Dec. 1932

27 AAU, 1926 Minutes, 9; and Lamb, *Amateurism* (Montreal 1925)

28 AAU, 1919 Minutes, 19–21, and 'Rather Than See a Split in Amateur Circles, Union Recognizes the Whitewash,' *Calgary Herald*, 27 Sept. 1919

29 Em Orlick, letter to John and Sheila Samela, 1 Aug. 1979

30 Frank Pugnucco, *Home Grown Heroes* (Sudbury 1985), 75; and Metcalfe, 'The Anatomy of Power in Amateur Sport in Ontario, 1918–1936,' 51

31 AAU, 1927 Minutes, 69
32 Ontario Sport and Recreation Centre, Toronto, Ontario Sport Oral History Project (OSOHP), Glynn Leyshon, interview with Bill Thorburn, 20 July 1990
33 Lou Marsh, 'How Amateur Are Canadian "Amateurs"?,' *Maclean's*, 15 Oct. 1926, 17
34 'Tourists Barred in Church League,' *Globe*, 13 Dec. 1921
35 AAU, 1924 Minutes, 4
36 AAU, 1926 Minutes, 21
37 Frederick Wilson, 'Scanning the Sport Field,' *Globe*, 10 Dec. 1926
38 'Our Sportsmen Visitors,' *Edmonton Journal*, 2 Dec. 1927
39 For an elaboration of this argument, see Rob Beamish and Bruce Kidd, Brief to the Commission of Inquiry into the Use of Performance-Enhancing Drugs and Other Banned Practices, Toronto, Jan. 1990
40 Henry Roxborough, 'Are Olympic Games Worth While?' *Maclean's*, 1 Nov. 1928, 55
41 AAU, 1921 Minutes, 31
42 AAU, 1931 Minutes, 121ff; and 'BC Branch Threatens to Withdraw, Claim Discrimination Shown at Meeting Held in Winnipeg,' *Winnipeg Free Press*, 8 Dec. 1931
43 AAU, 1922 Minutes, 6–7
44 AAU, 1934 Minutes, 51
45 Pierre Comte-Offenbach, 'Olympism, the Olympic Games, the Problems,' paper presented to International Conference, Fédération sportive et gymnastique de travailleurs, Paris, 11 May 1983
46 Roxborough, 'Are Olympic Games Worth While?' 55
47 Henry Roxborough, 'Where Are Canada's Field Athletes?' *Maclean's*, 15 April 1926, 65
48 AAU, 1924 Minutes, 8; and Roxborough, 'Where Are Canada's Field Athletes?' 65
49 Henry Roxborough, 'Our Olympic Hopes', *Maclean's*, 15 May 1928, 46
50 Maria Tippett, *Making Culture: English-Canadian Institutions and the Arts before the Massey Commission* (Toronto 1990), 127–55
51 Frank Cosentino and Glynn Leyshon, *Olympic Gold: Canada's Winners in the Summer Games* (Toronto 1975), 73–9
52 AAU, 1921 Minutes, 27
53 E.g., AAU, 1924 Minutes, 29–31
54 Bruce Kidd, 'Canadian Opposition to the 1936 Olympics in Germany,' *CJHSPE*, 9 no. 2 (1978), 31
55 AAU, 1928 and 1930 Minutes, 94–5 and 78

56 Henry Roxborough, 'An Empire Olympiad,' *Maclean's*, 1 Aug. 1930, 5 and 48

57 AAU, 1930 Minutes, 80ff, and Katharine Moore, " 'The Warmth of Comradeship": The First British Empire Games and Imperial Solidarity,' *International Journal of the History of Sport (IJHS)*, 6 no. 2 (1989), 242–51

58 AAU, 1934 Minutes, 54; Bruce Kidd, 'The Campaign against Sport in South Africa,' *International Journal*, 63 no. 4 (1988), 643–64; and William Baker, 'Muscular Marxism and the Chicago Counter-Olympics of 1932,' *IJHS*, 9, no. 3 (1992), 23.

59 '1942 Empire Games to Canada,' *Globe and Mail*, 30 Nov. 1939

60 Alison Wrynn, 'The Scientific Study of American Athletic Performance, 1920–1932,' paper presented to North American Society of Sport History, Albuquerque, New Mexico, 30 May 1993; Roberta Park, 'Athletes and Their Training in Britain and America, 1800–1914,' in Jack Berryman and Park, eds., *Sport and Exercise Science: Essays on the History of Sports Medicine* (Urbana, Ill., 1992), 57–107; and John Hoberman, *Mortal Engines: The Science of Performance and the Dehumanization of Sport* (New York 1992)

61 OSOHP, Glynn Leyshon's interviews with Jack Aubin, 13 Jan. 1990; Howard Bagguley, 18 July 1990; and George 'Shorty' McDonald 12 April 1990; and Leyshon, *Of Mats and Men*, 48–53

62 AAU, 1912 Minutes, 12 and 17; 1923 Minutes, 34

63 Ron Lappagge, 'Sport in Canada during the Depression,' paper presented to North American Society for Sport History, University of Windsor, 17–21 May 1977; and L.M. Grayson and Michael Bliss, *The Wretched of Canada* (Toronto 1973), vi

64 OSOHP, Glynn Leyshon's interviews with Harvey Charters, 30 Aug. 1989, and Scotty Rankine, 28 April 1989

65 Frederick Edwards, 'Bootleg Amateurs,' *Maclean's*, 1 Nov. 1930; and Henry Roxborough, 'That Bootleg Boogey,' and Bill Fry, 'An Official Reply to Mr. Edwards,' *Maclean's*, 15 Dec. 1930

66 Author's interview with Art Rice-Jones, 19 June 1988

67 Frank Cosentino, *Canadian Football* (Toronto 1969), 96; OSOHP, Glynn Leyshon's interviews with Scotty Rankine and 'Lefty' Gwynne, 1 Aug. 1989, and with Bill Fritz, 19 July 1989; and Floyd Williston, *Johnny Miles* (Halifax 1990), 69–70

68 Author's interview with W.E. 'Stuffy' Richards, 12 April 1987

69 Lou Turofsky and Nat Turofsky, *Sports Seen: Fifty Years of Camera Work* (Toronto 1960)

70 Charles L. Coleman, *Trail of the Stanley Cup*, vol. 1 (Sherbrooke 1966), 467

71 AAU, 1930 Minutes, 4 and 50–4
72 AAU, 1931 Minutes, 54 and 106–9
73 AAU, 1932 Minutes, 95–100, and 'Changes Opinion on Amateur-Pro Mingling Ruling,' *Calgary Herald*, 7 Dec. 1932
74 AAU, 1930 Minutes, 51
75 'Changes Opinion on Amateur-Pro Mingling Ruling'
76 AAU, 1933 Minutes, 71–83
77 'Moneyed Players Who Have Been Out of Sport for More Than Three Years Taken Back,' *Winnipeg Free Press*, 18 Nov. 1933
78 'Keen Debate Expected on Pro-Amateur Mingling Subject,' ibid., 15 Nov. 1933
79 Roxborough, 'Shamateurism,' *Maclean's*, 1 Feb. 1934, 32
80 AAU, 1934 Minutes, 74 and 81. On the Americanization of football, see Michael J. Rodden, 'It's a Scandal,' *Maclean's*, 1 Nov. 1936, and Frank Cosentino, *Canadian Football*, 89–96.
81 AAU, 1935 Minutes, 9
82 Henry Roxborough, 'We Revise Our Amateur Laws? No,' *Maclean's*, 1 Nov. 1936, 14
83 AAU, 1935 Minutes, 64
84 Henry Roxborough, 'Mat Money,' *Maclean's*, 15 Oct. 1931, 17 and 69
85 AAU, 1931 Minutes, 58
86 AAU, 1938 Minutes, 30
87 Author's interview with Sydney Halter, 25 Aug. 1988; and Cosentino, *Canadian Football*, 108
88 W.T. 'Tommy' Munns, 'Scanning the Sport Field,' *Globe*, 19 Nov. 1935
89 'Coming up To the Last Round,' *Halifax Herald*, 20 Nov. 1935
90 'Demoralizing' and 'Is Canada to Have Another Year of It?,' *Halifax Herald*, 25 Nov. 1935
91 NA, MG 28, I 151, Vol. 81, Canadian Amateur Hockey Association (CAHA), 1936 Minutes, 19–32 and 76–79
92 W.G. Hardy, 'Should We Revise Our Amateur Laws? Yes,' *Maclean's*, 1 Nov. 1936, 45; and Scott Young, *One Hundred Years of Dropping the Puck* (Toronto, 1989), 175–92
93 Letter from Sydney Halter to author, 19 July 1988
94 AAU, 1939 Minutes, 4
95 Ed Fitkin, 'Calder Sees Hockey under One Control,' *Globe and Mail*, 23 Nov. 1939
96 CAHA, 1935 Minutes, 74–81
97 Ralph Allen, 'Enter the Paid Amateur,' *Maclean's*, 1 Nov. 1940, 29
98 Cosentino, *Canadian Football*

99 E.M. Orlick, C.R. Melville, and E.H. Radford, 'Official Report of the Canadian Amateur Status Committee' (Ottawa 1949), 59

100 AAU, 1936 Minutes, 14–15, and 1939 Minutes, 13–14

101 Allen, 'Enter the Paid Amateur,' 29

102 Leslie Roberts, 'Does Sport Pay a Dividend?' *Canadian Magazine*, Aug. 1931, 46

103 NA, W.L.M. King Papers, vol. 274, 231684–5, 10 March 1939

104 Mark Dyerson, 'America's Athletic Missionaries: Political Performance, Olympic Spectacle and the Quest for an American National Culture, 1896–1912,' *Olympika* 1 (1992), 70–91

105 Vipond, 'National Consciousness in English-Speaking Canada,' PhD thesis, University of Toronto, 1974, 233

106 'Percy Williams Receives Showers of Civic Honours,' *Toronto Star*, 4 Sept. 1928; and Don Morrow, 'Newspapers: Selected Aspects of Canadian Sports Journalism and the Olympics,' in Roger Jackson and Tom McPhail, eds., *The Olympic Movement and the Mass Media* (Calgary 1989), 16–18

Chapter Three: 'Girls' Sports Run by Girls'

1 Dorothy N.R. Jackson, *A Brief History of Three Schools* (Toronto 1953), 13

2 Veronica Strong-Boag, *The New Day Recalled: Lives of Girls and Women in English Canada* (Toronto 1988)

3 Jean Cochrane, Abby Hoffman, and Pat Kincaid, *Women in Canadian Life: Sports* (Toronto 1977), 35

4 Marion Pitters, 'Women's Participation in Sporting Activities as an Indicator of a Feminist Movement in Canada between 1867–1914,' in Reet Howell, ed., *Her Story in Sport: A Historical Anthology of Women in Sports* (West Point, NY, 1982), 141–53; and Michele Landsberg, 'New Feminine Era for Women Athletes Replaces Strut and Color,' *Globe and Mail*, 5 Sept. 1963

5 'Can a Woman Win a T for Athletics?' *Varsity*, 15 Jan. 1924

6 E.g., Norman Reilly Raine, 'Girls Invade Track and Diamond,' *Maclean's*, 15 Aug. 1925; and 'Another Line of Sport Invaded by Women Now,' *Calgary Herald*, 20 April 1926

7 Henry Roxborough, 'Give the Girls a Hand,' *Maclean's*, 15 Feb. 1929, and 'The Illusion of Masculine Supremacy,' *Canadian Magazine*, May 1931; Provincial Archives of Alberta, Edmonton Grads Papers (EGP), 'Sitting on Top of the World, 1915–1940,' undated pamphlet; Cambridge (Ontario) Archives, Women in Sport File, 'Rivulettes ... A Hockey Success Story,' undated *Galt Reporter* clipping; and Alexandrine Gibb, 'No Man's Land of Sport,' *Toronto Star*, 6 Nov. 1930

8 Dora Easto, 'We Bicycled across Canada,' *Business Woman*, Aug. 1928; Cyndi Smith, *Off the Beaten Track: Women Adventurers and Mountaineers in Western Canada* (Jasper, Alta., 1989); and Jill Julius Matthews, 'They Had Such a Lot of Fun: The Women's League of Health and Beauty between the Wars,' *History Workshop*, 30 (1990), 22–54

9 Toronto Harbour Commission Archives, RG 3/3, Sunnyside Stadium records. And see Table 3.1, below.

10 *Toronto Star*, 16 April 1926; EGP, undated *Edmonton Journal* clipping; and Cathy Macdonald, 'The Edmonton Grads, Canada's Most Successful Team: A History and Analysis of Their Success,' MHK thesis, University of Windsor, 1976, 24

11 Sheila Mitchell, 'The Development of Women's Organized Sport in the 1920s: A Study of the Canadian Ladies Golf Union,' in Reet Howell, ed., *Her Story in Sport*, 564–71

12 Helen Gurney, *Girls' Sports: A Century of Progress* (Toronto 1982), 24–7; Ontario, *Department of Education Annual Report* (Toronto 1914), 669; Helen Lenskyj, ' "Femininity First": Sport and Physical Education for Ontario Girls, 1890–1930,' *Canadian Journal of the History of Sport* (*CJHS*), 12 no. 2 (1982), 4–17; Toronto Public School Girls' Athletic Association, 'History of the Association'; EGP, 'Sitting on Top of the World, 1915–40,' 3–7; Pauline Olafson, 'Sport, Physical Education and the Ideal Girl in Selected Denominational Schools, 1870–1930,' MA thesis, University of Windsor, 1990

13 Author's interview with Ann Clark, 18 May 1988; Jeff Wilkinson, 'She's No "Old Bat" and Here's Proof,' *Windsor Star*, 27 March 1979; author's interview with Gladys Gigg Ross, 21 June 1989; and Helen Lenskyj's interview with Doris Butwell Craig, 23 Jan. 1983; I am extremely grateful to Helen for the loan of her tapes.

14 Lenskyj, ' "Femininity First" '; Lois Banner, *American Beauty* (Chicago 1983); Sheila Fletcher, *Women First: The Female Tradition in English Physical Education, 1880–1980* (London 1984); Kathlene McCrone, *Sport and the Physical Emancipation of English Women, 1870–1914* (London 1988); Stephanie Twin, 'Jock and Jill: Aspects of Women's Sports History in America, 1870–1940,' PhD thesis, Rutgers State University of New Jersey, 1978; James Whorton, *Crusaders for Fitness: The History of American Health Reformers* (Princeton, NJ, 1982); Patricia Vertinsky, *The Eternally Wounded Woman: Women, Exercise and Doctors in the Nineteenth Century* (Manchester 1990); and Carolyn Strange, *Toronto's Girl Problem: The Perils and Pleasures of the City, 1880–1930* (Toronto 1995), 192–4

15 Senda Berenson, ed., *Spalding's Official Women's Basketball Guide, 1905–1906*

(New York 1906), 5–6; and Gurney, *Girls' Sports*, 21–2

16 Desmond Morton, 'The Cadet Movement in the Moment of Canadian Militarism,' *Journal of Canadian Studies*, 13 no. 2 (1978), 56–68; Don Morrow, 'The Strathcona Trust in Ontario,' *Canadian Journal of the History of Sport and Physical Education (CJHSPE)*, 8 no. 1 (1977), 72–90; and Strathcona Trust, *Syllabus of Physical Exercises for Schools* (Toronto 1911)

17 McCrone, *Sport and the Physical Emancipation of English Women*, 281; and Gurney, *Girls' Sports*, 22

18 City of Toronto Archives, Playground Scrapbook, 'Moss Park Recreation Centre Opening for Girls,' *Mail and Empire*, 15 May 1915, and 'Youthful Players in Moss Park Recreation Grounds,' *Globe*, 1 Aug. 1922; Elsie McFarland, *The Development of Public Recreation in Canada* (Ottawa 1970), 18–40; and author's interview with Florence Cutting, 13 June 1989

19 Gurney to author, 21 May 1988

20 Joan Sangster, 'The Softball Solution: Female Workers, Male Managers, and the Operation of Paternalism at Westclox, 1923–1960,' *Labour/Le Travail*, 32 (1993), 139–66; and Monys Ann Hagen, 'Industrial Harmony through Sports: The Industrial Recreation Movement and Women's Sports, PhD thesis, University of Wisconsin – Madison, 1990

21 Mabel Ray, 'This and That of Sport,' undated clipping, Mabel Ray Scrapbook in author's possession; Ray's role in the creation of the first softball and hockey leagues for women was subsequently confirmed by Phyllis Griffiths, 'The Girl and the Girl,' undated clipping.

22 Ontario Sport and Recreation Centre, Toronto, Ontario Sport Oral History Project (OSOHP), Glynn Leyshon's interview with Audrey Dearnley McLaughlin, 27 June 1990; Marie Parkes, *The Development of Women's Athletics at the University of Toronto* (Toronto 1961), 33; Judith Jenkins George, 'The Fad of North American Women's Endurance Swimming during the Post World War I Era,' *CJHS*, 25 no. 1 (1995), 52–72; and Morrow et al., *A Concise History of Sport in Canada* (Toronto 1989), 92

23 Author's interview with Magaret Lord, 21 June 1989; OSOHP, Cecil Smith's interview with Magaret Lord, 17 June 1986; Ontario Amateur Basketball Association, 'How It All Began,' undated mimeo; and Phyllis Griffiths, 'The Girl and the Game,' *Toronto Telegram*, 25 Nov. 1931

24 'Edmonton Girl Champions Here,' *Toronto Star*, 19 May 1922; and Louisa Zerbe, 'The 1930 University of British Columbia Women's Basketball Team: Those Other World Champions,' in Barbara Schrodt, ed., *Proceedings of the Fourth Canadian Symposium on the History of Sport and Physical Education* (Vancouver 1979). The Grads always claimed 502 victories in 522 games,

but Cathy Macdonald argues persuasively that 98 of the games were 'practice contests'.

25 Ray, 'This and That in Sport'; 'Ladies Ready for Hockey,' *Toronto Telegram*, 18 Dec. 1922; author's interview with Spalding, 9 July 1989; Parkes, *The Development of Women's Athletics at the University of Toronto*, 24; Cambridge Archives, Women in Sport File; Canadian Broadcasting Corporation, *The Inside Track*, 25 Jan. 1992; and Brian McFarlane, *Proud Past, Bright Future: One Hundred Years of Canadian Women's Hockey* (Toronto 1994)

26 Parkes, *The Development of Women's Athletics at the University of Toronto*, 2; Greater Vancouver Women's Grass Hockey Association, *Field Hockey Jubilee Booklet* (Vancouver 1956); and John McBryde, 'The Bipartite Development of Men's and Women's Field Hockey in Canada in the Context of Separate International Hockey Federations,' MPE thesis, University of British Columbia, 1986, 91–124

27 Author's interview with Joyce Plumptre Tyrrell, 10 June 1989

28 Helen Lenskyj, 'The Role of Physical Education in the Socialization of Girls in Ontario, 1890–1930,' PhD thesis, Ontario Institute for Studies in Education, 1983, 227–8; Gurney, personal communication, 18 Sept. 1989; and author's interview with Gladys Gigg Ross, 21 June 1989

29 Lois Brown, *Girls of Summer: In their Own League* (Toronto 1992), 5

30 THC Archives, Box 3/3, Sunnyside Ladies Softball Papers (SLS), correspondence 1923–24; and 'Girls' Baseball Match at Sunnyside Attracts Thousands,' *Globe*, 4 Aug. 1924

31 SLS, Minute of 24 July 1925, contract between the Toronto Women's Softball Association and the THC, 15 May 1928, and Gibb, 'In the No Man's Land of Sports,' *Toronto Star*, n.d.; and Griffiths, 'The Girl and the Game,' *Toronto Telegram*, 31 March 1930

32 Griffiths, 'The Girl and the Game,' *Toronto Telegram*, 13 Feb. 1931; James O'Mara, 'The Toronto Harbour Commission's Financial Arrangements and City Waterfront Development, 1910–1950,' Geography Discussion Paper No. 30, York University, 1984; and SLS, Report to Commissioners, 29 March 1939, and letter from E.H. Cousins to J.A. Grahamslaw, 4 July 1939. According to SLS, 'Operation of Sunnyside Softball Stadium 1925 to 1930,' the annual revenue produced by Sunnyside was slightly less than what it would have been if the commission had simply rented out the land at 5 per cent of its estimated value per year. But this calculation did not take into account the extent to which women's softball brought customers to the THC's other interest, the amusement park.

33 Letter from Beatrice Swinford to Harvey Haid, 25 June 1989, on loan to author

34 'Winnipeg Women Wield a Wicked Racket with Eye to Championships,'
   Winnipeg Free Press, 5 Dec. 1931; and Jack Purcell, 'Badminton Boom,'
   Maclean's, 1 March 1935

35 *Toronto Star*, 30 Aug. 1927; Bill Leveridge, *Fair Sport: A History of Sports at
   the Canadian National Exhibition since 1879* (Toronto 1978), 1–22 and
   315–20; and George, 'The Fad of North American Women's Endurance
   Swimming'

36 For football, see 'When Girls Play They Get Rough,' *Calgary Herald*, 22
   Nov. 1922. All the others were carefully recorded in Dorothy Medhurst's
   scrapbook. I am grateful to her daughter, Abigail Hoffman, for allowing
   me to use this scrapbook.

37 A.M. Hall and Dorothy Richardson, *Fair Ball: Toward Sex Equality in
   Canadian Sport* (Ottawa 1983); Lenskyj, *Out of Bounds*; Susan Cahn, *Coming
   On Strong: Gender and Sexuality in Twentieth Century Women's Sport* (New York
   1994); A.J. Young, 'Maritime Attitudes toward Women in Sport, 1920s–
   1930s,' in Bruce Kidd, ed., *Proceedings of the Fifth Canadian Symposium*
   (Toronto 1982), 228; and author's interview with Gladys Gigg, 21 June 1989

38 'Girl Sports,' *Toronto Star*, 26 Nov. 1927; Griffiths, 'The Girl and the
   Game,' *Toronto Telegram*, 25 Nov. 1931; and Edith Mackenzie Haid
   Scrapbook (EMHS), 'Winnipeg Girls' Basketball Schedule, 1931–2.' I am
   grateful to Harvey Haid for the loan of this scrapbook.

39 Cambridge Archives, Women in Sport File, 'Hurlbut Ladies Hockey Team,
   1921–22,' *Hurlbut Foot-Notes*, 1 no. 9, (1922); *Toronto Star*, 22 and 25 March
   1926; S.F. Wise and Doug Fisher, *Canada's Sporting Heroes* (Toronto 1974),
   286–7; and Tony Conacher Finlay Scrapbook, in author's possession

40 'In Girls' Sports Movement,' *Star Weekly*, 31 March 1928; Bobbie Rosenfeld,
   'Sports Reel,' *Globe and Mail*, 1 May 1943; author's interview with Joyce
   Plumptree Tyrrell, 10 June 1989; and Ontario Amateur Basketball
   Association, 'How It All Began'

41 *Toronto Star*, 11 Sept., 12 and 14 Nov. 1925, 10 and 24 March 1926; and
   Ray, 'This and That in Sport'

42 Author's interview with Margaret Lord, 21 June 1989

43 Olafson, 'Sport, Physical Education and the Ideal Girl,' 123–30

44 'Mrs. John Gibb Passes: Lifelong Ward 1 Resident,' *Toronto Star*, 17 Dec.
   1936; 'Leader in Girls' Sport Movement,' *Star Weekly*, 31 March 1928; and
   'Says She Is Not Allowed to Use Own Judgment,' *Toronto Star*, 12 Nov. 1934

45 Letter from Gus Ryder to H.C. Hindmarsh, *Toronto Star*, 15 Sept. 1954

46 On women's rights: author's interview with Ann Clark, 26 May 1989; Mary
   Boutelier and Lucinda SanGiovanni, *The Sporting Woman* (Champaign, Ill.,
   1983), 106–21; and author's interview with Gladys Gigg Ross, 21 June 1989

47 George Pallett, ed., *Women's Athletics* (London 1955), 14–30; and Mary H. Leigh and Therese M. Bonin, 'The Pioneering Role of Madame Alice Milliat and the FSFI in Establishing International Track and Field Competition for Women,' *Journal of Sport History* (*JSH*), 4 no. 1 (1977), 72–83

48 AAU, 1922 Minutes, 12 and 26; Pallett, ed., *Women's Athletics*, 23; and Virginia Lou Evans, 'The Status of the American Woman in Sport, 1912–32,' PhD thesis, University of Michigan, 1976, 221–30

49 AAU, 1923 Minutes, 13, 24–5, and 32; 1924 Minutes, 9, 20, and 28

50 Author's interview with Joyce Plumptre Tyrrell, 10 June 1989

51 Cited by Elmer Ferguson, 'I Don't Like Amazon Athletes,' *Maclean's*, 1 Aug. 1938, 32

52 'Ladies Ready for Hockey,' *Toronto Telegram*, 18 Dec. 1922

53 'Miss Alex Gibb Selected Manager of Canadian Girls Athletic Team,' *Mail and Empire*, 4 July 1925; Gibb, 'Report of Women's Athletic Team Which Competed in International Games Held at Stamford Bridge London, Eng. August 1st, 1925,' in J. Howard Croker, ed., *Report: Canadian Olympic Committee 1924 Games Held in Chamonix and Paris, France* (Montreal 1925), 63–71; and Pallett, ed., *Women's Athletics*, 25

54 E.g., Frederick Webster, *Athletics of Today for Women* (London 1930)

55 'Canadian Ladies A.C. of Toronto Organized,' *Toronto Star*, 26 Aug. 1925

56 AAU, 1925 Minutes, 25–6

57 Gibb, 'Plans Outlined for Women's AAU of C,' *Toronto Star*, 26 Sept. 1925; 'Constitution Is Drafted for Women's AAU of C,' *Toronto Star*, 26 Nov. 1925; and 'Ladies Athletic Group Is Formed,' *Globe*, 8 Dec. 1926

58 Author's interview with Joyce Plumptre Tyrrell, 10 June 1989; and Margaret Gillett, *We Walked Very Warily: A History of Women at McGill* (Montreal 1981), 225–7

59 University of Toronto Archives (UTA), Loudon Papers, Letter from Bellamy to Loudon, 11 April 1929; Gibb, 'No Man's Land of Sport,' *Toronto Star*, 29 Nov. 1928; 'Manitoba Branch WAA Is Formed,' *Winnipeg Free Press*, 5 Dec. 1931; and letter from Beatrice Swinford (Mackenzie's sister) to Harvey Haid (her husband), 25 June 1989

60 These are taken from press reports of the annual general meetings in those years. Except for the minutes of the 1928 meeting, which have survived in UTA, Marie Parkes Papers, few WAAF records remain. According to Margaret Lord, the main files were destroyed by Irene Wall in the late 1950s. Irene Moore McInnis kept copies of the Ontario and national constitutions, only to have them stolen from a sports history display in Thorold several years ago.

61 Fred Wilson, 'Sporting Views,' *Globe*, 9 Dec. 1926; Parkes Papers, WAAF, 1928 Minutes, 10–11; author's interviews with Joyce Plumptre Tyrrell, 10 June 1989, and with Margaret Lord, 29 April 1988

62 Fred Wilson, 'Discretion in Women's Athletics,' *Globe*, 10 Dec. 1926

63 Author's interview with Ann Clark, 26 May 1989; and Bob Elson, 'On the Sport Front,' *Vancouver Sun*, undated; 'Sport in Canada,' *New Zealand Herald*, undated; and 'Athletics in Canada,' unidentified Sydney paper, all from Ann Clark Scrapbook, copies in author's possession

64 Author's interview with Jim Worrall, 29 March 1990

65 Gibb, 'No Man's Land of Sport,' *Toronto Star*, 28 Nov. 1931

66 Griffiths, 'The Girl and the Game,' *Toronto Telegram*, 25 Nov. 1935

67 Paul Atkinson, 'Fitness, Feminism and Schooling,' in Sara Delamont and Lorne Duffin, eds., *The Nineteenth Century Woman: Her Cultural and Physical World* (London 1978), 92–113; Sheila Fletcher, *Women First*; and J.A. Mangan and Roberta J. Park, eds., *From 'Fair Sex' to Feminism* (London 1987)

68 UTA, Women's Athletic Association, 1930 Minutes; and 'Sports for Girls Develop Citizenship,' *Mail and Empire*, 6 Sept. 1928; 'Athletic Heart Not in Danger,' *Toronto Star*, 8 Jan. 1929; and 'Doctor Reluctant to Judge Venuses,' *Varsity*, 6 Dec. 1937

69 Wilson, 'Discretion in Women's Athletics'

70 'Lenskyj The Role of Physical Education in the Socialization of Girls and women,' 243

71 See also Cartwright, 'Athletics and Physical Education for Girls,' *Ontario Education Association Yearbook* (Toronto 1923), 274–81; and Herriott, 'The Department of Physical Education for Women,' *McGill News* (Autumn 1935), 38

72 'Ladies Athletic Group is Formed,' *Calgary Herald*, 9 Dec. 1929; Gibb, 'No Man's Land of Sport,' *Toronto Star*, 9 Dec. 1928; and interview with Helen Gurney, 11 July 1989

73 'Quebec Nominates Women Officials,' *Toronto Star*, 23 Nov. 1928; Parkes Papers, WAAF, 1928 Minutes, 2–4 and 17; 'No Man's Land of Sport,' *Toronto Star*, 3 Dec. 1928 and 27 Nov. 1931; and NA, MG 28, I 53, 3, X-24–8, CAHPER Collection, Women's Athletic Section, 'Report, 1940–1946'

74 Gurney, *Girls' Sports*, 37; and Ellen Gerber, 'The Controlled Development of Collegiate Sport for Women, 1923–36,' *JSH*, 2, no. 1 (1975), 1–28

75 Howard Savage, *American College Athletics* (New York 1929); and Gary Pennington, 'Rand Rogers: Educational Provocateur, 1894–1972,' *CJHS*, 12 no. 1 (1981), 24–50

76 Martha Verbrugge, 'A Gym of One's Own: Separatism and Women's Physical Education in Early Twentieth Century America,' paper presented to North American Society of Sport History, Halifax, 24 May 1992; the story about Bryans in Hart House is from David Smith, whose mother was the friend.

77 Wendy Dahlgren, *Report of the National Task Force on Young Females and Physical Activity* (Ottawa 1988); and Helen Lenskyj, 'Creating "Female-Friendly" Sport,' paper presented to Canadian Association for Health, Physical Education, and Recreation, Winnipeg, 1993

78 Pallett, ed., *Women's Athletics*, 30–7; Leigh and Bonin, 'The Pioneering Role of Madame Alice Milliat,' 74–80; and Joyce Sherlock's interview with Vera Seale, June 1987

79 'Women Vote to Send Team to Olympics,' and 'Miss Gibb, Manager; Miss Parkes, Escort,' *Toronto Star*, 26 Nov. 1927 and 10 April 1928, respectively; and Canadian Olympic Committee, *Official Report of the IX Olympiad 1925–29* (Hamilton 1929), 72–6 and 122

80 Parkes Papers, WAAF, 1928 Minutes; Phyllis Griffiths, 'Women Vote for Olympic Games,' *Toronto Telegram*, 1 Dec. 1928; and 'Women Favour Competition,' *Toronto Star*, 1 Dec. 1928

81 Gibb, 'No Man's Land of Sport,' *Toronto Star*, 10 Dec. 1928

82 Gibb, 'No Man's Land of Sport,' *Toronto Star*, 29 Nov. 1929; and 'Women's Amateur Federation Would Desert World Games for Full Olympic Program,' *Globe*, 14 Nov. 1934

83 Gibb, 'No Man's Land of Sport,' *Toronto Star*, 22 Nov. 1932

84 Leigh and Bonin, 'The Pioneering Role of Madame Alice Milliat,' 82

85 Smith's interview with Margaret Lord, 17 June 1986; author's interviews with Lord, 29 April 1988 and 21 June 1989

86 Author's interview with Lord, 29 April 1988

87 'Very Little Business Done at WAAF Meeting,' *Toronto Star*, 13 Nov. 1934

88 Author's interview with McInnis, 27 June 1989; Gibb, 'No Man's Land of Sport,' *Toronto Star*, 13, 14, and 15 Nov. 1934; and Phyllis Griffiths, 'The Girl and the Game,' *Toronto Telegram*, 13, 14, and 15 Nov. 1934

89 Jack Thomas, 'Storm Clouds Break When Women Gather,' and 'Rebellious Delegates Pacified,' *Halifax Herald*, 19 and 21 Nov. 1935, respectively

90 Alex Gibb, 'Reds and Ontario Votes Worry Gal Sport Solons' and 'Hamilton Girl Chosen after Squabble,' *Toronto Star*, 17 and 18 Nov. 1936, respectively

91 'Ultimatum: Ontario Will Quit WAAF If Demands Not Met,' *Winnipeg Free Press*, 15 Nov. 1938; and author's interview with McInnis, 27 June 1989

92 'No Man's Land of Sport,' *Toronto Star*, 17 Nov. 1938; 'Noel MacDonald Named Leading Woman Athlete,' *Calgary Herald*, 16 Nov. 1938; and Clem Shields, 'Edie Goes on the Warpath and Triumphs,' *Winnipeg Free Press*, 21 Jan. 1939

93 NA, RG 29, Vol. 783, File 184, Fitness and Amateur Sport Records, letter from Margaret Lord to Doris Plewes, 28 Nov. 1953

94 Canadian Ladies Athletic Club, *Souvenir Programme*, Ontario Women's Track and Field Championships, 16 Aug. 1930, Gladys Gigg Ross Scrapbook, copy in author's possession

95 'Women to Govern Sport for Women,' *Globe*, 1 Feb. 1928

96 Author's interviews with Florence Cutting, 14 June 1989; Mabel Beech, 14 June 1989; Gladys Gigg Ross, 21 June 1989; and Margaret Lord, 29 April 1988; SLS, letter from Ray to THC, 22 July 1930

97 'Censure Is Severe on W.J. D'Alesandro in Judicial Inquiry,' and 'D'Alesandro Banned from Amateur Sport, Committee Decides,' *Globe*, 18 Feb. and 3 Mar. 1931 respectively

98 'Barring of Miss Ray Protested By Women,' *Mail and Empire*, 10 March 1931; 'Mabel Ray Is Returned as Softball Body Head Executive Is Endorsed,' *Mail and Empire*, 31 March. 1931; 'Miss Ray Re-elected at Stormy Meeting; Four Leagues Quit?' *Globe*, 31 March 1931; and 'Accuse Grits of Meddling in Softball,' *Toronto Telegram*, 21 March 1931

99 Gibb, 'No Man's Land of Sport,' *Toronto Star*, 11 May 1931; SLS, letter from THC to Ray, 1 March 1929; internal THC memo, 7 March 1929; Solicitor's Memorandum for the THC General Manager, 17 Feb. 1932; letter from Robertson to Thomas Rennie, 26 Nov. 1931; and letter from Ray to THC, 16 May 1931

100 Phyllis Griffiths, 'The Girl and the Game,' *Toronto Telegram*, 28 March 1931

101 Author's interview with Spalding, 9 July 1989

102 Cahn, *Coming on Strong*, 164–84

103 Ferguson, 'I Don't Like Amazon Athletes,' *Maclean's*, 1 Aug. 1938; Atkins, 'Elmer, You're Goofy,' *Maclean's*, 15 Sept. 1938; Phyllis Griffiths, 'The Girl and the Game,' *Toronto Telegram*, 25 Nov. 1931; Gibb, 'No Man's Land of Sports,' *Toronto Star* undated columns, Irene McInnis Scrapbook, copy in author's possession; and Jim Thompson, 'Women Athletes Criticized,' undated (1931) clipping, Dorothy Medhurst Scrapbook, copy in author's possession

104 Lenskyj, *Out of Bounds*, 73–80

105 Mable Crews, 'The Family Purse: How the College Girl Can Make Money,' *Chatelaine* (June 1929), 34; and Mary Vipond, 'The Image of Women in Mass Circulation Magazines in the 1920s,' in Susan Mann Trofimenkoff

and Alison Prentice, eds., *The Neglected Majority* (Toronto 1977), 116–24

106 Hall and Richardson, *Fair Ball,* 37–48

107 Author's interview with Cathy Miller Ray, 4 July 1989

108 'Girl WAAF Camp' and 'Northern Ontario Girls to Attend Athletic Camp,' unidentified clippings, Gladys Gigg Ross Scrapbook, copy in author's possession

109 E.g., Cochrane, Hoffman, and Kincaid, *Women in Canadian Life: Sports,* 50–5; and Hall and Richardson, *Fair Ball,* 36

110 Bobbie Rosenfeld, 'Feminine Sports Reel,' *Globe and Mail,* 6 Nov. 1939; and 'Jimmie' Coo, 'Cherchez la Femme,' undated *Winnipeg Free Press* column, Edith Mackenzie Haid Scrapbook

111 Ruth Roach Pierson, *'They're Still Women after All': The Second World War and Canadian Womanhood* (Toronto 1986), 220

112 Sandra Kirby and Amanda Le Rougetel, *Games Analysis* (Ottawa 1993)

Chapter Four: Workers' Sport, Workers' Culture

1 Section 98 defined an 'unlawful association' as one whose purpose was to bring about any 'governmental, industrial, or economic change' by force or that advocated or defended use of force to accomplish such change. Anyone who attended a meeting or distributed the literature of any such association was 'presumed in the absence of proof to the contrary' to be guilty. The penalty was set at 20 years in prison. On five occasions between 1926 and 1930, W.L. Mackenzie King's government repealed the section, only to have Tories defeat the bill in the Senate. The jailing of Buck and his colleagues re-energized the pressure for repeal. In 1932, J.S. Woodsworth introduced two such measures. Finally in 1936, King delivered on a campaign promise and got it repealed. *Statutes of Canada* (SC), 9–10, George V, Ch. 46, S. 97A; F.R. Scott, 'Communists, Senators, and All That,' *Canadian Forum* (Jan. 1932), 127–9; Lita-Rose Betcherman, *The Little Band: The Clashes between the Communists and the Canadian Establishment 1928–32* (Ottawa n.d.), 171–211; A.E. Smith, *All My Life* (Toronto 1949)

2 *Toronto Star,* 3 Dec. 1934; *Worker,* 28 Nov. and 5 Dec. 1934; author's interview with Andrew Bileski, 3 Nov. 1977; and Gibb, 'No Man's Land of Sports,' *Toronto Star,* 28 Oct. 1935

3 Bryan Palmer, *Culture in Conflict: Skilled Workers and Industrial Capitalism in Hamilton, Ontario, 1860–1914* (Montreal 1979), 58; Mary Fallis Jones, *The Confederation Generation* (Toronto 1978), 70–9; David MacLeod, 'A Live Vaccine: The YMCA and Male Adolescence in the United States and

Canada,' *Histoire sociale/Social History*, 11, no. 2 (1978), 5–25; and Working Lives Collective, *Working Lives* (Vancouver 1985), 131–41

4 Alan Metcalfe, 'Working Class Physical Recreation in Montreal, 1860–1895,' *Working Papers in the Sociological Study of Sport and Leisure*, 1 no. 2 (1978), 14–16

5 Peter De Lottinville, 'Joe Beef of Montreal: Working Class Culture and the Tavern, 1869–1889,' *Labour/Le Travailleur*, 8/9 (1981–2), 9–40; and Gareth Stedman Jones, 'Working Class Culture and Working Class Politics in London, 1870–1900: Notes on the Remaking of a Working Class,' *Journal of Social History*, 7 (1974), 494

6 Gregory Kealey and Bryan Palmer, *Dreaming of What Might Be: The Knights of Labor in Ontario, 1880–1900* (Cambridge, Mass., 1983); and Roy Rosenzweig, *Eight Hours for What We Will* (Cambridge, Mass., 1983), 228

7 Lee Lowenfish and Tony Lupien, *The Imperfect Diamond* (New York 1980), 27–53, and Ted Vincent, *Mudville's Revenge* (New York 1981), 180–221

8 *Cotton's Weekly*, 5 Aug. 1909

9 *OBU Bulletin*, 22 June 1922; and David Bercuson, *Fools and Wise Men* (Toronto 1978), 217–19

10 *OBU Bulletin*, 9 Feb. 1922

11 E.g., 'OBU Athletic Notes,' *OBU Bulletin*, 1 May 1924, and author's interview with Ben Berck, 6 Oct. 1987

12 Horst Ueberhorst, *Frisch, Frei, Stark and Treu: Die Arbeiter sportbewegung in Deutschland, 1893–1933* (Dusseldorf 1973)

13 James Riordan and Arnd Kruger, eds., *International Workers' Sports* (Champaign, Ill., forthcoming)

14 *Arbeitersport und Sozialdemokratie* (Leipzig 1929), 4, cited by Jonathan Wagner, 'Prague's Socialist Olympics of 1934,' *Canadian Journal of the History of Sport* (*CJHS*), 23, no. 1 (1992), 4

15 J.G. Dixon, 'Prussia, Politics and Physical Education,' in Peter McIntosh et al. eds., *Landmarks in the History of Physical Education* (London 1981), 133–47; Bruce Kidd, 'The Popular Front and the 1936 Olympics,' *Canadian Journal of the History of Sport and Physical Education* (*CJHSPE*), 11 no. 1 (1980), 1–18; Bernard Rothman, 'Trespass – En Masse: Fight for Workers' Hiking Rights,' *Worker Sportsman*, May 1932; and Peter Donnelly, 'Access to the Countryside,' in Bruce Kidd, ed., *Proceedings of the Fifth Canadian Symposium on the History of Sport and Physical Education* (Toronto 1982), 490–500

16 *Populaire*, 22 May 1936. A collection of Marie's essays on sport was published as *Pour un sport ouvrier* (Paris 1934).

17 Harry Pollitt, *Worker Sportsman*, May 1932

18 Comité sportif international du travail, *Cinquante ans de sport ouvrier*

international (Brussels 1963); and Robert F. Wheeler, 'Organized Sport and Organized Labour: The Workers' Sports Movement,' *Journal of Contemporary History*, 13 (1978), 252–65

19 Coubertin, 'Olympic Memoirs: Legends,' *Olympic Review*, 134 (1978), 717–18

20 James Riordan, 'The Workers' Olympics,' in Alan Tomlinson and Garry Whannel, eds., *Five Ring Circus* (London 1984), 98–112; George Elvin Papers, British Library of Political and Economic Science, London; Wagner, 'Prague's Socialist Olympics of 1934,' *Canadian Journal of the History of Sports (CJHS)*, 23 no. 1 (1992), 7–9; and Erich Kamper, *Encyclopedia of the Olympic Games* (New York 1972), 297

21 *Worker*, 1 June 1922

22 David A. Steinberg, 'Sport under Red Flags: The Relations between the Red Sport International and the Socialist Workers' Sport International, 1920–39,' PhD thesis, University of Wisconsin, 1979, 44; see also Stephen G. Jones, 'The British Labour Movement and Working Class Leisure, 1918–39,' PhD thesis, University of Manchester, 1983, 128–9

23 G.A. Carr, 'The Spartakiad: Its Approach and Modification from the Mass Displays of the Sokol,' *CJHS*, 18 no. 1 (1987), 86–96

24 *Young Worker*, Oct. 1924

25 Ibid., 28 Feb. 1925; and Ivan Avakumovic, *The Communist Party of Canada* (Toronto 1965), 34

26 Author's interview with Dave Kashtan, 6 Oct. 1981

27 Toby Gordon Ryan, *Stage Left* (Toronto 1981); Richard Wright and Robin Endres, eds., *Eight Men Speak and Other Plays from the Canadian Workers' Theatre* (Toronto 1976), and Peter Krawchuk, *Our Stage: The Amateur Performing Arts of the Ukrainian Settlers in Canada* (Toronto 1984)

28 *Young Worker*, Dec. 1927

29 Author's interviews with Fred Kazor, 27 June 1977, Walter Kaczor, 3 Nov. 1977, Em Orlick, 11 Nov. 1979, Max Ilomaki, 17 Dec. 1985, Alex Hunnakko, 22 Nov. 1981; and *Worker*, 28 April 1928

30 Author's interview with Fred Kazor, 27 June 1977; and 'The Story of a Man,' *Universal Sportlite*, 1 Jan. 1939, 4 and 9. Kazor dropped the 'c' from his name during the Second World War.

31 Paula Unger Boelsems, 'Russ Saunders, Muscle Beach Alumnus Magna Cum Laude,' *Santa Monica Muscle Beach Alumni Association Newsletter*, 4 (Winter 1990). During a presentation on the history of Muscle Beach at the North American Society for Sport History, University of Long Beach, 27 May 1995, Saunders referred to the Universal Athletic Club as 'Muscle Beach Indoors.'

32 *Young Worker*, May 1928; and 'Urheilu ja canadan suomalainen,' in *Cana-*

dan Suomalainen Jarjesto 25 vuotta (Sudbury 1936), 155–6. I am grateful to Varpu Lindström for translating this and other Finnish documents.

33 *Worker*, 1 Oct. 1932, and *Young Worker*, 19 July 1933

34 Michael Ondaatje, *In the Skin of a Lion* (Toronto 1987), 20–2

35 Richard J. Evans, *The Feminists* (London 1977)

36 Varpu Lindström-Best, 'The Impact of Canadian Immigration Policy on Finnish Immigration, 1890–1978,' *Siirtolaisuus Migration*, 8 no. 2 (1981), 5–15, and *The Finns in Canada* (Ottawa 1985); Donald Wilson, 'Ethnicity and Cultural Retention: Finns in Canada, 1890–1920,' *Review Journal of Philosophy and Social Science*, 2 no. 2 (1977), 217–35; Auvo Kostianinen, *The Forging of Finnish-American Communism, 1917–1924* (Turku 1978); and Edward W. Laine, 'Finnish Canadian Radicalism and Canadian Politics: The First Forty Years,' in Jorgen Dahlie and Tissa Fernando eds., *Ethnicity, Power and Politics* (Toronto 1981), 94–112

37 Hannes Sula, Paavo Vaurio, and Jim Tester, 'The Federation through the Years,' in Jim Tester, ed., *Sports Pioneers: A History of the Finnish-Canadian Amateur Sports Federation, 1906–1986* (Sudbury 1986), 7

38 Myron Gulka-Tiechko, 'Ukrainian Immigration to Canada under the Railways Agreement, 1925–30,' *Journal of Ukrainian Studies*, 16 nos. 1–2 (1991), 29; Anthony Bilecki, William Repka, and Mitch Sago, *Friends in Need* (Winnipeg 1972); John Kolasky, *The Shattered Illusion* (Toronto 1979), and O.W. Gerus and J.E. Rea, *The Ukrainians in Canada* (Ottawa 1985)

39 K.W. Sokolyk, 'The Role of Ukrainian Sports, Teams, Clubs and Leagues, 1924–52,' *Journal of Ukrainian Studies*, 16 nos. 1–2 (1991), 133

40 Author's interview with Dave Kashtan, 26 May 1987

41 Fernando Claudin, *The Communist Movement: From Comintern to Cominform* (Harmondsworth 1975); E.H. Carr, *The Twilight of the Comintern* (New York 1982); Ian Angus, *Canadian Bolsheviks: The Early Years of the Communist Party of Canada* (Montreal 1981), 179–95; and Norman Penner, *The Canadian Left* (Toronto 1977), 77–100

42 *Worker*, 1 Nov. 1922, and *Young Worker*, May 1926

43 E.g., 'Political Resolution of the YCL National Executive,' *Young Worker*, Jan. 1929

44 *Young Worker*, June 1925; and National Archives of Canada (NA), CPC Archives, MG 28, IV4 54 I, 'Statement of Executive Committee of Young Communist International to Young Communist League of Canada,' 1926

45 *Young Worker*, Nov. 1929

46 Ibid., Feb. 1927

47 Ibid., June 1926

48 *Worker*, 23 Feb. 1924. This became a widely accepted criticism. According

to official YMCA historian C. Howard Hopkins, the Y 'completely allied itself with the employing class in a paternalistic service to workers ... International secretaries called upon and promoted the work with hundreds of railway officials, but never once met with organized labour.' *History of the YMCA in North America* (New York 1951), 239

49 E.g., *Worker,* 24 May 1924. Scholars have taken a similar view; see John Springhall, *Youth, Empire and Society* (London 1977).

50 Claudin, *The Communist Movement,* 71–91; and *Young Worker,* Sept.–Oct. 1928

51 *Young Worker,* Aug. 1930

52 Ibid., 24 July 1931 and 6 Aug. 1934; and William Baker, 'Muscular Marxism and the Chicago Counter-Olympics of 1932,' *International Journal of the History of Sport (IJHS),* 9 no. 3 (1992), 397–410

53 *Party Organizer,* May 1931, 24–5

54 *Worker,* 29 Aug. 1923

55 Hart Cantelon, 'Stakhanovism and Sport in the Soviet Union,' *Working Papers in the Sociological Study of Sport and Leisure (WPSSSL),* 2 no. 2 (1979), and 'The "Proletarian Culture" Movement and Its Influence on International Workers' Sports in the 1920s,' in Kidd, ed., *Proceedings of the Fifth,* 318–29; and Carmen Claudio-Urondo, *Lenin and the Cultural Revolution* (Brighton 1977)

56 *Young Worker,* Aug. 1925

57 Ibid., Aug. 1925; and *Worker,* 28 Oct. 1928

58 *Young Worker,* 20 Oct. 1931; *Worker,* 4 July 1931; *Young Worker,* 8 March 1932 and 15 June 1931

59 *Worker,* 9 May 1931

60 *Young Worker,* Oct. 1926 and Feb. 1928; *Worker,* 9 May 1931

61 Interview with Em Orlick, 11 Nov. 1979. The London YMCA subsequently took over the London Unemployed League, but Orlick claims that it wouldn't have done so if the WSA hadn't done the initial organizing; cf. Murray Ross, *The YMCA in Canada* (Toronto 1951): 'With very few exceptions, every YMCA in Canada was sensitive to the fact the number of unemployed young men was rapidly increasing,' 382.

62 Sheila I. Salmela and John H. Salmela, 'Emmanuel Orlick: Canada's Gymnastic Pioneer,' unpublished paper, Départment d'éducation physique, Université de Montréal, n.d.

63 Author's interview with Dave Kashtan, 6 Oct. 1981

64 *Young Worker,* 19 May 1931 and 17 Dec. 1932

65 Ibid., May 1930 and 20 April 1931

66 Avakumovic, *The Communist Party of Canada,* 35–8; Kolasky, *The Shattered Illusion,* 1–26; and Donald Avery, 'Ethnic Loyalties and the Proletarian

Revolution: A Case Study of Communist Political Activity in Winnipeg, 1923–36,' in Jorgen Dahlie and Tissa Fernando, eds., *Ethnicity, Power and Politics* (Toronto 1981), 68–93

67 Author's interview with Kirsti Niilsen, 21 Oct. 1982

68 Author's interview with Alex Hunnako and William Heikilla, 22 Nov. 1981, and Hannes Sula, *Canadan Suomalainen Jarjesto 25 vuotta* (Sudbury 1936), 155–7

69 *Clarion*, 3 Aug. 1937

70 Gibb, 'Soviet Athletes Prepare for World War on Russia,' *Toronto Star*, 16 Sept. 1935; Orlik, 'Open Letter to Canada's Sportsmen,' *London Free Press*, 8 Nov. 1935; 'The Personal Diary of Em Orlick Written during His Tour of the USSR When He Accompanied the WSA Delegation as Athletic Coach, 1935,' copy in author's possession; and 'Mass Physical Culture: A Russian Experiment,' *Health*, 19 Sept. 1939

71 Richard Mandell, *The Nazi Olympics* (New York 1971), 79

72 Bruce Kidd, 'Canadian Opposition to the 1936 Olympics in Germany,' *Canadian Journal of the History of Sports and Physical Education (CJHSPE)*, 9 no. 2 (1978), 20–40; and Irving Abella and Harold Troper, *None Is Too Many: Canada and the Jews of Europe, 1933–1948* (Toronto 1982)

73 NA, RG 28 V46, Vol. 59, File 40, Finnish-Canadian Workers Sports Association, *Sports Parade*, 1935–6; and *Clarion*, 28 Nov. 1936, 1 Jan. 1938, 18 Feb. 1937, 12 Nov. 1936, and 9 July 1937

74 *Young Worker*, 31 Aug. 1935, and *Clarion*, 16 April 1937

75 Canadian Ukrainian Youth Federation and the Universal Athletic Club, *Souvenir Program, Youth Pageant, Dec. 8, 1938*; and *Universal Sportlite*, April 1939, 2

76 *Clarion*, 4 July 1936

77 Mark Naison, 'Lefties and Righties: The Communist Party and Sports during the Great Depression,' *Radical America*, 13 (July–Aug. 1979), 47–59; and 'Sports for the Daily Worker: An Interview with Lester Rodney,' *In These Times*, 12–18 Oct. 1977, 12–19

78 George Pike, 'Robber Barons of Sport,' *Clarion*, 10 Nov. 1936

79 *Clarion*, 3 Aug. 1937

80 James Riordan, *Sport in Soviet Society* (Cambridge 1977), 142 and 162–6, and 'Rewriting Soviet Sport History,' *Journal of Sport History (JSH)*, 20 no. 3 (1993), 247–51

81 Sokolyk, 'The Role of Ukrainian Sports,' 136

82 Robert Harney, 'Homo Ludens and Ethnicity,' *Polyphony*, 7 (1985), 2

83 Rolf Lund, 'Skiing in Canada,' *Beaver*, Winter 1977, 48–53; Canadian Ski Association, 'The History of Skiing,' unpublished paper, n.d.; and Jorgen

Dahlie, 'Skiing for Identity and Tradition: Scandanavian Venture and Adventure in the Pacific Northwest,' in Elise Corbet and Anthony Rasporich, eds., *Winter Sports in the West* (Calgary 1990), 99–111

84 NA, Interview between George Nick and Stuart Davidson, 17 Nov. 1978

Chapter Five: Brand-Name Hockey

1 Brian McFarlane, *Fifty Years of Hockey: A History of the National Hockey League* (Toronto 1967), 25–6

2 Charles L. Coleman, *The Trail of the Stanley Cup* (Sherbrooke 1966), vol. 1, 306 and 312–13

3 *Globe*, 23 and 27 Nov. 1917; Coleman, *Trail of the Stanley Cup*, vol. 1, 332–3, 348–50, and 378; and *Toronto Telegram*, 23 Feb. 1920

4 National Archives of Canada (NA), MG 30, C129, Thomas Gorman Papers (TGP), Ottawa Hockey Club, 1918 Annual Report, 23 Oct. 1918; Archives of Ontario (AO), MU 5969, Series C Box 34, Conn Smythe Papers (CSP), 'Comparative Gross Receipts, Seasons 1931–32 to 1939–40 inclusive,' 7 March 1941; and Dick Beddoes, Stan Fischler, and Ira Gitler, *Hockey! Story of the World's Fastest Sport* (New York 1969), 35

5 While horseracing revenue fell during the Depression, it nevertheless far surpassed that of hockey. As a rough comparison, consider the taxes paid. The amount that the Ontario government collected in a flat daily levy on thoroughbred race meetings dropped from $314,804 in 1930–1 to $114,789 in 1933–4, and revenue from the 5 per cent tax on the pari-mutuel pool fell from $1.0 million in 1930–1 to $564,911 in 1933–4. But the taxes paid by the NHL in those years – the 5 per cent amusement tax and the 2 per cent Ontario Athletic Commission (OAC) levy – totalled only $39,974 and $30,888, respectively. In many years, the NHL paid more to the OAC than did all other sports combined.

6 Dink Carroll, 'Can Baseball Come Back?' *Maclean's*, 15 May 1937, 24; CSP, Maple Leaf Gardens Ltd. (MLG), 'Paid Attendance Professional Hockey,' 24 March 1953; 'Paid Attendance – All Attractions Years 1932 to 1955 Inclusive,' 9 Nov. 1956; and 'Schedule of Net Profits from date of inception to August 31, 1957,' 8 Nov. 1957

7 Beddoes, Fischler, and Gitler, *Hockey!*; Neil Isaacs, *Checking Back: A History of the National Hockey League* (New York 1977); McFarlane, *The Lively World of Hockey: A History of the National Hockey League* (Toronto 1968); Trent Frayne, *The Mad Men of Hockey* (Toronto 1974); and Frank Cosentino, 'A History of the Concept of Professionalism in Canada,' PhD thesis, University of Alberta, 1972

8 Bruce Haley, *The Healthy Body and Victorian Culture* (Cambridge 1978); and Keith Walden, 'The Road to Fat City: An Interpretation of the Development of Weight Consciousness in Western Society,' *Historical Reflections/Reflexions historiques*, 12 no. 3 (1985), 331–73

9 F.H. Leacy, ed., *Historical Statistics of Canada*, 2nd edition (Ottawa 1983), 420–3

10 Chrys Goyens and Allan Turowitz, *Lions in Winter* (Scarborough 1986), 25

11 David Cruise and Alison Griffiths, *Net Worth: Exploding the Myths of Pro Hockey* (Toronto 1991), 26–40

12 David S. Savelieff, *A History of the Sport of Lacrosse in British Columbia* (Vancouver: Author, n.d.), 14; and Frank Cosentino, *Lionel Conacher* (Toronto 1978), 47

13 Bruce Kidd, *Tom Longboat* (Toronto 1980), 43–9

14 Alan Metcalfe, *Canada Learns to Play* (Toronto 1987), 133–45

15 Ibid., 238, n. 1

16 Excerpts from *Globe* grouped as 'Ned Hanlan and National Pride,' in Michael Cross, ed., *The Workingman in the Nineteenth Century* (Toronto 1974), 225–7

17 Rob Beamish, 'The Political Economy of Professional Sport,' in Jean Harvey and Hart Cantelon eds., *Not Just a Game: Essays in Canadian Sport Sociology* (Ottawa 1988), 141–58

18 Author's interview with Frank Carlin, former Victorias' secretary-treasurer, 1972, quoted in Bruce Kidd and John Macfarlane, *The Death of Hockey* (Toronto 1972), 105

19 Glenbow Alberta Institute (GAI), Tom Phillips Collection (TPC), 'Kenora Wins the Stanley Cup,' undated clipping; R.S. Lappage, 'The Kenora Thistles' Stanley Cup Trail,' *Canadian Journal of Sport History* (*CJSH*), 19 no. 2 (1988), 86–92; Eric Whitehead, *Cyclone Taylor: A Hockey Legend* (Toronto 1977), 54–76; and Brenda Zeman, *Hockey Heritage: Eighty-eight Years of Puck-Chasing in Saskatchewan* (Regina 1983), 22–3

20 Trevor Bailey, *A History of Cricket* (Boston 1978); Tony Mason, *Association Football and English Society, 1863–1915* (Brighton 1980); and Leonie Sandercock and Ian Turner, *Up Where Cazaly? The Great Australian Game* (Sydney 1981)

21 Harold Seymour, *Baseball: The Early Years* (New York 1960); Steven Reiss, *Touching Base: Professional Baseball and American Culture in the Progressive Era* (Westport, Conn., 1980); and Robert Burk, *Never Just a Game: Players, Owners and American Baseball to 1920* (Chapel Hill, NC, 1994)

22 Foster Hewitt, *Hockey Night in Canada* (Toronto 1961), 34–7; see also Eric

Whitehead, *Cyclone Taylor*, 34–53; and Frank Selke, *Behind the Cheering* (Toronto 1962), 28–39.

23 Coleman, *Trail of the Stanley Cup*, vol. 1, 117–58

24 Ibid., 178–92; and Whitehead, *Cyclone Taylor*, 103–29

25 Scott Young and Astrid Young, *O'Brien* (Toronto 1969), 63

26 TGP, Annual Report of the Ottawa Hockey Club, 23 Oct. 1919

27 Coleman, *Trail of the Stanley Cup*, vol. 1, 250

28 Eric Whitehead, *The Patricks* (Halifax 1983), 89–118

29 Seymour, *Baseball: The Early Years*, 317-21

30 Don Morrow, *A Sporting Evolution* (Montreal 1981), 77–82

31 TGP, 'Memorandum of Agreement between St. Patrick's Professional Hockey Club ... ; and Hamilton Professional Hockey Club ... ; and Ottawa Hockey Association ... ; and Canadien Hockey Club,' 10 Nov. 1923

32 Coleman, *Trail of the Stanley Cup*, vol. 1, 375–6

33 CSP, Agreement between Arena Gardens of Toronto Ltd. and Toronto Maple Leaf Hockey Club Ltd., 23 July 1927

34 TGP, Agreement between Gorman and Ahearn, 18 April 1922; and *Ottawa Journal*, 14, 15, and 29 Dec. 1923

35 NA, 28 III, 57, Vol. 239, Molson Papers, Leo Dandurand, unpublished manuscript, and Canadian Arena Company, Capitalization, 8 Nov. 1924; and Hewitt, *Hockey Night in Canada*, 86

36 TGP, *The Weather Vein* (Carrier Engineering Corp.), 6 no. 2 (1926), 23–8; and Conn Smythe with Scott Young, *If You Can't Beat 'Em in the Alley* (Toronto 1981), 102–3

37 Whitehead, *The Patricks*, 81–7 and 98–103

38 Thomas Foster, 'Why Our Soldiers Learn to Box,' *Outing*, 72 (May 1918), 114–16; Glynn Leyshon, *Of Mats and Men* (London 1984), 53; and Bert Sugar, *Hit the Sign and Win a Free Suit of Clothes from Harry Finkelstein* (Chicago 1978), 139–80

39 Cruise and Griffiths, *Net Worth*; and Barney Nagler, *James Norris and the Decline of Boxing* (New York 1964)

40 TGP, 'One for the Hockey Archives'; and NA, Trent Frayne Papers (TFP), NHL Minutes, 31 Aug. 1924

41 TFP, NHL Minutes, 12 Oct. and 18 Dec. 1924; 15 and 25 Jan. and 11 April 1925; and Whitehead, *The Patricks*, 143

42 *Hamilton Spectator*, 12–14 March 1925; and Meyer Siemiatycki, 'The Stanley Cup Strike of 1925,' in Dan Diamond, ed., *The Official National Hockey League Stanley Cup Centennial Book* (Toronto 1993), 60–7

43 'Hamilton Syndicate Would Purchase Club,' 'Sale of Hamilton Club Failed

to Materialize,' and 'Hamilton Franchise Has No Ties On It,' *Hamilton Spectator*, 16, 17, and 18 Sept. 1925, respectively

44 Walter McMullen, 'The Sport Trail,' *Hamilton Spectator*, 18 Sept. 1925

45 TFP, NHL Minutes, 26 Sept. 1925 and 7 Nov. 1925

46 Tom Traves, *The State and Enterprise: Canadian Manufacturers and the Federal Government, 1917–1931* (Toronto 1979), 81–6; and Bryan Palmer, *Working-Class Experience: The Rise and Reconstruction of Canadian Labour, 1800–1980* (Toronto 1983), 186–7

47 Zeman, *Hockey Heritage*, 51; Coleman, *Trail of the Stanley Cup*, vol. 1, 417; and Whitehead, *The Patricks*, 143

48 Zeman, *Hockey Heritage*, 51–9

49 Whitehead, *The Patricks*, 151–60

50 United States, *Statistical Abstract of the United States* (Washington 1927), 43

51 *Saskatoon Star-Phoenix*, 10 March 1924; cited in Zeman, *88 Years*, 55; GAI, Calgary Exhibition and Stampede Papers (CESP), Western Canada Hockey League, Financial Statements, 1921–27; and NA, MG 30, C84, Harry Connor Scrapbook (HCS), '27,610 Fans take in Pro Puck Games Here,' undated *Phoenix* clipping. Connor was later traded to Boston Bruins.

52 CSP, 'Maple Leaf Hockey Club, Season 1927–28.' The Leafs did not seem to keep their own records of attendance before 1931–2, when they got their own rink.

53 Max Foran, *Calgary: An Illustrated City* (Toronto 1978), 117–24; Ron Lappage, 'Sport as an Expression of Western and Maritime Discontent in Canada between the Wars,' *Canadian Journal for the History of Sport and Physical Education* (*CJHSPE*), 8 no. 1 (1977), 50–71; and Cosentino, *Canadian Football* (Toronto 1969), 60–124

54 'The Sport Trail,' *Hamilton Spectator*, 30 Sept. 1925; and Charles Good, 'Will US Cash Cripple Our Hockey?' *Maclean's*, 1 March 1926

55 Whitehead, *The Patricks*, 159–60

56 Selke, *Behind the Cheering*, 76

57 Cosentino, 'A History of the Concept,' 146-8; Thomas Vellathottam, 'A History of Lacrosse in Canada prior to 1914,' MA thesis, University of Alberta, 1968, 105–6; Selke, *Behind the Cheering*, 58; S.F. Wise and Doug Fisher, *Canada's Sporting Heroes* (Toronto 1974), 28–32; and Metcalfe, *Canada Learns to Play*, 204–11

58 Foster Hewitt, *Down the Ice* (Toronto 1934), 16

59 Whitehead, *The Patricks*, 74–5 and 127–30

60 In his marvellous memoir, *The Game*, written in the early 1980s, Ken Dryden argues that Canadian hockey players and coaches had not fully transcended the strategic limitations imposed by the original offside rule

and so were unprepared for Soviet teams unburdened by the same history.
I am always attracted to arguments that respect the weight of tradition,
but Dryden does not consider that when many commentators first saw the
Soviets in 1972 they were reminded of the New York Rangers of the 1920s
and 1930s. That team was managed by Lester Patrick, one of the men who
dreamed up the new rule.

61 E.g., Henry Roxborough, 'Is Pro Hockey on the Level?' *Maclean's*, 1 Jan.
1936

62 CSP, Maple Leaf Gardens, 'Paid Attendance Professional Hockey,' 24
March 1953

63 CESP, Letter from E.L. Richardson to J.T. Ganguish, 13 Jan. 1933, and
Memorandum of Agreement between NHL, Canadian-American Hockey
League, International Hockey League, American Association of
Professional Hockey Clubs, and Western Canada Hockey League, 3 Oct.
1932. The revived WCHL operated only one season. See Andy Lytle,
'Sardonic Laughter Greets Demands of International,' *Toronto Star*, 1 Nov.
1935.

64 J.C.H. Jones, 'The Economics of the National Hockey League,' in R.S.
Gruneau and J. Albinson, eds., *Canadian Sport: Sociological Perspectives* (Don
Mills 1976), 225–58; Roger Noll, ed., *Government and the Sport Business*
(Washington, DC, 1974); and James Quirk and Rodney D. Fort, *Pay Dirt:
The Business of Professional Team Sports* (Princeton, NJ, 1992)

65 Lee Lowenfish and Tony Lupien, *The Imperfect Diamond* (New York 1980),
25–53; Ted Vincent, *Mudville's Revenge* (New York 1981), 180–223;
Coleman, *Trail of the Stanley Cup*, vol. 1, 201; and 'Contract Adopted by the
National Hockey Association of Canada,' 1910, reproduced by Cosentino,
'A History of the Concept,' 521–32

66 TFP, NHL Minutes, 28 Dec. 1925

67 In a study of the major commercial leagues in North America between
1900 and 1970, James Quirk and Mohamed El Hodri found a strong
correlation between market population size and team standings, which
they attributed to the ability of franchises located in more profitable
markets to buy better players; the one exception was the NHL between
1939 and 1967. Because of the uneven spread of hockey in the United
States, they argued, larger population did not automatically mean a larger
demand. See their 'The Economic Theory of a Professional Sports
League,' in Roger Noll, ed., *Government and the Sports Business*
(Washington, DC, 1974), 33–80.

68 TFP, NHL Minutes, 7 Nov. 1925. On the salary cap, the minutes state that
the motion was '*unanimously* carried' and then 'Col. Hammond of New

York requested that his protest against the adoption of this measure be recorded.'

69 Joe Gorman, quoted by Goyens and Turowitz, *Lions in Winter*, 55 and 59–60
70 TFP, NHL Minutes, 12 Oct. 1924
71 Coleman, *Trail of the Stanley Cup*, vol. 2 (Sherbrooke 1969), 144–50. The records of the Stanley Cup trustees have never been found; letter to author from Joseph Romain, curator of the Hockey Hall of Fame, 10 Dec. 1987.
72 Author's interview with Ted Reeve, 1972; Selke, *Behind the Cheering*, 76; and Hewitt, *Hockey Night in Canada*, 65
73 Author's interviews with Spicer and Laprade, 1972
74 Smythe with Young, *If You Can't Beat 'Em in the Alley*, 102
75 TGP, 'One for the Hockey Archives'; 'By Eddie MacCabe,' *Ottawa Journal*, 24 Oct. 1974; Whitehead, *The Patricks*, 170–4; author's interview with Reeve, 1972
76 Selke, *Behind the Cheering*, 77
77 Author's interview with Richards, 12 April 1987
78 Bruce McFarlane, 'The Sociology of Sports Promotion,' MA thesis, McGill University, 1955. McFarlane's analysis focuses on the relationship among promoters, and sportswriters and broadcasters, but subsequent scholarship has placed the production of sports information in the broader context of the capitalist mass media. See, in particular, Sut Jhally, 'The Spectacle of Accumulation: Material and Cultural Factors in the Evolution of the Sport/Media Complex,' *Insurgent Sociologist*, 12 no. 3 (1984), 41–56
79 Smythe with Young, *If You Can't Beat 'Em in the Alley*, 115–16; and Ross Harkness, *J.E. Atkinson of the Star* (Toronto 1963), 277–86 and 373–5
80 Smythe with Young, *If You Can't Beat 'Em in the Alley*, 85–6
81 Ibid., 102; CSP, Memorandum of Agreement between Arena Gardens and Maple Leaf Hockey Club, 30 Nov. 1929; and Maple Leaf Gardens Ltd., undated prospectus
82 Smythe with Young, *If You Can't Beat 'Em in the Alley*, 102–9; Selke, *Behind the Cheering*, 81–99; and Cruise and Griffiths, *Net Worth*, 85–6
83 Selke, *Behind the Cheering*, 92
84 Scott Young, *Hello Canada: The Life and Times of Foster Hewitt* (Toronto 1985), 48–50; E. Austin Weir, *The Struggle for National Broadcasting in Canada* (Toronto 1965), 85; Hewitt, 'Sports on Radio,' *Toronto Star*, 13 Oct. 1928; and Lawrence Perry, 'What Radio Is Doing to the World of Sport,' *Popular Radio*, 7 no. 3 (1925), 211–19
85 Young, *Hello Canada*, 47; Selke, *Behind the Cheering*, 85; and Scott Young, *The Boys of Saturday Night: Inside Hockey Night in Canada* (Toronto 1990), 38–45

86 F.H. Leacy, *Historical Statistics of Canada 2nd Edition*, R730–43

87 Alice Goldfarb Marquis, 'Written on the Wind: The Impact of Radio during the 1930s,' *Journal of Contemporary History*, 19 (1984), 392; and Russell B. Adams, *King C. Gillette: The Man and His Wonderful Shaving Device* (Boston 1978), 185–94

88 Stuart Ewan, *Captains of Consciousness: Advertising and the Social Roots of the Consumer Culture* (Toronto 1976), 23–30. As large-scale industrialial production has been transformed in the course of the computer revolution and the globalization of finance capital, the term 'post-Fordism' has taken on much broader meanings; see Stuart Hall, 'Brave New World,' *Socialist Review*, 21 no. 1 (1991), 57–64

89 John Thompson and Allen Seager, *Canada, 1922-1939* (Toronto 1985), 138

90 Ibid., 342-3; William L. Marr and Donald G. Patterson, *Canada: An Economic History* (Toronto 1980), 290–7 and 355–74; James Cowan, 'The Battle for Canadian Film Control,' *Maclean's*, 1 Oct. 1930, 7; and Mary Vipond, 'Canadian Nationalism and the Plight of Canadian Magazines in the 1920s,' *Canadian Historical Review*, 58 no. 1 (1977), 43–63

91 Traves, *The State and Enterprise*, 81-6; and Palmer, *Working-Class Experience*, 186–7

92 NA, MG 28, I 151, Reel C-4852, Vol. 1, George Dudley Papers (GDP), CAHA Collection, 'Suggestions for a CAHA-NHL Agreement,' 1936; Canada, National Council of Fitness and Amateur Sport, *Report of the Hockey Study Committee* (Ottawa 1967); and Kidd and Macfarlane, *Death of Hockey*, 55

93 Mark Lavoie, 'Stacking, Performance and Salary Discrimination in Professional Ice Hockey: A Survey of the Evidence,' *Sociology of Sport Journal* (*SSJ*), 6 no. 1 (1989), 17–35

94 Rob Beamish, 'The Impact of Corporate Ownership on Labor-Management Relations in Hockey,' in Paul Staudohar and James Mangan, eds., *The Business of Professional Sports* (Chicago 1991), 175–201; Cruise and Griffiths, *Net Worth*, 52–140; Gruneau and Whitson, *Hockey Night in Canada*, 109–52; and Douglas Hunter, *Open Ice: The Tim Horton Story* (Toronto 1994), 34–51

95 Paul Rutherford, *The Making of the Canadian Media* (Toronto 1978), 54–5; 'Baseball Scores by Radio,' *Radio News of Canada*, 2 no. 2 (1924), 3; Stacey Lorenz, ' "Bowing Down to Babe Ruth": Major League Baseball and Canadian Popular Culture, 1920–1929,' *CJHS*, 26 no. 1 (1995), 22–39; John W. Key, 'Socio-Cultural Characteristics and the Image of the Urban Anglo-Canadian Athletic Hero, 1920–39,' MHK thesis, University of Windsor, 1982; and Maria Tippett, *Making Culture: English-Canadian*

Institutions and the Arts before the Massey Commission (Toronto 1990), 127–55

96 Selke, *Behind the Cheering*, 76

97 Metcalfe, *Canada Learns to Play*, 223–4

98 David Shoalts, 'NHL, Players Strike Deal,' and James Christie, David Shoalts, and Rhéal Séguin, 'Les Nordiques Say Finis,' *Globe and Mail*, 12 Jan. 1995 and 26 May 1995

99 David Whitson and Don Macintosh, 'Becoming a World Class City: Hallmark Events and Sport Franchises in the Growth Strategies of Western Canadian Cities,' *SSJ*, 10 no. 3 (1993), 221–40; William Houston and David Shoalts, 'Canadian Cities Play on Thin Ice,' *Globe and Mail*, 4, 5, 6, and 7 Jan. 1994; and David Roberts, 'Jets to Stay Put One More Season,' *Globe and Mail*, 16 Aug. 1995

Chapter Six: Capturing the State

1 Canada, *House of Commons Debates*, 13 Feb. 1936, 158–9; Kidd, 'Canadian Opposition to the 1936 Olympics,' *Canadian Journal of History of Sport and Physical Education* (*CJHSPE*), 9 no. 2 (1978), 20–40; and P.J. Mulqueen, 'Foreword,' in W.A. Fry, ed., *Canada at Eleventh Olympiad 1936 in Germany* (Dunnville, Ont., 1936), 3

2 Kevin Walmsley, 'Legislation and Leisure in 19th Century Canada,' PhD thesis, University of Alberta, 1992

3 Canada, *Statutes of Canada* (SC), 1906, Ch. 27, 145–9; Barbara Schrodt, 'Sabbatarianism and Sport in Canadian Society,' *Journal of Sport History* (*JSH*), 4 no. 1 (1977), 22–33; Gene Homel, 'Toronto's Sunday Tobogganing Controversy of 1912,' *Urban History Review*, 10, no. 2 (1981), 25–34; and Chris Armstrong and Viv Nelles, *The Revenge of the Methodist Bicycle Company* (Toronto 1977)

4 Elsie Marie McFarland, *The Development of Public Recreation in Canada* (Ottawa 1970); and National Archives of Canada, (NA), MG 28, I 25, Vol. 105, File 101, NCW

5 Helen Lenskyj, '"Moral Physiology" in Physical Education for Girls in Ontario 1890–1930,' in Bruce Kidd, ed., *Proceedings of the Fifth Canadian Symposium on the History of Sport and Physical Education* (Toronto 1982), 139–49; and Neil Sutherland, '"To Create a Strong and Healthy Race": School Children in the Public Health Movement,' *History of Education Quarterly*, 12 no. 3 (1972), 304–33

6 Marianne Valverde, 'The Mixed Economy as a Canadian Tradition,' *Studies in Political Economy*, 41 (1995), 33–60; and Bruce Kidd, 'The Philosophy of

Excellence: Olympic Performance, Class Power, and the Canadian State,'
in Pasquale Galasso, ed., *Philosophy of Sport and Physical Education* (Toronto
1988), 11–31

7 NA, MG 28, I 150, AAU, Minutes of the Reconstruction Committee

8 *House of Commons Debates*, 4 April 1919, 1164–5; and Arthur Ford, 'Venom
against Rowell Fails to Delay Bill,' *Times*, 5 April 1919

9 Roxborough, 'What Happened at LA,' *Maclean's* 1 Oct. 1932

10 *House of Commons Debates*, 18 May 1922, 1972–8

11 Archives of Ontario (AO), RG 3, Box 98, 1926, International Labour
Conference Recommendations, 16 June–5 July 1924; and Canada, Privy
Council Report 220, 15 Feb. 1926

12 *House of Commons Debates*, 20 Jan. 1937, 114–26

13 Statutes of Ontario (SO) 1919, Ch. 55, 336–8; Minutes of the Reconstruction Committee; 'A Social Centre for Rural Life,' *Globe*, 25 March 1919;
and Alan Metcalfe, 'The Urban Response to the Demand for Sporting
Facilities,' *Urban History Review*, 12 no. 2 (1983), 31–45

14 *Debates of the Senate*, 13 Dec. 1880, 52. See also S.F. Wise, 'Sport and Class
Values in Old Ontario and Quebec,' in W.H. Heick and Roger Graham,
eds., *His Own Man* (Montreal 1974), 101–2.

15 *R. v. Wildfong and Lang* (1911), 17 CCC 251 (Ont. CC)

16 *Steele* v. *Maber* (1901), 6 CCC 446 (Que. Mag. Court); *R. v. Littlejohn* (1904)
8 CCC 212 (NB Co. C.); *R. v. Wildfong and Lang* (1911), 17 CCC 251 (Ont.
CC); *R. v. Fitzgerald* (1912), 19 CCC 145 (Ont. Co. C.); *R. v. Pelkey* (1913)
12 DLR 780 (Alb. SC), and *R. v. Fleming and Wallace* (1916), 30 DLR 418
(Que. Mag. C.); and AO, RG 23, E85, 1.1, correspondence between
Premier James Whitney and Superintendent J.E. Rogers, Jan. 1910

17 *R. v. Littlejohn*

18 *Bithel* v. *Butler* (1918) 30 CCC 275 (Que. SC)

19 Paul Rutherford, 'Tomorrow's Metropolis: The Urban Reform Movement
in Canada, 1880–1920,' Canadian Historical Association, *Historical Papers
1971*, 206; Jeffrey Sammons, *Beyond the Ring: The Role of Boxing in American
Society* (Urbana, Ill., 1988), 16–29; and Steven Riess, 'In the Ring and Out:
Professional Boxing in New York, 1896–1920,' in Donald Spivey, ed., *Sport
in America: New Historical Perspectives* (Westport, Conn. 1985), 95–128

20 'Would Teach Boxing in Ontario Schools,' and Francis Nelson, 'Value of
Sports in Common Welfare,' *Toronto Star*, 6 April 1920 and 3 May 1920,
respectively

21 Peter Oliver, *Public and Private Persons: The Ontario Political Culture,
1914–1934* (Toronto 1975) 64–90; and Charles M. Johnston, *E.C. Drury:
Agrarian Idealist* (Toronto 1986), 51–82

22 SC 1933, Ch. 53, p. 287

23 AO, RG 49, 1–7, B2, Ontario Athletic Commission (OAC), 'Rules and Regulations of Professional Boxing and Wrestling in Ontario, 1920'; Minutes of 28 Dec. 1921; and 1923–24 Annual Report

24 SO 1923, Ch. 19, pp. 48–9

25 AO, RG 49, 19, no. 35, OAC, 927–28 Annual Report, and N.A. Beach, 'Background to the Ontario High School Track and Field Championship Meets,' personal communication, 17 Nov. 1980

26 AO, RG 49, 19, no. 35, OAC, 1927–28 and 1929–30 Annual Reports

27 For example, in 1923, when the 5 per cent gate tax yielded $5,275.54, the income from licences and fines was $5,463.15. In 1928, the 2 per cent tax produced $4,364.20, while fees and fines totalled $6,448.66.

28 'Future of Province Declared Dependent on Healthy Boyhood,' *Globe*, 26 Feb. 1927; SO 1927, Ch. 72, 585–6; and 'Scanning the Sports Field,' *Globe*, 16 Feb. 1927

29 Bruce Kidd, ' "Making the Pros Pay" for Amateur Sport: The Ontario Athletic Commission 1920–1947,' *Ontario History*, 87 no. 2 (1995), 105–28

30 Barbara Schrodt, 'The Origins of British Columbia's Pro-Rec,' in Schrodt, ed., *Proceedings of the Fourth Canadian Symposium on the History of Sport and Physical Education* (Vancouver 1979); and Ron Lappage, 'British Columbia's Contribution to the Dominion-Provincial Training Program through the Provincial-Recreation Program,' *Canadian Journal of the History of Sport and Physical Education* (*CJHSPE*), 9 no. 2 (1978), 86–92

31 NA, RG 27, Vol. 3349, 'Forms and Reports,' BC Department of Recreational and Physical Education, 1936–1937 Report; and *Gymnast*, 2 no. 3 (1937)

32 Jean Harvey, 'Sport Policy and the Welfare State: An Outline of the Canadian Case,' *Sociology of Sport Journal*, 5 no. 2 (1988), 315–29; Canadian Youth Congress, *Declaration of the Rights of Canadian Youth* (Ottawa 1936), 6; Susan Markham, 'Pressure Groups and Canadian Recreation Services in the 1930s,' paper presented to North American Society of Sport History, Saskatoon, 28 May 1994

33 James Struthers, *No Fault of Their Own: Unemployment and the Canadian Welfare State* (Toronto 1983); Rebecca Coulter, 'Youth Employment: State Response in Canada, 1936–1941,' unpublished paper: and OA, RG 65–15, RCMM30, TBMM30, 15–36–2–11, J.J. Heagerty, 'History of the National Fitness Movement'

34 NA, RG 29, Vol. 882, File 210-8-1, vol. 1, letter from Power to L. Rajchman, 2 May 1938

35 Harvey, 'Sport Policy and the Welfare State'; OA, RG 3, Box 213, Canada,

Department of Labour, Review of the Dominion-Provincial Youth Training Programme and the National Forestry Programme, 1940

36 Canada, Special Committee on Social Security, Minutes of Proceedings and Evidence No. 1, 16 March 1943, 32–4: National Physical Fitness Council, Minutes, 29–30 Aug. 1944; and Shirley Tillotson, 'Citizen Participation in the Welfare State: An Experiment, 1945–47,' *Canadian Historical Review*, 75 no. 4 (1994), 511–42

37 Bruce Kidd, 'A History of Government in Recreation,' unpublished paper, University of Toronto, 1965; Alvin Finkel, 'Paradise Postponed: A Re-examination of the Green Book Proposals of 1945,' Canadian Historical Association, *Historical Papers*, 1993, 120–42; and NA, MG 28, I10, Vol. 115, File 840, Canadian Welfare Council, Recreation Division, Citizens Research Institute of Canada, 'Abolish the National Physical Fitness Undertaking?' *Effective Government*, 16 Nov. 1951, 1–5

38 Austin Weir, *The Struggle for National Broadcasting in Canada* (Toronto 1965), and Frank Peers, *The Politics of Canadian Broadcasting, 1920–1951* (Toronto 1968)

39 Scott Young, *Hello Canada: The Life and Times of Foster Hewitt* (Toronto 1985), 61; and Peers, *The Politics of Canadian Broadcasting*, 197–200

40 Peers, *The Politics of Canadian Broadcasting*, 442; Mary Vipond, *Listening In: the First Decade of Canadian Broadcasting, 1922–1932* (Montreal 1992), 286; Dallas Smythe, *Dependency Road: Communications, Capitalism, Consciousness and Canada* (Norwood, NJ, 1981), 160–5; and Russell Johnson, 'The Emergence of Broadcasting Advertising in Canada, 1920–1932,' paper presented to the Canadian Historical Association, 1994

41 'Political and Controversial Broadcasting Policies and Rulings, 8 July 1930, as Revised 21 Feb. 1944,' in Roger Bird, ed., *Documents of Canadian Broadcasting* (Ottawa 1988), 186

42 *House of Commons Debates*, 18 May 1932, 3035

43 Ralph Allen, 'Enter the Paid Amateur,' *Maclean's*, 1 Nov. 1940, 29

44 Scott Young, *Hello Canada* (Toronto 1985), 95, and Frank Selke, *Behind the Cheering* (Toronto 1962), 126–7

45 Vipond, *Listening In*, 102; Young, *Hello Canada*, 95; and Young, *The Boys of Saturday Night: Inside Hockey Night in Canada* (Toronto 1990)

46 George Gerbner, 'The Dynamics of Cultural Resistance,' in G. Tuchman, A.K. Daniels, and J. Benet, eds., *Hearth and Home: Images of Women in the Mass Media* (New York 1978), 44

47 *Winnipeg Tribune*, 3 June 1935

48 Ron Powers, *Supertube: The Rise of Television Sports* (New York 1984), 28; and Sut Jhally, 'The Spectacle of Accumulation: Material and Cultural Factors

in the Evolution of the Sport/Media Complex,' *Insurgent Sociologist*, 12 no. 3 (1984), 41–56

Conclusion: The Triumph of Capitalist Sport

1 Author's interview with Johnny Miles, 14 May 1990
2 Richard Gruneau, 'Modernization or Hegemony: Two Views on Sport and Social Development,' in Jean Harvey and Hart Cantelon, eds., *Not Just a Game: Essays in Canadian Sport Sociology* (Ottawa 1988), 22
3 Canada, National Advisory Council on Fitness and Amateur Sport, *Report of the Hockey Study Committee* (Ottawa 1967)
4 Important exceptions include Brian McFarlane, *Proud Past, Bright Future: One Hundred Years of Canadian Women's Hockey* (Toronto 1989); Scott Young, *War on Ice* (Toronto 1976) and *One Hundred Years of Dropping the Puck* (Toronto 1989); Brenda Zeman, *Hockey Heritage: Eighty-eight Years of Puck-Chasing in Saskatchewan* (Regina 1983); and Gary Zeman, *Alberta on Ice* (Edmonton 1985).
5 But see Raymond Boulanger, 'Class Cultures and Sporting Activities in Quebec,' and Suzanne Laberge and David Sankoff, 'Physical Activities, Body *Habitus*, and Lifestyles,' in Harvey and Cantelon, eds., *Not Just a Game*, 247–65 and 267–86, respectively
6 John Thompson and Allen Seager, *Canada, 1922–1939* (Toronto 1985), 190
7 Linda Hutcheon, *As Canadian as Possible ... under the Circumstances* (Toronto 1990), 23
8 Frank Cosentino, *The Passing Game: A History of the Canadian Football League* (Winnipeg 1975)
9 National Archives of Canada, MG 28 III 57, Vol. P240, Molson Papers, David Molson to H. deM. Molson, 29 Dec. 1971, and Selke to Miss Taylor, 1 Feb. 1973
10 These developments are examined in Bruce Kidd, 'Confronting Inequality in Sport and Physical Activity,' *Avante*, 1 no. 1 (1995), 1–19.

Illustration Credits

Author's collection: Percy Williams; Beatty, Willingdon, Bennett, and Ferguson; Edmonton Grads; Women's Amateur Athletic Federation

Canada's Sports Hall of Fame: Toronto Granites; Lester Patrick; Walter Knox

City of Toronto Archives: Josie Dyment and Myrtle Cook; permanent bleachers, 1930; 1924 women's baseball game (*Globe and Mail*, 1 August 1924); first women's Olympic team (*Globe and Mail*, 11 July 1928), 14109

Hockey Hall of Fame: Hamilton Tigers, 1.248; Frank Calder, 5.980; Hugh Plaxton, 1.928; Conn Smythe, 44; Foster Hewitt, 20.341

Irene McInnis: Canadian team travelling to London; Dorothy Wilson

Multicultural History Society of Ontario: Jewish Workers' Sports Association, MSR 9161; Camp Tarmola, MSR 7393; Finnish-Canadian pyramids, FCHS 874; South Porcupine ski race, MSR 7399

National Library: Tim Buck (Toronto *Worker*, 8 December 1934)

The Toronto Star Syndicate: 'Bobbed-Headed Athletes' (*Toronto Star Weekly*, 24 April 1926)

University of British Columbia, Hilda Kealty Materials: Pro-Rec Mass Display

Index